THE GARDEN TREE

AN ILLUSTRATED GUIDE TO CHOOSING, PLANTING AND CARING FOR 500 GARDEN TREES

ALAN MITCHELL & ALLEN COOMBES

PHOTOGRAPHY BY ANNE HYDE

CONTENTS

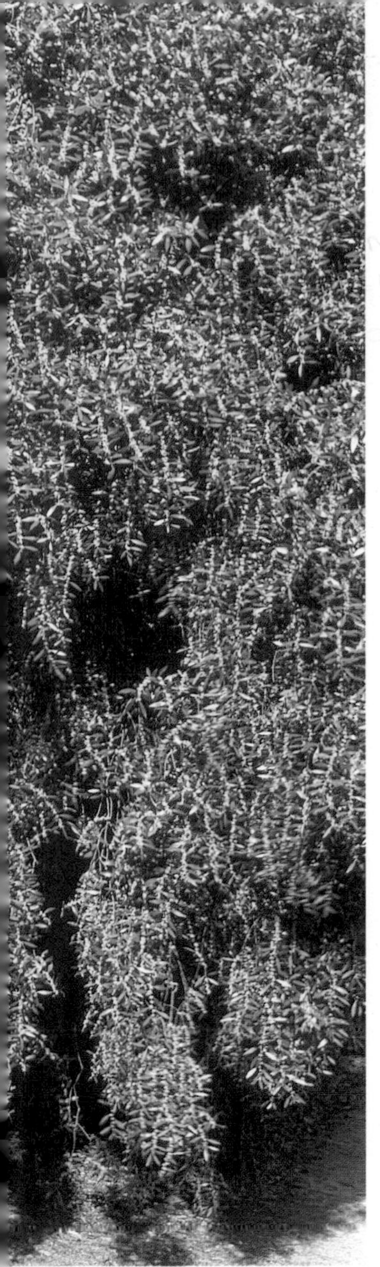

I have great pleasure in dedicating this book to the memory of Alan Mitchell, without doubt, the 'champion of trees' in Britain. In spite of my tinkering this is still, very much, his work.

Allen Coombes

First published in Britain in 1998 by
George Weidenfeld & Nicolson Ltd

This paperback edition first published in 1999 by
Seven Dials, Cassell & Co.
The Orion Publishing Group
Wellington House, 125 Strand
London, WC2R 0BB

A CIP catalogue record for this book is available from the British Library.

ISBN 1 84188 007 8

Designed and produced by Blackjacks
Illustrations by Ian Sidaway
Edited by Tessa Clark
Colour reproduction by Blackjacks
Printed and bound in Italy by Printer Trento Srl

Acknowledgements
I would like to thank all those whose efforts and inspiration helped to make this book what it is. Susan Haynes of Weidenfeld and Nicolson; Jonathan Baker of Blackjacks; The Sir Harold Hillier Gardens and Arboretum for making available such a splendid location for photography; Brian Gibbons for helping to locate material; Mike Buffin for preparing captions; Anne Hyde for her photographs.

INTRODUCTION

Trees are the most enduring living things we handle, and can be prominent features through five or six generations after the death of the planter. Unlike the making of a stone monument or mansion, the planting of a grove of trees requires no special physical skills, no gangs of labourers and no long years of work. It can be done by one gardener in one afternoon. A grove cannot, however, be made in the form in which it is to endure. Architect and gardener both envisage the final effect for which they aim: but whereas the architect can ensure that this comes about as the work goes on, the gardener has to leave it in the hands of the trees he plants to mature in the way he hopes.

Planting a tree is, or should be, an irrevocable act. It is unwise and difficult to move it even after two or three years, and after thirty or so it is quite impracticable. The only change possible is to fell it.

Trees are the entire framework and background and the largest features of all large gardens and parks, so the choice of the right one for each position is vital at the outset. Mistakes will live on and affect the overall design for its lifetime, for the removal of an unsuitable tree results in an unplanned gap followed by years when the tree that replaces it is smaller than was intended.

The aim of this book is to make such mistakes less likely, by provoking thought and airing ideas on patterns of planting and what to avoid, and to show the great diversity of trees that can be used for different requirements. Every planting is unique in the details of its situation; aspect, altitude, soil and climate will rarely all be similar, while local topographies can never be the same. Precise recommendations are therefore of less value than general ideas and guidance as to the merits and demerits of each species.

A subsidiary aim, but an important one, is to remove the great discouragement to tree-planting enshrined in the commonly held fallacy that trees grow very slowly. This leads to the belief that the results of planting are appreciated only by one's grandchildren and that newly planted trees must be big, staked, ugly and expensive. None of these ideas are true and this cannot be said too often.

It is hoped, also, that by describing a proportion of the huge number of trees available, a greater interest in them will be aroused in the reader and he or she will realize that tree-watching is a rewarding pastime in towns, cities and suburbs as well as in rural areas, and one that can be pursued every day without the need to visit well-known gardens and collections. By giving brief historical details about the discovery and introduction of some of the world's trees, it may be that they will come to be seen as individual personalities with a romance behind them. The ones generally seen in this country are not just remnants of the old native woodland; they have mostly been brought here by colourful characters, often in diverse circumstances, from all parts of the temperate world.

Inclusions and Exclusions

This book cannot hope to include all the trees in cultivation and therefore must select rigorously. To merit mention, the following criteria must apply:

1. The tree must be a tree, not a shrub, and although there is no absolute distinction between the two, some shrubs often masquerade as trees – the Wayfaring tree (*Viburnum lantana*) is an example. These are firmly excluded because all the space available is needed for the inclusion of proper trees. A suitable criterion for a tree is that it is a woody plant which is commonly capable of growth to over 6 m on a single stem. On this basis dwarf conifers are also excluded.

2. It must either be garden-worthy and distinctive, with positive merits, or have been much planted and so worthy of mention, if only as a warning against further planting.

3. It should not, in general, be so rare that only one or two specimens are known in specialist, often private, collections. Some trees only a little less rare will be included where they are of special merit and really ought to be better known, for unless they feature in books like this they will never be planted more widely.

PART 1

CHOOSING AND PLANTING GARDEN TREES

This section of the book is an introduction to trees in gardens. It describes where our trees came from and how they arrived, going on to explain the role of trees in gardens and the landscape. The important subject of planting and caring for trees is also covered. The names of trees are explained, why we use scientific names and why they sometimes have to change.

Finally there are lists of trees recommended for particular situations and soils, and of trees with particular characteristics, such as an upright habit or variegated foliage. These trees and many more are described in part 2, the Tree Directory.

A brief history of trees in the British landscape

ONLY 12,000 YEARS AGO there were no trees in Britain as it is known today. The ice was at its greatest extension, reaching south to the Chiltern Hills, to the south and west of which was glacial outwash and tundra. There was then land south and west of Cornwall and Ireland, which was a refuge for a few species like the strawberry tree and, possibly, the Cornish elm. With the retreat of the ice the strawberry tree migrated into western Ireland and, unless it was brought there by a tribe in the Iron Age, as has been put forward, the Cornish elm moved into the valleys of south-western Ireland where it is now common. The rest of the land that is now England would have been growing nothing but dwarf willows and dwarf birches. The first pioneers would have been the downy and silver birches and the Scots pine, which advanced rapidly northwards. The birches left large populations on sandy and heath areas but the Scots pine ones were crowded out during subsequent climatic changes. Those now flourishing on Lower Greensand in Surrey and on Bagshot Sands and other recent beds in Hampshire, Berkshire and elsewhere derive from recent reintroductions, probably in 1663 in Surrey and in 1777 in the New Forest.

Also early to arrive were the aspen, bay willow, rowan, sallow, juniper, hazel and sessile oak. Pollen analysis cannot distinguish between the two native oaks but the present distribution, with the sessile oak predominant in the north, west and (with the exception of Dartmoor) at higher altitudes, suggests that the sessile preceded the common oak, which is found mainly in lowland areas and more in the south and the east. During a warm early period, the small-leafed lime was dominant over large areas and spread north, and the wych elm and bird cherry were other early arrivals. The ash, field maple, yew, and hawthorn arrived with time to spare, probably with the wild cherry and crack willow, but the English Channel was now threatening the land-bridge. This was of chalk and, apart from holly and hornbeam, the last trees to cross it were those that thrive on chalk and are often now found wild only near chalk hills – the wild service tree, whitebeam, beech and, probably last, the box.

The total complement of native trees was about thirty-five. Europe was unfortunate during the Ice Ages because the great mountain systems run from east to west. The flora and fauna were somewhat trapped between the northern ice and the mountain ice. The Mediterranean Sea also prevented access to Africa as a refuge. In Canada and the northern USA, which experienced the same Ice Ages, the mountains run north to south. Trees migrated southwards along mountains or valleys at their preferred climate, and afterwards migrated back again. Hence there is an immense wealth of species, broad-leafed and coniferous, in North America. Britain could be recolonized only by species hardy enough to survive on the plains that stretch from France to Germany, and even then only by those near enough and sufficiently fast-moving to migrate back in the 6000 years available before the Channel opened.

JUNIPERUS CHINENSIS 'NEABORIENSIS' (left), the Chinese Juniper is much more tree-like than the native *J. Communis* and has given rise to many selections. This form is a compact, conical tree to about 5m tall.

The native trees in Britain would have covered all the country except the highest peaks and some swampy valleys before man made his inroads. Increasingly, the forests were cleared for agriculture, the making of charcoal, the smelting of iron for fuel, and for timber to build ships. Although the remnant forests in the north and west, and a few others, probably redressed the balance, it is evident from topographical views, and plans by the Dutch engraver Kip and others, that by the eighteenth century much of the lowlands was far more denuded of trees than it is now. Beyond the complex parterres and knot gardens, the patterned orchards and parkland, lay a landscape of the utmost desolation. Whilst this may have been partly a desire on the part of the designer of the parks and gardens to emphasize the contrast between his well-treed demesne and the windswept surroundings, it is probably true that at this period there were fewer trees in southern England than there had been since the Ice Ages. By 1920, only four per

QUERCUS PETRAEA (below), the sessile oak makes a finer specimen than common oak (*Q. robur*) but is less frequently planted.

cent of Britain was under woods of one sort or another, and this included the parks and plantations made in the eighteenth century and the copses and spinneys valued as game coverts. At the present time, about eight per cent of the land is under managed forest.

By 1700, a small and growing proportion of woodlands was not of native tree species. The exotic sweet chestnut made up large areas of coppice, and Norway spruce and European larch formed many coverts, shelter-belts and plantations. Parklands increasingly used a wide range of exotics and the sycamore had long spread wild. Today, the production-forests of the west and north are almost entirely composed of exotic species and other examples of these are accepted as part of the landscape. In large parts of the south-west and near all coasts, the Monterey pine and cypress from California and the holm oak from southern Europe are a dominant part of the scenery. In British gardens, native trees are rare or almost absent. A grove of beech, a big old oak or ash, may be part of the garden, but there are entire vistas in famous gardens without a native tree in sight. This is fine – gardens are meant to be decorative and should not be restricted by the vagaries of ice 12,000 years ago and the grain of the European mountain chains. Britain has one of the very best climates in the world for the development of a huge variety of plants. It would be a gratuitous waste of a superb asset were gardeners not to take advantage of this and create some unique landscapes by judicious blending of the floras of the temperate parts of the world. In using these floras, we are enabled to select the best species in the world for particular sites or features; there is no need to try and make do with the minute proportion of trees that made their own way to Britain.

CASTANEA SATIVA (right), the sweet chestnut, was an early introduction to Britain, probably brought by the Romans for its edible fruit, and is now naturalised in many areas.

The invasion of exotic trees

THE FIRST ADDITIONS to the native tree flora were various elms from the Continent, brought by Iron Age tribes and used as boundary-markers and for fodder. The grey poplar and the white poplar may also have been brought here during this time, but the Romans are credited with the introduction of the sweet chestnut and the walnut and, possibly, the fig. The interest in trees was strictly medicinal or culinary from Roman times until after 1500, so it is unlikely that with so much virgin woodland around, a tree would have been brought here just for its timber. Hence the Romans are unlikely to have brought the sycamore, although this too has been suggested, because its value lies entirely in its timber and the shelter it gives on coasts and high land.

There is a period of 1500 years between the Roman introductions in the early years of the millennium and the first ones with known or accepted dates. The many trees that are undated, but are known to have grown in Britain for 400 years or more include the Italian cypress, maritime and stone pines, bay, almond and peach, Norway spruce, cherry laurel, black and white mulberries, Judas tree, oriental plane and holm oak. The 'Turkey merchants' were trading actively from Aleppo in the fifteenth and sixteenth centuries and a number of trees from Asia Minor are thought to have come along the trade routes. Four species from this region have, however, presumed precise dates: common laburnum 1560; Turkish hazel 1582; Scotch laburnum 1596; and phillyrea 1597. The rather few trees of central Europe arrived at long intervals afterwards: silver fir 1603; European larch about 1620; Norway maple before 1683; arolla pine 1746; and grey alder 1780. Surprisingly, the Austrian pine, so common now, was not in cultivation until 1835.

A few American trees came before 1600 but their numbers increased from then on. John Tradescant the Younger brought the swamp cypress and, in 1656, the red maple. There were two periods of intensive introduction, the first from about 1675 to 1713 when Henry Compton was Bishop of London. His friend John Banister was an ardent collector and Compton put him in charge of missionaries in the Carolinas. Together they arranged the Atlantic crossings of returning missionaries so that plants could be brought to England at the right time. Hickories, maples, oaks, sweet gum and many more American trees stocked the Bishop's garden at Fulham Palace. The practice was continued from 1730 or so until 1768 by Peter Collinson, who planted at Mill Hill and received plants from the

CORYLUS COLURNA (bottom left), the Turkish hazel, has been cultivated in Britain for more than 400 years, its compact, conical habit making it a popular tree.

ACER RUBRUM (below), the red maple, was among the earliest introductions from eastern North America where it contributes to the spectacular displays of autumn colour. This form, 'Schlesingeri', produces exceptional and very early, autumn colour.

HALESIA MONTICOLA (right), snowdrop tree, was a relatively late introduction to Britain, only arriving in 1897, probably because of confusion with another species, introduced earlier.

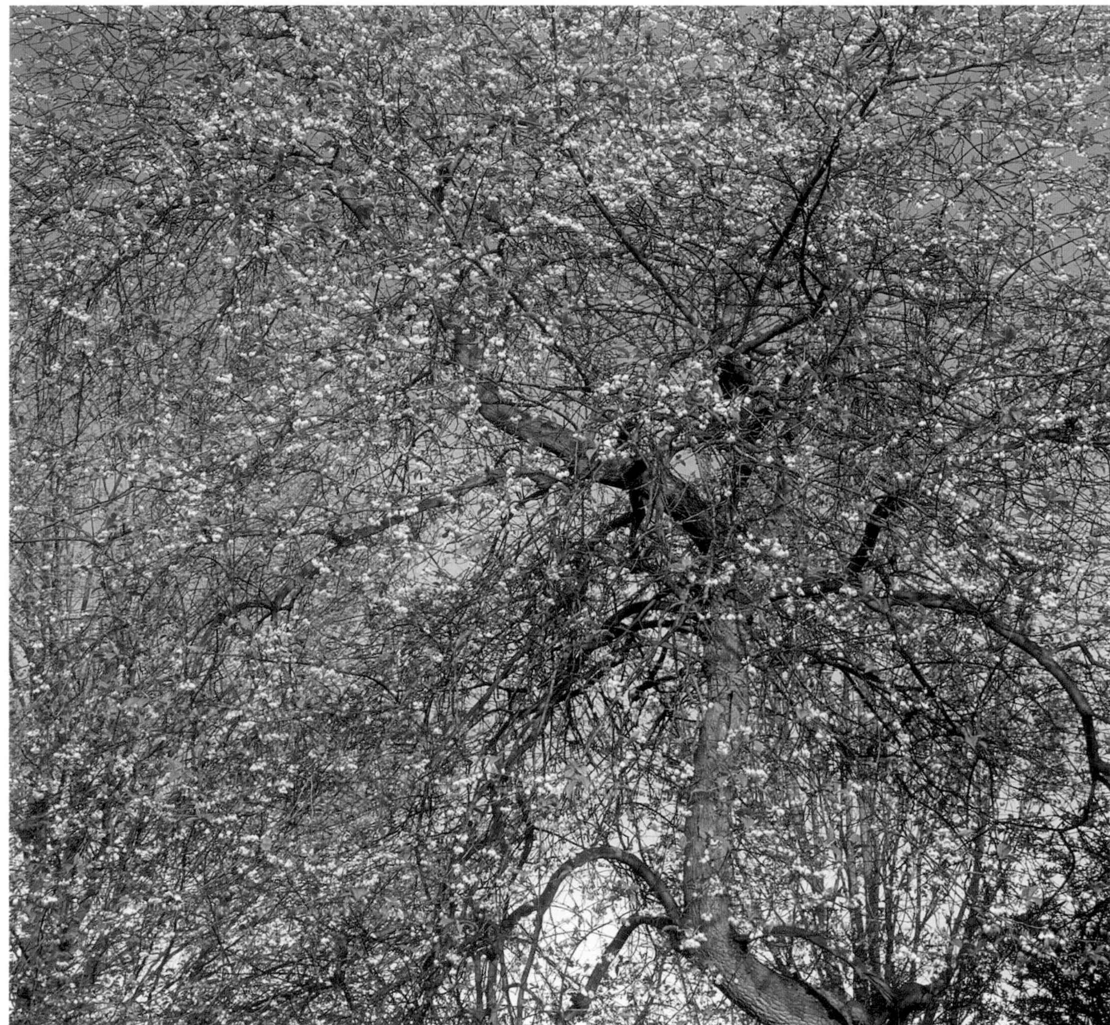

Bartrams, father and son, in Philadelphia. From 1785 to 1796 André Michaux sent large numbers of trees from America to France, some of which were then sent on to England. With John Fraser bringing trees back from his dozen or so journeys to America before 1811, most of the eastern American trees were growing here by 1820. Two notable late arrivals are the snowdrop tree, 1897, and western catalpa, 1880.

The Pacific slopes of the Rocky Mountains are the home of the finest forests in the world and proved a rich source. It was Archibald Menzies who first saw the giant conifers that grow there and collected foliage for description in 1792, but the first man to collect their seeds was David Douglas. He travelled mostly alone and in two journeys, 1825–1827 and 1829–1833, he sent back seeds of Douglas fir, sitka spruce, sugar pine, western yellow and western white pines, grand and noble firs, and, when based in Monterey, California, the digger, Coulter and Monterey pines. No other collectors went to the Pacific coast for a period and, apart from the mysterious appearance of an envelope of seed in 1838 on a desk at Kew which turned out to be of Monterey cypress, no more seeds arrived until 1846 when Theodor Hartweg, the German collector for Kew, sent bishop pine from southern California.

By 1850 the original Douglas trees were about 20 years old and showing extraordinary promise, especially in the gardens and policies around Douglas's native Perth and further north. The lairds had become great enthusiasts for western American conifers and more were badly needed. In 1850, they formed the Oregon Association and selected and trained a collector to send to Oregon. He was John Jeffrey and he managed to repeat all the Douglas imports and to find new ones. He sent back ten crates of seeds in the next four years, finding and introducing Jeffrey pine, mountain hemlock, red fir and others and sending the first western hemlock, nootka cypress and western red cedar.

The nursery trade also saw the potential of trees from the western United States and many collectors were sent out to the West Coast. William Lobb of Veitch's Nurseries sent back many of the same trees as Jeffrey and is given the credit for their introduction, although in some cases Jeffrey was first. Lobb also remained convinced all his life that it was he who sent the first giant sequoia in December 1853, but a Scottish landowner, J. D. Matthew, had been to Oregon himself and collected its seeds in August of the same year. However, it was Lobb who introduced the Santa Lucia fir, the California nutmeg tree and Low's white fir among others.

One major conifer from the Pacific north-west that featured in this flood of imports had, nonetheless, a very different early history in Europe. The coast redwood was, it is now known, brought to Portugal in about 1780 by the missionaries who discovered the coast of California. This was even before Menzies, sailing with Captain Vancouver, saw and took specimens of it as well as the sitka spruce, Douglas fir and others in 1792. David Douglas had collected seeds and plants of the redwood in 1832 but these, together with his journals, were lost when a boat was swamped. The coast redwood was sent to England by Theodor Hartweg with other discoveries in 1846, but it had already reached there by a roundabout route in 1843. Russia had a colony at Fort Ross in Canada where the redwood belt is relatively broad, and Russian botanists had taken seeds many years before and were growing the tree in the Crimea. Dr Fischer of Leningrad sent some seeds to the London nurseries of Knight and Perry in 1843. Several specimens planted from these seeds in 1844 and 1845 are known in British collections, although most of our biggest trees derive from other collectors' packets and date from after 1850.

From the Caucasus, Caucasian zelkova was the first to arrive, in 1760. The rampant Caucasian wing-nut followed via France in about 1785 and the elegant Caucasian ash came in 1815. The chestnut-leafed oak was first sent, to Kew, in 1846 and this original tree is now a monumental specimen. The vigorous and variable Caucasian alder came in 1860 and Van Volxem's maple, with large, sycamore-like leaves, in 1873.

China was a closed country until about this time, except for a few coastal areas, but some trees had come along the old trade routes to the Middle and Near East in or before the Middle Ages. The peach and the white mulberry, for example, were widespread in those regions before plant-mapping began. Between 1751 and 1753, d'Incarville, a French Jesuit missionary, had introduced from northern China the tree of heaven, the Chinese thuja and the pagoda tree as well as the first ginkgo. From the treaty ports on the south coast came the Chinese privet in 1794, brought by Sir Joseph Banks; the Cunninghamia and Chinese juniper in 1804, brought by John Kerr; the chusan palm in 1836, the cryptomeria in 1849 and the golden larch in 1854,

SEQUOIA SEMPERVIRENS (above), coast redwood, was introduced on to Portugal in 1870 but only reached Britain, via Russia, 1843.

brought by Robert Fortune. But the amazing abundance of plants in China, particularly in the centre and west where they are most concentrated, remained unknown until d'Incarville's successors began to describe some of them after 1860.

In 1885 Augustine Henry, a doctor with the Customs service, travelled through south-west China and introduced a few of the trees he discovered.

In 1898 it was decided that the time had come for some serious collecting in China, to follow up the tales and specimens brought back by Jesuit fathers like David Farges and Delavay and sent by Augustine Henry; and in 1899 Ernest Wilson was appointed collector by Veitch's Nurseries, trained and sent to China. In four journeys between 1900 and 1911 Wilson discovered and sent back 400 new species of trees and shrubs and 800 others. Every suburban road has plants owed to Wilson and among the more notable species are the paperbark maple, Chinese tulip tree and Sargent spruce. George Forrest made seven expeditions from 1904 to 1932, approaching China from the Burma border, and collected in areas slightly further south and west; he sent back numerous silver firs, spruces and other conifers, and vast numbers of rhododendrons. Joseph Rock and Kingdon Ward collected in the same areas and beyond, from 1923 until 1958. Further collecting expeditions are continuing and new plants still arrive.

The first tree from the botanically rich Himalayan region was received in 1818 when Dr Govan was sent cones of the morinda spruce by his son and gave the seed to the earl of Hopetoun; at his home near Edinburgh the two original trees and an early graft of one of them on to a Norway spruce still flourish. The Himalayan pine followed in 1823 and the deodar in 1831, the Himalayan hemlock in 1838 and other trees rather sporadically afterwards.

Japan was a country virtually closed to the West until 1854 so that little was known of the wealth of plant forms there. A few Japanese trees came to Europe from a botanic garden established on Java, in 1843. Some filtered out with occasional travellers,the most important of whom was Philipp von Siebold, a German eye-surgeon whose wanderings were tolerated from time to time as his services were so much in demand. It was he who brought to Europe the (smooth) Japanese maple in 1820, and much more. The Japanese had long cultivated many Chinese trees and the paulownia was first introduced from there to France in 1834, and thence to Britain in 1840. After 1854 the collectors arrived in Japan and the sudden eruption of its plants dates from 1860. In 1861 numerous conifers and cultivars of maples were sent back by Robert Fortune and John Gould Veitch. But the interior was still not open and these collectors naturally concentrated on nurseries, so the wild species in the mountains were less collected than the cultivars. When the country was fully available to collectors a flood of species of maple, oak, birch, silver firs and others was sent to Britain by Charles Maries and Harry James Veitch between 1877 and 1892 and, via the Arnold Arboretum in Massachusetts, by Charles Sargent.

LIGUSTRUM LUCIDIUM (below), Chinese privet, was one of the first introductions from China because it was cultivated in coastal areas to which early travellers had access.

Korea has a tree flora which includes some species found otherwise only in Japan, and some which range far to the south, in China, and to the north, in Mongolia. The trees tend to be very small, very hardy and attractive. Charles Oldham first collected in Korea, for Kew, in 1860–1862, and Ernest Wilson was there in 1917.

Taiwan has a flora of mixed Japanese and Chinese origin, together with some endemics like Taiwania. Wilson visited the island in 1917 but the Formosan cypress, which grows quite well in all parts, had already been introduced to Britain in 1910 by Admiral Clinton-Baker.

southern hemisphere forests and has provided many fine trees. The first to be introduced, the Chile pine or monkey puzzle, arrived in England in 1795 brought by Archibald Menzies. He took five nuts from the table during a banquet in Valparaiso and raised the trees on the voyage home. This is ironic. He had been the first to see many of the giant conifers of the north-west, like Douglas fir and coast redwood, but at the time had been unable either to collect seeds or store them on the voyage home – and never saw the one tree he did introduce, the Chile pine, growing wild. In 1843 and 1849, Sir Joseph Hooker and William Lobb collected in Chile and the Argentine, and quantities of Chile pine seeds, as well as seeds of many other trees like Fitzroya and Saxegothaea, were sent back by Lobb. The most vigorous South American trees, the roble and the rauli, were much later imports, in 1902 and 1913 respectively.

The first tree from Mexico was the cedar of Goa, which came via Portugal between 1650 and 1700, but the first direct imports were brought by the German collector, Theodor Hartweg, in 1846. These included the cedar of Goa but were mainly pines, including the Montezuma, Mexican and Mexican white pines. There is a huge assembly of pine species and forms in the mountains of Mexico, and various imports of Montezuma pine have grown in Europe under thirty different names, while several more are well-marked varieties. In 1962 *Pinus durangensis*, *P. engelmannii* and *P. cooperi* were introduced in Britain and may be seen in some pineta growing strongly. Many of the numerous Mexican oaks continue to arrive. The best of these so far, *Quercus rhysophylla*, came in 1978 and is already more than 10 m tall.

Arrivals from Australasia began in 1775 with *Sophora tetraptera*, but have been sporadic and not well recorded since. The cabbage tree, so familiar near the west coast of England, on the Isle of Man and in Ireland, was sent from New Zealand in 1823 and the blue gum from Tasmania in 1829. All three of the King William pine (*Athrotaxis*) group of strange redwood relatives were sent from their Tasmanian mountain in 1857. The cider gum came in 1846 but other eucalypts have been sent at various times and new ones still arrive.

The use of exotic trees

THE PARKS AND GARDENS in the British Isles rely for their beauty primarily on exotic trees from every part of the temperate world. Many well-known garden vistas have no native species in sight. These gardens are unsurpassed for the variety and excellence of their trees. And no other country has anything approaching the number of gardens with fine trees or tree collections that can be found in these islands. At least a thousand were visited before this book was written but there are as many more, if mostly smaller, yet to be seen. In Sussex there are five tree collections, among the best in the world, within about 16 kilometres of Haywards Heath, a concentration almost equalled around Exeter, Truro, and Crieff in Perthshire. The skill of the designers of British and Irish gardens has been in making full use of the peculiarly benign climate in which they work and achieving blends and contrasts among the great wealth of the world's plants which flourish here.

The probability of finding several good trees for any particular purpose or situation makes the designing of plantings very much simpler than if the gardener were restricted to native species, and the results more varied and nearer actual requirements. There are, however, grave dangers, both aesthetic and ecological, in using a world flora too liberally. The native flora, however restricted in variety, has been the setting of unique country scenery and has supported, and grown with, the native fauna. The scenery is now very man-made and one typical view, unique to England and much admired until disease struck the wide lowland valleys heavily sprinkled with elms, relied in fact on an exotic elm – an immigrant but one of the longest standing. Any unique natural feature is inherently of the utmost value and must be preserved. Most large-scale countryside views are basically of native species and an important feature of contrasting, obviously exotic, trees is disruptive and out of place.

Land usage, on the other hand, demands crops over wide areas and these must usually be highly exotic, whether potato fields or plantations of larch or sitka spruce, in order to produce the crop required. Large regions under this sort of crop are therefore unavoidable and, to most people, quite acceptable as their features and their effects on fauna and flora are by no means all negative. In other regions, however, there has not been, and need not be, a big incursion of exotics. All plantings which are a visible part of the landscape need sensitive treatment and should at least appear to be native species or be visually acceptable as native, like sweet chestnut, Norway maple or even, perhaps, in hill country, European larch. In this connection it is appearance rather than time of arrival which must be the guide. The horse chestnut has been in Britain for over 300 years and is regarded by many laymen as a native but it is visually quite out of keeping with native trees, while the rauli, new in 1913, fits very well. The general rule is to keep all fancy planting and bright colours to enclosed or small-scale features.

NOTHOFAGUS OBLIQUA (left), roble beech, has no fancy flowers or spectacular foliage, apart from some good colour in the autumn and so associates well with native trees.

AESCULUS DISCOLOR (below), and other horse chestnuts, having showy flowers and obviously exotic foliage do not blend well in the native landscapes and associate better with more ornamental plants.

The importance of trees

TREES ARE THE most important scenic features that can be added easily in almost every part of the land. They add diversity and increase wildlife in general. There should never be any doubt as to whether to plant a tree or not, except where there is obviously not enough room, but only doubt as to which is the best one to plant. At worst a tree can always be cut down, but a gap cannot be filled so easily. It may need emphasizing that trees, once properly established, look after themselves. They do not need endless attention and they grow just as well when the ground around them is deep in nettles and brambles as they would if it were kept clean. In fact, many of the finest trees in Britain are exactly so placed. A herbaceous garden disappears in two years of neglect but a tree thrives on 200 years of it. It is normal for an old one to carry some dead branches. They need be removed only if the tree is in a public place, for safety reasons. Broken branches look better trimmed back and remedial surgery can save a tree badly damaged by storms, but no amount of care will prevent one dying in the end and it will go about it in its own way. No one need refrain from planting trees for fear that they will not be looked after. They will look better if cared for, but will survive even if they are not.

CEDRUS LIBANI (far right), cedar of Lebanon, has proved its value as a tree for large gardens over many years.

QUERCUS VARIABILIS (right), Chinese cork oak, is of fast growth, soon making an imposing specimen with attractive foliage and bark.

Trees in the landscape

THE BRITISH ISLES has a uniquely varied geology, contained within small areas, and scarcely a rock series, from the most ancient to recent, is missing. From the Malvern Hills to the New Forest – a distance of only about 130 kilometeres – one traverses rocks of every age from Pre-Cambrian, the earliest geological era, to recent sands. The scenery is thus likely to be exceedingly diverse and in fact lacks only towering peaks and glaciers and active volcanoes. Within the great range of scenic features only cliffs and rugged peaks owe nothing to trees. Every other form of scenery, every other picture on a scenic calendar, relies heavily on them. Pictures of fens or saltings usually include, or are framed by, an old hedgerow tree or two to give contrast and aid composition. Even the scenery of bare rolling hills, so admired by ramblers and hill-walkers, gains immensely from little patches of trees under bluffs or by becks and burns; a view without them is bleak, unvarying and monotonous. When we look at a panoramic landscape our eyes roam over it seeking some prominent feature, from which to distance the components and to which to return. This is so important to our enjoyment that it operates in surprising circumstances. The view from the part of the Chiltern Hills in Oxfordshire, for example, is a broad sweep of lowlands, quite featureless except for the cooling towers of Didcot power station. Although we may not choose a clutch of cooling towers as an aesthetic feature, they are the focus to which the eye returns and by which it distances the middle and background. Without them, the view would be of much less visual interest.

Similarly, the ramblers' glorious bare hills – which are in fact a man-made semi-desert resulting from centuries of misuse by clearing, burning and over-grazing – gain as scenery if the valley sides are in many places clothed with woods, which provide changes in colour and texture and emphasize the form of the land, affording some resting place and distancing reference for the eye. Woods also provide much-needed cover for wildlife and increase the number of species of plant, insect, mammal and bird. Many birds which hunt over moorland need trees in which to breed and roost.

ABIES KOREANA (left), Korean fir, is a good choice where a small evergreen tree is required and has the advantage of producing its ornamental cones when still a small plant.

Trees in gardens and parks

TREES GIVE A GARDEN style and substance. A single well-chosen specimen, skilfully sited, can transform a scene from one of little visual interest to a vista of great impact. A park or garden may be designed to be a continuation of the surrounding countryside, but it is much more usual for it to define itself and differ radically from what is beyond, whether open fields or part of a town, and to be seen to do so. The outside world should not obtrude but, rather than being blocked out, views should be filtered; even the worst industrial or urban scenery can be interesting as a glimpsed backdrop to a garden. All this is done by trees, which will also define major features like glades, vistas and lawns. Trees are thus the backbone of every garden design. They are also, when evergreen, the most important part of the winter aspect.

QUERCUS ROBUR (right), English oak, will blend into any natural area, large park or garden with space for it. Wherever it is found it supports an enormous range of associated wildlife.

Trees add a third structural layer, above shrubs and herbs, and increase immensely the varieties of foliage, flowers and fruit. This three-layer structure is best developed and applied in Cornish-type gardens, many of them in Sussex and other counties, where rhododendrons are important in the scheme, and allows the maximum amount of plant material to be enjoyed in the minimum space. Wildlife, particularly the number of birds, increases greatly as the trees grow. This is more because of the food and cover provided by the spreading canopy than the greater number of nesting places, since many of our best songbirds nest only in shrubs or long grass. Tree-creepers, nuthatches and woodpeckers are the important exceptions.

CERCIS SILIQUASTRUM (right), Judas tree, is very much a plant for the more formal part of a garden where its ornamental qualities can be appreciated. 'Bodnant', shown here, has profuse deep pink flowers.

Trees in towns and among buildings

THE VITAL ROLE OF TREES in urban areas is to provide welcome change. Change in shape, with the rounded or conic crowns breaking the very rectilinear outlines and features of buildings; change in form, with the light and airy tracery of shoots and crowns in winter relieving their massive solidity; similar changes in texture and colour; and, above all, change with the seasons.

The use of trees in the downtown areas of clustered skyscrapers in American cities is of relevance and great interest here. They cannot hope to screen or compete with 300 m buildings and are not meant to. The ginkgos, honey-locusts, American and small-leafed limes planted in the canyons between the skyscrapers provide a different environment, on a human scale, where people walk. They give the scenic changes outlined above, and shade and relief from monotony, but they also afford fascinating views of the buildings, framed by or through their crowns – a new and rather thrilling form of landscape.

Trees in city and town parks and in churchyards also increase the number of bird species in the surrounding areas. Greenfinches would be less likely to be found on the suburban nut-bag if there were no Lawson cypresses in which they breed. The same trees, so ubiquitous around towns, may have bred the goldfinches sparkling and tinkling over thistles on wasteland, and may also have provided sites for the great majority of successful early nests of thrushes, blackbirds and dunnocks. More recently, the collared dove has moved into Lawson cypresses and now frequents towns.

The trees in a suburban road, in the street or in front gardens, transform these areas from monotonous rows of similar houses into something more akin to a glade in a garden – and places of real beauty when cherries and laburnums are in flower.

CHAMAECYPARIS LAWSONIANA 'POTTENII' (above), is one of numerous forms of Lawson cypress popular in gardens which provide ideal nesting sites for many birds.

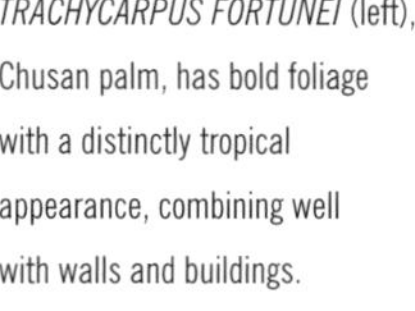

TRACHYCARPUS FORTUNEI (left), Chusan palm, has bold foliage with a distinctly tropical appearance, combining well with walls and buildings.

LARIX X EUROLEPIS (below), the hybrid larch, provides attractive cone which persist over winter and can be used in decorations.

The tree as a plant

Definition

A tree is a woody perennial plant, a form of growth found in numerous botanical families. The definition does not, therefore, imply any relationship between the various tree species, and there is no class 'trees' in the same way that there is a category of 'mosses' or 'ferns'. This manner of growth is absent or very rare in such major families as Compositae, Cruciferae and Primulaceae. It is frequent in some families, like Rosaceae, with many herbaceous species and it is dominant, almost universal, in Aceraceae (maples), Tiliaceae (limes), Fagaceae (oaks, beeches, etc.) and in the class Coniferae.

Whether a plant is a tree or a shrub is often influenced by where it is growing. Many plants which are trees in valleys may be shrubs on mountain-tops. Nevertheless, there are many plants which even in the best conditions will never be more than shrubs and others with the potential to grow into trees, and these need to be distinguished by definition. A tree is here taken to be a plant which is capable of growth on a single stem from the ground, to a height exceeding 6 m.

Names

Old-established popular names of trees are usually only general. The name oak, ash, elm or pine does not specify which of many oaks, ashes, elms and pines is intended. To be specific involves the use of a second name: red oak, manna ash, wych elm or Scots pine. In the course of time, most languages have applied names very loosely; for example, colonists in North America named some of the new trees they found after the homeland ones that they most resembled, and even repeated the process, using the same names for other trees found further afield. It was easier to sell a new coniferous timber under the old, well-known name of a highly valued wood like cedar, so the eastern parts of America, explored first, soon had two 'white cedars' and a 'red cedar'; this last is a juniper, but when the west was opened up a thuja was also called 'red cedar' and a cypress was called 'yellow cedar'. The confusion is great and none of the trees is a true cedar at all. To shed all this ambiguity and to have tree names the same all over the world, scientific names are used instead.

Early botanists described plants in Latin but some used descriptive phrases to specify the actual plant in its group. It fell to the Swedish botanist Linnaeus to implement a concise, more logical arrangement and he named all the forms of life known to him in *Systema Naturae,* published in 1758. The Linnaean system gave every organism a name in two parts, the generic and the specific, which is consistently included as a summary after the usual long description. The common oak was

QUERCUS ACUTA (top), the slow growing Japanese evergreen oak can be recognised by its untoothed leaves.

QUERCUS MYRSINIFOLIA (middle), this very hardy evergreen oak produces its bronzy young foliage late in the year, missing late frosts.

QUERCUS RYSOPHYLLA (bottom), loquat oak, is a fast-growing Mexican species still rare in cultivation but deserving to be more widely planted.

Quercus robur: 'Quercus' the genus (plural 'genera') and 'robur' – the rugged, strong one – the species (plural 'species'). With botanists everywhere actively naming plants, it was likely that the term 'robur' could have been used to describe another oak. Confusion could thus return, so the whole subject of naming organisms, the science of nomenclature, evolved certain strict rules, one being that the specific epithet always carries, as part of itself, the author's name. Since Linnaeus's work is the foundation stone of the system, his name is shortened to 'L.', hence the common oak is *Quercus robur* L., while others are identified by the first syllable of a botanist's name or other acceptable abbreviations; when two or more botanists have the same name, initials need to be added.

Of course, in 1758 neither Linnaeus nor anyone else knew more than a small proportion of the animals and plants of the world. Few conifers were then known, and only one cedar, two larches, a few spruces and several pines, so it was sensible to consign these woody-coned trees into one genus and the few known scale-leafed conifers into another. Thus Linnaeus had only three genera of conifers – *Pinus*, *Juniperus* and *Cupressus* (apart from the rather different yew, *Taxus*) – and named the larch *Pinus larix*, the cedar of Lebanon *Pinus cedrus*, the Norway spruce *Pinus abies* and the deciduous or swamp cypress *Cupressus disticha*. When it was found that there were several other larches, many other spruces and cedars and that more were likely to be discovered, it became evident that this system was inadequate. A spruce was not only a type of pine; there were in fact a large number of spruces and it was necessary to recognize these as a group distinct from pines. The cedar and the larch, likewise, each had to move up the hierarchy from being a species in the genus *Pinus* to being a genus with its own species. *Pinus* was restricted to those conifers that bear leaves arising in a common sheath, in bundles of two, three or five; that is, the true pines as we know them today. The cedars, larches, spruces and others which had been in the genus *Pinus* are now genera in the family Pinaceae, of which *Pinus* is the typical genus.

Botanical names had to be altered to reflect new relationships, and status and names follow the rules of the science of nomenclature. One basic rule is that a species always retains the specific epithet that was given to it when it was first described and named validly, provided this does not infringe any other rules of nomenclature. Thus, even when later revisions move a plant to another genus, it is always known from its specific name. The bluebell, for example, is *non-scripta* whether in *Scilla* or in *Endymion*. However, there is frequent conflict with other rules when a large genus like *Pinus* is divided into many smaller genera, and the old specific epithet often has to be dropped and replaced by the second valid published name.

PINUS PINEA (left), the stone or umbrella pine is a familiar tree in Mediterranean regions but is occasionally found in British gardens

The cedar of Lebanon was first named by Linnaeus as *Pinus cedrus*. To make the cedar a genus, the logical step is to promote its specific name to that of the new genus and call cedars in general *Cedrus*. This is straightforward for *Cedrus* and for *Larix* (the larches from *Pinus larix* L.) as both names were used as descriptive nouns. It would not do, however, for the hemlocks where the first one to be named was *Pinus canadensis* L. because 'canadensis' is an adjective and would not be suitable for use as a generic name. The eastern hemlock thus became *Tsuga canadensis* (L.) Carr., the 'L.' in parentheses because Linnaeus originally named the plant (as *Pinus canadensis*) but Carrière transferred it to the genus *Tsuga*.

Both *Cedrus* and *Larix* run into another difficulty. It would be logical, and would preserve the original names, to make the cedar of Lebanon '*Cedrus cedrus*' and the European larch '*Larix larix*'. Zoologists follow this practice and are at home with names like that of the wren, *Troglodytes troglodytes*. Botanists, however, are opposed to such repetition or 'tautology' so the next available name for the cedar of Lebanon is used: *Cedrus libani* Rich. (for Richard). For European larch, Miller's name is used *Larix decidua* Mill.

It will be noticed that *Pinus decidua* (the early name for the larch) which was so descriptive of the tree when it was among evergreen pines, spruces, silver firs and so on, loses its aptness when named by Miller as *Larix decidua*, since all larches shed their leaves in winter. Nomenclature is concerned only with correct naming according to a set of defined rules and not at all with distinguishing plants botanically. Similarly, Linnaeus put the swamp cypress in his big genus *Cupressus* and distinguished it as *C. disticha*, with parted leaves, not by its deciduous habit. When it was found to be a redwood, not a cypress, it was made into a genus of its own, *Taxodium distichum*. The coast redwood, on the other hand, was seen to be closely related to the 'deciduous cypresses', *Taxodium*, but its greatest single distinction was in being evergreen. It was therefore well-named as *Taxodium sempervirens,* but when it was

later transferred to the genus *Sequoia*, the term 'sempervirens' lost its significance because the other *Sequoia* then in the genus *S. gigantea* (now *Sequoiadendron giganteum*) is equally evergreen.

VARIETIES AND CULTIVARS

A species with a wide geographical range is likely to show some minor differences when individuals from remote parts of this range are compared. The western yellow pine, *Pinus ponderosa*, for example, ranges throughout the vast Rocky Mountain complex within the USA. A specimen from the Oregon coast is, not surprisingly, slightly different from one in the Black Hills of South Dakota and both differ from one by the Grand Canyon in Arizona. The differences are not considered sufficiently fundamental for each population to be made into a full species of its own, nor are the boundaries always definite between such forms, so they are regarded as 'varieties' of *Pinus ponderosa* and need to be named accordingly. They become *P. ponderosa* var. *scopulorum* from South Dakota and *P. ponderosa* var. *arizonica* from Arizona. Strictly the Oregon form, the one described first as *Pinus ponderosa*, then becomes var. *ponderosa*, while the name *Pinus ponderosa* includes all forms of this species. These geographical varieties are named in Latinized form, in italics, and (strictly speaking) are followed by the name of the botanist who gave them that name. In each case there is a wild population to provide seeds if the variety is needed for growing in a collection.

With 'garden varieties' the case is wholly different. These are forms like weeping, erect, golden or variegated-leafed trees of which there is no wild population. Each has been found as a single oddity, rarely seen again, or as a single shoot growing on a normal tree. Obviously there is no seed source and, with very few exceptions, any seeds produced yield normal trees. These forms are propagated by grafting or from cuttings or layers. They need to be named in a fashion that distinguishes them from true varieties. They are called 'cultivars' and are named by adding a third name to the species name, as before, but in Roman type and enclosed in single quotes. The cultivar epithet should be in the language of the person who names it, not in Latin, but old-established Latinized names given before 1959 are accepted. Hence the weeping beech can be *Fagus sylvatica* 'Pendula' as that is the earliest correct name. The cultivar epithet must begin with a capital letter. Recent cultivars have vernacular names like *Gleditsia triancanthos* 'Sunburst' and *Fraxinus angustifolia* 'Raywood'.

In some cases, with cultivars of unknown origin or very mixed or uncertain parentage, the specific epithet is dropped. Many Japanese cherry cultivars are in both categories and their names become, for example, *Prunus* 'Kanzan', *Prunus* 'Tai Haku' or *Prunus* 'Ukon'.

CUPRESSUS MACROCARPA 'LUTEA' (below right), is one of several yellow-foliaged forms of the Monterey cypress.

JUNIPERUS WALLICHIANA (below), Wallich's Juniper, is a small tree uncommon in cultivation, and much larger in its native Himalayas.

Looking at trees

IN NO COUNTRY in the world is there anything comparable to the number of fine gardens available in Britain to the public. Most of our stately homes are set among splendid trees and Scottish castles tend to have huge conifers in their policies and more in separate pineta. The botanic gardens are generally open, and a huge number of private gardens are now open on certain days under various schemes for charities. The royal parks in London, and many other city parks, are first-class arboreta, and most town parks have a number of unusual trees. Many suburban roads with front gardens and street-planting are virtually linear arboreta and it is fascinating to see how many really quite rare trees may be found in them.

To those who have no real interest in trees, it is axiomatic that a tree enthusiast walks the countryside woods and copses to see the trees, but compared with those in streets and gardens there is little of interest here – only the few native species and the common exotics like sycamore, horse chestnut and Turkey oak, and remarkably few will be well-grown specimens. Little

CORNUS NUTTALLII 'COLRIGO GIANT' (left), is one of the flowering dogwoods, in which the heads of small flowers are surrounded by prominent bracts.

AESCULUS X CARNEA (left), pink horse chestnut, is actually a hybrid between the common horse chestnut, *A. hippocastanum* and *A. pavia*, a red-flowered American species.

EUCALYPTUS PAUCIFLORA subsp. *NIPHOPHILA* (above), the snow gum, is fast growing but not very large and has striking peeling bark attractive throughout the year.

CHAMAECYPARIS PISIFERA 'SQUARROSA' (right), is a form of the Sawara cypress with distinctive blue-grey foliage, a type which is normally only found in young seedlings of this species.

new will be seen or learned of trees, however delightful it is to be in woods, without visiting areas better stocked with a variety of them.

The visits to large collections and gardens have value in more ways than the enjoyment of rare, beautiful or imposing trees. They are essential in learning to identify the less common species as well as enabling the gardener to see them in various stages of growth and health and in varying climates and soils. To someone who is planting trees, there are great areas of knowledge to be gained in this way: the wealth of species possible for each particular situation; the shapes, growth and health which can be expected; and ideas in design to be gathered and judged. Most major gardens plant continually and these are where the new cultivars can be seen and assessed as established trees used in designs, rather than as young ones in lines or containers at a nursery.

Apart from studying trees with a view to planting them, tree-watching becomes an addictive and absorbing hobby, which can be indulged in at any time of the year and in almost any place in the British Isles.

Planting trees

MOST TREES make very rapid growth when young. However, there is a generally held myth that all trees are slow growing and this often leads to great expense and difficulties in establishing garden ones. If trees did grow slowly there would be some advantage in buying and planting a large specimen. Since they do not, this common practice merely proliferates unsightly, gaunt, staked cripples scarcely able to grow, where one should see sturdy, unstaked, well-furnished and thriving small trees.

Too often a gardener will seek the largest specimen available of a particular tree. Perhaps this is needed to replace a lost one, to fill a gap or to provide an instant planting. Without realizing it he or she is creating problems for the future, for although a large specimen will fulfil immediate needs it is not usually realized that a small tree will almost certainly have reached the same size as, and overtake, the large specimen within a few years, and result in a much more healthy tree.

In a tree, as in any other plant, the roots feed the leaves and the leaves feed the roots. Should some part of the crown be lost through accident, the roots, now in excess for the needs of the crown, can provide extra nutrients and water for the required additional shoot growth. If, however, part of the root system is destroyed, the situation is more serious. Fewer nutrients and less water from the roots mean that fewer and smaller shoots are produced. This cuts down the amount of nutrients from the leaves available for root production and, if these conditions continue, the growth of the tree is permanently retarded.

When a large tree is transplanted, part of its root system, and often the most essential part, can be left behind. The first year's growth, therefore, is often poor, and at a time when the roots need abundant nutrients to re-establish they are provided with a minimum. They put on little growth and are unable to support active shoot growth the following year. This vicious spiral is seldom, if ever, broken, and can be crippling for as much as 20 years.

In contrast to this a young sapling loses little of its root system when moved and, although there will be a slight check in growth the first year, by the following year the roots will have established themselves enough to support vigorous top growth.

SELECTING A TREE

In buying a tree, whatever its size and almost independent of the species, there is one golden rule. There must be a good, strong, single leading shoot. This is the prime indication of healthy growth in the nursery and of strong growth and good shape in the garden. A tree without a leading shoot should be shunned absolutely.

When looking at a tree in a nursery, try to imagine the effect you aim to create in the garden. Whether it is destined to be a single specimen in a lawn, to be part of a group or to form an upper canopy to a shrubbery, its task is to grow as rapidly as possible as a single stem resulting in a straight bole which leads the eye to the crown. It is therefore important to avoid trees with broken or twisted leading shoots, or with more than one leader. To buy a maple with three or four equal leading branches is, as one so often sees, to buy a tree incapable of ever making a good bole and crown.

When planted correctly and looked after, a young tree such as this cherry (above), should soon be growing strongly.

1 Here a two- or three-year-old tree has been planted in a hole that is only slightly larger than its existing roots. The surrounding soil is enriched with garden compost or leaf mould.

2 A stake was inserted into the soil, slightly off-centre, before the tree was planted. The tree is tied to the stake with a tree tie and watered well. It is essential when backfilling the hole that the tree and stake remain vertical.

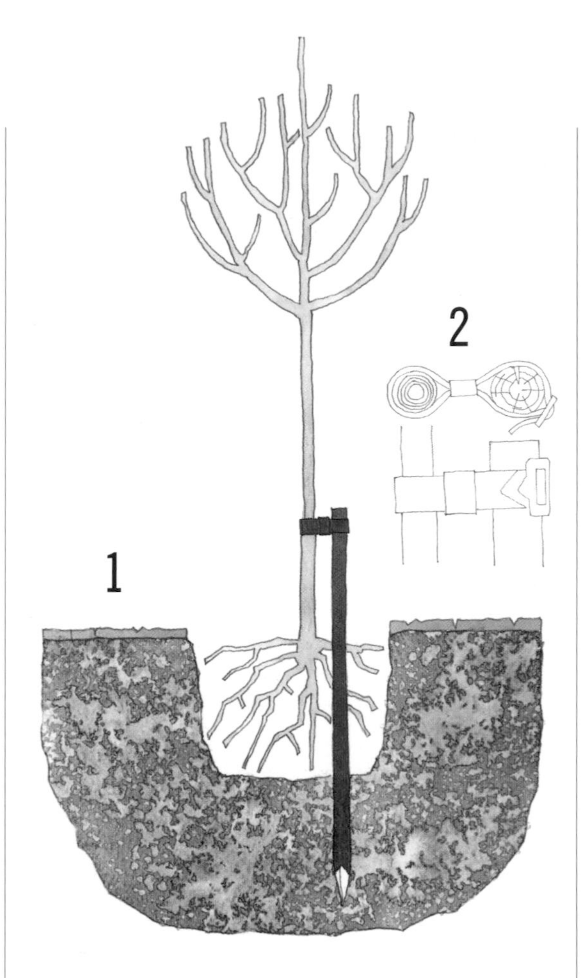

HOW TO PLANT

To ensure as great a success as is possible with a tree, care must be taken of it even before planting. Never let the soil around the roots become dry if the tree is in a container or rootballed, and make sure the soil is wet before planting. A tree which is bare-root needs greater care as its roots can dry out easily. To prevent this, keep them covered with damp sacks or soil even while the tree is laid beside the planting hole.

A two- to three-year-old tree needs a hole only slightly larger than the spread of its roots and some soil enriched with compost or leaf mould. On very sandy, open soils it is worthwhile digging a much deeper hole and adding several buckets of old turf, weeds, compost or leaf mould to the soil to increase water retention for several years. Most importantly, firm the tree in really hard by ramming your heel into the soil around it, taking care not to damage the base or leave the tree out of vertical.

Planting a large tree is a much bigger task. Roots in a ball, and particularly any that curve round the edge of a container, should be spread out and damaged ones cut off. The hole should be at least twice as wide as the fully spread roots. The depth of the hole should be such that when the tree is planted the soil level at its base is the same as it was in the nursery. This can usually be seen at the base of the trunk. The hole will often reach the subsoil and this should be broken up and some good topsoil or compost added and worked in. If drainage is poor, add a layer of coarse sand.

If a stake is used, insert it slightly off-centre before the tree is planted, then place the tree next to it and spread its roots out over the prepared soil. Backfill the hole gradually in layers of about 15 cm, using good topsoil mixed with organic matter. Ensure that all spaces between the roots are filled and that the tree and stake remain vertical. Firm the soil around the base of the tree gently to avoid damaging any roots. Tie the tree to the stake using a tree tie and water well.

WHEN TO PLANT

There is often a great deal of confusion over the best time to plant trees. This is often unnecessary as most good nurseries will not supply them when they cannot be planted. Today many trees are grown in containers and have the advantage that they can be planted at any time of year, as there is only minimal disturbance to their roots. When planting large container-grown trees, in particular, care must be taken to avoid disturbing the roots – because there is a larger proportion of foliage than in smaller specimens, the roots will lose more water and dry out more quickly. All container-grown trees need regular watering after planting.

Deciduous trees that are supplied bare-root can be planted whenever they are dormant – that is, when they are leafless – normally between October and April, as long as the soil is not frozen or waterlogged. At any other time too much water will be lost and the tree will be likely to die. October is a good time to plant as the soil is still warm and some root growth can occur before the onset of winter, giving the tree an excellent start the following year.

Evergreens are normally supplied in containers or rootballed. They are much more susceptible than deciduous trees to water-loss during winter and therefore, unless grown in containers, are best planted when their root systems are active. This is in either early October or March.

ACER NEGUNDO var. *VIOLACEUM* (far right). The visual effect of a tree has to be considered when planting. This one, for instance, grows well on most soils but would not fit in with every setting. It is too striking to be assimilated into a fully rural landscape.

Tree care

FERTILIZING

In general, trees seldom require fertilizers except for a brief period at each end of their lives, when a judicious application can make a big difference in growth and appearance.

Phosphates (P) are important for good root growth, and are notably lacking in peaty and other acid soils but generally adequate in loams and clays. On sandy soils, therefore, it is as well to mix a little phosphatic fertilizer in the bottom of the planting hole and in the backfill. The one tree for which this is unnecessary is the Lawson cypress and its legion cultivars.

Nitrates (N), too, are essential for vigorous growth and production of foliage and so are most beneficial in the first few years when the shape and vigour of the young tree are of greatest importance. Nitrates leach out of well-drained soils very readily and only rich loams and clays retain enough. On all other soils, and particularly on open sands and heathy soils, nitrate in some form should be supplied for the first few years. Even on clays, trees of normal vigorous and leafy growth like poplars, willows and wing-nuts will benefit from nitrate. Eucalypts, on the other hand, do not; they have low nutrient requirements and, providing they have a root-run completely clear of vegetation for two or three years, will manage best on their own, as will alders, locust trees and other legumes. These equip themselves with bacteria in nodules on their roots which extract nitrogen from the air. On sandy soils all other trees show clearly the good effects of nitrates. Larches, spruces and many silver firs among conifers grow much faster if given nitrate. Leaching away as it does, it needs to be given when it can be taken up immediately, which is from about early April. The only way in which a tree planted in autumn can be given useful nitrate at planting is by mixing bone meal with the soil as this releases the nitrogen slowly.

The last of the three major nutrients is potash (K), which is needed for flower and fruit production, ripening and hardening off, and resistance to disease in general. It is seldom really short in garden soils except on the poorest sandy ones. Potash, it will be seen, in most ways works as a curb on the action of nitrates, and vice versa; their effects are opposed. Where nitrates promote shoot and leaf growth at the expense of flowers and fruit, and soft growth liable to fungal disease, potash promotes flowers and fruit at the expense of foliage, stops late growth and hardens it against disease. This state of affairs demonstrates a vital factor in fertilizing – the nutrients must be balanced.

This is simple to achieve through the use of balanced fertilizers, which are easily obtained. For general use a fertilizer like National Growmore does well. For sandy, light soils short of nitrate, a formula relatively high in N is needed for early growth. At planting, bone meal is highly beneficial because the nitrate leaches away more slowly in this form than in the more soluble forms which are given when growth has started. Bone meal also yields a trace of P.

Senility can set in at almost any time in the life of a tree and when one looks as if it may soon die, it usually will. However, its ill-health may be due to a shortage of nutrients, possibly through long years of closely mowing a lawn over its root-run without replacing the nutrients that are removed as a result. If so, fertilization may help the tree to better health and growth, and prolong its life.

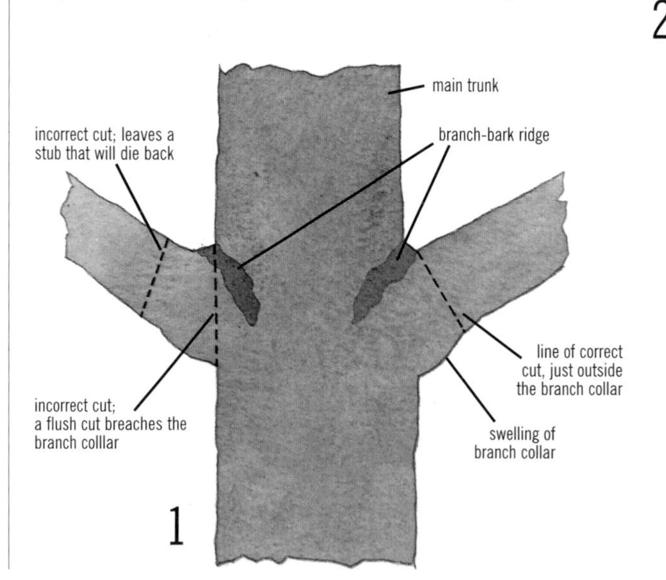

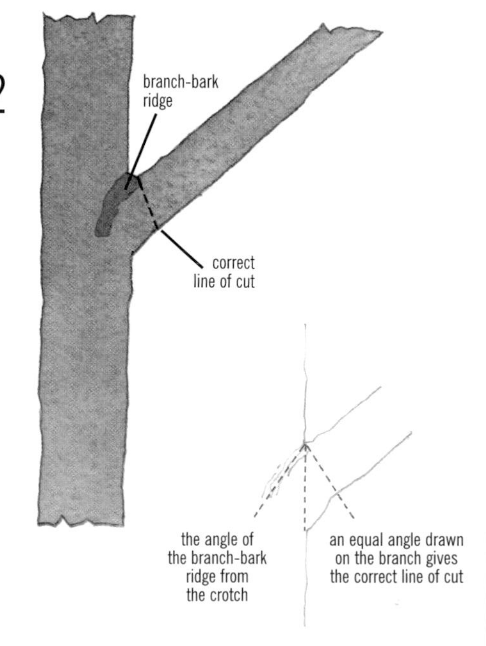

REMOVING UNWANTED TREE BRANCHES

1 It is usually quite easy to see the swelling of the branch collar where a large branch joins the main trunk. When removing branches, *do not* cut into the collar – this will breach a tree's natural defences – or leave too long a stub which will die back.

2 On small branches the branch collar is seldom obvious, but at the branch base you will see a wrinkle of bark known as the branch-bark ridge. Observe the angle that it makes from the crotch into the main stem. Make your final cut at an equal and opposite angle on the branch.

Pruning

Arboricultural pruning is quite different from that done in orchards and shrubberies to promote larger and fewer flowers and fruit within easy reach, and is very much simpler to carry out. There are only two aims, one of which – to promote a strong, single, central stem and shapely crown – the tree should be capable of achieving by itself. The other is to achieve rapidly a straight, smooth, clean stem uncluttered by shaded-out twigs and heavy low branches.

In order to mature into a good specimen, a tree must be planted out when small and young and must have a good, strong leading shoot from the start. Only if the leading shoot fails, or forks into two, or if an extra strong shoot grows out at an awkward angle, does pruning become necessary. Where two or more new shoots compete as leaders, the strongest and straightest (a balance between the two factors may have to be struck) must be selected and the others cut out.

Nearly all trees grow naturally in groups or in woods and it is normal for the lower branches to be shaded out and die and then to fall, leaving a clean stem. In amenity planting many trees are grown in the open. The interior of the lower branches dies but the tips are still in the light and continue to grow, although often feebly, and this keeps the branches alive and prevents their being shed. The result is a bole cluttered with masses of dead twigs which become a thicket of nettles, elderberry and brambles and a haven for rabbits. The tree needs help in shedding these useless shoots and the earlier it is given, the better.

Even when a tree on a lawn is required to be 'furnished to the ground', it does this best, and with more luxuriant foliage, when the bottom 2 m of the stem is clean and the branches arising above it bend to the ground under their own weight. The bole will then have space around it which can be kept clear of weeds, and the low foliage benefits from the light and air.

Trees other than lawn specimens, and particularly those grown among shrubs or in groups, need to have their crowns raised. and the clean straight boles which are their unique contribution to the garden made, as soon as possible. It does a tree no harm to remove a third of its crown by cleaning 1 m of bole when the tree is 3 m high; a tree that grows to 9 m will probably end with 3 m of clear bole from ground level. The advantages are many. The shoots cut off close to (but not flush with) the bole are small and the scars heal within a year and need no treatment at all. Trees grown for their bark will show this feature much more quickly on clean boles, and in all cases the space around the tree becomes available for planting, mowing or walking. It should then mature without further help into a shapely specimen.

Pruning should rarely be necessary to restrict size. The constant cutting back of branches is a necessity to shape pleached *allées*, topiary and similar features, but otherwise the need for shaping is a sign that the wrong tree has been planted. A tree should be chosen for a site where its normal growth will not cause obstruction, and no other form of pruning should be required but the cleaning up of the bole.

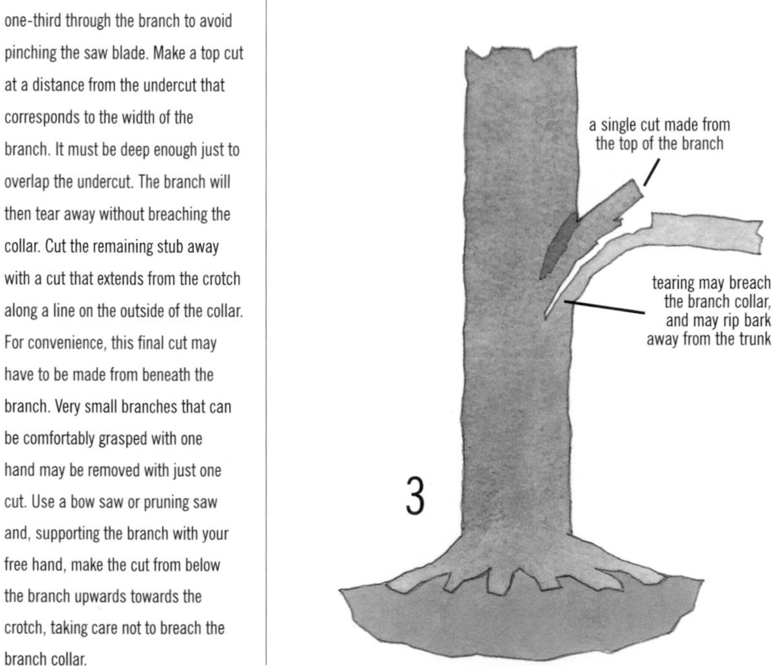

3 A branch removed with one cut will tend to tear along the grain of the wood, pulled down by its own weight before the cut is complete. This may extend into the trunk and breach the branch collar. Do not attempt to remove large branches from mature trees, or any branches that cannot comfortably and safely be reached from the ground. If in *any* doubt, consult a professional tree surgeon.

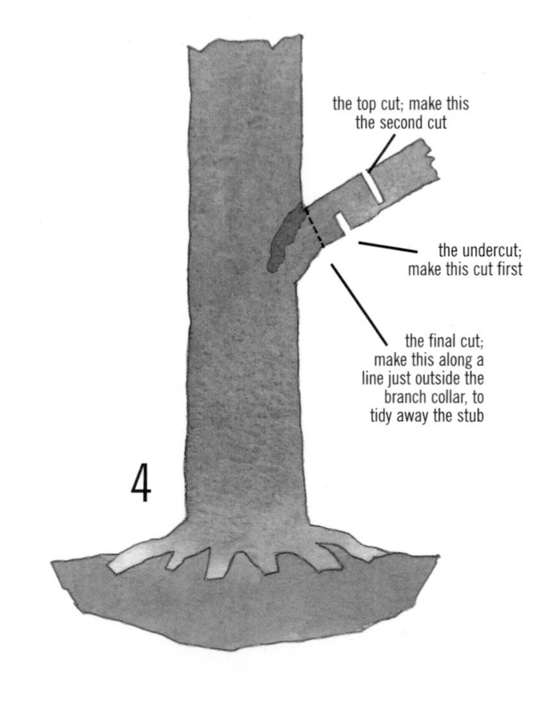

4 Using a bow saw, make an undercut at a convenient distance from the branch collar, no more than one-third through the branch to avoid pinching the saw blade. Make a top cut at a distance from the undercut that corresponds to the width of the branch. It must be deep enough just to overlap the undercut. The branch will then tear away without breaching the collar. Cut the remaining stub away with a cut that extends from the crotch along a line on the outside of the collar. For convenience, this final cut may have to be made from beneath the branch. Very small branches that can be comfortably grasped with one hand may be removed with just one cut. Use a bow saw or pruning saw and, supporting the branch with your free hand, make the cut from below the branch upwards towards the crotch, taking care not to breach the branch collar.

Ivy and trees

The growth of ivy on trees causes frequent worry and may lead to well-meant expeditions to cut it away from roadside and other ones, inspired by the mistaken idea that ivy kills trees. However, in general, healthy trees have little or no ivy, sickly and senile ones have a fair quantity and dead trees are festooned with it. A rational explanation for this is that a healthy tree shades its bole and prevents the growth of ivy. As it weakens it lets in more light, and when it dies the ivy can luxuriate.

Whether or not to remove ivy is a matter of aesthetics together with a large element of conservation. A fine bole has its looks spoiled; attractive bark is hidden. In general, specimen trees should be kept free of ivy, especially those that are prominent on a lawn, but countryside and woodland trees should be left to grow it. In a country with very few native evergreens thick ivy is a vital winter refuge for insects and birds. It is important for nesting birds and its late flowers provide insects with the last nectar of the year, through them enabling fruit to ripen throughout the winter to feed birds in hard times. Deer browse ivy and the trailing stems on the ground hold snow, keep the soil warm and allow small mammals to burrow. Ivy is therefore a valuable plant in woodland ecology.

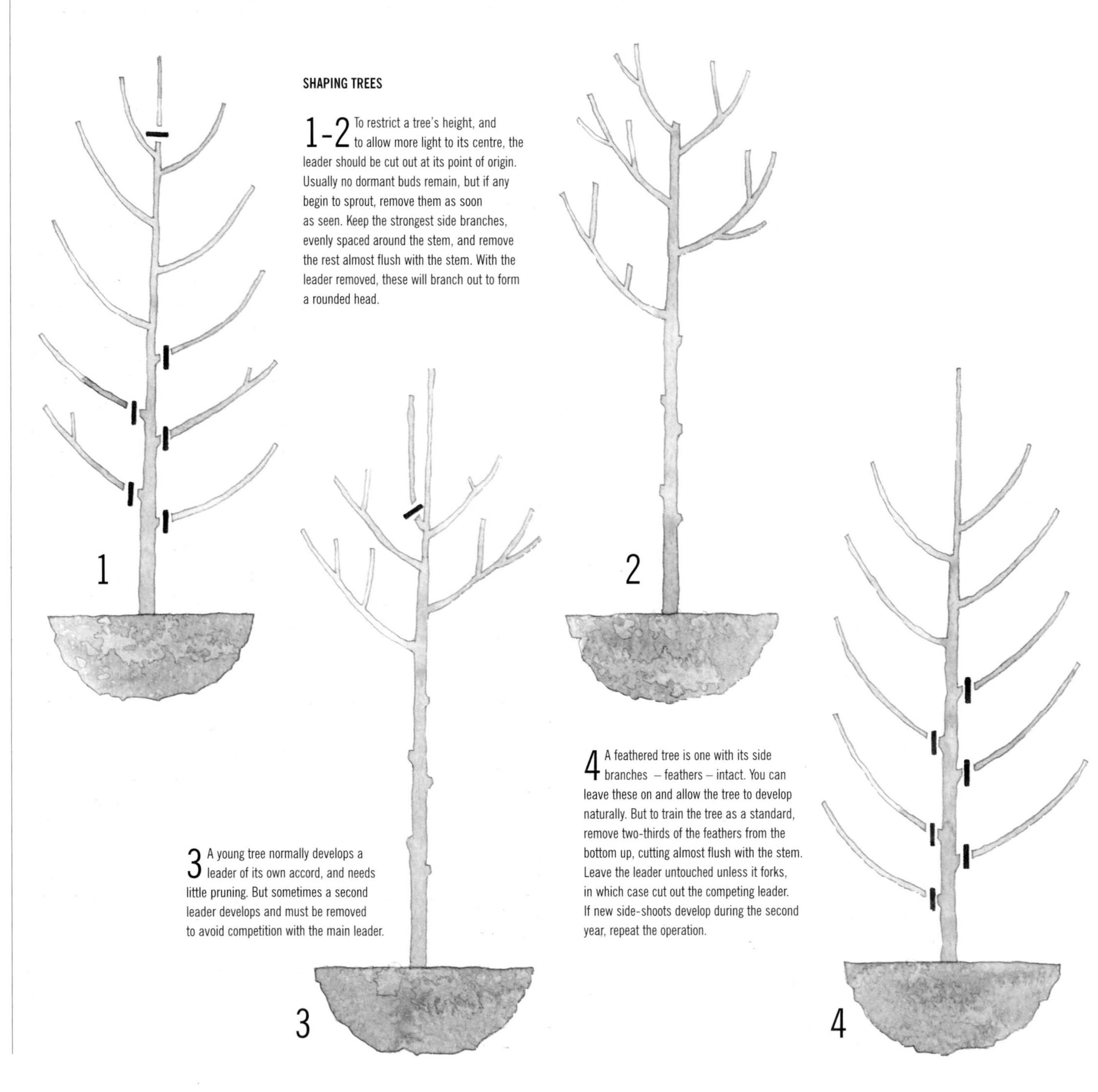

SHAPING TREES

1-2 To restrict a tree's height, and to allow more light to its centre, the leader should be cut out at its point of origin. Usually no dormant buds remain, but if any begin to sprout, remove them as soon as seen. Keep the strongest side branches, evenly spaced around the stem, and remove the rest almost flush with the stem. With the leader removed, these will branch out to form a rounded head.

3 A young tree normally develops a leader of its own accord, and needs little pruning. But sometimes a second leader develops and must be removed to avoid competition with the main leader.

4 A feathered tree is one with its side branches – feathers – intact. You can leave these on and allow the tree to develop naturally. But to train the tree as a standard, remove two-thirds of the feathers from the bottom up, cutting almost flush with the stem. Leave the leader untouched unless it forks, in which case cut out the competing leader. If new side-shoots develop during the second year, repeat the operation.

Landscaping with trees

Planning

With very few exceptions, trees need full light overhead in order to grow properly and in any case the taller-growing ones will need clear space above into which to grow. A shady corner under other trees is thus not the place to plant a new one. It will also be dry from the shading and from the roots of the old trees.

The site for a new tree must be able to contain it without constricting its natural spread until it is a reasonable age. Except in trees of fixed rather formal shape, the spread of a mature specimen depends on the individual tree and its surroundings. Oaks in a wood take up the space available, whereas oaks in open parkland, unhindered by others, vary from being rather less broad than their height to being enormously spreading – two or three times as broad as they are tall – with long low branches.

There are two opposing approaches to spacing trees at planting. They can be planted at the distances that will be required when they are fully mature; or they can be positioned much more closely. For many large trees planting for the ultimate size usually means leaving a clear space of 20–30 m round each plant, and restricts the number of trees per hectare to thirty or less; but it does permit the tree unhindered growth throughout its life and avoids the possibility of valuable specimens having to be felled for the benefit of others.

NYSSA SYLVATICA 'SHEFFIELD PARK' (below), has grown here to be a well-shaped specimen. Requiring a lot of sun to be at its best, its habit could easily be spoiled by planting it too close to another tree.

Those with limited land and a less assured future for their planting will prefer the closer option. In practice, the gardener with limited space usually packs in a variety of trees and, by judicious placing of erect and small ones among the others, achieves for his or her lifetime a planting of endless fascination. Nevertheless, great care is required in tree-planting. It is folly to plant a black walnut within 10 m of a Hungarian oak for, as anyone who appreciates these species knows, one or the other must be doomed within a few years. Favourite trees should be set as widely apart as possible and the infilling done with less choice species which can be sacrificed when their time comes.

Placing

The golden rule is that it is where you do NOT plant that makes or breaks a design. Anyone can plant trees that grow into a wood, lose their individual character and fail to make a good picture. Successful vistas depend on the unplanted areas, the glades and lawns and prospects, and these must be kept open. To look its best, a tree needs to be viewed from varying distances and allowed to develop its crown evenly all round. Both requirements imply the absence of other trees from certain areas. Lawns, in particular, must be kept unplanted and any external vista in the design obviously needs to be kept clear of trees.

Large-scale features

In planning an extensive prospect it is important that the main features, or framework, should be on a proportionately bold scale. A single tree of the largest size may sometimes be required, as a skyline feature, for example, on the crown of a bare knoll, at the end of a lake, in the centre of a glade or at a large cross-rides. To carry off such a solitary position, it must not only be capable of reaching a large size, and that as soon as possible, but it must have character. Big trees are also necessary in lining or defining a long glade, and particularly in narrowing one with false perspective, for the effect is greatest at the most distant point and will be lost unless they are prominent. The trees chosen for a long avenue must also be of the largest ultimate stature, as should those for background plantings. If the species chosen for clumps and roundels is, like the larch, of only moderately large growth, the area the trees cover should be increased to avoid a spotty effect and, in the case of a roundel on a knoll, to clothe the upper slopes and prevent the feature being a mere tuft on the top.

Framework trees

IN A LARGE GARDEN not every tree can be an individual, planted as a specimen. Many are what are referred to as 'framework' trees, those that make up the basic structure of a planting or are used to create certain features, such as boundary screens, avenues or groups. Depending on how they are planted they screen the garden or open up and highlight views of the external landscape, which can be very effective whether the scene is rural or urban.

These are reliable trees that fit naturally into the landscape even though they may not be native, and that will grow well in the given soil and conditions. So no garishly coloured, yellow or purple trees should be used. Framework trees differ according to area, so in high rainfall ones, where conifers may be common and thrive, many of these would work very well. On the other hand, beech would be more in keeping in a dry, chalky area. Traditionally, trees of more exotic appearance are grown in more formal areas, closer to the house, and those that fall in between, such as upright or weeping forms of native trees, can be effectively used to link the two.

Framework trees can also be used to create avenues, planted in two or more rows of individual trees or, if the avenue is large, in groups. If space allows, groups are better because they are accident-proof – failure of a tree here and there has no real effect on the planting as a whole, whereas long lines of individual trees depend on 100 per cent success and good growth. Broad-leafed trees and conifers can be mixed in an avenue, either where a long, informal one of mixed species includes a few Scots pines or Atlas cedars, or in a clumped avenue where some of the groups can be made up of a number of conifers of a stature similar to the other trees.

While an avenue should be planted with consideration of the path or road between the trees, the same does not apply to a line where light need not be the main factor in determining the choice of tree and the spacing. The hedgerow approach, with trees of mixed stature, form and spacing, is the best way of planting a belt of trees when an avenue is desired but only one side of the thoroughfare can be planted. A line can also be a good feature where a hillside of beech woods or other high forest ends at a field. If the wood is liable to be felled, a permanent line along the base softens the sudden clearance and strengthens the contour and division between field and wood or scrub. In lowlands broad-leafed trees would be preferable, with small-leafed lime, beech and oak among the first choices. In hills western hemlock or giant sequoia are probably best, although Douglas fir is often a good choice and silver fir, Norway spruce and thuja may be seen.

Roundels are clumps of trees roughly circular in outline and usually crowning a knoll. The traditional roundel is of beech on chalk downlands but in other parts Scots pines, oak, larch, birch and, very occasionally, monkey puzzle are used. Beech on top of chalk cannot grow by itself at first, and must have a nurse species such as Scots pine, ash, sycamore or Lawson cypress. Beech and larch are two of the best species for roundels but in coniferous areas the giant sequoia can be the most commanding, and the monkey puzzle the most unusual.

Some of the best framework and avenue trees are listed below with their various advantages and disadvantages.

Acer platanoides (Norway maple) is a good tree for clumps and short avenues but has not quite the stature for the biggest scale features, and in a boundary planting

AESCULUS HIPPOCASTANUM (above) The flowers and fruit of the horse chestnut are great favourites with the public. The fragility of its branches, however, means that it is not a wise choice for widespread planting on public land.

ACER DAVIDII 'GEORGE FORREST' (far right). Any species, like this Chinese maple, which is too exotic in form and colour is unsuitable as a framework tree. Reliability rather than individuality is the essential attribute for one that has to make up the basic structure of a planting.

it needs to be mixed with other trees. Its merits are fast early growth, whether on acid or chalky soils, a good densely domed crown of light green leaves (a foil for the dark sycamore) and splendid autumn colours – scarlet here and there, but mostly gold and orange. However, its best point may be its abundant bunches of bright yellow flowers before it, or most other trees, has any leaves.

Acer pseudoplatanus (Sycamore) may be dull but it is of immense value in severe conditions because it is so extraordinarily tough. Neither strong sea winds nor badly polluted air seem to affect it, and it makes the biggest tree in many city parks. It has a very dense crown, is good as a screen and will grow well as a crowded clump that, if thinned, will contain some splendid boles. Its branches are safer than those of most trees and it is very long-lived and almost never blows down.

Acer saccharinum (Silver maple) has, foremost of its merits, an abundant vigour of upward growth so that it soon has long, erect and arched slender branches and a stout bole. The prettily lobed and toothed leaves are light green above and silvery beneath, giving the fully foliaged tree an ethereal aspect, and turn soft yellow with some pink, or sometimes red, in autumn. It is, however, somewhat fragile and short-lived and will lose branches in an exposed position.

Aesculus hippocastanum (Common horse chestnut) is often a framework tree around, and in the interior of, town and city parks and in old parkland. It has a good tolerance of soils and can achieve the necessary size and be an effective screen. Its flowers and fruit are great favourites with the public. Nonetheless it is not a wise choice for widespread planting on public land. Its branches tend to crash down if suddenly weighted by a summer shower. Many trees are senile when they are not much more than 100 years old and still in reasonable shape.

Castanea sativa (Sweet chestnut) is a good framework tree and can be seen in avenues and clumps of considerable age. It is long-lived, if not nearly as long as is often claimed – 400–500 years is as much as any old specimen really indicates. It decays slowly and when heavy branches have been lost the stump makes sprouts and survives as a picturesque relic. Although it is best on light soils, many old trees have grown well in city parks on gravels and clay. It makes a good screen, has prominent flower catkins and fruit and turns fine yellows and browns in autumn.

Fagus sylvatica (Common beech) is the most widely used tree, and one of the best, for boundary planting, clumps and roundels. It withstands considerable exposure, even on the coast, and will make a large specimen nearly everywhere. It also gives good shelter with its dense leafage and its leaf fall makes a great contribution to the soil for quite a distance around the tree. As it is a native species it blends with the countryside and adds a rural aspect to a city park, growing well either on acid and sandy soil or on chalk and limestone. Unfortunately, beeches are relatively short-lived and many old trees now 200 years old shed large branches dangerously.

Fraxinus excelsior (Common ash) has a limited role. It grows well in cities, given a retentive soil, and in exposure and on chalk. It can have a fine straight bole and be 25 m tall even under some adversity, making a good clump if thinned judiciously. It is not long-lived – about 230 years, like the beech – and is somewhat ungainly as a single tree. It is late into leaf and any autumn golds will be brief.

Larix decidua (European larch) and other species will unfortunately not flourish in large towns, but in more rural areas this is a first-class perimeter tree, ideal for roundels, clumps and irregular copses. It grows fast, is attractive to many birds, can support a dense growth of bluebells and is bright in early spring and late autumn.

Platanus x *acerifolia* (London plane) is of utmost value and much used in urban parks, where many species may not flourish. It has as great a stature as any tree and

can thrive in the most difficult conditions. It has come to look urban because of its very success in cities, and is therefore desirable in country parks only if mixed with other trees in framework and clumps.

Populus x *canadensis* 'Serotina Aurea' (Golden black poplar) can be 30 m tall and has a dense crown of bright yellow leaves. It is very much a city park or a garden tree, but a group in the right place is highly attractive.

Populus x *canescens* (Grey poplar) has great possibilities as a framework tree. It has the rapid growth and final stature required and makes a fine, imposing tree of character. The purple cast of its expanding catkins is marked and unusual in early spring, while the emergence of silvery foliage is a striking feature. It has, for a poplar, a dense crown that is effective as a screen, and turns quite a good gold in autumn. A clump or belt soon becomes effective and the tree has a reasonably long life.

Pseudotsuga menziesii (Douglas fir) will make an imposing avenue, mainly in regions with cool, moist summers, but needs to be widely spaced, about 20 m between trees, as it can lose shape with age and the avenue will become informal. It can be a perimeter and general framework tree in a park or garden in a valley, provided it is not planted in heavy, dull, solid belts which would hide the surrounding mountains. It is not suitable for lowland areas.

Quercus cerris (Turkey oak) resists city air very well. There are some fine trees in London parks and it makes an imposing avenue in Central Park, New York. It has rapid growth and usually a good bole in its favour, but the foliage is a little too dull and dark for it to be planted in large belts. It is excellent as a roundel tree.

Quercus robur (Common oak) is frequently seen as a framework tree, mostly in lowland clay areas unsuited to the growth of beech. It does not become as tall as beech, and a wider belt is needed to provide the amount of shelter that the latter would give, but it lives for twice as long. The leaf fall is just as beneficial as that of beech and the autumn colour is later and nearly as good. The sessile oak (*Quercus petraea*) has rarely been used as a framework tree but, given the same or somewhat lighter soil as the common oak, it makes a much more handsome tree and ought to be more used. The leaves are regularly spaced, unlike those of the common oak, and cast a more even shade. A group or copse will have a grass floor with few shrubs – which attracts pied flycatchers and redstarts.

Sequoia sempervirens (Coast redwood) has not been seen planted as a grand avenue, and this may be for the best since the quite wide variation in its habit of growth makes an uneven avenue likely; the crown does not taper like that of the Sierra redwood so would give less light, and to avoid a gloomy atmosphere the trees would need to be more widely spaced. However, in good redwood country the huge red boles are impressive and in small groups, widely spaced or among other trees, the coast redwood can be the major feature of an informal avenue. It is excellent in clumps or roundels but is much too thin in large urban areas.

TILIA X EUROPAEA (above), common lime, is very fast growing and a common parkland tree. However, the profuse sprouts borne around its base make it difficult to maintain and its parents (*T. cordata* and *T. platyphyllos*) would be better in many situations.

Sequoiadendron giganteum (Sierra redwood or Giant Sequoia) has no rivals for avenues on the largest scale. It is also excellent for small roundels and clumps, but is quite unsuited as a perimeter-belt tree and too thin in smoky air to be advisable in a city park.

Tilia cordata (Small-leafed lime) would make a splendid tree for framework plantings but has rarely been used. It can exceed 30 m in height and its foliage is small, prettily heart-shaped and slightly silvered beneath. Unlike the other big limes, its starry little flowers spray out at all angles. As a single tree its clean straight main branches and big stature add to its good foliage, and it has been omitted from the selection of 'single specimen' trees only because its crown is a little shapeless and shares some of the defects of the common lime.

Tilia x *europaea* (Common lime) is widely planted in urban parks, lines, avenues and old parkland. As a screen, it does well for height but the narrow upper crowns allow regular gaps if the trees are in a line rather than a belt. The poor shape of the middle and lower crowns and the vigorous sprouting around the base render this lime too untidy to make a pleasing single tree despite the great size it can attain. It is very long-lived and rarely sheds any but well-decayed light branches.

Tilia platyphyllos (Broad-leafed lime) is inferior to the common lime only in stature. It clearly surpasses it in its fine hemispheric crown, clean growth, and the fact that it attracts fewer aphids.

Trees for screens and windbreaks

PYRUS USSURIENSIS (above), is a vigorous pear, valued for its early flowers in spring and is capable of reaching a height of 15 m.

TRADITIONALLY, screens in large gardens are composed of fast-growing large trees such as beech, larch, Austrian pine and Turkey oak. The belts are broad enough to absorb the occasional loss of ones which will inevitably be blown down. Today, the tendency is to plant a narrow belt of evergreen conifers, usually thuja or a cypress. These are not so effective because a solid wall of foliage creates strong eddies of wind around its edges and over the top, and actually increases locally the speed of the wind. Secondly, a narrow belt will suffer damage and random losses when gusts cannot penetrate the dense foliage and so exert sudden high pressures. Thirdly, a uniform line of cypress or thuja foliage is dull and monotonous and not what one would choose for an end to a vista.

A filter rather than a barrier has none of these drawbacks. The wind filters through the gaps without building up damaging speeds or pressures, and each group of trees can be varied and attractive in shape and colour. The planting need not be restricted to native countryside species. This is as well, for the most effective trees will be exotic evergreens and of columnar, conic or other distinct shape and of the tallest growth.

For a windbreak there is no reason to avoid more uniform plantings and they can be entirely of species which give rapid and effective shelter. In sites exposed to sea winds these are Monterey and bishop pines for early effect and holm oak for long-term. Monterey cypress tends to be vulnerable to wind throw when grown in groups but is more stable on its own, when it makes a hugely broad tree in western areas. Leyland cypress is also liable to be unstable but usually only where the soil is shallow or where trees have been planted in a line. Its foliage is thicker and creates more of a barrier than that of the Monterey cypress or the two pines mentioned, so it must be planted in small groups.

Deciduous trees give adequate shelter to plants which are dormant in winter, but evergreens should be chosen where it is necessary to shelter tender plants. Even when bare, deciduous trees break the force of the wind significantly and a broad belt of beech, larch or birch has a beneficial effect over a great distance. In a new and exposed garden, deciduous trees are invaluable for early and temporary shelter. Vigorous and rugged pioneer species like larch, birch and sallow are cheap and easily found and give early shelter with minimum summer shade. They allow main plantings to be made reasonably close to them and so do not interfere with the final plan. They are removed when the permanent shelter trees have grown enough to be effective.

If a windbreak is made into a decorative feature there rarely is any need to reduce it to a single line. Fortunately, the best trees for this purpose have conic crowns and this allows the desired ratio to be achieved: the tapering tops form less than half of the windbreak while the bases occupy more than half, providing shelter where it is most needed. By using such conic trees as the golden-barred thuja and many of the best coloured forms of Lawson cypress, three-quarters of the boundary can be planted yet it will never present more than half a solid barrier to the wind when the trees grow. If deciduous trees are used, they should also be conical ones such as larch and metasequoia.

It is very much easier to plan an effective and attractive windbreak where space can be made, at least in parts, for more than a single row of trees. The ideal is to have varied clumps which will withstand loss more effectively than a line would. This also allows variety in shape, texture and colour, and helps to create a windbreak that is a major feature as well as being useful. The more strikingly coloured conifers which are so useful for eye-catching and shelter plantings are, on the whole, not among the fastest growers, but early rapid growth is of value in shelter and screen plantings. Each clump should therefore include one or more rapid-growing specimens on the outer or windward side of the colour feature.

PINUS SYLVESTRIS 'FASTIGIATA' (below), the erect Scots pine, has a narrow, formal habit which lend it very well to planting in formal situations and near buildings.

Single specimen trees

MONUMENTAL SIZE

In the traditional parkland landscape trees are planted to become enormous, widely spaced single specimens, or occasionally a garden will call for a tree of the largest size as its major feature. To carry off a solitary position, a species must not only be capable of reaching a large size, and that as soon as possible, but it must also have character. In any situation a single huge tree should meet the following requirements:

Imposing stature
Its ultimate height must be at least 30–40 m and it must be reliable in attaining it.

Longevity
The chosen tree will not do its job properly if it has to be replaced every 150 years.

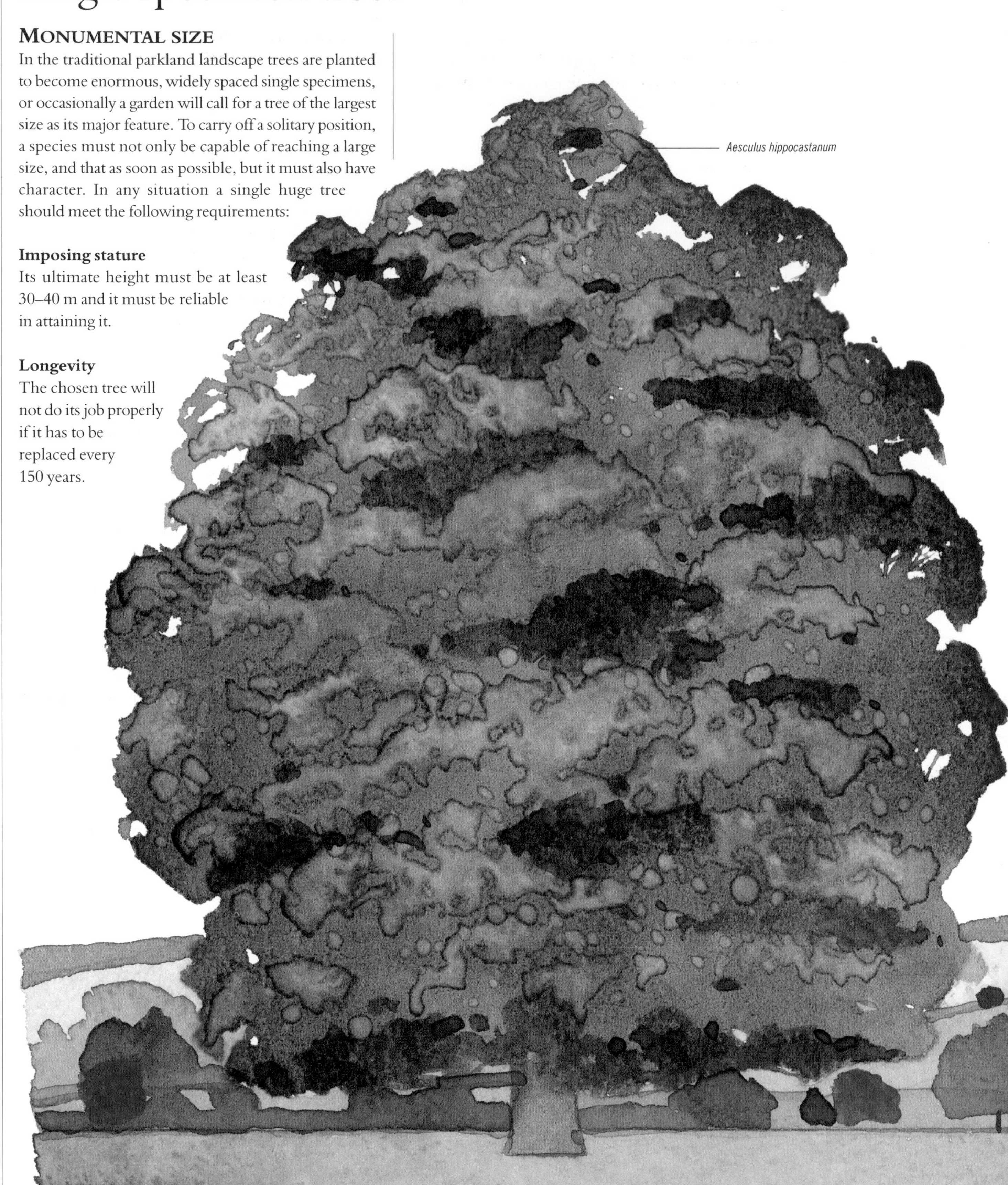

Character
This includes individuality of shape – formal or striking – foliage, flowers, fruit and autumn colour. Its winter aspect is important.

General robustness
It must be firm against wind throw.

Other features which are desirable, rather than necessary, are a tolerance of varying soil types and rapid early growth. No single species earns top marks in every feature. Conifers tend to rate highly because they are mostly evergreen, they grow fast with a spire form from the persistent bole, which makes them tall, and they are mostly undemanding of soils. The list below is a selection of trees that can be recommended.

Abies grandis (Grand fir)
Aesculus hippocastanum (Common horse chestnut)
Cedrus libani (Cedar of Lebanon)
Eucalyptus globulus (Blue gum)
Fagus sylvatica (Common beech)
Juglans nigra (Black walnut)
Liriodendron tulipifera (Tulip tree)
Pinus jeffreyi (Jeffrey pine)
P. ponderosa (Western yellow pine)
Platanus x *acerifolia* (London plane)
Quercus cerris (Turkey oak)
Q. frainetto (Hungarian oak)
Q. petraea (Sessile oak)
Sequoiadendron giganteum (Sierra redwood)
Tilia cordata (Small-leafed lime)
T. x *europaea* (Common lime)
T. tomentosa 'Petiolaris' (Silver pendent lime)
Tsuga heterophylla (Western hemlock)
Zelkova carpinifolia (Caucasian zelkova)

MEDIUM-SIZE

This category includes trees which rarely achieve 30 m in height but can be expected to culminate at around 25 m. The list that follows is a short selection of the more choice medium-size trees.

Aesculus flava (Yellow buckeye)
Alnus cordata (Italian alder)
Araucaria araucana (Monkey puzzle)
Betula maximowicziana (Monarch birch)
Calocedrus decurrens (Incense cedar).
Carpinus betulus 'Fastigiata' (Fastigiate or Pyramidal hornbeam)
Cercidiphyllum japonicum (Katsura tree)
Chamaecyparis lawsoniana 'Wisselii' (Wissel cypress)
Corylus colurna (Turkish hazel)
x *Cupressocyparis leylandii* (Leyland cypress)
Cupressus glabra (Smooth Arizona cypress)
Fagus sylvatica 'Dawyck' (Dawyck beech)
Ginkgo biloba (Maiden hair tree)
Liquidambar formosana (Chinese sweet gum)
L. styraciflua (Sweet gum)
Metasequoia glyptostroboides (Dawn redwood)
Nothofagus nervosa (Rauli)
Nyssa sylvatica (Tupelo)
Picea breweriana (Brewer spruce)
P. omorika (Serbian spruce)
Pinus leucodermis (Bosnian pine)
P. peuce (Macedonian pine)
Populus nigra 'Italica' (Lombardy poplar)
Pseudolarix amabilis (Golden larch)
Quercus palustris (Pin oak)
Q. robur 'Fastigiata' (Cypress oak)
Salix 'Chrysocoma' (Weeping willow)
Taxodium distichum (Swamp cypress)
Thuja plicata 'Zebrina' (Golden-barred thuja)
Tilia oliveri (Oliver's lime)

Trees in small gardens

MANY OF THE DECISIONS necessary when planting a large garden will also apply to smaller ones. For example, it is essential before choosing trees to consider which views are to be kept, which to be hidden. A small garden can be made open by including the external landscape, whether it is rural or urban, or secluded by hiding it. Many gardens are traditionally screened by dense, and often unattractive, hedges which use valuable space and require constant attention. In all but the smallest gardens, a few skilfully placed trees can accomplish the same effect and, with space beneath and between them, leave room for an interesting selection of shrubs.

In a small garden, the first consideration should be size. Never be tempted to plant a tree that will outgrow the space available for it. It will soon create problems, require cutting back which will undoubtedly spoil it, and will reduce the amount of space available for growing other plants, thus restricting the diversity on which a small garden must rely. Also, resist the temptation to plant an oversized tree for 'instant' effect. A smaller specimen will establish more quickly and make a more attractive tree.

If only one or a few trees can be grown, they should have ornamental features over more than one season – for example, spring flowers and autumn colour or attractive fruit.

Bark is very useful as it can be attractive all year round, but provides particular interest in winter. The temptation to plant mostly variegated or yellow-leaved trees should be avoided and they should, ideally, not be the central feature in a garden. It is much more effective to use a single example as a focal point to highlight one particular area or incorporate it into a screen, and contrast it with dark green foliage.

Acer cappadocicum 'Aureum'

The following trees are suitable for smaller gardens. For details of eventual size and ornamental characteristics refer to the Tree Directory.

Abies koreana
Acacia dealbata
Acer buergerianum
A. capillipes
A. cappadocicum 'Aureum'
A. crataegifolium
A. ginnala
A. griseum
A. negundo 'Auratum'
A. negundo 'Elegans'
A. negundo 'Flamingo'
A. palmatum
A. pensylvanicum
A. pseudoplatanus 'Brilliantissimum'
A. pseudoplatanus 'Prinz Handjery'
Alnus glutinosa 'Imperialis'
A. incana 'Ramulis Coccineis'
Arbutus x *andrachnoides*
A. unedo
Betula medwediewii
B. pendula 'Youngii'
Catalpa bignonioides 'Aurea'
Cercis siliquastrum
Chamaecyparis lawsoniana (yellow-leaved forms)
Crataegus (most)
Cupressus glabra 'Pyramidalis'
Eucryphia glutinosa
Fagus sylvatica 'Aurea Pendula'
Genista aetnensis
Ilex (most)
Juniperus chinensis 'Aurea'
J. recurva var. *coxii*
J. squamata 'Meyeri'
Koelreuteria paniculata
+ *Laburnocytisus adamii*
Laburnum x *watereri* 'Vossii'
Ligustrum lucidum
Luma apiculata
Magnolia grandiflora
M. x *loebneri*
Malus (most)
Oxydendrum arboreum
Picea pungens 'Koster'
Pinus sylvestris 'Fastigiata'
Pittosporum tenuifolium
Prunus (most)
Pyrus calleryana 'Chanticleer'
P. salicifolia 'Pendula'
Quercus cerris 'Variegata'
Q. pontica
Robinia pseudoacacia 'Frisia'
Sophora japonica 'Pendula'
Sorbus (most)
Stuartia pseudocamellia
Thuja orientalis 'Elegantissima'

Trees of very rapid growth

FAST-GROWING TREES can create a feeling of maturity very quickly in a new garden. It is much better to plant a few, even if they are not required to grow to full size, than to attempt to establish large specimens. Not all of these trees eventually reach a very large size. Some, such as the snake-bark maples (*Acer*), are small.

Abies grandis
Acer davidii
A. grosseri var. *hersii*
Ailanthus altissima
Alnus (most)
Betula pendula
x *Cupressocyparis leylandii*
Cupressus macrocarpa
Eucalyptus globulus
E. gunnii
E. nitens
Larix decidua
L. x *eurolepis*
L. kaempferi
Metasequoia glyptostroboides
Nothofagus nervosa
N. obliqua
Paulownia tomentosa
Picea sitchensis
Pinus muricata
P. radiata
Populus x *canadensis* 'Robusta'
P. x *canescens*
Pseudotsuga menziesii
Pterocarya x *rehderiana*
Quercus castaneifolia
Salix alba
Sequoia sempervirens
Sequoiadendron giganteum
Tsuga heterophylla

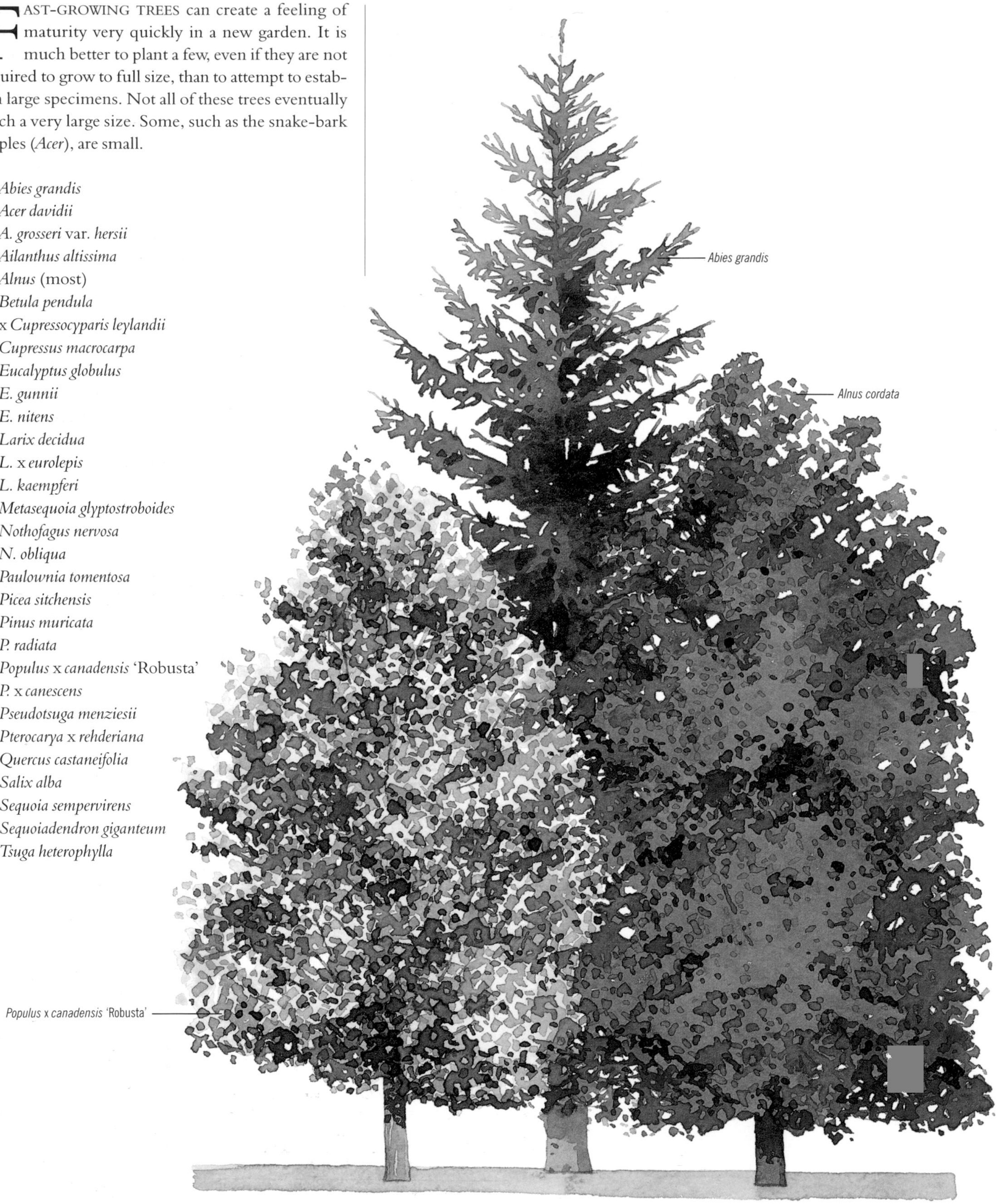

Lawns and trees

A LAWN IS IN EFFECT a clearing in the woods, a glade surrounded by trees. It is emphatically not a place for central specimens. It must be kept largely open to remain a lawn as a feature, rather than just an area of mown grass. Too many lawns of no great size have a blue Atlas cedar right in the centre; this will grow to be a very big tree that fills much of the air space and thus obliterates the prime purpose of the lawn. Small lawns often have a central clump of pampas grass or a small cherry; these will not undo the effect of the lawn as they grow but look as wrongly placed as large trees. The lawns of some mansions have huge cedars of Lebanon and these only look right if they are isolated from other trees or if they are grouped on either side of a broad open space.

If the lawn is the only site available for a tree it must be encroached upon from the side. Ideally, the surroundings will be big trees outside smaller trees (both sizes in scale with the area of grass) with one or two big trees set forward among the smaller ones to prevent too much of an arena effect. The edges should form generously sweeping bays. The front positions should be reserved for species selected for their good foliage, bark or year-round appearance. A very large lawn can afford a promontory or two of trees, like most of the Japanese cherries, that have spectacular but short seasons but whose appearance is indifferent at other times. Around a small lawn these should be behind low trees or big shrubs that are good to look at all summer.

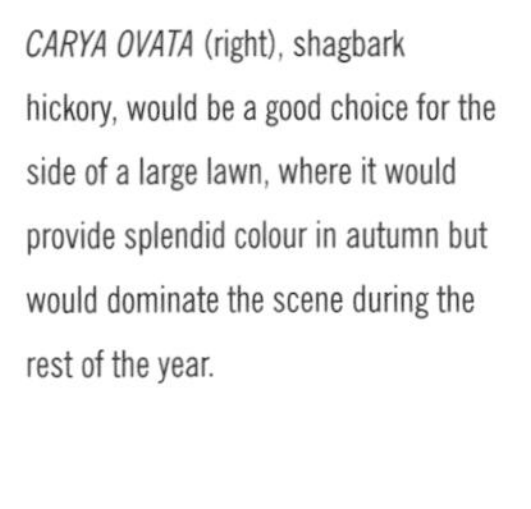
CARYA OVATA (right), shagbark hickory, would be a good choice for the side of a large lawn, where it would provide splendid colour in autumn but would dominate the scene during the rest of the year.

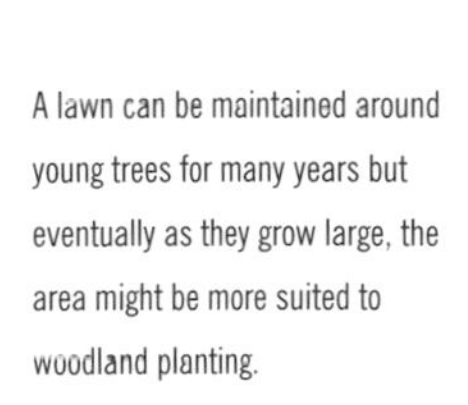
A lawn can be maintained around young trees for many years but eventually as they grow large, the area might be more suited to woodland planting.

Waterside trees

A GARDEN LUCKY ENOUGH to have a lake, pool, stream or river needs to make the best use of it. A small lake should ideally be set into, or run alongside, a lawn, and trees should be kept well clear of it except for one or two specimens towards the distant end. Part of their function is to be seen in reflection, and weeping trees are especially effective in this respect. Autumn colour is also a great advantage.

The traditional tree for a waterside setting is the weeping willow and in places none is a better choice. It will weep well over water but surprisingly, in view of how commonly it does so, there is said to be a danger to fish from toxins released by rotting willow leaves. Leaves of any kind are a nuisance, if unavoidable, especially in standing water, and a weeping willow set back from the edge will weep just as well. The white willow and its cultivar the coral-bark willow, which is especially good for winter colour, are also good choices. In small gardens, or if growth needs to be restricted for any reason, white willows can be pollarded, that is, cut to about 2.5 m, either annually or every few years to create an old riverside scene as in a Bewick woodcut.

Another weeping tree, but one that is much smaller than the willow, is Young's weeping birch, which lends itself to a place beside a small pool so that it can be seen in reflection.

Another good choice for waterside planting is the swamp cypress. It is completely at home next to water and, where flooding is frequent, will often produce the familiar wooden 'knees' over quite a distance once it is 40 years old. It is distinctive, although twiggy, in winter and takes a very long winter rest, but it makes up for this by its fresh green delicate foliage after June and rich foxy red-brown colours in late autumn. Of similar effect, but without the 'knees' and in leaf for much longer, is the dawn redwood.

Poplars are well-known waterside trees but the Lombardy poplar needs to be planted with discretion. It grows rapidly to 30 m tall and one on its own will soon make a small pool look ridiculous. A group on a lawn behind a lake, or a single one where a stream enters a fairly large pool, are very effective. The poplar 'Robusta' makes a good alternative although it is broad-conic and not columnar. It grows even faster than the Lombardy, has large handsome leaves which are bright orange-red to brown when they emerge, and is liberally hung with big dark-red catkins before the foliage appears.

The Caucasian wing nut is a splendid tree for a lakeside but, unless kept in check, will need some 50 m of bank to itself for it throws up strong suckers to make a thicket. Its merits are very rapid growth, big compound bright green leaves and bright yellow autumn colour.

TAXODIUM DISTICHUM (above), swamp cypress, makes an ideal waterside tree by a lake. As here, when planted in the water, it will grow more slowly than if planted on the margin, and will often colour earlier in autumn.

The hybrid wing nut is also suitable for growing by a lake, but grows even faster and is eventually taller.

The sweet gum looks exceptionally good on a lakeside lawn and grows best there. Given full light, it should be a blaze of scarlet or deep red in autumn.

The golden alder is rare and rather slow, but makes a useful change of colour at a lakeside. Although the golden form of the grey alder (*Alnus incana* 'Ramulis Coccineis') is probably more at home on sites that are rarely flooded, it has the advantages of scarlet winter buds and catkins and less slow growth. The weeping form of the same species will also grow well and is useful for places where the weeping willow is too large.

Red maple is a tree of swampy bottoms in North America and, while the crown of mature trees is a little untidy and dull in winter, the summer foliage is good. In autumn, given sunshine, it is a fine blaze of yellow, orange and scarlet.

LIQUIDAMBAR STYRACIFLUA (left), sweet gum, is a splendid tree for a large lawn next to a lake as it prefers moist soil. A position in full sun will ensure striking autumn colour.

Trees for special conditions

CHALK AND LIMESTONE

The limiting effects of alkaline soils on the growth of some trees are due to free lime – the calcium ions – making iron less available to them. Iron is an ingredient in the vital chlorophyll, the major and distinguishing feature of green plants.

When too much calcium prevents a plant from obtaining enough iron for the chlorophyll it needs, its leaves turn yellow. This is 'lime-induced chlorosis' and is seen where plants that are not tolerant of lime are grown on shallow soils over chalk.

There are many types of alkaline soil, ranging from dry chalk to limestone. Shallow chalk soils are the most limiting and many plants that will not tolerate these will grow on good, deep soils over chalk, even if they are alkaline, or on soils based on the harder limestone. A soil depth of only 60 cm is quite enough to accommodate most of even the larger trees. Although lime will inhibit the growth of some plants, it is actually beneficial to others, such as Common ash (*Fraxinus excelsior*).

Trees which are particularly recommended for alkaline soils include:

Abies cephalonica
A. grandis
A. homolepis
A. pinsapo
Acer
Aesculus
Arbutus unedo
A. x *andrachnoides*
Carpinus
Carya
Castanea
Cedrus
Cercis
Chamaecyparis
Crataegus
x *Cupressocyparis*
Cupressus
Fagus
Fraxinus
Ginkgo biloba
Juglans
Juniperus
Larix
Ligustrum lucidum
Malus
Metasequoia glyptostroboides (not in dry soils)
Morus
Picea omorika
P. pungens
Pinus leucodermis
P. nigra
Populus
Prunus
Pterocarya
Pyrus
Quercus
Salix
Sorbus
Taxodium distichum (not in dry soils)
Taxus
Thuja
Thujopsis

HEAVY SOILS

In heavy clay soils aeration is poor and insufficient for deep root-growth; their density also makes it difficult for roots to penetrate. Clays therefore restrict rooting and, although they retain moisture well, if they do dry out the plants, with their shallow rooting, will suffer from drought. This is made worse if the clay shrinks as large cracks open out and more moisture is lost.

In their favour, clays retain their base salts since water can scarcely move through and leach them. This means that any tree able to grow on clay should seldom lack nutrients and with water readily available, as it usually is, an extensive root system is not as necessary to good growth as it is on other types of soil.

Trees particularly recommended for heavy clay soils include:

Abies
Acer
Aesculus
Alnus
Betula
Carpinus
Carya
Cercidiphyllum
Chamaecyparis
Crataegus
Eucalyptus
Fraxinus
Ginkgo biloba
Ilex
Laburnum
Larix
Liquidambar
Liriodendron
Magnolia
Malus
Pinus
Platanus
Populus
Prunus
Pterocarya
Quercus
Salix
Sorbus
Taxodium
Taxus
Tetradium
Thuja
Tilia
Tsuga heterophylla
Zelkova

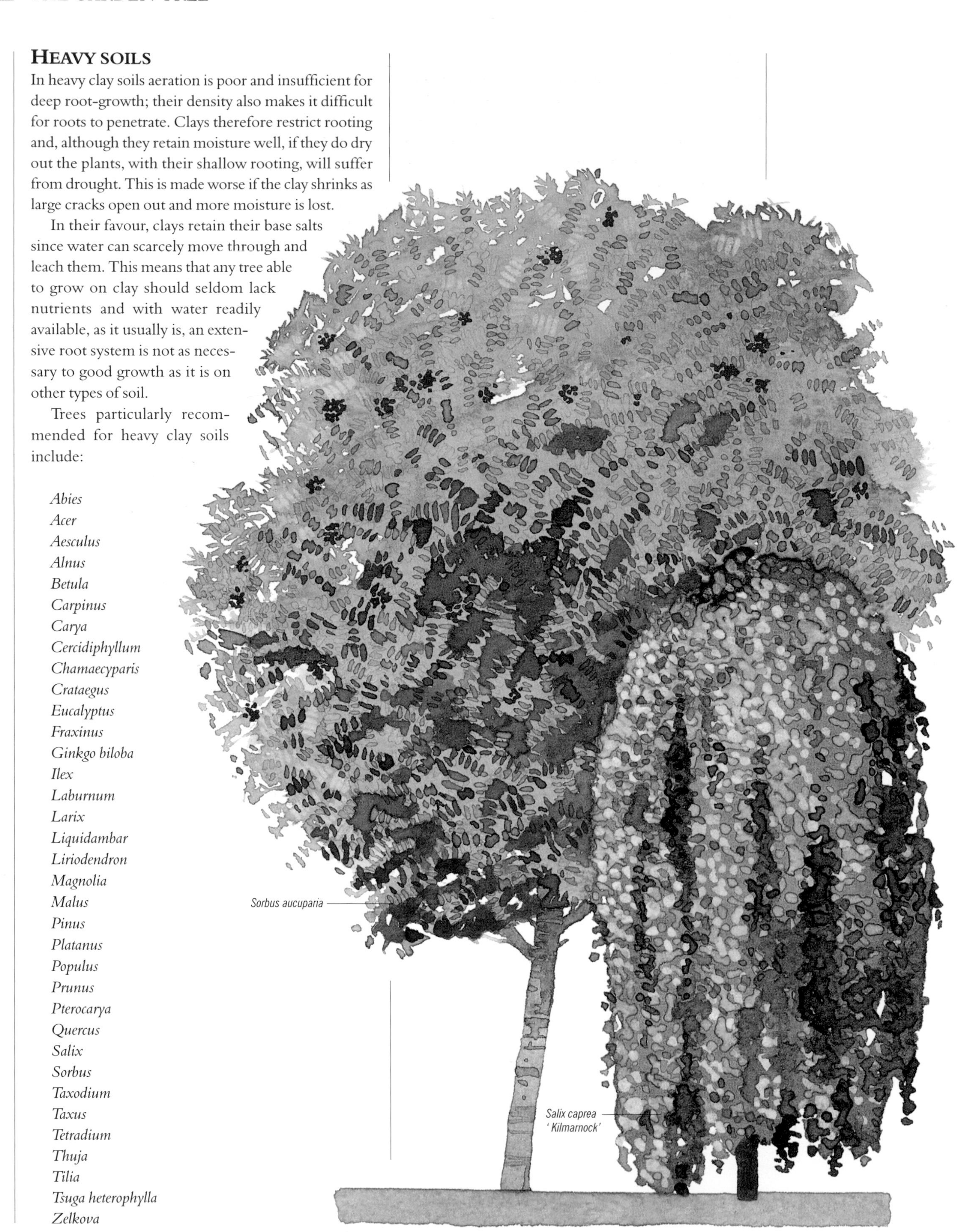

Acid sandy soils

Acid soils drain rapidly so are poor in nutrients but, because they are well aerated and open, they allow roots to penetrate deep and wide. They are not always more severe sites in drought than are clays as the quality most needed in a tree in order to grow well is the ability to grow at low levels of nutrients.

Trees recommended for these soils include:

Ailanthus
Betula
Castanea
Cupressus
Gleditsia
Nyssa
Pinus
Quercus
Robinia
Salix
Sequoiadendron
Sorbus aucuparia
Tsuga

CITIES AND INDUSTRIAL AREAS

Airborne solid matter and gases both have harmful effects on plant growth. The solids include lime and concrete dust, and the output of factories, but the main particulate matter is soot. Inner cities and large towns were as polluted as purely industrial areas until clean-air legislation brought about striking improvements. Today much urban pollution comes from traffic.

Some trees are adapted to cope with these effects to a certain extent. Smooth, shiny leaves collect less soot and are washed clean by rain. The foliage of trees which normally leaf out late and shed early is active only for a short time, and that in the hottest time of the year when least fuel is burned. Bark that is shed readily starts clean again every year; bark that is craggy clogs more slowly and resists soot in its deepest crevices.

Trees recommended for urban and industrial areas include:

Acer pseudoplatanus
Aesculus
Ailanthus
Alnus
Catalpa
Crataegus
Ginkgo
Gleditsia
Ilex
Ligustrum
Magnolia
Platanus
Populus
Prunus
Pyrus
Robinia
Taxodium
Tetradium

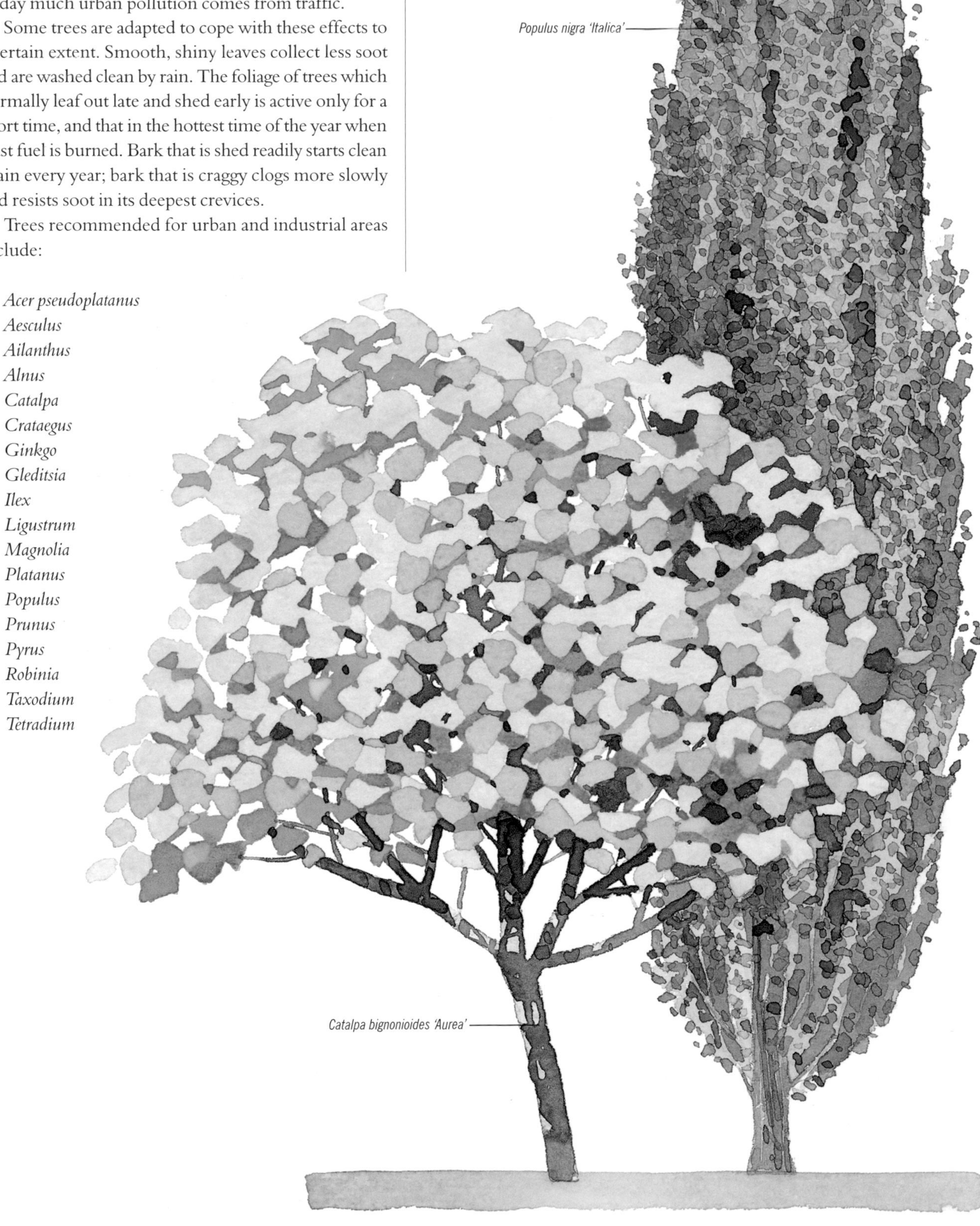

MARITIME EXPOSURE

The adverse aspects of a seashore site arise from salt and wind. Salt is carried inland for many miles by gales, in damaging quantities, so a tree does not have to be on the shore or cliff-top to suffer maritime exposure. Wind and salt are nearly always combined, so resistance to both is a necessary condition for good growth.

Resistance to wind is largely a matter of having evolved in an area exposed to it, and so is most likely to be found in species native to mountain ridges and coastlines. Beyond a tendency towards hard leaves and away from big ones, there are no evident features common to such trees. Resistance to salt is associated with leaves that are glossy and wash clean easily. The soils in maritime areas are liable to contain some common salt after gales, and there are some trees to which this is fatal and which are unable to grow near the sea.

Trees recommended for exposed coastal sites include:

Acer pseudoplatanus
Arbutus unedo
Chamaecyparis lawsoniana
Cryptomeria japonica
x *Cupressocyparis leylandii*
Cupressus macrocarpa
Eucalyptus
Ilex x *altaclerensis* 'Hodginsii'
Picea sitchensis
Pinus muricata
P. nigra
P. radiata
P. thunbergii
Populus alba
P. x *canescens*
Quercus cerris
Q. ilex
Q. robur
Q. petraea
Q. x *turneri*
Sorbus aria

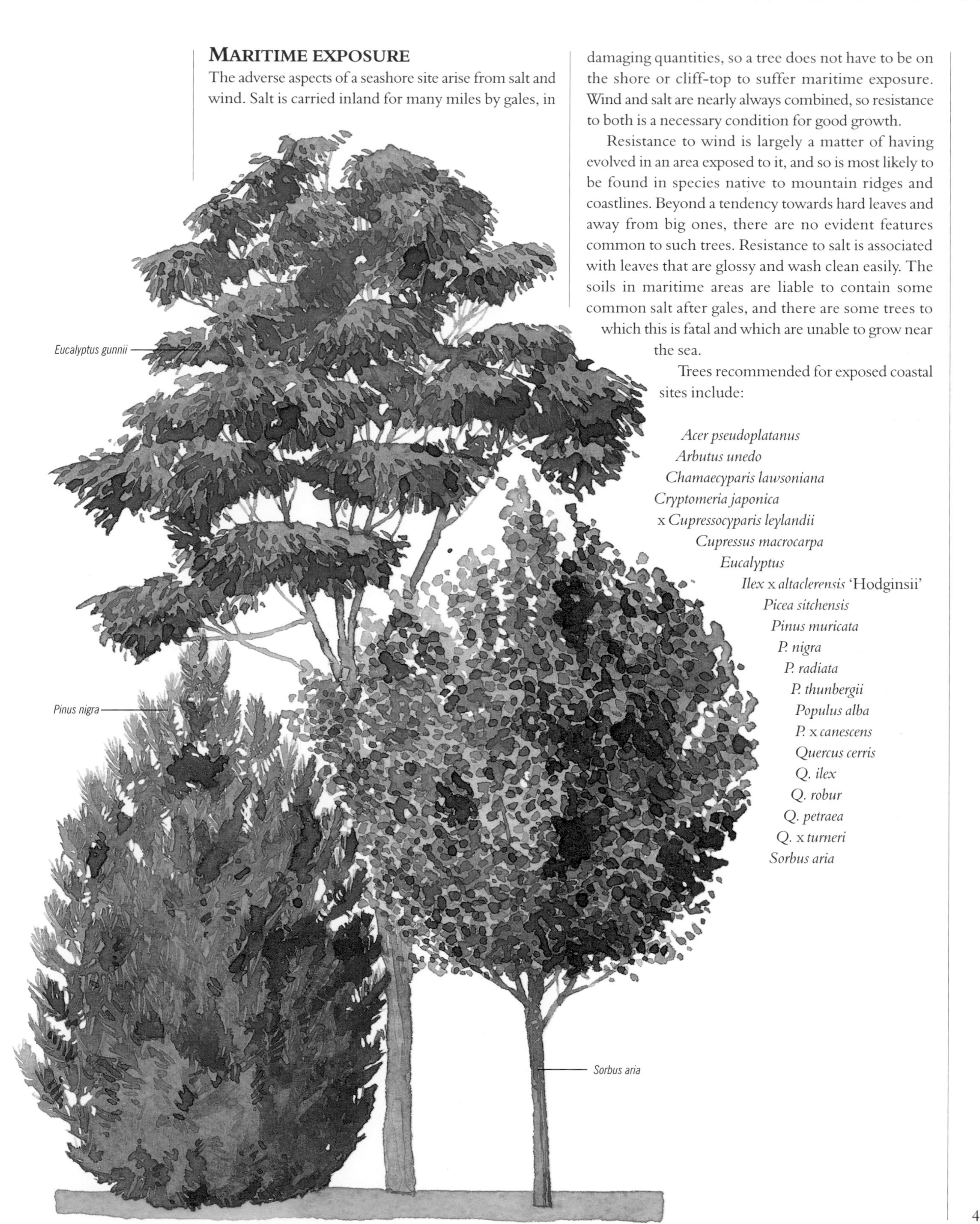

Trees for autumn colour

AUTUMN COLOUR is an important asset that many trees provide. After the lush greenness of summer it brings many gardens to life before the onset of winter. The season naturally extends over several months so the greater the variety of trees that can be planted, the greater the length of time that autumn colour can be enjoyed. A mixed planting of trees that colour well can be a great joy, as their foliage turns many shades over a long period. On the other hand good autumn colour, together with other ornamental features, can make a single specimen worth planting in a small garden. While many trees give autumn colour, the following is a list of some of the best, of all sizes.

Acer buergerianum
A. capillipes
A. cappadocicum
A. crataegifolium
A. davidii
A. ginnala
A. griseum
A. grosseri var. *hersii*
A. japonicum
A. maximowiczianum
A. palmatum
A. pensylvanicum
A. platanoides
A. rufinerve
A. saccharinum
A. saccharum
Aesculus flava
Betula (most)
Carya (all)
Cercidiphyllum japonicum
Cornus controversa
Crataegus crus-galli
C. phaenopyrum
C. x *persimilis* 'Prunifolia'
Cryptomeria japonica 'Elegans'
Fagus orientalis
F. sylvatica
Fraxinus angustifolia 'Raywood'
F. excelsior 'Jaspidea'
Ginkgo biloba
Koelreuteria paniculata
Larix (all)
Liquidambar (all)
Liriodendron (all)
Malus florentina
M. trilobata
M. tschonoskii
M. yunnanensis
Metasequoia glyptostroboides
Nothofagus antarctica
N. obliqua
Nyssa sinensis
N. sylvatica
Oxydendrum arboreum
Parrotia persica
Photinia villosa
Picrasma quassioides
Populus alba
P. x *canadensis* 'Serotina Aurea'
P. x *canescens*
Prunus sargentii
Pseudolarix amabilis
Quercus alba
Q. coccinea 'Splendens'
Q. palustris
Sassafras albidum
Sorbus alnifolia
S. aria
S. aucuparia
S. commixta
S. folgneri
S. 'Joseph Rock'
S. sargentiana
S. scalaris
Stuartia pseudocamellia
S. sinensis
Taxodium ascendens
T. distichum

ACER JAPONICUM (below), downy Japanese maple, as well as giving excellent autumn colour, provides spring interest with its fresh unfolding leaves and small red flowers.

Carya cordiformis
Acer platanoides
Malus tschonoskii

Trees with purple foliage

PURPLE-LEAVED TREES are distributed very unevenly among plants. There are many maples, beeches and crabs, and a few cherries, but no conifers. The range of sizes is enough to provide a purple tree for every garden should one be wanted. However, they are not always easy to place. They look rather out of place with more natural plantings, and in a large garden tend to be positioned near the house, where they create a sombre effect. In small gardens with few trees they tend to dominate other plants.

Many of the trees in the following list are not preferable to their green-leafed counterparts and some, such as *Betula pendula* 'Purpurea' and *Pittosporum tenuifolium* 'Purpureum', are poor compared to the typical forms. Others, however, make splendid trees. Two examples are *Fagus sylvatica* 'Dawyck Purple', a striking column of deep purple, and *Acer platanoides* 'Schwedleri', whose leaves start off deep red-purple, turn to dark green and give good autumn colour.

Acer campestre 'Schwerinii'
A. platanoides 'Crimson King'
A. platanoides 'Faassen's Black'
A. platanoides 'Goldsworth Purple'
A. platanoides 'Schwedleri'
A. pseudoplatanus 'Atropurpureum'
Betula pendula 'Purpurea'
Catalpa x *erubescens* 'Purpurea'
Fagus sylvatica 'Dawyck Purple'
F. sylvatica 'Riversii'
Malus 'Liset'
M. 'Profusion'
M. x *purpurea*
Pittosporum tenuifolium 'Purpureum'
Prunus cerasifera 'Nigra'
P. cerasifera 'Pissardii'
P. padus 'Colorata'

FAGUS SYLVATICA ATROPENICEA GROUP, (above), purple beech, comes in varying shades of purple when grown from seed, and being a large tree, is best viewed from a distance.

PRUNUS CERASIFERA 'NIGRA' (left), is one of the purple-leaf forms of the cherry-plum, which although rather dull in foliage during summer give an unrivalled display in early spring and are among the first trees to flower.

Fagus sylvatica 'Dawyck'
Prunus cerasifera 'Pissardii'

Trees with blue, grey or silver foliage

GREY OR SILVER is a natural colour in trees and is therefore relatively easy to place in the garden without looking artificial. In nature it is generally an adaptation to high light levels and often, but not always, hot sunny positions. Trees with this foliage colour are therefore generally at their best in full sun. By selectively planting species with grey or silver foliage some striking combinations can be achieved, and the trees can be effectively used to tone down, and contrast with, purple-leaved shrubs.

Abies concolor
A. lasiocarpa var. *arizonica*
A. magnifica
A. pinsapo
A. procera
Acacia dealbata
Cedrus atlantica Glauca Group
C. atlantica 'Fastigiata'
Chamaecyparis lawsoniana 'Alumii'
C. lawsoniana 'Columnaris'
C. lawsoniana 'Pembury Blue'
C. lawsoniana 'Triomf van Boskoop'
C. pisifera 'Squarrosa'
Cunninghamia lanceolata 'Glauca'
Cupressus glabra 'Pyramidalis'
Eucalyptus cordata
E. gunnii
E. pauciflora subsp. *niphophila*
Juniperus deppeana
J. virginiana 'Burkii'
Picea likiangensis
P. pungens 'Hoopsii'
P. pungens 'Koster'
P. koraiensis
P. parviflora
Populus alba
P. x *canescens*
Pyrus salicifolia 'Pendula'
Salix alba 'Argentea'

ABIES CONCOLOR 'CANDICANS' (left), is a striking French selection of the Colorado fir with bright silvery blue foliage. For the best effect ensure that trees of this colour get as much sun as possible.

PICEA PUNGENS 'HOOPSII' (below left), is one of many forms of blue spruce grown for their brightly coloured foliage, particularly striking when the young leaves are just emerging.

CHAMAECYPARIS LAWSONIANA 'PEMBURY BLUE' (below), has bright silvery blue foliage making it a choice selection of Lawson cypress. Although blue-foliage forms are usually slower growing than green ones, they can still reach a considerable size.

Cedrus atlantica
Populus alba
Picea pungens

Trees with yellow foliage

UNLIKE THOSE WITH PURPLE FOLIAGE, many yellow-leaved trees are conifers. Yellow foliage can be used very effectively in a garden but should not be overdone. It is certainly easier to place the trees in a large garden where a dark green background can be used for contrast, or a yellow specimen can be partially hidden in a glade to draw the eye into another part of the garden. Trees of narrow habit work particularly well and some striking combinations can be made by placing a yellow-leaved conifer, or even a small group of them, among dark green trees. The Weeping beech, (*Fagus sylvatica* 'Aurea Pendula') can also be very effective when used in this way.

When choosing yellow-leaved trees it should always be remembered that they are slower growing than their green counterparts and will develop their best colour in a sunny position, although some can burn in intense heat.

Acer cappadocicum 'Aureum'
A. x *hillieri* 'Summergold'
A. negundo 'Auratum'
Aesculus hippocastanum 'Hampton Court Gold'
Alnus glutinosa 'Aurea'
A. incana 'Ramulis Coccineis'
Catalpa bignonioides 'Aurea'
Cedrus atlantica 'Aurea'
C. libani 'Aurea'
Chamaecyparis lawsoniana 'Lane'
C. lawsoniana 'Lutea'
C. lawsoniana 'Stewartii'
C. lawsoniana 'Westermannii'
C. obtusa 'Crippsii'

C. obtusa 'Tetragona Aurea'
C. pisifera 'Aurea'
x *Cupressocyparis leylandii* 'Castlewellan'
x *C. leylandii* 'Golconda'
x *C. leylandii* 'Robinson's Gold'
Cupressus macrocarpa 'Lutea'
C. macrocarpa 'Donard Gold'
C. sempervirens 'Swane's Gold'
Fagus sylvatica 'Aurea Pendula'
F. sylvatica 'Dawyck Gold'
F. sylvatica 'Zlatia'
Gleditsia triacanthos 'Sunburst'
Juniperus chinensis 'Aurea'
Picea orientalis 'Aurea'
Pinus densiflora 'Aurea'
P. sylvestris 'Aurea'
Pittosporum tenuifolium 'Warnham Gold'
Populus alba 'Richardii'
P. x *canadensis* 'Serotina Aurea'
Quercus robur 'Concordia'
Q. rubra 'Aurea'
Robinia pseudoacacia 'Frisia'
Sorbus aucuparia 'Beissneri'
Thuja occidentalis 'Lutea'
T. orientalis 'Elegantissima'
T. plicata 'Aurea'
Thujopsis dolabrata 'Aurea'

ACER CAPPADOCICUM 'AUREUM' (above), one of the finest of all trees with yellow leaves, is better, not as a central feature, but where it will draw the eye.

FAGUS SYLVATICA 'AUREA PENDULA' (far left), is a very choice form of common beech, the bright yellow foliage of which is ideal for lighting a woodland glade.

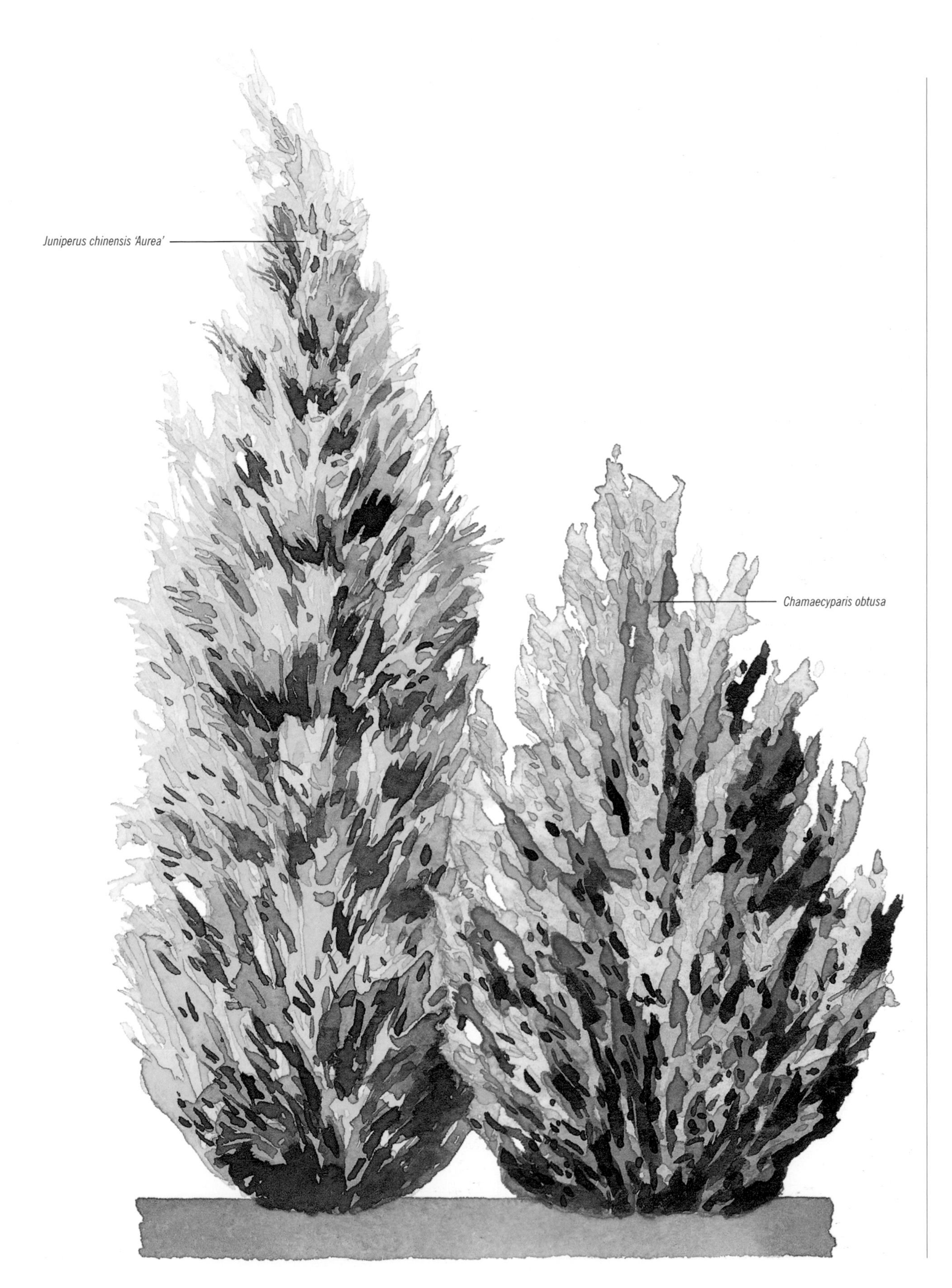
Juniperus chinensis 'Aurea'
Chamaecyparis obtusa

Trees with variegated foliage

LIKE YELLOW-FOLIAGED TREES, variegated ones should be used with care in gardens. Again, they should not, ideally, be dominant but should be used to contrast with others, perhaps providing a focal point away from the main area. They are slow-growing compared to their green-leaved forms and this should be taken into account when siting them. *Quercus cerris* 'Variegata' will, for example, grow to nowhere near the size of a green-leaved *Q. cerris*, and would quickly become out of place if associated with large trees. This slow growth can be an advantage as it allows some variegated forms to be grown in gardens too small to accommodate green-leaved ones.

Variegated plants will often produce shoots of completely green, white or yellow foliage and these should always be removed as soon as they appear.

Acer negundo 'Elegans'
A. negundo 'Flamingo'
A. negundo 'Variegatum'
A. platanoides 'Drummondii'
A. rufinerve 'Albolimbatum'
Calocedrus decurrens 'Aureovariegata'
Castanea sativa 'Albomarginata'
Cornus controversa 'Variegata'
Ilex x *altaclerensis* 'Belgica Aurea'
I. x *altaclerensis* 'Golden King'
I. aquifolium 'Argentea Marginata'
I. aquifolium 'Golden Queen'
Ligustrum lucidum 'Excelsum Superbum'
Liquidambar styraciflua 'Variegata'
Liriodendron tulipifera 'Aureomarginatum'
Platanus x *hispanica* 'Suttneri'
Populus x *candicans* 'Aurora'
Quercus cerris 'Variegata'
Taxus baccata 'Adpressa Aurea'
Thuja plicata 'Zebrina'
Thujopsis dolabrata 'Variegata'

Variegated trees such as this *LIQUIDAMBAR STYRACIFLUA* 'VARIEGATA' (left) are slower growing than their green-leafed counterparts and rarely grow as large.

LIRIODENDRON TULIPIFERA 'AUREOMARGINATUM' (below right), not only has a very striking variegation, but also has the advantage of not growing as quickly or as tall as the form with green leaves.

ACER NEGUNDO 'VARIEGATUM' (below left), must be watched closely for the production of shoots with green leaves. These would soon dominate the tree and must quickly be removed.

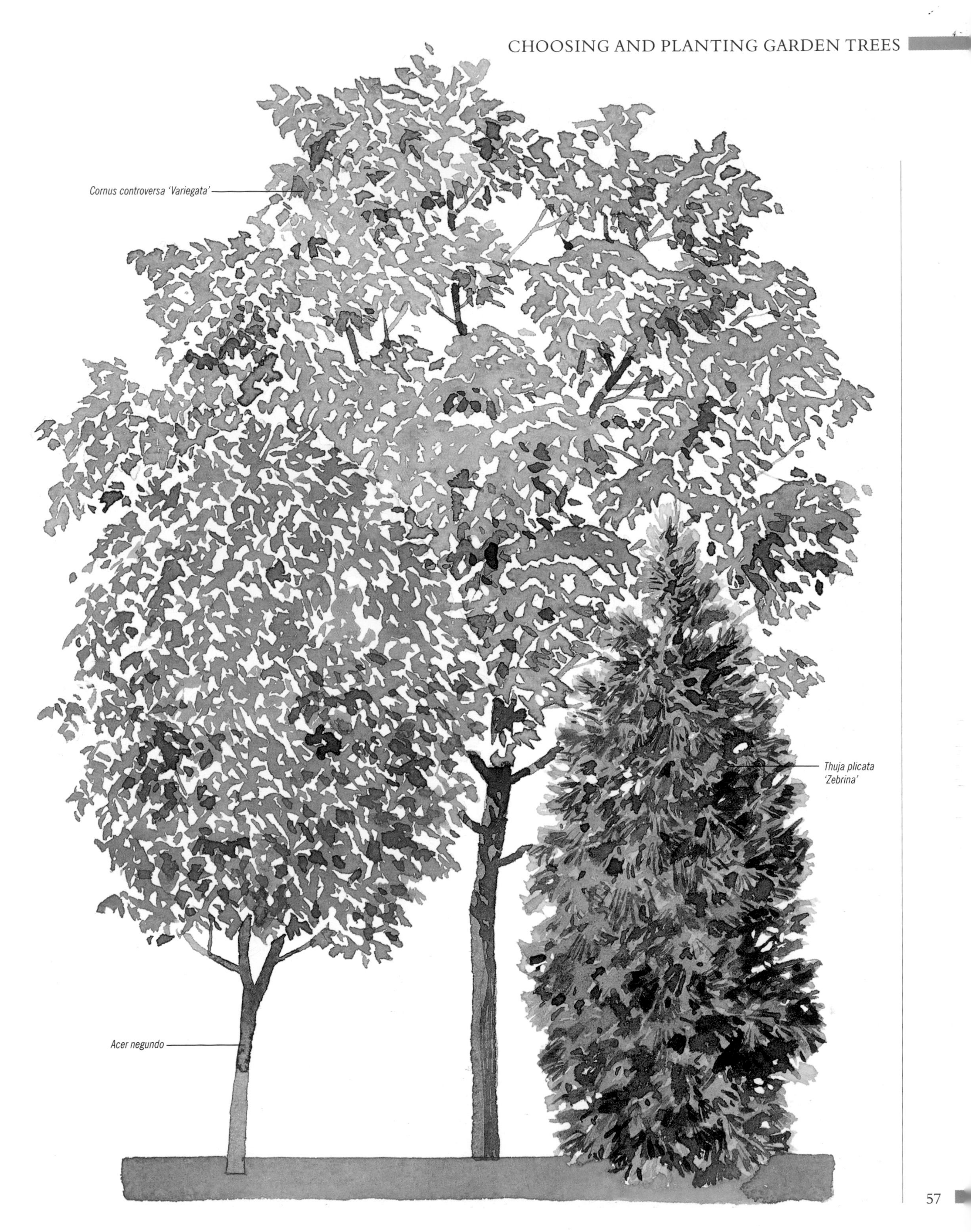
Cornus controversa 'Variegata'
Thuja plicata 'Zebrina'
Acer negundo

Trees of upright habit

WHILE MANY TREES are of naturally upright habit, others which are normally spreading have given rise to selected forms with upright branches. They provide excellent focal points, for example at the end of a vista or to create an imposing entrance either to a garden or part of it. Their narrow habit makes them suitable for planting near or between buildings where their strong vertical lines will contrast with, and complement, those provided by a wall or house. They can also be accommodated more easily in a small garden, but it should be remembered that their root spread is no less than it would be if they were spreading in habit. In addition to the trees listed below most conifers in the genera *Calocedrus*, *Chamaecyparis*, x *Cupressocyparis*, *Cupressus* and *Thuja* have a narrow columnar to conical habit.

Acer lobelii
A. platanoides 'Columnare'
A. rubrum 'Scanlon'
Carpinus betulus 'Fastigiata' (when young)
Cedrus atlantica 'Fastigiata'
Fagus sylvatica 'Dawyck'
F. sylvatica 'Dawyck Gold'
F. sylvatica 'Dawyck Purple'
Ginkgo biloba 'Fastigiata'
Juniperus chinensis 'Aurea'
J. virginiana
Liriodendron tulipifera 'Fastigiatum'
Malus trilobata
M. tschonoskii
M. 'Van Eseltine'
Metasequoia glyptostroboides
Picea omorika
Pinus sylvestris 'Fastigiata'
Pittosporum tenuifolium
Populus alba 'Pyramidalis'
P. nigra 'Italica'
Prunus 'Amanogawa'
P. cerasifera 'Lindsayae'
P. sargentii 'Rancho'
P. x *schmittii*
Pyrus calleryana 'Chanticleer'
Quercus castaneifolia 'Green Spire'
Q. frainetto 'Hungarian Crown'
Q. petraea 'Columna'
Q. robur 'Fastigiata'
Sequoiadendron giganteum
Sorbus aucuparia 'Sheerwater Seedling'
Taxodium ascendens
Taxus baccata 'Fastigiata'
Tilia cordata 'Greenspire'

FAGUS SYLVATICA 'DAWYCK GOLD' (above), combines a compact columnar habit with yellow spring foliage to give a very ornamental and garden-worthy tree.

METASEQUOIA GLYPTOSTROBOIDES (above left), the dawn redwood, is not only very fast growing and suitable for wet soil but retains its narrow conical habit.

ACER LOBELII (left), is a fast growing maple with a strictly upright habit making a tough and adaptable tree suited to a wide variety of soils and positions.

Pinus sylvestris 'Fastigiata'
Populus nigra 'Italica'
Acer rubrum
Acer lobelii

Weeping trees

WEEPING TREES ARE SO DIVERSE that one can be found for most gardens and situations. Trees that weep naturally such as Silver birch (*Betula pendula*) and Brewer spruce (*Picea breweriana*) are able to fit into informal plantings without looking out of place. Others, such as Silver weeping pear (*Pyrus salicifolia* 'Pendula') and *Betula pendula* 'Youngii', are better in more formal areas or small gardens where they can form a significant feature.

Alnus incana 'Pendula'
Betula pendula
B. pendula 'Tristis'
B. pendula 'Youngii'
Cercidiphyllum japonicum 'Pendulum'
Chamaecyparis nootkatensis 'Pendula'
Fagus sylvatica 'Aurea Pendula '
F. sylvatica 'Pendula'
Fraxinus excelsior 'Pendula'
Ilex aquifolium 'Pendula'
Larix kaempferi 'Pendula'
Picea breweriana
Prunus cerasifera 'Pendula'
P. x subhirtella 'Pendula'
Pyrus salicifolia 'Pendula'
Quercus pyrenaica 'Pendula'
Q. robur 'Pendula'
Salix caprea 'Kilmarnock'
S. 'Chrysocoma'
Sequoiadendron giganteum 'Pendulum'
Sophora japonica 'Pendula'
Tilia tomentosa 'Petiolaris'

PRUNUS CERASIFERA 'PENDULA' (left), is very rarely seen weeping form of the cherry plum, suited for the smallest of gardens and toughest of positions.

QUERCUS PYRENAICA 'PENDULA' (left), is an unusual weeping oak with particularly ornamental foliage, softly grey-felted when young.

SEQUOIADENDRON GIGANTEUM 'PENDULUM' (left), is more commonly seen as a narrow upright tree with drooping shoots but occasionally, as here, specimens sprawl over a wide area.

Picea breweriana
Betula pendula
Pyrus salicifolia
'Pendula'

Trees with ornamental bark

Ornamental bark is an important feature of several trees and can be used with great effect in gardens. Provided they are of a suitable size, species with striking bark are often popular for small gardens which can accommodate few trees, as they extend the season of interest: the bark is attractive all year round but particularly noticeable during winter. In larger gardens the possibilities increase: a group of white-barked birches can be an impressive sight, for example. It is a good idea to plant trees grown for their bark close to a path where it can easily be admired and where, by gentle stroking, it will be kept clean.

Acer crataegifolium
A. davidii
A. griseum
A. grosseri var. *hersii*
A. pensylvanicum
A. rufinerve
Arbutus andrachne
A. x *andrachnoides*
Betula (most)
Cryptomeria japonica
Cupressus glabra
Eucalyptus (all)
Juniperus deppeana
Luma apiculata
Malus trilobata
Parrotia persica
Photinia serratifolia
Platanus x *hispanica*
Prunus maackii
P. x *schmittii*
P. serrula
Quercus variabilis
Sequoia sempervirens
Sequoiadendron giganteum
Sorbus aucuparia 'Beissneri'
Stuartia pseudocamellia
S. sinensis

EUCALYPTUS JOHNSTONII (above), is very fast growing with a clean bole which shows off to perfection the attractive bark, it will not, however, survive in the coldest areas.

CRYPTOMERIA JAPONICA 'ELEGANS' (above), is a juvenile form of Japanese cedar with strikingly coloured bark which is complimented in winter by purple foliage.

BETULA UTILIS (above), Himalayan birch, has bark ranging from pure white to cream and pink, which can often be seen peeling in sheets on the trunk.

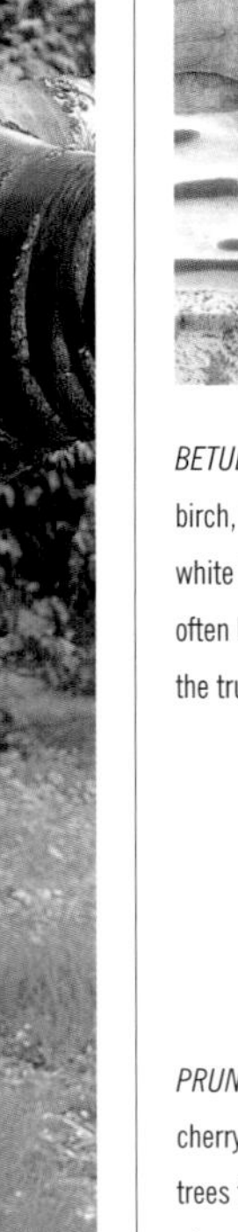

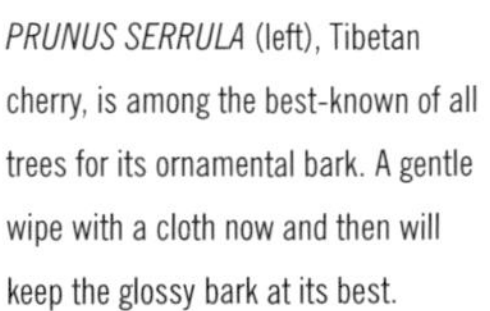

PRUNUS SERRULA (left), Tibetan cherry, is among the best-known of all trees for its ornamental bark. A gentle wipe with a cloth now and then will keep the glossy bark at its best.

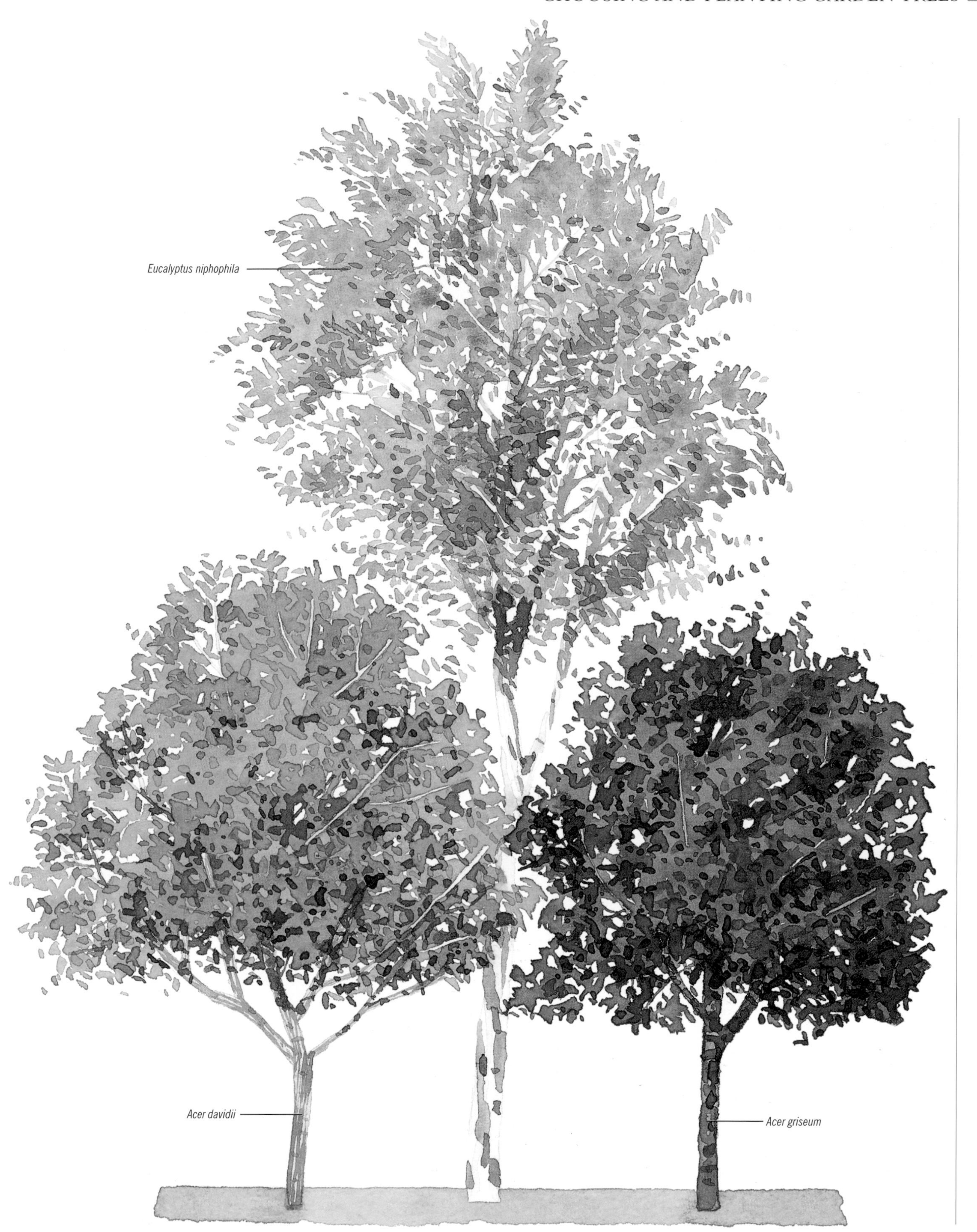

Eucalyptus niphophila
Acer davidii
Acer griseum

Trees for winter effect

MANY TREES are effective in winter, even without leaves. It is difficult to beat the delicate tracery of birch or beech when outlined by frost or snow. There are some, however, which are particularly outstanding at this time of year, either for flowers, fruit or their winter shoots. In addition to these, of course, there are numerous conifers with brightly coloured winter foliage and all the trees with ornamental bark.

Acacia dealbata
Acer palmatum 'Senkaki'
A. pensylvanicum 'Erythrocladum'
Alnus incana 'Ramulis Coccineis'
Arbutus unedo
Crataegus x *lavallei*
Ilex (most)
Magnolia campbellii
M. dawsoniana
Parrotia persica
Pinus sylvestris 'Aurea'
Pittosporum tenuifolium 'Warnham Gold'
Prunus x *subhirtella* 'Autumnalis'
P. x *subhirtella* 'Autumnalis Rosea'
Pyrus calleryana 'Chanticleer'
Salix 'Chrysocoma'

PRUNUS X SUBHIRTELLA 'AUTUMNALIS' (above), is not only a good tree for small gardens but has the advantage of producing flowers from late autumn through winter t spring, whenever the weather is mild.

PYRUS CALLERYANA 'CHANTICLEER' (far left), will flower profusely in late winter following a hot summer. Its good autumn colour, upright habit and tough constitution make it a good all round small tree.

PARROTIA PERSICA (left), Persian ironwood, produces small red flowers in late winter, adding to the year-round interest of this tree.

Salix 'Chrysocoma'
Prunus x subhirtella
Ilex aquifolium

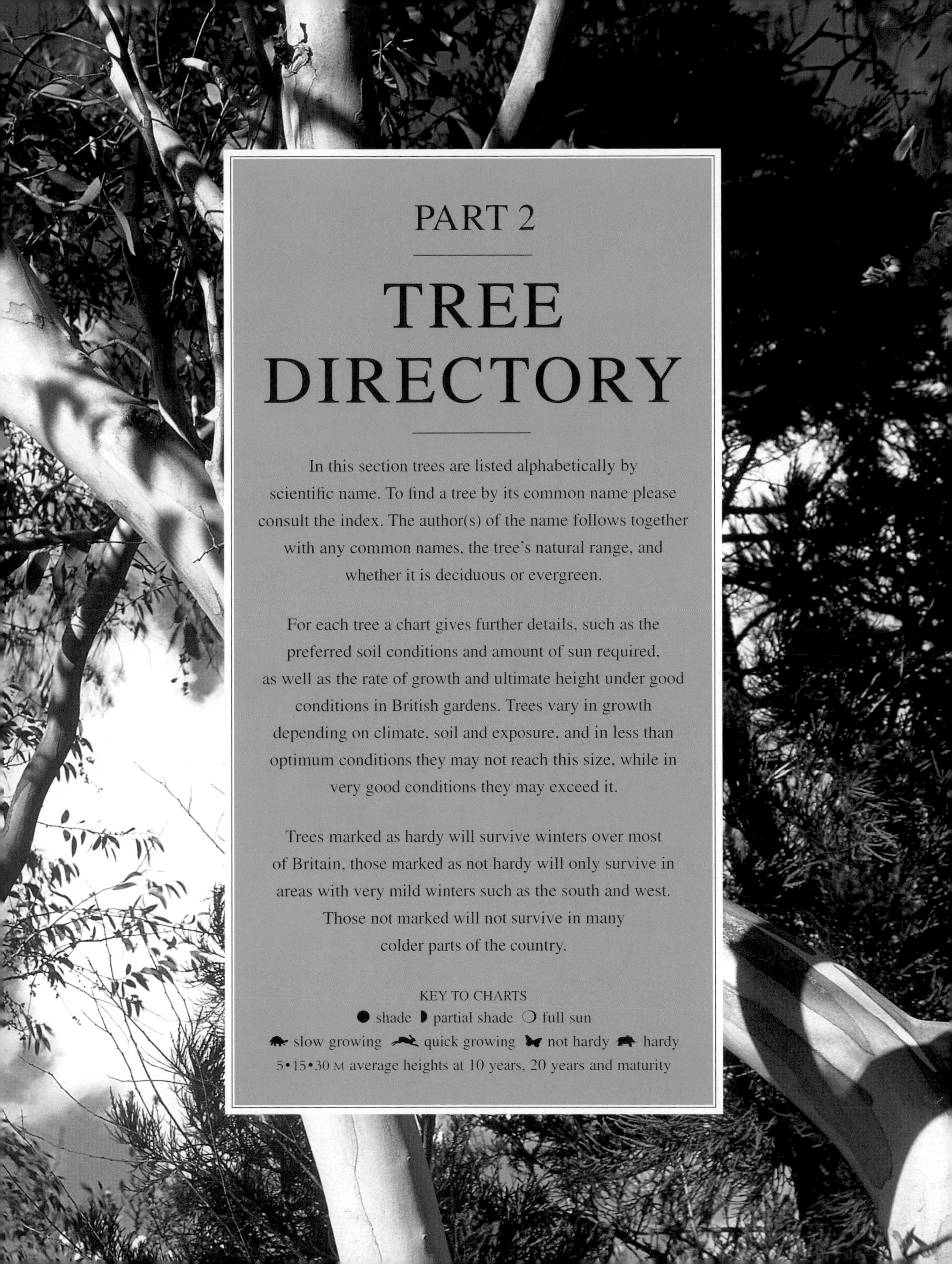

PART 2

TREE DIRECTORY

In this section trees are listed alphabetically by scientific name. To find a tree by its common name please consult the index. The author(s) of the name follows together with any common names, the tree's natural range, and whether it is deciduous or evergreen.

For each tree a chart gives further details, such as the preferred soil conditions and amount of sun required, as well as the rate of growth and ultimate height under good conditions in British gardens. Trees vary in growth depending on climate, soil and exposure, and in less than optimum conditions they may not reach this size, while in very good conditions they may exceed it.

Trees marked as hardy will survive winters over most of Britain, those marked as not hardy will only survive in areas with very mild winters such as the south and west. Those not marked will not survive in many colder parts of the country.

KEY TO CHARTS

● shade ◗ partial shade ❍ full sun

slow growing · quick growing · not hardy · hardy

5•15•30 M average heights at 10 years, 20 years and maturity

Abies/Silver firs

THE SILVER FIRS are a group of evergreen conifers that generally make trees of conical habit, frequently of large size. Often confused with the spruces (*Picea*), they are most easily distinguished by their upright cones, often very ornamental as they ripen, which break up before they fall.

Cultivation They are generally best in a good, moist soil and most species reach their largest size on lime-free soils in areas of high rainfall and cool summers. *A. cephalonica* and *A. pinsapo* are the best for growing on chalky soils.

ABIES ALBA MILL.

EUROPEAN SILVER FIR, COMMON SILVER FIR; EUROPE. EVERGREEN.

This was first planted in 1603 and has been grown in Britain longer than any other silver fir. Around 1770 it was commonly planted in gardens and woods and, until the conifers from the American north-west overtook it, was the biggest and tallest tree anywhere in Britain and Ireland. Some remain in the Coniferous Areas, but in the east and south there are none, and very few younger ones. Although commonly seen in Scotland, this fir is less frequently planted today and is susceptible to attack by adelgids and damage by late frosts. The foliage is about the dullest of that of any silver fir: grey shoots with scattered blackish pubescence, with thin rows of dark green leaves lying nearly flat each side.

5•15•45 M

ABIES ALBA (above). This once commonly planted tree will outgrow any of the other silver firs, although it is often damaged by late spring frosts.

ABIES AMABILIS (far left). This fir is more situated to milder areas with high rainfall, and like most other firs, will not thrive on shallow chalk soils.

A. AMABILIS FORBES

BEAUTIFUL FIR, PACIFIC SILVER FIR; NW NORTH AMERICA. EVERGREEN.

This is a variably successful tree in Britain, with most vigorous and shapely specimens in areas of high rainfall. It has a slender, regularly conic crown with whorls of light branches level and very short near the top of the tree. The stout shoots bear long spreading glossy dark green leaves, brilliantly banded silver beneath and fanning out forward over the shoot. When newly unfolded they are often soft blue-grey. This is a tree for a park or garden among the western and northern mountains, and needs an acid, damp mineral soil. As a young tree it is one of the most attractive of all silver firs with a crown of luxuriant foliage to the ground.

4•12•30 M

ABIES BRACTEATA (above). Although slow to establish and susceptible to frost damage when young, it is worth the wait as it quickly develops into a very ornamental tree.

ABIES CEPHALONICA var. *APOLLINIS* (far right above and below). This once commonly planted tree will outgrow any of the other silver firs, although it is often damaged by late spring frosts. It is more situated to milder areas with high rainfall, and like most other firs, will not thrive on shallow chalk soils.

A. BRACTEATA (D. DON) POITEAU

SANTA LUCIA FIR; CALIFORNIA. EVERGREEN.

The wild population of this splendid silver fir is a relic of those found near the heads of damp canyons in the Santa Lucia Mountains of Monterey, California. Hence the tree grows best in the Coniferous Areas with plenty of summer rain. Elsewhere it flourishes only in moist and sheltered places and is relatively short-lived. It is unique among the silver firs in the long, narrow, protruding bracts of its cones and in having slender acute buds like a beech, while the hard leaves with spined points are very unusual.

The bark is smooth and almost black, prominently marked by rings of branch scars. The crown, after some 30 years, is in two parts. The top is a slender spire with very short, level side-shoots and rises from long, down-swept branches holding fans of foliage that sweep to the ground. The foliage is on a large scale; the stout shoot – olive-brown then dark red-brown – bears parted ranks of 5 cm spine-ended leaves, dark green above and with two narrow but bright white bands beneath.

The Santa Lucia fir is slow to start and susceptible to frost damage as a young plant, but once established it grows very fast and is extremely ornamental at all times.

soil: ACID — ALKALINE; DRY — WET

5•10•40 M

A. CEPHALONICA LOUDON

GREEK FIR; SE EUROPE. EVERGREEN.

This grows into a coarse, huge and widely branched tree liable to have high branches broken. It makes a very vigorous tree, quite shapely for years, and unlike many firs grows well in dry, warm regions as well as in the Coniferous Areas. It has rigid acute, dark green leaves radiating all round an orange-brown shoot.

Variant var. *apollinis* Beissner has better foliage, thicker and more crowded above the shoot, and makes a much better tree.

soil: ACID — ALKALINE; DRY — WET

5•12•30 M

ABIES CONCOLOR (GORDON) HILDEBRAND

WHITE FIR; W NORTH AMERICA. EVERGREEN.

The typical tree grows from Colorado south and westwards and is uncommon in gardens. When growing well it has fine long, 5–6 cm, upstanding leaves that are dark blue-green on both sides and is decorative as a young tree. var. *lowiana* (Gordon) Lemmon (Low's fir) is the form from mid-Oregon south along the Sierra Nevada. It was introduced in 1851 and is the commoner and better form in gardens. Trees with a black bark have narrowly columnar tall crowns and flat-spreading 5 cm leaves, dark green above. Those with a corky thick bark, grey with deep brown fissures, are conic to the tip and have grey-blue-green leaves that curve up each side of the shoot. In high rainfall areas this is one of the fastest growing and biggest silver firs, and is remarkably shapely even when 45 m tall. At all ages it is a first-class specimen tree and will grow some of the finest boles to be seen.

Variant 'Violacea' is slower growing with long upstanding leaves, bright blue-grey or silvery. It is remarkably handsome as a young tree but apt to thin before reaching any great size.

soil
ACID ALKALINE
DRY WET
8•15•45 M

A. FORRESTII COLTMAN-ROGERS ex CRAIB

FORREST'S FIR; SW CHINA. EVERGREEN.

In high rainfall areas this tree grows on to be a fine specimen, while in drier areas it fades and dies back when about 16 m tall. However, it is worth growing for its best period, from 6 to 25 years of age, when it is a sturdy regular cone of whorled, slightly ascending branches bearing orange-red or dark red shoots with densely held, deep green, notch-tipped leaves that are broadly banded beneath with the clearest snow-white. Furthermore, at a surprisingly young age, about10 years, it bears a number of big erect barrel-like cones. It needs a moist acid soil and is best in some shelter.

soil
ACID ALKALINE
DRY WET
5•12•20 M

ABIES CONCOLOR var. *LOWIANA* (above). This is one of the fastest and most impressive of the firs if grown in mild, moist areas. It can be quite variable in bark and foliage colour as well as in habit.

ABIES CONCOLOR (far left). Although a very attractive large tree it is seldom seen in gardens as it is often difficult to grow successfully.

ABIES CONCOLOR 'CANDICANS' (above). A striking form of French origin with very bright silvery-blue foliage. Its strong growth soon gives an impressive specimin tree.

ABIES FORRESTII (left). Provide the right conditions, and even from a young age you will be rewarded with a stunning display of large, deep violet blue-purple cones.

ABIES GRANDIS (right). Since its introduction this fir has been widely planted. It is more at home in a protected woodland setting and is easily distinguished by its scented foliage when crushed.

A. GRANDIS LINDLEY

GRAND FIR; W NORTH AMERICA. EVERGREEN.

One of the giant trees of the world, this has been known to be 90 m tall in the wild and was first sent to Britain by David Douglas in 1830. It is one of the fastest growing trees there. It is a fine specimen among other trees but it can be rather thin on its own. In a small group it is very effective, as it grows such a fine bole, but is less windfirm. Its bright green leaves stand out each side of slender olive-brown shoots. They are of mixed lengths, and have a strong scent of orange peel when crushed

ABIES HOMOLEPIS SIEBOLD & ZUCC.

NIKKO FIR; JAPAN. EVERGREEN.

This is a very sturdy tree with parallel raised branches, from a bole with a bark that scales crisply in pale pink-orange patches. Unlike several Japanese conifers it usually remains very healthy, and seems to be long-lived. It is one of the best silver firs for warm dry regions. Excellent foliage: cream, plated stout shoots with two somewhat parted dense rows of dark blue-green leaves. It bears cones sooner than many of its relatives, and more of them spread over the crown. They are cylindric, domed dark blue-purple.

A. KOREANA WILSON

KOREAN FIR; S KOREA. EVERGREEN. 10 M.

This grows at some 50–60 cm a year into a charming, slender tree but it is the ones from the offshore Cheju-do (Quelpaert Island) that are mostly desired. They begin to flower when scarcely 1 m high and five or more years old and will be only 10 m tall when 60 years old. The female flowers may be red, pink, green or white. The cones are 6 cm barrels, deep blue but much hidden by large brown bracts. The leaves are slender and rather sparse for a silver fir, but pure white beneath.

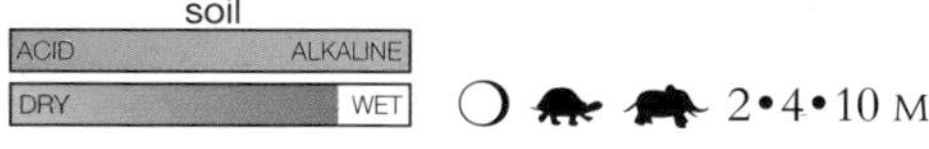

A. LASIOCARPA (HOOKER) NUTTALL

SUBALPINE FIR; W NORTH AMERICA. EVERGREEN.

The typical form of this species neither lives long nor grows well; The most commonly grown form is var. *arizonica* (Merriam) Lemmon (Arizona fir, Cork fir), which is moderately slow growing but soon shows a creamy brown, thick, corky bark and a slender crown. It grows best in warmer, drier areas.

A. MAGNIFICA MURRAY

RED FIR; OREGON & CALIFORNIA. EVERGREEN.

In foliage this serves the same garden purposes as the Noble fir (*A. procera*) but it differs in its crown which is slender-conic to the tip and strongly layered. The leading shoot has at its base a ring of quite level short stubby shoots 1 m or so above a slightly longer ring, and so on. The bole is so stout it can appear to swell or may even be slightly barrelled, and is prominently marked by rings of branch scars.

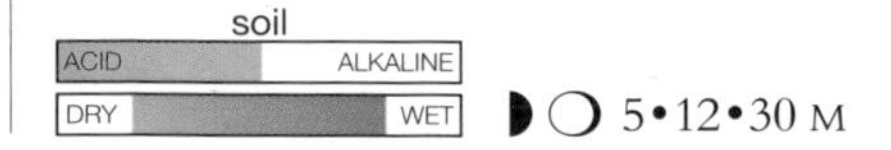

ABIES HOMOLEPIS (left). This is arguably the best silver fir for warmer, dryer areas, and it is quite tolerant of pollution, making it a wise choice for larger gardens in industrial areas.

ABIES LASIOCARPA. This species seldom does well in Britain as it is more at home on the snowline in the Rocky Mountains; var. *arizonica* (below) is a better choice.

ABIES KOREANA (far left). This is the best of the silver firs for the smaller garden. Attractive deep blue cones are produced, often in abundance.

ABIES MAGNIFICA (below). Maximising the true grace of this tree requires high rainfall and a mild climate, when it will reveal its strongly layered branch habit.

ABIES MARIESII (far right). Requiring less rainfall to promote healthy growth this fir is tolerant of a wide range of climatic conditions.

A. MARIESII MASTERS

MARIES'S FIR; JAPAN. EVERGREEN.

This is a Japanese version of the Pacific silver fir (*A. amabilis*) and differs mainly in having browner thicker pubescence on its shoots, shorter leaves which are glossy green above and blue-white beneath, and speckled grey bark marked by branch scars. It is less vigorous but more reliable for a shapely specimen outside the Coniferous Areas.

A. NORDMANNIANA (STEVEN) SPACH

CAUCASIAN FIR; CAUCASUS, SW ASIA. EVERGREEN.

This is in effect a healthier, less branchy version of the European silver fir (*A. alba*) with more leathery, glossier leaves across the top of the shoot. A large import of seeds

in 1854 enabled gardens everywhere to plant it and since then few European silver firs have been planted. In the Coniferous Areas the Caucasian tree is big and richly foliaged. It grows very well elsewhere too, although it is less heavily foliaged and is a good specimen for any mixed planting of the bigger conifers. Plants are now commonly offered in the Christmas tree trade.

ABIES NORDMANNIANA (right). Now a common substitute for the Christmas tree, this tree is more widely planted than the European silver fir (*A. alba*).

ABIES NUMIDICA (left). This is the best of the firs for hot, dry conditions with its attractive dark green foliage and masses of brown cones.

ABIES NUMIDICA DELANNOY ex CARRIÈRE

ALGERIAN FIR; ALGERIA. EVERGREEN.

This bears shoots that are remarkably densely covered in short, thick, broad leaves with white bands above and broader ones beneath. It usually grows a good clean bole and a regularly conic narrow crown, and is one of the best silver firs in hot, dry areas and near towns. It is very attractive as a small tree, often coning prolifically.

soil
ACID ALKALINE
DRY WET
5•12•25 M

A. PINDROW (ROYLE) SPACH

PINDROW FIR; W HIMALAYAS. EVERGREEN.

ABIES PINDROW (left). This native of mixed woodland in the Himalayas requires a protected location. It is seldom seen in gardens.

Although this high-altitude tree is strictly for coniferous areas so far as long life and great size are concerned, its foliage is so handsome that it is worth growing elsewhere in a group as a short-term tree. Big specimens have dark grey bark, scaling in curves, and strictly conic crowns, and even when 30 m tall the leading shoot – straight, stout and short – can be seen to be shaggy with the long, loosely held leaves. These are also on very stout, pale pink lower shoots and are bright shiny green, thick, hard and leathery, springing up and forwards from the shoots in two loose ranks, to 7 cm long.

soil
ACID ALKALINE
DRY WET
5•10•25 M

A. PINSAPO BOISSIER

SPANISH FIR; S SPAIN. EVERGREEN.

This very distinct species is confined in the wild to three small stands near Ronda in southern Spain and is one of the best firs for growing in hot, dry, even chalky areas. Its very rigid, blue-grey leaves are densely borne, standing out all around the shoot. Although not as fast-growing as some of the other species in moist areas, it will rapidly make a very beautiful tree.

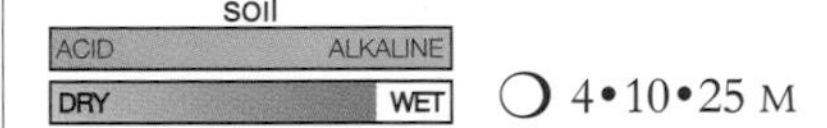

ABIES PROCERA (right). This fir was introduced to Britain with the Grand Fir (*A. grandis*). Although quick growing it will not attain the same height.

ABIES PINSAPO (far right). With distinctive foliage and a tolerance of lime soils, this is one of the best firs for hot, dry exposed areas.

A. PROCERA REHDER (*A. NOBILIS* LINDLEY)

NOBLE FIR; W UNITED STATES. EVERGREEN.

This tree was sent to Britain by David Douglas in 1830. It is a distinct blue-grey from a distance so is valuable among green-leaved species to vary the coniferous landscape. It grows a stout bole rapidly although height growth is slower – at best 1 m a year. The bark on smaller trees is smooth silvery-grey with a few dark fissures; the biggest trees have hard square scales. The slender leaves, blue-grey on both sides, rise sharply from and hide the orange brown, densely short pubescent shoots. The leaves are flattened and grooved, so will not roll between finger and thumb, unlike those of the similar Red fir (*A. magnifica*) which are more rounded, with a rib, and can be rolled (they also spread widely, revealing the shoot). Thrives anywhere except on chalky or dry soils and is quite good in exposed sites.

A. VEITCHII LINDLEY

VEITCH'S SILVER FIR; JAPAN. EVERGREEN.

Although an attractive tree when young, this species is relatively short-lived. The bole is unsightly with deep ribs and pockets but young trees start away fast. Its leaves are notched and their undersides are bright white. With the branch ends sweeping up in an elegant curve, this underside shows well with an effect like frost.

ABIES VEITCHII (below). Although fast growing this fir is seldom long lived, and will not attain the same stature as its North American relatives.

Acacia dealbata link

MIMOSA, SILVER WATTLE; SE AUSTRALIA, TASMANIA. EVERGREEN.

On its own this will make a 12 m tree on a sinuous warm brown bole, liable to lean and be blown down. The long snaking, budless shoots of a young or regrowing plant are silvery blue-green with narrow ridges below each leaf. The leaves are feathery, and doubly compound with about a dozen pairs of pinnae, each bearing about 30 pairs – many scarcely parted – of oblong, narrow, bright blue-green leaflets. The yellow flowers are 3 mm globules, 20–30 on a head, and open in January in Torquay or Penzance and April in Surrey.

Cultivation Coming from south-east Australia, this really needs a south-facing wall unless it is close to the south or south-west coasts of England and Wales or in southern Ireland; it is in every other garden on the Isle of Wight, and common in the south of Devon and Cornwall and in Ireland, where it can be grown as a free-standing tree. Elsewhere it can grow rapidly in years with mild winters but will be cut to the ground or lose most of its top in cold ones.

soil
ACID ALKALINE
DRY WET
10•12•15 M

ACACIA DEALBATA (left). Requiring a protected location such as against a south-facing wall, large clusters of tiny, vibrant yellow flowers bloom in winter or early spring.

Acer/Maples

ACER BUERGERIANUM (far right). This rare trident maple should be more widely grown as it has many attractive features including a wide soil tolerance.

ACER CAMPESTRE 'COMPACTUM' (below), is a dwarf, shrubby form of the Field maple sometimes grafted on a stem to give a small bushy tree.

WITH MORE THAN 100 species, the maples provide some of Britain's finest garden trees for foliage and there are examples to fit every size of garden. The opposite leaves are normally lobed, but some are not and some are divided into distinct leaflets. Many of them give excellent autumn colour. Though individually small, the flowers are often highly ornamental when viewed close-up and are followed by characteristic winged fruit.

Cultivation Most maples are easy to grow, very hardy and fast on any good soil.

ACER BUERGERIANUM MIQ.

TRIDENT MAPLE; CHINA, JAPAN. DECIDUOUS.

The Trident maple is rare but so attractive that this ought to be rectified. It was first sent to Britain in 1896 and even the oldest trees are scarcely 13 m tall so suitable for small plantings. The crown is domed and carries a dense mass of leaves on a rather short bole with a flaky, pale orange and brown bark. The leaf tapers to a slender petiole and at its end has three forward-pointing triangular lobes. Three prominent veins spring from the base of the leaf, which is often slightly cupped showing the pale or bluish underside. In autumn the leaves turn crimson and dark red. The flowers open

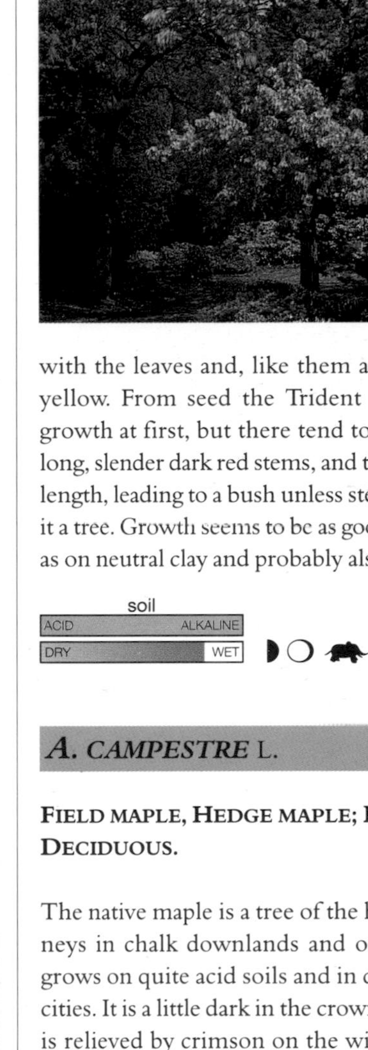

with the leaves and, like them at that time, are pale yellow. From seed the Trident maple makes rapid growth at first, but there tend to be too many of the long, slender dark red stems, and they are too similar in length, leading to a bush unless steps are taken to make it a tree. Growth seems to be as good on acid sandy soils as on neutral clay and probably also in limy soil.

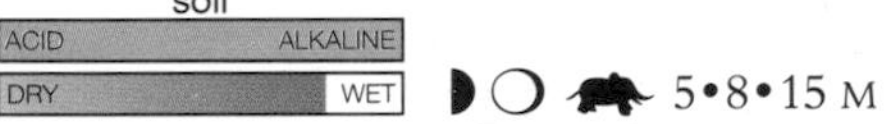

ACER CAMPESTRE 'SCHWERINII' (below). This form of our native field maple has delightful bronze new foliage and attractive autumn tints.

A. CAMPESTRE L.

FIELD MAPLE, HEDGE MAPLE; EUROPE. DECIDUOUS.

The native maple is a tree of the hedgerows and spinneys in chalk downlands and on limestone. It also grows on quite acid soils and in clay and is healthy in cities. It is a little dark in the crown in summer but this is relieved by crimson on the wings of the clustered fruit. The leaves turn yellow, old gold, russet or even purple in autumn. It is therefore very valuable as a background tree. Trees left to grow in hedges at wide intervals develop good boles and broad, domed crowns about 16 m tall, but in wooded gardens can reach 25 m. Trees grown as specimens or as a group in a woodland garden may need relieving of suckers around their boles. This should not be neglected.

Variants Most variegated and yellow-leaved forms can scarcely be considered as trees but one worth mentioning is 'Schwerinii' which has bronze foliage.

ACER CAPILLIPES MAXIM.

RED SNAKE-BARK MAPLE; JAPAN. DECIDUOUS.

This is the most attractive of the many snake-bark maples in several ways and the only one with such shiny leaves and regular rows of parallel veins. Its bark is clearly and brightly striped, white on grey-green, and the shoots are dark red. The petioles are scarlet and stand out among the bright, glossy green leaves. Their undersides are pale and slightly glaucous, and have little red or green pegs in the axils of the main veins. Pairs of arched catkins of yellow flowers are borne from an early age at almost every node, and ripen to tiny winged fruit which are, pink and yellow in summer and quite a feature. In autumn the foliage turns yellow, orange, bright red and crimson.

Introduced to Britain from Japan via the Arnold Arboretum in Boston in 1894, this maple grows rapidly when young but its branches arch over and it has not exceeded 15 m in height. A few of the oldest trees have boles 40 cm in diameter.

Although a good choice for a fast-growing tree of only moderate size, it is often not long-lived in gardens.

A. CAPPADOCICUM GLEDITSCH

CAPPADOCIAN MAPLE; TURKEY TO CHINA. DECIDUOUS.

This tree has a unique breadth of range since no other grows on both sides of the Hindu Kush massif. It was introduced in Britain in 1838 from Asia Minor and is uncommon here even though it is found in most of the largest gardens and many smaller ones and parks. The untoothed margin of the taper-pointed leaf lobes is unusual but the most marked feature of the tree is its propensity to sucker. In the absence of cattle, mowers or gardeners, each tree becomes enclosed in a thicket.

The value of this tree, where there is room for it, lies in its soft grey, smoothly crinkled bark, its bronzy young foliage and, particularly, in its reliable bright butter-yellow autumn colour. It grows notably well in western gardens with high rainfall and cool damp summers but is equally at home in the north-east and drier areas. It also grows in chalky soils.

Variants 'Aureum' is delightful in spring and, as a young tree at least, throughout the summer. The leaves emerge bright yellow and to some extent turn green with time, but young trees continue to make new growth through much of the summer so their outer crowns remain bright yellow; some old trees remain bright throughout.

Other species *A.* x *hillieri* Lancaster 'Summergold' is a small tree to about 10 m with very bright yellow foliage, red when young. It can sometimes burn in too much sun.

ACER CAPILLIPES (far left). Like other highly ornamental snake bark maple, *A.capillipes* requires an acid soil, in a cool, moist location.

ACER CAPPADOCICUM (below) With its dramatic autumn colours and alkaline tolerance, this maple should be more widely planted.

ACER CAPPADOCICUM 'AUREUM' (below). This is an improved selection of the parent plant and is more desirable as a garden tree due to its foliage and reduced suckering habit.

ACER CARPINIFOLIUM (above). Often resembling a large shrub, this maple has unusually shaped leaves and good autumn tints.

A. CARPINIFOLIUM SIEBOLD & ZUCC.

HORNBEAM MAPLE; JAPAN. DECIDUOUS.

This normally looks more like a large bush than a tree but is technically a tree because it is on a single stem. It is Japanese and its handsome leaves suggest a hornbeam (*Carpinus*) until it is noticed that they are in opposite pairs. They are a good fresh green, turning yellow-brown in autumn, and 8–10 cm long, unlobed but sharply toothed with a tapered tip, and have 20 or more pairs of parallel veins. The flowers are green and star-shaped on slender catkins. The merits of the Hornbeam maple, apart from its apparent disguise, are its fine foliage and good soft yellow autumn colour.

soil
ACID ALKALINE
DRY WET 4•6•8 M

A. CISSIFOLIUM (SIEBOLD & ZUCC.) K. KOCH

VINE-LEAF MAPLE; JAPAN. DECIDUOUS.

This little Japanese tree is one of a group of maples in which the leaves have three leaflets. Its tiny yellow flowers are borne profusely, and the pairs of arched catkins with their tiny winged fruit dominate the foliage until autumn when the leaves turn pale yellow then brown. It is of unusual aspect, but in a small planting it takes up more room than it justifies ornamentally and its best role is as a group on a broad bank.

A. CRATAEGIFOLIUM SIEBOLD & ZUCC.

HAWTHORN MAPLE; JAPAN. DECIDUOUS.

Although one of the snake-bark maples from Japan, this makes such a slender stem that the bark is of little note. The foliage is carried on short, twiggy shoots close above each slender branch. The finely pointed leaf is only 6 x 3 cm and is faintly lobed and finely toothed. It is borne on a scarlet stalk and is tinged red from the time it unfolds. The thinness of the foliage is reduced by numerous catkins of level-winged fruit.

Variant 'Veitchii' is a striking form which has leaves mottled with white and pink.

ACER CISSIFOLIUM (right). In keeping with other maples from Japan, it will not thrive on a chalk soil. Its masses of tiny, winged fruit persist long into autumn.

ACER CRATAEGIFOLIUM (far right). Although there are maples with better bark striations, the mixture of reddish fruits and foliage are a bonus.

ACER DAVIDII FRANCH.

PÈRE DAVID'S MAPLE; CHINA. DECIDUOUS.

This Chinese species is among the best known of the snake-bark maples, introduced in Britain in 1879. Generally of arching habit, it has green bark striped with white and red. Its leaves are unlobed, and in some forms turn orange or yellow in autumn.

Variants There are everal forms of this variable species. Examples are 'Ernest Wilson' with pale green leaves; 'George Forrest' with dark green, red-stalked leaves; and 'Madeline Spitta' which is narrowly upright with orange leaves in autumn.

A. GINNALA MAXIM.

AMUR MAPLE; CHINA, JAPAN. DECIDUOUS.

Whether a small tree on a pale grey-barked bole or more of a bush, this very hardy plant from northern China and Mongolia is highly desirable for small gardens. It comes into leaf yellowish with numerous erect rounded heads of pale yellow scented flowers, and by the time the leaves are dark green the bunches of fruit are tinged red. The leaves, 6–8 cm long, have a long, slender, pointed central lobe and a small triangular one on each side near the base; all three are deeply and irregularly toothed. In autumn this is among the first trees to show colour, the leaves turning deep red.

Much planted, often in tubs, where winters are really cold, the Amur maple has a crown of rather dense, twisting branches on which the bark is smooth silvery-grey.

soil
ACID ALKALINE
DRY WET
3•5•10 M

A. GRISEUM (FRANCH.) PAX

PAPERBARK MAPLE; CHINA. DECIDUOUS.

This outstanding species is one of the most sought-after trees for its bark. Introduced in Britain from China in 1901, it is now frequently seen in parks and gardens. Although slow-growing it is worth persevering with for its beautiful cinnamon-coloured bark which peels on even the smallest branches. The leaves have three leaflets which are bluish beneath and softly hairy. They can, but do not always, turn red in autumn. The green flowers open in small clusters as the young leaves expand in spring, and are followed by conspicuous green-winged fruit which are usually infertile.

ACER DAVIDII (above left). This species is one of the most widely planted snake bark maples. While handsome, 'George Forrest' fails to colour in autumn.

ACER GINNALA (above). This versatile, very hardy maple can be grown as a tree or shrub and exhibits vibrant autumn tints.

ACER GRISEUM (left). This is one of the most desirable of the maples. It is outstanding in shape, bark and autumn colour, but must be planted on acid soil.

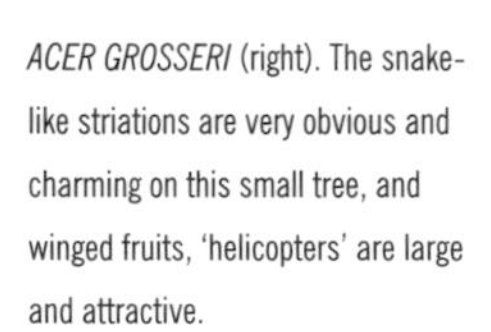
ACER GROSSERI (right). The snake-like striations are very obvious and charming on this small tree, and winged fruits, 'helicopters' are large and attractive.

A. GROSSERI PAX VAR. *HERSII* (REHDER) REHDER (*A. HERSII* REHD.)

HERS'S MAPLE; CHINA. DECIDUOUS.

This tree is named from the French collector who found it in China and introduced it in 1927. It is one of the best of the snake-barks and very distinctive. The bright white stripes are on a smooth green background which is retained until the bole is some 30 cm in diameter, after which corky patches of brown and grey appear and angular pits become prominent.

The crown develops long arching branches well clothed with leaves, but with few or no lateral shoots, and they sweep down as a fine fountain of green. The singular character of Hers's maple among the snake-barks is its devotion to olive-green. It leafs out olive-green, not red like Père David's maple (*A. davidii*), and its shoots and leaf stalks, flowers and fruit all remain this colour. The leaves are rather densely held and grow to 17 x 9 cm with a broad central lobe and a small acute triangular lobe on each side, or are unlobed. It is entirely glabrous and in the basal vein axils beneath there is a purple spot. The abundant flowers on paired, arched catkins (strictly racemes, they have tiny side-branches as in all the maples with 'catkins') ripen to big broad-winged fruit, 5 cm across, yellow-green until tinged pink, then brown.

Hers's maple grows strongly in any reasonable soil and is known so far to have reached a height of 17 m. Its value lies in its splendid shape, bark and foliage, and very much in its autumn colours. The leaves turn yellow, then bright orange, then some turn crimson. With its shapely crown this tree is spectacular in autumn.

8•10•10 M

ACER JAPONICUM THUNB.

DOWNY JAPANESE MAPLE; JAPAN. DECIDUOUS.

This often shrubby species is less common in gardens than the Smooth Japanese maple (*A. palmatum*) and is mainly grown as a few selected forms, of which the following is the most striking and tree-like.

Variants 'Vitifolium' is an old selection from Japan which was sent to Britain in about 1863 but is still uncommon. This is despite a well-placed group up to 15 m tall at Westonbirt, Gloucestershire, which attracts such crowds for its wonderful autumn display that it should be known as 'Kodak's Benefit'. It has a very short bole before breaking into two or three sinuous, stout, upright main branches with pale grey bark. The flowers, in drooping clusters, have quite big dark red petals that open as the young leaves expand. The bold, dark green leaves with 7–9 pointed lobes are silky hairy when young and can reach up to 10 x 15 cm, or even 22 x 24 cm. In autumn, the outer leaves which receive sunshine turn scarlet and deep red, while those a little inside the crown turn pink, lilac and yellow; those further in are green, then yellow. Another selection, 'Aconitifolium', has very deeply cut leaves but is usually a shrub.

3•6•10 M

ACER JAPONICUM (right). Requiring the same conditions as the more widely planted *Acer palmatum* forms, the autumn tints are equally good.

ACER JAPONICUM 'VITIFOLIUM' (far right). With leaves resembling a grape vine, and vibrant scarlet autumn tints, this maple should be more widely planted.

ACER LOBELII TEN.

LOBEL'S MAPLE; S ITALY. DECIDUOUS.

As a young tree, Lobel's maple is strictly upright with rather few branches and even fewer side-shoots. It is therefore highly suitable for restricted sites despite the fact that it grows 1–1.3 m a year. Later it grows more slowly and its branches begin to spread. The biggest trees are 25 m tall with a spread of less than 10 m. The shoots are bloomed lilac in the first year. Its leaves, which are held level from little spurs on the erect branches, resemble those of Norway maple (*A. platanoides*) except that the five lobes are nearly entire with wavy margins, and the whiskers into which the lobe-tips are drawn curve upwards or sideways. The leaves are dark green in summer and show some yellows in autumn, but nothing brilliant.

Any well-drained soil, alkaline or acid, will grow this tree well but on a dry site it will need watering for a few years to establish strongly. Lobel's maple is recommended where a tall tree is wanted in limited space.

8•12•25 M

A. MACROPHYLLUM PURSH

BIG-LEAF MAPLE, OREGON MAPLE; W NORTH AMERICA. DECIDUOUS.

Conic, with a strong leader when it is young, the Oregon maple matures with a hugely domed crown on radiating and arched branches. Its stout shoots bear very big but thinly textured leaves, divided almost to the base into five lobes, the central and two outer ones tapering much towards their bases with a large acute tooth on each side at their broadest part and a few smaller ones from there to the leaf-tips. They can be more than 25 x 30 cm on petioles of 30 cm which expand at the base to enfold the shoot and hide the bud. In May the large expanding buds bear among the emerging leaves an erect, substantial inflorescence which bends over and hangs 25 cm bearing yellow-green flowers. Before falling in autumn the leaves turn brown, or sometimes yellow to orange – briefly in Britain although in Oregon, especially, they are a blaze of orange for weeks.

As an open-grown specimen this vigorous tree needs much space. Although it is a little dark in summer, the big leaf makes it interesting and the flowers and fruit are conspicuous. Leafing out and in flower, it is striking. It can be grown to mature among a group of other trees, where its foliage will still show and its fine bole with orange-brown square plates can be well displayed.

soil
ACID ALKALINE
DRY WET

6•12•25 M

ACER LOBELII (far left). Lobel's maple can be used where a tall tree is sought within a limited space. Its autumn colour is an added bonus.

ACER MACROPHYLLUM (left). If grown to maturity with other trees, its large foliage is its greatest attribute, but is is also very ornamental in flower and fruit.

ACER MAXIMOWICZIANUM (above). Grown where many Japanese maples fail to thrive, this maple has bright deep red autumn colour.

ACER NEGUNDO 'VARIEGATUM' (far right). In spring, often coinciding with the flowering of magnolias, masses of bright pink, male tassels hang from naked branches.

ACER NEGUNDO var. *VIOLACEUM* (below). The box elders will thrive in very harsh conditions. The variegated forms are less vigorous and can be grown as shrubs if pruned annually.

A. MAXIMOWICZIANUM MIQ. (*A. NIKOENSE* (MAXIM.) MIQ.)

NIKKO MAPLE; JAPAN. DECIDUOUS.

One of the trifoliate maples, this is an excellent medium-small tree. It colours bright deep reds in autumn even when growing on chalky soils.

Other species *A. triflorum* Komar., from Manchuria and Korea is a striking small maple with ornamental flaking bark, unfortunately rare in gardensIts leaves emerge yellow then turn very dark green above, while the leaflets beneath are blue-white and densely hairy like the dark red, stout petiole. The flowers are cup-shaped and yellow, and hang in threes below the leaves. The fruit are 5 cm across with broad pubescent wings. The bark is smooth, tight and dark grey.

A. NEGUNDO L.

ASH-LEAFED MAPLE, BOX ELDER; NORTH AMERICA TO MEXICO. DECIDUOUS.

This is one of the trees received by Bishop Henry Compton at Fulham Palace where it arrived in 1688. Its native range is remarkable – from northern Alberta to California where it becomes a thickly pubescent variety, from Texas to Mexico, and from Quebec to Florida. In the Allegheny Mountains and New England the leaves are handsome, a rich shiny green, but in Britain this is a dull, shapeless and short-lived tree not worth planting in its typical form. It is distinct among the maples in having leaves with 3–5 leaflets. Male and female flowers are borne on separate plants before, or as, the leaves emerge. The males, with long, drooping stamens, are the more ornamental.

Variants 'Auratum' is a choice tree, and the bright feature of some colour-plantings at Kew. With its upswept upper crown and level-branched lower crown, it covers itself in leaves of a rich bright yellow that fade to greenish in late autumn. 'Elegans' has leaflets broadly edged with yellow. 'Variegatum' is about the most conspicuously white-variegated tree grown. It is entirely female and carries masses of small fruit, the wings of which are mainly white and tinged pink. 'Flamingo' is a more recent introduction, similar to 'Variegatum', but the young leaves are edged with pink. Unfortunately all of these variegated forms are liable to revert and are often seen as neglected trees that have been overtaken by more vigorous shoots with green foliage. var. *violaceum* (Kirchn.) Jaeg. is a very vigorous and handsome form which occurs scattered in the wild. It has lilac-bloomed shoots, deep green leaves with red petioles, and soon makes a stout bole and a good tree. The male form has conspicuous pink tassels of flowers before the leaves emerge.

ACER PALMATUM THUNB.

SMOOTH JAPANESE MAPLE; JAPAN. DECIDUOUS.

The typical form of this Japanese species is most commonly seen in gardens in a wide array of forms with variously cut, purple or variegated leaves. It makes a handsome small tree. The small, red-purple flowers open in drooping clusters in spring as the leaves emerge and are followed by fruits which can have red wings. The 5–7 lobed leaves provide brilliant autumn colour.

Variants Most are shrubby but those worth considering as trees include 'Atropurpureum' with deep purple foliage which turns brilliant red in autum; 'Osakazuki' with reliable red autumn colour and red-winged fruit; and 'Senkaki', Coral-bark maple, with small pale green leaves that turn orange-yellow in autumn and bright pink winter shoots.

A. PENSYLVANICUM L.

MOOSEWOOD; E NORTH AMERICA. DECIDUOUS.

The only snake-bark maple native to North America was introduced in 1755 and was the first snake-bark to be cultivated in Britain. It is a fast-growing rather upright tree, with green bark prominently streaked with white and red. The bright green leaves have three tapered lobes and briefly turn bright yellow in autumn.

Variant 'Erythrocladum' is a striking selection with brilliant pink winter shoots and yellow, streaked bark. This form is, however, best as a shrub as it grows weakly as a tree.

A. PLATANOIDES L.

NORWAY MAPLE; EUROPE. DECIDUOUS.

Found through much of Europe, this species has several features which combine to make it one of the amenity trees of greatest value. It will thrive equally on thin soils over chalk and on acid soils. It grows well on clays and tolerates a largely paved root-run. It transplants well as a big tree 2–4 m. It is easily pruned to give a clean, smooth bole in a few years. In appearance, it approaches the spectacular when it is thickly covered in bunches of bright acid-yellow-green flowers towards the end of March, when few other trees are flowering and before

ACER PALMATUM (far left), makes a handsome small tree and is especially attractive in the autumn.

ACER PALMATUM 'ATROPURPUREUM' (far left). Only the most vigorous of the smooth Japanese maples will thrive on chalk soils. 'Atropurpureum' is an example of one, although the normally spectactular autumn tints may not be as vibrant.

ACER PENSYLVANICUM 'ERYTHROCLADUM' (far left) . With its striking winter stems this form of the moosewood should be pruned annually to promote pink shoots.

ACER PLATANOIDES 'SCHWEDLERI' (top). Known for its later flowering time, and distinctive red winter buds.

ACER PLATANOIDES 'LORBERGII' (above). This is one of the most attractive of the Norway maples.

ACER PSEUDOPLATANUS (far right). An excellent pioneer species which thrives in harsh conditions.

ACER PSEUDOPLATANUS 'BRILLIANTISSIMUM' (below). Unsurpassed in spring with its salmon pink foliage, the leaves fade to yellow, before turning green for the summer.

the leaves emerge. The flowers turn to green as the leaves unfold, and darken with them. In early autumn a few trees turn bright orange while the majority are reliably butter-yellow all over during most of October. The broad leaves are thin in texture and the five lobes of each have a few large teeth which, like the lobes, are tipped by a finely drawn-out whisker.

Variants 'Columnare', which arose in France, is slender with erect branches. 'Crimson King' has deep purple-red foliage and red-flushed flowers. 'Faassen's Black' and 'Goldsworth Purple' are similar. 'Drummondii' remains of very moderate size, with a neat dense crown and brightens everything around it with its small leaves spotted with pale cream or white. Occasional shoots can revert to green and must be removed. 'Globosum' has a tightly spherical dense crown and is seen increasingly in the landscape. 'Lorbergii' has its leaves deeply cut into five lobes. 'Schwedleri' has deep red buds in winter and opens its flowers two weeks later than the typical form; they are on red pedicels with red calyces and yellow petals. In autumn, foliage turns early to orange and then crimson.

A. PSEUDOPLATANUS L.

SYCAMORE, GREAT MAPLE; EUROPE. DECIDUOUS.

The Sycamore or Great maple ranges from the Caucasus Mountains to central and southern Europe near Paris and may have been brought to Britain by the Romans. It is remarkably resistant to maritime exposure, polluted air and high altitude. It yields hard, white first-class timber, which neither gives nor receives taint from foods, dyes well and takes a fine finish. It can be invasive in fertile woodland soils where it seeds abundantly.

The Sycamore is the best hardwood tree for the extreme maritime winds and cool summers of the Western Isles and in cities. It cannot be said to be ornamental, and its only contribution to wildlife is to provide a perch for town pigeons and house sparrows, but it will grow and make smooth, reasonably good boles on limestone as well as on acidic city soils, gravels or clay, so it has a great value for less favourable sites.

The heavily leafed, domed crown of the Sycamore makes it suitable for screens and for clumps and roundels. Although a small clump can be pure Sycamore, the sward beneath will be poor as the trees' big, leathery leaves can form mats that are very slow to break down; woods or lines or peripheral belts should be small-sized if only Sycamores are planted. If the trees are used more extensively they should be mixed with ones with lighter crowns, like birch or larch. Thinning is a lengthy procedure as cut trees sprout strongly and, if left, the sprouts deaden the surrounding area by shading out other plants and are of no interest to birds. They must be cut back several times early in the year.

Variants The Sycamore has given gardens a number of forms, several of which are particularly valuable. 'Atropurpureum' has purple undersides to its leaves and a large specimen makes an interesting contrast with smaller trees. No garden should be without 'Brilliantissimum', a remarkable cultivar that is among the most spectacular of foliage trees for nearly two months in late spring. Grafted on a 2 m stem of ordinary Sycamore, it forms a small, tight, bun-shaped crown on a leg for some years. It gradually becomes less odd-looking and makes a shapely, if bushy, tree nearly 12 m tall in 60 years. The buds open with the leaves and are bright pink as they expand, then become red and pink for a few days. After that they begin to change through orange to yellow, a fine spectacle which lasts for two weeks; they remain a clear yellow for up to three weeks then fade to white for about a week before turning a rather poor dull green. A similar form, 'Prinz Handjery', is a little more open and bears numerous 'catkins' of yellow flowers when the leaves are at their reddest. It has more sharply lobed leaves, which are often purple underneath.

Both these trees are invaluable for brightening up a corner of a shrubbery. As single specimens they suffer from very dull foliage after July, so despite their long period of glory they are better when not prominently solitary. Quite undemanding of soil and will tolerate light shade.

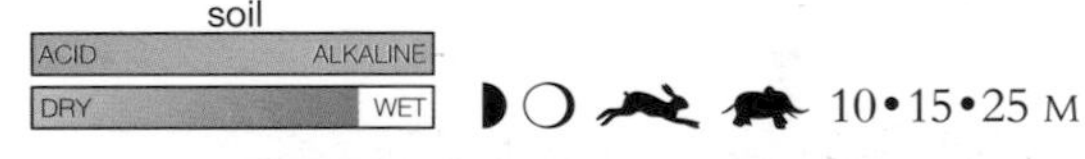

ACER RUBRUM L.

RED MAPLE; E NORTH AMERICA. DECIDUOUS.

First brought to Britain by John Tradescant in 1656, this tree ranges throughout eastern North America. The name is due to its red flowers, males and females on separate trees, which wreathe the shoots in spring before the leaves unfold. In most young plants autumn colours are spectacular, with scarlet outer foliage and orange and yellow interior leaves until the trees are briefly deep red all over. The leaves are pale orange when unfolding, after which they are dark green above and silvered beneath. They have three main large but shallow lobes, coarsely toothed, and may have two smaller basal lobes. The petiole is slender and red. The crown is somewhat narrow with long, slender and often curved whip-like shoots. The pale, dull grey bark is smooth at first but becomes fissured and flakes in strips.

A tree of rapid growth and with these features should be very popular, but the Red maple is little known and therefore seldom planted. It has a reputation for not succeeding on chalky soils but will in fact grow well on them, although it may colour less riotously in autumn. It can achieve 22 m without spreading far, but the autumn display of old trees is more limited, and the outer tips of foliage turn early to crimson-red. It is a good tree, nonetheless, to have in a group of specimens, or above shrubs, as it casts little shade until old. In a park, a drift of these along a bank would form a notable feature.

ACER RUBRUM 'SCHLESINGERI' (above). Grown for its dramatic, but very early autumn colour, this red maple seldom exceeds 10 m.

ACER RUBRUM 'COLUMNARE' (far left),is very vigorous, little-branched and very upright, becoming a pillar of fire as the leaves turn orange and red in autumn.

Variants There are many selections, mainly made for improved autumn colour. 'Scanlon' is a columnar one with upright branches; 'Schlesingeri' has brilliant, very early autumn colour and only makes a small tree that grows to 10 m or less.

6•12•20 M

A. RUFINERVE SIEBOLD & ZUCC.

GREY-BUDDED SNAKE-BARK MAPLE; JAPAN. DECIDUOUS.

This Japanese tree is somewhat variable, or perhaps there are two forms. One has pink stripes on very pale grey bark, large firm leaves and a good constitution. The other, which is rather more usual, has green stripes on dull grey bark, smaller darker leaves and a bad tendency for the upper branches to die back. Both forms make a fine show of orange and scarlet autumn colours. This tree is distinguished from other similar snake-barks by its leaf, which is broader than it is long; by its shoot and buds, which are bloomed pale grey, and quite blue on the buds of old wood; and by the rusty down at the base of the underside of its leaf, which is reduced by midsummer to rust-brown patches between the basal veins. The fruit, usually copiously borne in dense bunches, are very small, up to 2 cm across the widely angled wings which turn from green to red in summer.

Variant 'Albolimbatum' is rare and much sought after. The leaves are margined and sometimes spotted with white, and turn to pink and purple in autumn.

ACER RUFINERVE 'ALBOLIMBATUM' (right). This very delightful variegated selection is less common in gardens than the species, although it is equally good, if not better.

ACER SACCHARINUM 'WIERI' (far left). This is the most commonly grown of the Laciniatum Group, chosen for its deeply incised leaves and quick growing habit.

ACER SACCHARINUM L.

SILVER MAPLE; E NORTH AMERICA. DECIDUOUS.

This close relative of the Red maple (*A. rubrum*) has more strongly silvered leaf undersides and a gust of wind can make a tree seem suddenly white with frost. The flowers are greenish-yellow, and are clustered on short spurs at the nodes of the shoots before the leaves unfold, as early as February in some years. The leaves emerge reddish-orange before assuming the pale green upper surface of summer. In autumn they become mostly pale yellow and brown, although a few are scarlet. The broadly winged fruit are rare in Britain.

The deep lobing and toothing of the leaf, together with the distinctively silvered underside, make the Silver maple a good foliage tree, and its great vigour is a useful asset, but it also has some less desirable features. The tall crown of upright arched branches is often too thin to be a good screen and is liable to breakage in gales. The stout bole is often sprouty and looks better if kept clean, and the tree is unlikely to live more than 150 years. However, a tree which grows so well on clays or sands and in city air has its uses.

Variants Laciniatum Group has deeply cut leaves and is a frequent variant, but the extreme form 'Wieri' is the one grown. It is very vigorous with brown, pendulous shoots, and deeply incised leaves. The crown is long-pendulous. 'Wieri' is just as vigorous as the type and will reach the same sort of size.

soil
ACID ALKALINE
DRY WET
10•15•30 M

A. SACCHARUM MARSH.

SUGAR MAPLE; E NORTH AMERICA. DECIDUOUS.

Few trees are more underrated than the Sugar maple from the eastern United States. Many gardens and estates have a fine specimen or two unknown to the owner. Although many gardeners in Britain think of it as a failure, it grows quite fast for many years. The finest specimen in the country was, until recently, labelled 'Norway maple' (*A. platanoides*). However, although the Sugar maple resembles this tree, its bark is very distinct with long open fissures and dark grey shaggy plates. The leaves are matt blue-green, not glossy green, beneath and have fewer teeth than the Norway, all minutely rounded and not whisker-tipped. It is a fine foliage tree of moderate size and some specimens

ACER SACCHARUM subsp. *LEUCODERME* (below), from the south-east United States. makes only a small tree, usually less than 10 m tall with pale bark but giving good autumn colours.

ACER SACCHARUM (above). The sugar maple is a fine foliage tree of moderate size. The autumn colour is variable and not as good as seen in its native habitat as it requires hot summers.

briefly show bright orange or scarlet autumn colour. However, none of the trees in Britain achieves the flame-orange scarlet which is perhaps the most brilliant of all the New England fall colours.

A. TRAUTVETTERI MEDWED.

TRAUTVETTER'S MAPLE, RED-BUD MAPLE; TURKEY AND CAUCASUS. DECIDUOUS.

This Caucasian tree resembles a sycamore but has two good features which that tree lacks. Its bold leaves can be up to 20 cm across and are deeply divided into five lobes, making the summer crown less heavy and more interesting visually; and it has decorative fruit with broad wings, each 5 x 2 cm, at an acute angle which turn bright rosy pink in early summer. It is not, in fact, a close relative of the sycamore and this is shown by the flowers, which are in erect, loose panicles, and by the sharply acute dark brown buds. Its alternative name, the Red-bud maple, refers to the bright red bud scales. It makes a good parkland tree, and grows well in any ordinary soil. To show at its best, it needs to be isolated from, or well in front of, other trees and where the full light on its crown encourages flowering.

A. X *ZOESCHENSE* PAX

ZOESCHEN MAPLE; CULTIVATED ORIGIN. DECIDUOUS.

This hybrid was raised in a German nursery by crossing a Field maple (*A. campestre*) with, probably, Cappadocian maple (*A. cappadocicum*). It's tendency to sucker is usually suppressed by the broad crown. The leaves are five-lobed and glossy, and are held level on 10 cm red stalks. It adds dark handsome foliage to a mixed group.

Variant A frequently seen form is 'Annae' which has deep bronze-purple young foliage.

ACER TRAUTVETTERI (top right). To encourage masses of flowers this tree should be planted at the front of a group with full sun on its crown

ACER X ZOESCHENSE (bottom right). Like the cappadocian maple, this tree has a tendency to sucker, but luckily, these are less problematic, due to a dense crown.

Aesculus/
Horse chestnuts, Buckeyes

THE HORSE CHESTNUTS are distinguished by their opposite leaves which are palmately divided into several leaflets and by their conspicuous panicles of flowers. The seeds of all are the familiar conkers, which in the case of the Common horse chestnut (*A. hippocastanum*) in particular, can sometimes be a problem when they seed themselves freely in gardens.

Cultivation Given a good soil Horse chestnuts are easy to grow in sun or light shade.

AESCULUS X *CARNEA* HAYNE

RED HORSE CHESTNUT; CULTIVATED ORIGIN. DECIDUOUS.

This commonly planted hybrid is a cross between Common horse chestnut (*A. hippocastanum*) and Red buckeye (*A. pavia*). Smaller than the common horse chestnut it can be distinguished, by its smaller leaves which often have twisted, puckered leaflcts. The typical form has rather dull pink flowers followed by smooth or only sparsely prickly fruits.

Variants 'Briotii' with bright red flowers or 'Plantierensis' which has pale pink flowers.

soil

5•8•20 M

A. + *DALLIMOREI* SEALY

CULTIVATED ORIGIN. DECIDUOUS.

Although rarely available at the moment, mention is made of this tree because it deserves to be more widely planted. It arose in Kent and is thought to be a graft hybrid of Common horse chestnut (*A. hippocastanum*) and Sweet buckeye (*A. flava*). A vigorous tree, similar to the common horse chestnut, it is distinguished by creamy yellow flowers which fade to nearly white.

soil

6•10•20 M

A. FLAVA SOL.

YELLOW OR SWEET BUCKEYE; E UNITED STATES. DECIDUOUS.

This splendid American tree has been in Britain for some 240 years. It would be of immense benefit visually if every dull red horse chestnut (*A.* x *carnea*) had been a Yellow buckeye. It is frequently grafted on to horse chestnut because of the difficulty in importing fresh seed. The five leaflets are elegantly lanceolate and taper evenly to a fine point; they have slender stalks of 1–2 cm, very fine toothing, are a bright glossy green in summer and turn orange and crimson in autumn. The flowers are not spectacular but are highly attractive as pale yellow spikes among the bright green leaves.

soil

5•8•20 M

AESCULUS X *CARNEA (above).* Smaller than the common horse chestnut, it can be distinguished by its smaller leaves which often have twisted, puckered leaflets.

AESCULUS + *DALLIMOREI* (bottom left). A vigorous tree, it is distinguished by creamy yellow flowers which fade to nearly white.

AESCULUS FLAVA (below). Although the flowers are not as spectacular as the red horse chestnut, it is highly ornamental in leaf and form.

AESCULUS HIPPOCASTANUM 'HAMPTON COURT GOLD' (right). A young tree, striking in spring just as the new foliage emerges.

A. HIPPOCASTANUM L.

COMMON HORSE CHESTNUT; SE EUROPE. DECIDUOUS.

So familiar is the Common horse chestnut that it was made one of the four 'British trees' in a set of postage stamps. It grows freely into a big tree in every part of the British Isle. Yet it is native only to mountains in northern Greece and Albania, was unknown to northern European botanists until described in 1596 and did not grow in England until about 1616. At its best, on deep, damp soils in a warm, sheltered site it can be a very fine specimen, growing to 35 x 2 m or more, but it will achieve 25 x 1 m almost anywhere that is not too exposed and can seed itself in woodlands. Young plants grow straight, sturdy 60 cm shoots but old trees grow very slowly. Its life span is unusually variable. A few trees which are known to date back to 1662 are in full health, whereas many shed branches and break up when they are probably no more than 120 years old. The weak wood renders a tree in full leaf liable to shed a branch when it is weighted with water from a sudden storm.

The leaves colour well in autumn but vary with individual trees: a few turn scarlet early but the majority turn yellow then orange from mid-September to early November. The 30 cm panicles of flowers never fail to be prolific on old trees but some years are better for the resulting conkers than others. The sticky, resinous dark red-brown buds are not found on any of the numerous relatives of this tree in America – the buckeyes – nor are they so well developed in the Indian or Japanese horse chestnuts. The bark on old trees is pinkish-brown with hard scales. This is unlike the bark of the Red horse chestnut (*A.* x *carnea* Hayne) or the Yellow buckeye (*A. flava*), both of which are often grafted on to the horse chestnut at 1–2 m, resulting in a smoother dark red-brown bark.

Variants 'Baumannii' is the form with double flowers without conkers. One at Westonbirt, Gloucestershire, reached 30 m but no other has been seen of this size and it is not yet a common tree. 'Hampton Court Gold' has leaves variegated with pale yellow or that are even entirely this colour and is rare and slow-growing.

A. INDICA (WALL. ex CAMBESS.) HOOKER

INDIAN HORSE CHESTNU; HIMALAYAS. DECIDUOUS.

Brought to Britain from the Himalayas in 1856 this tree is popular with those planting city and resort parks because it flowers nearly two months later than the common horse chestnut, in late June when parks are most visited. It also has the advantage of being a good orange-brown colour when it comes into leaf. The lanceolate leaflets have slender, usually red stalks and are often dark and hanging, with slightly silvered undersides. Some trees bush out with strong low branches and need early attention to give them shape. The flowers are on narrow, 30 cm panicles and are often so flecked with pink that the tree seems to be pink-flowered. It grows fairly vigorously in any normal soil.

Variant 'Sydney Pearce' is a very sturdy form selected at Kew in 1928. It differs in its larger heads of whiter flowers and broader leaflets on stout green stalks, which are less pale beneath.

AESCULUS INDICA 'SYDNEY PEARCE' (far right). An improved selection of *A. indica* as it has larger heads of whiter flowers and better foliage.

AESCULUS X NEGLECTA 'ERYTHROBLASTOS' (left). A popular small chestnut grown for the bright pink colour of its young foliage.

AESCULUS X NEGLECTA LINDLEY

SE UNITED STATES. DECIDUOUS.

This is thought to be a naturally occurring hybrid between two North American species, the Red buckeye (*A. pavia)* and(*A. sylvatica),* and is represented in gardens mainly by the following form.

'Erythroblastos' is among the most popular of the smaller buckeyes. A slender, conical tree that reaches about 6 m, it is grown entirely for the colour of its young foliage. The leaves emerge bright pink and turn gradually to cream, then green flushed with yellow. The pale cream flowers in small panicles are relatively inconspicuous.

AESCULUS TURBINATA (left). This is the cream of the horse chestnuts with huge leaves and rich orange autumn colour.

A. TURBINATA BLUME

JAPANESE HORSE CHESTNUT; JAPAN. DECIDUOUS.

In most respects this can be regarded as a rather superior Common horse chestnut (*A. hippocastanum*) with huge leaves and rich orange autumn colour. It differs in having a smooth grey or grey-pink bark, narrower flower panicles and leaflet-tips that taper gradually to a long acute, not abrupt, point, but shares the common tree's sessile leaflets. The conkers are smaller, with a bigger white circular patch which covers more than a third of the seed, borne in smooth, pear-shaped fruits.

The leaves can be 40 cm across on 42 cm petioles and there are small tufts of orange hair at the base of the veins on the undersides of the leaflets. The tree seems to grow with considerable vigour on any normal soil and is well worth planting for its vast leaves and as a change from the common horse chestnut.

Ailanthus altissima (Mill.) Swingle

TREE OF HEAVEN; N CHINA. DECIDUOUS.

This tree from northern China likes a hot summer, so makes little growth in the north or west of Britain and is big only from Devon to East Anglia. It is common, and grows very rapidly, in London – fortunately not as fast as in cities in the hottest parts of the USA and other countries where it can be a considerable nuisance.

The long bole is smoothly circular in section, with a few stout branches.The bark is pewter-grey with shallow fissures marked with streaks of white. The dark red leaves emerge very late and expand to 30–40 cm, bearing between 11 and over 40 leaflets up to 15 cm long, each with a distinctive, minutely swollen large tooth or two near the base; the leaves fall, fairly early without changing colour. Male trees have dense clusters of small white flowers on spikes. Female trees have greenish flowers which ripen to big bunches of winged fruits that turn from green to scarlet in summer and are dull brown from autumn to winter.

For luxuriant foliage at shrub height, stump back a Tree of heaven annually; the rods will bear huge leaves. As a tree it is suitable only in large spacious sites in southern Britain and is in leaf too briefly to be a good screen. Suckering is often a problem and these can occur some distance from the tree.

ALINTHUS ALTISSIMA (right). Tolerant of city conditions, large leaves emerge in late spring. Female flowers give way to big bunches of scarlet winged fruits.

Alnus/Alders

SEVERAL SPECIES OF ALDER are useful for providing fast-growing windbreaks while ornamental selections provide some attractive foliage trees. They all bear catkins – early in the year, before the leaves emerge, in the case of the species that follow. Those of the male trees are long and pendulous.

Cultivation The main garden value of the alders is their ability to grow in wet soils where few other trees will thrive. *A. cordata* and *A. incana*, however, will grow equally well in dry soils.

ALNUS CORDATA DESF.

ITALIAN ALDER; CORSICA, ITALY. DECIDUOUS.

The tallest and most shapely of the alders, this tree also has the most distinctive and decorative foliage, and its thick, bright yellow catkins are among the best. The leaves are small, 5–8 cm, and heart-shaped; late leaves are pale orange when they unfold, and all mature to a smooth, glossy, usually dark, green. The catkins are out early and lengthen to 8–10 cm. The fruit arc big, 2.5 cm long, and glossy dark green, turning nearly black when woody and old, with numerous separated scales. The bark is dark grey or brownish-grey and smooth between the few, broad dark fissures. The crown is conic or narrowly domed.

The Italian alder is a remarkably useful tree. It grows very fast when young, to 15 m in 15 years; beyond this it slows much less than other alders. It is not dependent on a wet site, but grows best in normally drained but fairly retentive soil and about as well on thin loams over chalk. Completely hardy and apparently wind-firm, it is early into leaf and late to shed.

soil
ACID ALKALINE
DRY WET
10•15•25 M

ALNUS CORDATA (above). The fast growing Italian alder is a remarkably useful tree.

ALNUS FIRMA (far left). This striking but little known species should be more widely grown for its numerous bright gold catkins.

A. FIRMA SIEBOLD & ZUCC.

JAPANESE ALDER; JAPAN. DECIDUOUS.

The Japanese alder is rare in Britain and none of those present are so far known as big trees. Well worth growing for its numerous catkins, these are neither very long (to 8 cm) nor stout, but the brightest gold of any alder, or perhaps any catkin. The leaves are remarkably decorative with numerous prominent parallel veins.

soil
ACID ALKALINE
DRY WET
5•8•10 M

A. GLUTINOSA (L.) GAERTN.

COMMON ALDER; EUROPE, W ASIA, N AFRICA. DECIDUOUS.

This is not a good tree for normal planting, as it lacks grace and any positive feature as well as autumn colour. It has one useful purpose and that is too hold the banks of lakes and rivers firm against erosion. It will also grow in much-flooded water margins or hollows. It grows very strongly for a few years, especially as sprouts from a cut tree, and has a good conic crown. However this flattens with age. The bole should be cleaned of all branches as high as can be reached. The male flowers, on catkins, open brownish-yellow over a long period, from February on some trees to April on others. Female flowers are tiny, dark red globules on short, branched stalks. The broadly rounded and indented end to the leaf distinguishes it from other alders grown in Britain.

Variants 'Aurea', Golden alder, is rare, slow and small. It is a good foliage tree with rich golden leaves. 'Laciniata', Cut-leaf alder, is much more attractive than the normal form as the foliage is transformed by regular triangular lobes which are cut halfway to the midrib, giving an interesting effect. It should not be confused with 'Incisa', which is sometimes grown under this name, and has small lobed and toothed leaves. 'Imperialis' is altogether different. It is a slender, rather graceful little tree, often leaning out at the top, with light branches that bend to become level.

ALNUS GLUTINOSA 'IMPERIALIS' (above), is a slender, rather graceful little tree.

ALNUS GLUTINOSA 'LACINIATA' (below). Lacking grace, *A glutinosa*'s one useful purpose is to hold river and lake banks firm against erosion. *A glutinosa* 'Laciniata', often confused with 'Incisa', has better, and more interesting foliage.

ALNUS GLUTINOSA 'AUREA' (centre right). The seldom seen, golden leaved alder is slow in growth, making it a good choice for the smaller garden.

ALNUS INCANA 'PENDULA' (right) This delightful, weeping tree is dramatic in leaf as well as in winter when the framework of branches can be seen.

A. INCANA (L.) MOENCH

GREY ALDER; EUROPE. DECIDUOUS.

Although of little merit itself in the garden, and included largely for its cultivars, the Grey alder from Europe is unusually tough and grows vigorously on the inhospitable soils of mine-tips and rubble. Young branches are a good smooth silvery grey and the acute well-lobed leaves are pleasant, but they are held loosely and from a distance the crown is dull. The grey pubescence on the shoots and on the undersides of the leaves, especially on the veins, is an unusual feature in an alder. The male catkins are variably early and quite attractive. This is a tree for fast growth on a really difficult site – 9 m in nine years is known.

Variants 'Aurea' and 'Ramulis Coccineis' are almost identical, but the catkins of the latter, are more prominent and brighter. Both have bright orange-red winter shoots and scarlet leafbuds that make a pinkish haze in late winter, followed by soft yellow leaves. Both make rather bushy small trees. 'Pendula' is an attractive, very pendulous weeping tree of no great size, and is particularly ornamental when in flower.

soil
ACID ALKALINE
DRY WET
10•15•20 M

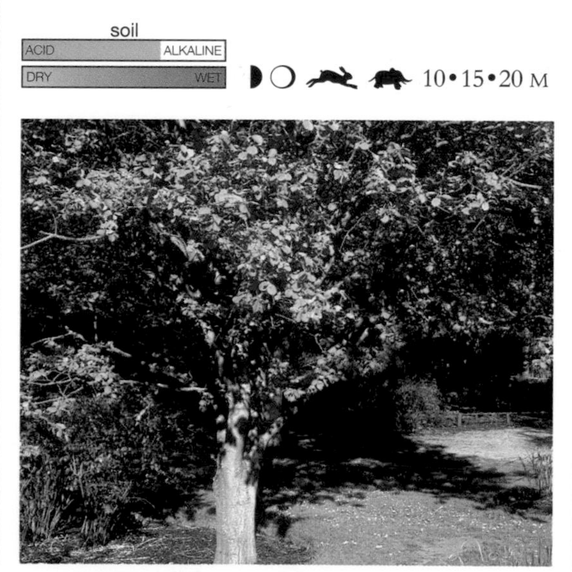

ALNUS INCANA 'RAMULIS COCCINEIS' (far right). A bushy small tree with bright orange-red winter stems and distinctive red-blushed catkins.

ALNUS RUBRA BONG.

OREGON ALDER, RED ALDER; W NORTH AMERICA. DECIDUOUS.

Even on poor wet peats or clay over chalk,the Oregon alder starts in great style with shoots to 1.5 m long (one at Westonbirt, Gloucestershire, reached 18 m after 12 years) and huge leaves, sometimes 15 x 12 cm, but it rarely keeps its promise. It was introduced in Britain in 1880 but the oldest at present on record dates from 1930 and is only 19 m tall. The leaf is like that of the grey alder (*A. incana*), but broader with bigger lobes. In its native, damp wooded valleys along the Coast Range and Cascade Mountains, south from Washington State and especially through Oregon, the bark of even young trees is silvery white but in Britain it is always leaden grey.

The value of the Oregon alder is to raise rapid shelter in wet, peaty hollows, and few trees are better for the purpose if they are combined with longer term species like sitka spruce or shore pine, which grow much the better for having it among them. Alders fix nitrogen in nodules on their roots and their leaf-litter acts as a nitrogenous fertilizer.

A. SUBCORDATA C.A. MEYER

CAUCASIAN ALDER; CAUCASUS, IRAN. DECIDUOUS

This alder is little known in Britain as yet and four 50- to 60-year-old trees at Kew are almost the only indication that it does, to some extent, retain its great early vigour of growth. The shape of its big leaves varies greatly: some are broad and floppy, others narrow and willow-like. In its third year from seed one in Surrey grew a leading shoot 2 m long with leaves to 25 cm long and after 14 years it reached 15 m.

ALNUS RUBRA (above). A pioneer tree, this alder will have rapid growth even on poor wet peats or clay over chalk.

ALNUS SUBCORDATA (left). Growing an average of 1m each year when young, this alder is little known in Britain.

Araucaria araucana (Molina) K. Koch

MONKEY PUZZLE, CHILE PINE; CHILE, ARGENTINA. EVERGREEN.

Distinctive with its stout whorled shoots densely clothed in rigid, sharp-pointed leaves, it makes a prominent lawn specimen in many gardens. Its effect depends less on its unusually broad, domed crown than on its almost cylindrical bole, always rigidly straight and very rarely forked, which arises from a base like an elephant's foot and is encased in tight, finely roughened or horizontally wrinkled bark. There is plenty of light on the bole when the lower crown has been shed so it needs to be kept clear of ivy. The bottom 2 m of the bole of a young Monkey puzzle must be cleared of branches even if the tree is to be grown with foliage to the ground.

Most Monkey puzzles are either male or female. There is no way of telling which until a tree flowers and some do not flower. Very broad-crowned ones have been noted to be female, but there are males that are equally broad. In 1967 the mean height and girth of all the trees in the Bicton Avenue were both, by a strange chance, precisely the same for all the males as a group and all the females. A tree needs to grow and flower within 100 m or so of one of the opposite sex for its seed to be fertile. When the sexes are adjacent 95 per cent germination may be expected, and up to 200 seeds in a cone. Very occasionally a tree is found with both male and female flowers.

There are several Monkey puzzle avenues other than the one at Bicton. At Castle Kennedy, County Wigtown, for example, there is a short narrow one near the old Loch Inch Castle and an enormously broad 'grand avenue' with only a few trees missing from the original 21 pairs. Many are 26 m tall and some are 95 cm in diameter, but they need to be taller yet to be in proportion as an avenue.

Cultivation Any soil suits the Monkey puzzle and it withstands a good deal of exposure. Big trees are rarely blown down and, where they have been, in most cases were probably dead already. Uniquely amongst conifers in Britain, the Monkey puzzle can take two years to grow from one whorl of shoots to the next, or it can make two whorls in three years or the standard one whorl a year. As a result, unlike most other conifers, the age of a tree cannot be determined by counting the whorls down its stem. A clump is sometimes seen crowning a knoll in open country and is an interesting feature. If the trees are planted fairly closely the interior lower crowns become shaded and dead. Cleaning them out is quite a problem but cattle will do this to 1.5 m or so by pushing around and scratching. In the absence of cattle, the trees will suddenly clean themselves.

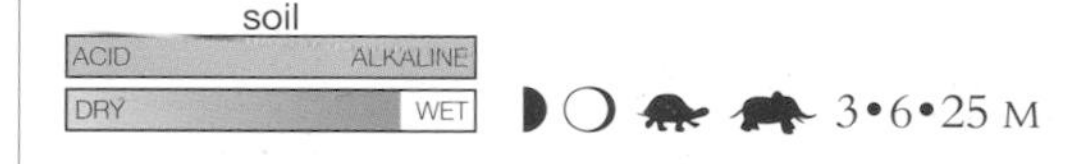

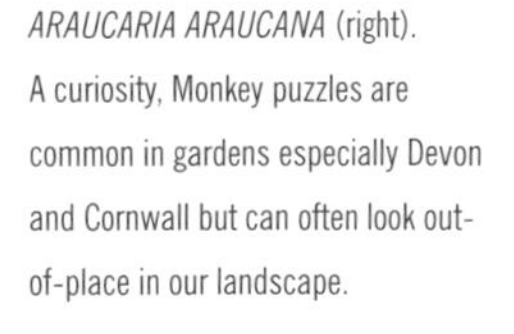
ARAUCARIA ARAUCANA (right). A curiosity, Monkey puzzles are common in gardens especially Devon and Cornwall but can often look out-of-place in our landscape.

Arbutus/Strawberry tree

THE CULTIVATED MEMBERS of this genus are fine evergreen trees for the garden and offer a range of ornamental features, including small white flowers, red fruit and peeling bark.

Cultivation Unlike most members of the Rhododendron family, all strawberry trees, apart from *A. menziesii,* are suitable for chalky soils. Grow them in full sun, ideally protected from strong winds.

ARBUTUS ANDRACHNE L.

GREEK STRAWBERRY TREE; E MEDITERRANEAN REGION. EVERGREEN.

This little tree is rather tender and is suited only to warm, dry south-eastern gardens. The main attraction is its bright rufous-orange bark, which flakes away each year to show whitish or pale lemon, smooth patches. Halfway through this moult the stem is remarkably beautiful. The bark of branches in the crown is yellow-green, in contrast to the only other Strawberry tree with entire leaves, the Madrona (*A. menziesii*), where the branches are orange-red. The Greek species has small, white, urn-shaped flowers in nodding heads in mid-spring and 1 cm, smooth red berries in autumn.

With its glossy, dark green foliage, this is a tree of abundant attraction. Its rarity in Britain is only partly due to its climatic needs, and there should be more in gardens near the south coast of England.

soil
ACID ALKALINE
DRY WET
3•5•10 M

ARBUTUS X ANDRACHNOIDES (above). This is good as a substitute for the madrona or the Greek strawberry tree where neither can be grown.

A. X *ANDRACHNOIDES* LINK

HYBRID STRAWBERRY TREE; GREECE. EVERGREEN.

This hybrid occurs in the wild in Greece where its parents, the Greek strawberry tree (*A. andrachne*) and the Common strawberry tree (*A. unedo*) both grow. It is much more robust than either parent. It has rich dark red, slightly purplish, ridged and scaly bark that flakes here and there to leave bald, smooth, orange-brown patches. The flowers are similar to those of both parents and may open at the times appropriate to either – that is, in spring or late autumn. The matt, pale leaves are serrated. This is good as a substitute for the madrona or the Greek tree where neither can be grown.

A. MENZIESII PURSH

MADRONA, PACIFIC STRAWBERRY TREE; W NORTH AMERICA. 15 M.

Although fast-growing, the Madrona is an uncommon tree in British gardens. Short as we are of reasonably hardy, large, decorative evergreen broad-leaf trees, it

ARBUTUS ANDRACHNE (far left). This little tree is rather tender and is suited only to warm, dry, south-

ARBUTUS MENZEISII (above and top). Although fast-growing and with much to commend it, the Madrona is an uncommon tree in British gardens.

should be planted more often, in the south-east at least. The bark is pinkish-orange or orange-red and sheds big flakes to leave large, irregular, bald, green then yellow-pink areas; on branches within the crown it is rich orange. The evergreen untoothed leaves can be up to 12 cm long and crowd rather towards the tip of the shoot. They are deep shiny green, becoming yellower and paler and often blotched black before being shed, and glaucous blue-grey beneath. The numerous small flowers are prominent in spring, crowded on and spreading from an erect 20 x 15 cm panicle. The small and globose fruit are dark green, and ripen to orange-red in August in some years; in others they remain green until October, both in Britain and in the tree's native habitat.

Its striking bark, good evergreen foliage, plentiful flowers and fruit, and its vigour and stature undoubtedly make the Madrona a first-class tree for town parks and general planting except in greatly exposed sites in the north of Britain, and it is not fussy about soil. The only difficulty is the minor one that for three or four years from seed it can be killed by frost if it is growing in tall grass.

A. UNEDO L.

COMMON STRAWBERRY TREE; MEDITERRANEAN REGION, SW IRELAND. EVERGREEN.

This has become very much a village tree in England, found more often in small, old-fashioned gardens and churchyards than in larger gardens. Unlike other species it does not give a good display of coloured bark as the bole is soon grey-brown scaly ridges or largely dark grey, but it does present a unique and cheerful aspect in late autumn. At that time its nearly black foliage is decorated with nodding heads of white flowers and also with the fruit of the previous year's flowers which turn yellow, orange and scarlet.

'Unedo' means 'I eat one', an academic joke implying 'one only' – the fruit tempt, but are insipid with a not very pleasant after-flavour. Grown on a cleaned-up 'leg' of 2 m or more it would make a far better single specimen than is usually seen.

Variant 'Rubra', with pink flowers, is seen occasionally.

ARBUTUS UNEDO (right). Unlike other species, it does not give a good display of coloured bark, but the flowers and fruit are delightful.

Betula/Birches

FOR AIRINESS AND GRACE there is little to rival the birches. Fast-growing, hardy and with numerous ornamental features like striking catkins, showy bark and autumn colour, they are valuable trees for any garden. Birches will not cast a dense shade and are therefore useful for associating with other plants. They are traditionally used in areas such as heather gardens to create very effective combinations.

Cultivation Birches will grow well in most well-drained soils. They prefer ones that are light and are particularly useful on sandy soils. Most are best in full sun but species such as *B. alleghaniensis*, *B. lenta* and *B. maximowicziana* prefer woodland conditions. It may take a few years for young trees to show their bark colour.

BETULA ALBOSINENSIS BURK.

CHINESE RED-BARK BIRCH; W CHINA. DECIDUOUS.

Introduced in Britain from China in 1901, this highly ornamental tree has taper-pointed rather glossy leaves which are sharply toothed and turn yellow in autumn. The bark is distinct from that of most other species as it is coppery red and peels attractively.

Variant var. *septentrionalis* Schneider is similar but has paler bark, a mixture of cream and grey-pink.

B. ALLEGHANIENSIS BRITT. (*B. LUTEA* MICHX.)

YELLOW BIRCH; E NORTH AMERICA.

The main differences between this and the very similar Cherry birch (*B. lenta*) are outlined in the latter's entry. The leaf of the Yellow birch is noticeably flat with 12–15 pairs of parallel veins; rounded at its base and irregularly double-toothed, it is ovate and acute rather than acuminate. Its autumn colour, earlier than in the cherry birch, is a fleeting but brighter gold.

B. ERMANII CHAM.

ERMAN'S BIRCH; NE ASIA, JAPAN. DECIDUOUS.

Erman's birch grows over wide areas of Manchuria and Korea as well as in Japan, which is where the first seeds came from. It therefore tends to be variable in British gardens but retains several distinctive features. The leaves taper to the base with prominent, impressed parallel veins in 7–11 pairs and are densely borne with

BETULA ALLEGHANIENSIS (below left). Its autumn colour, earlier than in the cherry birch, is a fleeting but brighter gold.

BETULA ALBOSINENSIS (below). The bark is distinct from that of most other species as it is coppery red and peels attractively.

BETULA ERMANII (right). This tree tends to be variable in British gardens but retains several distinctive features including bark, attractive foliage and catkins.

BETULA LENTA (below right). When crushed, stems emit a strong scent of oil of winter-green and leaves are bright yellow in autumn. Bark is glossy mahogany when young.

many spreading out level. The fruit are compact cylinders 4 cm long. They are usually abundant and persist through the winter during which, from a distance, they are a good indicator of the species. In young trees the bark of the branches and bole is clear white. In somewhat older trees the branches remain white while the bole becomes dull pink and beribboned with loose, fine horizontal papery strips. When the lower branches are stout with age they also have strips hanging in fringes.

Erman's birch is grown more for its very white bark in youth than for its attractive foliage. It has ascending branches and grows vigorously on any well-drained soil including poor sands.

soil
ACID ALKALINE
DRY WET
8•12•20 M

B. LENTA L.

CHERRY BIRCH, SWEET BIRCH; E NORTH AMERICA.

This has much in common with the Yellow birch (*B. alleghaniensis*) including a similar range in eastern North America and the strong scent of oil of wintergreen when shoots are skinned or crushed. In the wild woods the two are easily distinguishable by the bigger, broader leaves of the yellow birch, but in cultivation there is less difference in the leaf. The barks are different although both are partly grey and roll horizontally into strips; that of the Cherry birch has a purple shade or dark red patches while that of the yellow birch has a yellow-grey, silvery cast. The Cherry birch has a broad crown of level branches at the base and ascending ones above. The fruit are erect, ovoid-oblong and 3.5 m long, with spreading tips. The foliage is bright yellow briefly in autumn. The leaves are narrow-ovate-acuminate and slightly cordate with 9–12 pairs of parallel veins.

BETULA MAXIMOWICZIANA REG.

MONARCH BIRCH; JAPAN. DECIDUOUS.

A good specimen of the Japanese Monarch birch is indeed the king of the birches with big, substantial broad leaves like those of the lime, up to 15 x 12 cm. They are glossy rich green and elegantly toothed; each of the 10–12 veins on either side of a leaf ends in a fine bristle of a tooth projecting beyond the several sharp teeth between. The male catkins, 10–12 cm long when open, are yellow among freshly unfolded leaves. The crown is more strongly branched than in other birches, with the branches rising at a fairly wide angle. The bark is at first dark red-brown but soon becomes smooth and white, striped with grey-brown.

B. MEDWEDIEWII REG.

TRANSCAUCASIAN BIRCH; CAUCASUS. DECIDUOUS.

The Transcaucasian birch can make a short-stemmed, broad, upright bushy tree although it is more often shrubby. It has a dull silvery grey bark that flakes in ridges. Large dark green leaves, up to 14 x 11 cm, are ovate to nearly round and deeply set with about 12 parallel veins on each side. It is slow-growing and, in view of its shape, is best planted where a large shrub is needed. It is particularly striking when the stout, drooping male catkins emerge in late spring.

soil
ACID ALKALINE
DRY WET
2•4•8 M

B. NIGRA L.

BLACK BIRCH, RIVER BIRCH; E UNITED STATES.

This tree is rarely seen away from south-eastern England, where it is still scarce and only a few mature trees are known. It prefers a damp soil and warm, sheltered site but must be more adaptable than is commonly thought for a few have grown quite well in the pavement of a road near Woking. It grows a broad crown with pendulous outer shoots. The characteristics for which it might be planted are its bark and foliage. Young trees have pale orange to brown bark with peeling blackish scales. When a tree is around 30 years old the bark is deep red-brown with papery rolls and strips which hang from the branches in translucent tatters. The leaves are unusual rather diamond-shaped, lobulate and often silvered beneath.

Variant 'Heritage' is a relatively recent selection with particularly striking bark.

BETULA MAXIMOWICZIANA (above left). The bark is at first dark red-brown but soon becomes smooth and white, striped with grey-brown.

BETULA MEDWEDIEWII (above). This shrubby tree is particularly striking when the stout, drooping male catkin emerge in late spring.

BETULA NIGRA (below). Widely used in North America, this decorative tree is little planted here; it likes damp soils and a warm, sheltered site.

B. PAPYRIFERA MARSH.

PAPER BIRCH; NORTH AMERICA. DECIDUOUS.

Almost the whole of Canada from coast to coast is the home of this birch. In most of this range the bark is chalky white. In the New England states, as in northern Alberta, it is bright white, banded by black rings and grey-stippled faint ridged rings, with black moustaches over branch scars. In gardens in Britain, however, the bark is seldom white for long but has orange tones, pink or pale brown areas or is largely dark purple. The Paper birch is known by its large, few-veined leaves with relatively stout, sparsely long, silky-haired petioles and its rough, warty shoots. It is occasionally 23 m tall but is probably short-lived.

BETULA PAPYRIFERA (right). Young, bright white bark contrasts sharply with surrounding foliage.

B. PENDULA ROTH.

SILVER BIRCH; EUROPE, N ASIA. DECIDUOUS.

BETULA PENDULA (below right). Of the two birch tree native in Britain, only the Silver birch is of garden and landscape value.

BETULA PENDULA 'LACINIATA' (below). A remarkably decorative specimen, pendulous and adaptable, this birch needs a location in full sun for proper growth.

Of the two birches native in Britain (a third species, *B. nana* L., is a shrub) only the Silver birch is of garden and landscape value except where trees are needed in a boggy patch of sandy soil. It is the only species with the characteristic, gracefully pendulous shoots and the black diamonds at the base of the white trunk also distinguish it from the Downy birch (*B. pubescens*). The Silver birch grows rapidly, at 1 m a year when young, on almost any soil including chalk and clay as well as acid light sand. On fairly good soil the light shade it casts allows good growth of bulbs and herbs. On hungry sands, however, the tree's strong root system gathers wherever good soil is placed, so shrubs planted in leafmould are soon sitting on a mass of birch roots and suffer accordingly. This, together with the fact that the Silver birch seeds itself frequently and can become a nuisance, means it would be wiser to choose a less vigorous species in such a situation.

This is a good tree for extending planting into the edges of a lawn or for framing a vista as a natural edge to thicker woods. As a lawn specimen it responds to early cleaning of all growth from the lower bole, not only because the tree looks better for losing shaded-out twiggy shoots but also because this produces cleaner and whiter bark which is enhanced by exposure to winds, and makes the Silver birch more visible. In late autumn the leaves turn yellow and remain longer than on most birches.

Variants 'Laciniata', Cut-leaf birch, has also been grown as 'Dalecarlica' a different and rarer form. It has a pretty, deeply cut leaf and a smoothly rounded, white-barked long bole. It makes a remarkably decorative specimen, very pendulous and adaptable, and needs only full light for its proper growth. Because it is so light and airy, it makes more impact in a large garden spaced some 7–8 m apart in groups of three. 'Purpurea' has glossy purple foliage, and 'Tristis' has long, slender shoots that hang down like streamers. 'Youngii', Young's weeping birch, has a low, wide-spreading head of arching and weeping shoots.

BETULA UTILIS (left and above). The Himalayan birch has reliably good bark even after reaching maturity. Several forms have been selected for their clean white bark and belong to var. *jacquemontii*.

BETULA UTILIS

HIMALAYAN BIRCH; HIMALAYAS TO CHINA. DECIDUOUS.

This wide-ranging species is extremely variable, especially in bark colour, but all forms are particularly valuable as single specimens with winter interest and autumn colour, or in small clumps. They are also some of the very best trees for the edges of glades.

The forms are not easily distinguishable but the most commonly grown, which belong to var. *jacquemontii* (Spach) Winkler (*B. jacquemontii* Spach), have a strikingly white smooth bark and good leaves marked by 10–12 pairs of impressed parallel veins. The Himalayan birch has strong, steeply rising branches and firm, shiny leaves on stout, grooved and often dark red stalks covered, like the shoots, in long hairs. In autumn the leaves turn pale then bright yellow. Other forms in cultivation, from the eastern Himalayas and China, may have pinkish to coppery brown bark, but are less common.

Variants Several selections have been made for particularly good white bark. These include 'Doorenbos', commonly supplied from Holland, 'Grayswood Ghost', 'Jermyns' and 'Silver Shadow'. Some of these have been distributed simply as *B. jacquemontii*.

soil
ACID ALKALINE
DRY WET
8•12•20 M

B. SZECHUANICA (SCHNEID.) JANSSON

SICHUAN BIRCH; CHINA. DECIDUOUS.

This tree was sent to Britain from China in 1908 and is decidedly rare. Although vigorous, it is not a very shapely tree. Its good points are its pure white bark, unmarked over large areas, and solid, leathery, dark, nearly round leaves. The leaves turn a good yellow in autumn.

soil
ACID ALKALINE
DRY WET
6•10•20 M

BETULA SZECHUANICA (left). This rare tree should be grown more for its white bark and good, crisp, yellow autumn colour.

CALOCEDRUS DECURRENS (right). Growing well on almost any soil, the Incense cedar is a good feature tree and when planted in groups.

Calocedrus decurrens (Torr.) Florin (*Libocedrus decurrens* Torr.)

INCENSE CEDAR; W NORTH AMERICA. EVERGREEN.

This cypress, related to *Thuja* and not a cedar at all, is the biggest of the erect, narrowly columnar conifers. In their native Oregon and California nearly all trees have open crowns of level branches unlike the tight columns in eastern England. In general, the further west and north the trees are in Britain, the more open or loose their crowns. In Ireland they are broad columnar and the branches are at a wide angle. In Scotland they tend to grow two or three heavy ascending branches. There are some very narrow ones as far west as Westonbirt, Gloucestershire, where the group, planted at 4 m spacing in 1910 and now 25–27 m tall, is the classic example of the use of columnar trees in groups. The bright green, scale-like foliage emits a strong scent of shoe-polish on the lightest handling. If the bole is cleaned of dense erect shoots growing on the bottom 2–3 m it shows rich purplish-brown long plates and is a fine sight. However, a single lawn tree may be more impressive clothed nearly to the ground. The Incense cedar is a good tree for a feature. It is also excellent planted in groups.

Cultivation Grows well on almost any soil, but on shallow, dry soils the crown begins to thin in patches when the tree is about 26 m tall until only some tufts near the top are green, and the cedar finally dies.

Variants 'Aureovariegata' may be worth having as a small tree when the blotches on the green foliage are bright yellow, but they become dull and sparse making a big tree look diseased. 'Berrima Gold' is an interesting variation with bright yellow foliage introduced to Britain from Australia but is slow-growing.

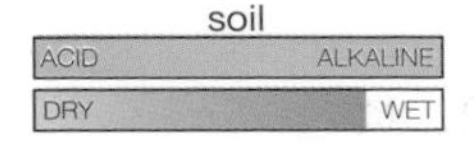

5•10•30 M

Carpinus betulus L.

HORNBEAM; EUROPE. DECIDUOUS.

This native tree was one of the last to enter England before the land-bridge was eroded and is wild only in the south-east and perhaps west to Somerset and north to Hereford. It is the typical tree of the fragments of old forest on London clay in Hainault and Epping where there was a long history of lopping – cutting back periodically at 2.5 m from the ground. Hornbeam wood is among the hardest known and immensely strong. It was used for cogwheels in mills and for the centres of cartwheels. It is still used for the hammers in pianos and in butchers' chopping blocks, where the hornbeam centre is set in beech; the beechwood is softer and wears away to leave the raised centre required for chopping meat.

The Hornbeam is an attractive tree in winter, with its leaden grey bark patterned with dark streaks and broadly domed crown of fine, straight shoots. In early spring the small, brownish catkins open in profusion. The female flowers are in slender, down-curved green catkins and ripen into dark green Chinese lanterns which adorn the crown. The leaves have fine, sharp teeth and prominent parallel veins. In autumn the leaves turn yellow, then orange-brown.

Cultivation The Hornbeam grows quite well to a moderate size in town parks. It is a little dull for planting in numbers but is a useful background tree, especially on heavy soil. It is of great value, although little planted until recently, in that it likes to grow on heavy clay but will thrive on any reasonable soil.

Variants 'Fastigiata', Pyramidal hornbeam, is a splendid form which makes a fine specimen tree of moderate size but great distinction. It is usually seen grown on a clean stem of 2 m, from which the very shapely crown grows as a tall ovoid. It has all the good features of the hornbeam and a strikingly dense, formal shape that makes it ideal for short avenues and groups. Young trees are strictly columnar, which is confusing because 'Columnaris' makes a shrubby and untidy small tree quite unlike 'Fastigiata'. Its only fault is that with age it becomes very broad.

Other species *Carpinus japonica* Blume, Japanese hornbeam, is both rare and slow-growing – unfortunately, because this little tree has particularly attractive leaves. They are oblong-lanceolate, up to 10 cm long, and have 20 or more pairs of parallel veins; each vein runs to a longer tooth than the two between, and the ends curl above the surface of the leaf. The bark is smooth and dark grey or dark green marked by pink wavy stripes. The fruit are broad cylindric bunches, 3 cm long, of in-curved, bright green, coarsely toothed bracts that are flushed crimson after midsummer. Like the similar Chinese species *C. cordata* Blume, which has leaves that are twice as broad and deeply cordate, the Japanese hornbeam is better regarded as a shrub than as a tree in isolation.

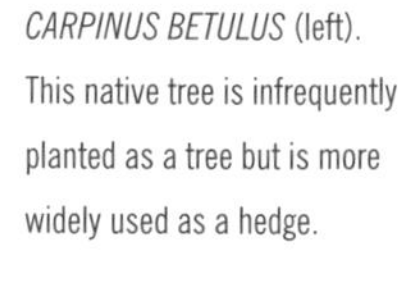

5•10•25 M

CARPINUS BETULUS 'COLUMNARIS' (above). Although columnar when young, with age this hornbeam develops a rounded head as broad as it is tall.

CARPINUS BETULUS (left). This native tree is infrequently planted as a tree but is more widely used as a hedge.

Carya/Hickories

THE HICKORIES ARE RELATED to the walnuts (*Juglans*) and are distinguished from them by the solid pith of their shoots and by having the male catkins in threes. They reach a large size and their stately habit and autumn colour make them valuable as specimen trees in large gardens. In addition, some have unusual bark. Male and female flowers are separate on the same plant; the females are small and at the ends of the young shoots as they emerge, the males are in pendulous, green, three-pronged catkins borne on the previous year's shoots. Pecans are derived from *C. illinoinensis* (Wangenh.) K. Koch, which really needs the hot summers found in the United States to thrive.

Cultivation Hickories like good, deep soil, preferably in full sun. Because they quickly develop a taproot which can be damaged if they are transplanted, they should be established early as young plants, preferably from a container.

CARYA CORDIFORMIS (far right). Preferring hotter summers than are frequent in Britain, this bitternut is slow-growing even on good soils.

CARYA LACINIOSA (below). Grown for its shaggy bark and large, seven-parted leaves, this is hickory is from eastern North America.

CARYA CORDIFORMIS (WANGENH.) K. KOCH

BITTERNUT; E NORTH AMERICA. DECIDUOUS.

This hickory is easily distinguished from all others likely to be seen in Britain by its slender, bright yellow buds, and because it usually has nine leaflets, the terminal leaflet cuneate down its stalk to the base. The bark, also distinctive, is a network of grey-brown to brown shallow ridges. The Bitternut is an elegant tree with long slender branches that are raised at a steep angle and arch out at the top. Hence, although the tree is conic when immature it later becomes vase-shaped. Even on good soils it is slow-growing and ideally prefers hotter summers. The fruit ripen to pear-shaped, yellow-green 4 cm long with four flanges on the outer half.

C. LACINIOSA (MICHX. F.) LOUDON

BIG SHELL-BARK HICKORY; E UNITED STATES. DECIDUOUS.

This is one of the two hickories from the eastern United States that have very big seven-parted leaves; the other is the Mockernut (*C. tomentosa*). Like the shagbark, the Big shell-bark has dark grey shaggy bark which is pale grey with adhering slender curving strips when the tree is young. The leaves can be 75 cm long and are rather thin: the rachis and petiole are densely but softly pubescent and the terminal leaflet has a stalk 1 cm long or less.

CARYA OVATA (left). A good shade tree, the shagbark hickory has leaves which turn bright yellow in autumn.

CARYA OVATA (MILL.) K. KOCH

SHAGBARK HICKORY; E NORTH AMERICA. DECIDUOUS.

From an early age the Shagbark hickory's grey bark accords with its name and when the tree is fairly old dark grey surfboards seem to be growing on its bole. The only other hickory – in fact, the only tree – in Britain with similar bark is the Big shell-bark hickory (*C. laciniosa*). The Shagbark hickory from eastern North America has big five-parted leaves 45–65 cm long which are either smooth and thick or, less commonly, thin and dark. The oily leaves are yellow-green. There are minute tufts of hair between the teeth of the leaf and often rings of pale brown hair near the node on the stout green young shoot. The crown is broad with stout level branches. The leaves turn bright yellow in autumn, making this a foliage tree of some worth. Given good conditions it can be fast-growing, and will fruit prolifically.

soil
ACID ALKALINE
DRY WET
4•6•25 M

C. TOMENTOSA (POIR.) NUTT.

MOCKERNUT; E NORTH AMERICA. DECIDUOUS.

The feature that immediately separates the Mockernut from other hickories is its smooth dark grey bark, which is unfissured, ridged or plated even when the tree is 50 years old. Only very old trees in their native woods in eastern North America acquire shallow ridges. The leaf is no longer than 50 cm and its rachis and stalk, like the shoot, are covered in dense and hard pubescence. The terminal leaflet has a slender, 2–4 cm stalk. The leaves are hard, thin and dark and pleasantly aromatic when crushed. The crown tends to be tall-conic and in autumn it becomes a tower of brilliant gold. Although slow to reach a good size, the Mockernut is a goodlooking tree any time it is in leaf and is spectacular in autumn.

5•8•25 M

CARYA TOMENTOSA (below). The Mockernut is a good looking tree in leaf and is spectacular in autumn when it becomes a tower of gold.

CASTANEA SATIVA (above). The Sweet chestnut makes a very good background tree as it is fast-growing and exceedingly robust.

Castanea sativa Mill.

SWEET CHESTNUT, SPANISH CHESTNUT; S EUROPE, N AFRICA. DECIDUOUS.

The Sweet chestnut is a member of the beech and oak family and native to southern Europe, but thrives in Britain's mild northern climate. Probably introduced by the Romans, it is a common woodland tree over most of the British Isles. The oldest known tree of any sort in Britain with a documented planting date is a Sweet chestnut at Castle Leod in Easter Ross, north of Dingwall. Planted in 1550 it was 2.47 m in diameter in 1980. . The Sweet chestnut is evidently a long-lived tree but the age of over 1000 years credited to one specimen must be mythical as the bole is not nearly big enough to indicate such an age.

The Sweet chestnut makes a very good background tree, as it is fast-growing, exceedingly robust and capable of making a fine clean bole when grown in a group. It also has a broad crown of quite dense and very handsome foliage which is ornamented each June with sprays of pale creamy yellow male catkins. The arrangement of the flowers is unusual. The prominent long catkins that are seen first are strung with male flowers. Female flowers are white stigmata from bright green bracts – on shorter catkins nearer the tip of the shoot. The outer parts of these catkins bear closed buds at that time but weeks later these may open as white male flowers on erect spikes.

In late autumn the leaves turn a good yellow, then pale brown or sometimes orange. This tree is not in the first rank as a single specimen; open-grown, it seldom makes great height growth but spreads far on big, low branches and it is nondescript in winter. The oldest trees have become picturesque in their senility but it is a long time to wait. By then the bark is in spiralled grooves at a small angle from the ground. The grooves start as vertical fissures in the smooth grey bark of the tree when it is about 40 years old and 60 cm in diameter. Gradually the bark turns brown and the ridges and fissures begin to lean into a spiral which may be at an angle of about 45° when the bole is 1.5 m through, but is ever nearer the horizontal with increasing age.

Cultivation The Sweet chestnut grows best on light soils and gravels and is not good on heavy clay or chalk. However, it is fairly tolerant and will grow in city parks. It coppices freely and a chestnut coppice is an optimum habitat for bluebells and nightingales if some oak standards are also grown.

Variants 'Albomarginata' has leaves margined with white but can revert. A few forms are sometimes grown for their edible nuts.

soil
ACID ALKALINE
DRY WET
8•12•30 M

CASTANEA SATIVA 'ALBOMARGINATA' (right). This form may produce plain green leaves from time to time; remove these to maintain variegation.

Catalpa

CATALPAS ARE BOLD-FOLIAGED TREES ideally suited to large gardens and parks and valuable for their showy, bell-shaped, two-lipped flowers in summer. These are borne in large, upright panicles and are followed by bean-like, hanging fruit which persist through winter.

Cultivation Grow Catalpas in a good, deep soil in a position sheltered from very strong winds and with as much sun as possible. They are ideally planted in position as one-year plants so that they can make their second year big growth of shoot and root without further disturbance. Unfortunately, the market is geared towards selling big trees and new plants thus have big tops but have been shorn of the feeding roots to support them, and there is a check while new roots are grown. North of the English Midlands the Catalpa is a short season foliage tree only, as it will not flower freely. It is not a tree to consider in cool areas.

CATALPA BIGNONIOIDES WALT.

SOUTHERN CATALPA, INDIAN BEAN TREE; SE UNITED STATES. DECIDUOUS.

Coming as they do from the American Deep South, it is not surprising that the best Southern catalpas in Britain, with plenty of flowers, are in the cities and sheltered gardens of the southern counties where they grow very fast but rarely live long. The tree branches low unless it is pruned to one strong bud every year, for although a young plant will grow a single rod 2 m long it grows on too late in the season to harden off the last 15 cm or so. Consequently, there is never a terminal bud active in spring and two or three shoots emerge from lower whorls. These have to be sorted out before any one of them has dominated and become strong. This can be done for only a few years; after that even a single shoot makes but weak growth and the crown inevitably starts to bush out. It is soon broader than it is tall and old trees are usually very spreading. Since catalpas require all the sun they can have in order to bear a worthwhile crop of flowers, they do need space. If they are grown for their foliage they are summer trees only. The Southern catalpa is gaunt and often shapeless in winter, and rarely has time to show any autumn colour.

This is an excellent tree in its season because its large ovate leaves, up to 25 cm long, are fresh yellow-green and a change from the general run of foliage in a garden. The frilled white flowers in late summer, spotted yellow and purple, on panicles 20 cm high, are an added bonus.

CATALPA BIGNONIODES 'AUREA' (above). The glorious Golden catalpa tends to have a lower and proportionately broader crown than the green leaved form. Flowers are low enough to enjoy as well.

Variant 'Aurea', Golden catalpa, is even more restricted to the south and east, with their warm summers, than the Southern catalpa if it is to be effective. The leaf is pale green when it expands, then firms up to a bright butter-yellow, greening a little during the summer. Flowering – white among yellow leaves – is no asset unless it is profuse, as can happen in a very hot summer. The leaves sometimes scorch in hot sunshine; a little shade from the midday sun will help to prevent this but will decrease the gold colour. The Golden catalpa tends to have a lower and proportionately broader crown than the green-leaved form.

C. X *ERUBESCENS* CARR.

HYBRID CATALPA; CULTIVATED ORIGIN. DECIDUOUS.

The form now grown of this hybrid between Southern catalpa (*C. bignonioides)* and Yellow catalpa (*C. ovata)* is known as 'J.C. Teas' and arose in 1879 in Indiana. Where space is available, this is the catalpa to choose. It has decidedly larger leaves than the northern or southern trees, flowers earlier in life – although later in the year – and grows more vigorously into a big tree. It may either be tall or hugely spreading, rarely both. The leaves are mostly shallowly five-lobed and broader than long, to 35 x 30 cm. They emerge dark purple from the bud and turn pale green until they fall. The flower panicles are 30 x 20 cm, open and bear, rather sparsely, highly fragrant flowers much like those of the

CATALPA X ERUBESCENS (right). This is the catalpa to choose, if you have a large garden.

CATALPA OVATA (below). In southern counties this is a useful alternative to other catalpas as it has the largest leaves, and flowers from a young age.

CATALPA SPECIOSA (below). Not well suited to the British climate, large heart shaped leaves grace this tree.

northern and southern catalpas. The bark is dull grey and deeply ridged.

Variant 'Purpurea' has blackish-purple young foliage which turns dark green.

soil: ACID – ALKALINE; DRY – WET. 8•12•20 M

C. *OVATA* G. DON

YELLOW CATALPA; CHINA. DECIDUOUS.

This tree is scarce even in the south of Britain, although one is the central tree in Leatherhead, Surrey. It has dark leaves with purple blotches at the base of their undersides, and dark reddish petioles. The rather small flowers are whitish with yellow spots. In southern counties it is a useful alternative to the other catalpas.

soil: ACID – ALKALINE; DRY – WET. 5•8•12 M

C. *SPECIOSA* (WARDER ex BARNEY) ENGELM.

NORTHERN CATALPA; UNITED STATES. DECIDUOUS.

Britain received the wrong catalpa when the southern species was sent in 1726 for by the time the northern form arrived in 1880 the southern tree was firmly entrenched. Although the Northern catalpa experiences much colder winters in the wild than the southern catalpa, the summers there are much hotter than those in Britain where it remains uncommon.

The Northern catalpa foliage is very like that of the southern tree except that the leaf-tip is longer drawn-out and more acuminate and the base more often deeply cordate, while the petiole, at first at least, is pubescent and the leaves become yellowish late in the summer and bright pale yellow in autumn. The bark is a much more positive point of difference between the two trees. The southern has pink-brown or grey-brown, thin scaly bark whereas that of the northern is dark grey and willow-like with deep spiral ridges. The flowers of the Northern catalpa open in midsummer, a month before those of the southern, and at 6 cm across are a little bigger, on a slightly smaller, more open panicle which thus does not carry so many.

soil: ACID – ALKALINE; DRY – WET. 4•8•15 M

Cedrus/Cedars

THE CEDARS ARE magnificent evergreen trees for large gardens and parks where they have been widely planted. They are easily recognized by their foliage, with leaves produced in whorls on short, slow-growing side-shoots but singly on long, leading shoots. Flowers are borne in autumn and in some years trees are conspicuously brown with them. The barrel-like cones, which stand upright on the shoots, take about two years to mature and break up on the tree.

Cultivation Cedars prefer a good, deep and not too dry soil but will also grow on dry, chalk soils.

CEDRUS ATLANTICA (ENDL.) CARR.

ATLAS CEDAR; NORTH AFRICA. EVERGREEN.

Although not now planted as frequently as the blue cedar, this is common as a large tree in many parks and gardens. Conical when young, it spreads with age and becomes more like the Lebanon cedar (*C. libani*). It normally grows with a single bole from the base. The foliage is bright green and the grey bark eventually cracks into scaly plates. It is the best cedar for town gardens.

Variants Glauca Group, Blue Atlas cedar, is the blue-grey form, it is the one to plant and selections that are almost blue-white have been made. It is not a tree for the centre bed of the rose garden: although the big plants that are sold usually deceive by growing very slowly for many years. The Blue Atlas cedar grows better in the warm, dry summers of non-coniferous areas like East Anglia, which makes it valuable in such places. In any garden its cool blue foliage is a fine foil to the green leaves and varied colours of flowers. 'Aurea' is a superb but rarely seen cultivar which grows at less than half the speed of the blue cedar. It is bright pale yellow or gold on the outer crown and blue-grey on the inner. This is better than the golden cedar of Lebanon (*C. libani* 'Aurea') for general use. 'Fastigiata', a slender conic-columnar tree with fine branching and good blue-grey foliage, is much too seldom planted.

C. DEODARA (D. DON) G. DON

DEODAR; W HIMALAYAS. EVERGREEN.

This tree makes a fine young specimen and an imposing old one. Young trees are attractively pendulous and usually glaucous grey. They grow fast, at about 1 m a year, and become dark green, less markedly pendulous and rather twiggy. A group planted not too closely – at 6 m apart or more – makes a fine little grove or roundel with good boles. A lawn specimen should have its bole cleared of branches for 1 m by the time it is 4 m tall and for 2.5 m before it is 10 m; the remaining lower branches will bend down around a good bole.

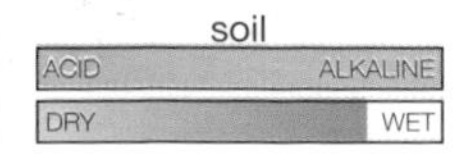

CEDRUS ATLANTICA 'FASTIGIATA' (top). This slender columnar tree with fine blue-grey foliage is elegant yet seldom planted.

CEDRUS ATLANTICA GLAUCA GROUP (middle). The Blue atlas cedar grows better in warm, dry summers.

CEDRUS DEODARA (left). This tree, with lax, drooping branches, makes a charming young specimen.

C. LIBANI A. RICH.

CEDAR OF LEBANON; SW ASIA. EVERGREEN.

The traditional hugely spreading cedar on the mansion lawn starts as a slender, conic young plant with a thin open crown. It is not a good tree at this stage and should be planted only where a big open space demands a huge specimen. The young tree is very fast-growing; the branches soon thicken greatly and extend and the bole expands to support them. Most of the vast old trees in Britain were planted after 1810 and very few date from before 1760. Growth is much better outside the cool areas and the trees grow well in a variety of soils from clay and chalk to light, dry sand, provided they are well drained. The crown tends to be on five or six vertical boles and this is acceptable, but far too many old cedars are ruined when these boles start from the ground; the trees have no true bole and are really giant bushes. On the other hand, cedars with single boles of 3 m or more are enormously impressive when these are 2 m through. However, the secateurs need to be active to ensure growth. A few Cedars of Lebanon have been planted in beech woods or wooded ravines and more should be grown in this way as they can make grand trees with very long boles and narrow crowns more like those of the larch. The foliage varies from dark green to blue-grey.

Variants 'Aurea', Golden cedar of Lebanon, is usually very slow-growing and not very brightly coloured but on a good damp site, may grow fairly fast into a spreading tree that is little more than tinged with gold, except in spring when the new growth is brighter. Unless a big tree is required, the Golden Atlas cedar (*C. atlantica* 'Aurea') is to be preferred every time

CEDRUS LIBANI (right). Grows well in a variety of soils from clay and chalk to light, dry sand, provided they are well drained.

Cercidiphyllum japonicum Siebold & Zucc.

KATSURA TREE; HIMALAYAS TO JAPAN. DECIDUOUS.

The Katsura tree was introduced in Britain in about 1864 and a larger quantity was sent in 1881.This is an important tree in garden design as it imparts an air of elegance and adds a distinctively different kind of foliage as well as providing a great display of autumn colours. It looks delicate, but is remarkably robust and grows very fast. The bark is dull grey and stripping. The crown varies. It may be a superb spire right to the tip of a single bole, or a tall bush on many nearly equal stems, or it may rise from big low branches. The leaves are small, nearly round and are borne in opposite pairs all down the shoots and on spurs along the branches, making a crown that is deep and dense but that looks light and dainty. It flushes coral pink or deep red, and is a fresh green in summer. Young plants usually turn bright deep red but older ones may turn yellow, or yellow followed by pink and red, or yellow and pink. Some trees with many yellow leaves remain green until late in the season then turn lilac or purple. Dry autumns can make the leaves shrivel before they colour, and a damp soil solves this problem as well as being best for growth. When the leaves are dry after falling they have a strong smell of burnt sugar.

Several specimens are now 22–24 m tall, and the tree is scarce at this size only because few were planted more than 50 years ago; by now almost every large garden has one (Westonbirt in Gloucestershire has at least thirty that are over 15 m tall) and in time big trees will become quite common.

The Katsura is botanically primitive and as with many, but by no means all, such trees has female and male flowers on different trees. They open with, or just before, the leaves and are dark red bunches of stamens with grey anthers, or dark red slender up-curved styles, 5–6 mm long. The fruit are little claw-like pods, 4–6 per bunch, and close along the shoot in pairs. They are blue-grey tinged crimson during summer, ripen to a shiny green and persist after the leaves, then turn brown. If there is a flowering male tree in the vicinity seed will be fertile.

In winter the Katsura is eye-catching with its tracery of numerous up-curved slender long shoots – whether it is a fine spire on one bole or a broader tree on several stems.The shoots are made the more unusual by regularly spaced, paired buds like knots along a cord.

Cultivation Katsuras will grow on moist soils as long as they are not too dry, and can tend to wilt in bad droughts. Many of the finest specimens are beside open water or in moist hollows and, given such positions, trees are not fussy about lime or strongly acid sands. Young plants can quickly develop several stems from the base and if a single-stemmed tree is required it therefore needs to be watched at first, with secateurs at the ready. Katsuras tend to come into leaf very early and late frosts can kill the flushing leaves, although most trees will quickly recover.

Variants var. *magnificum* Nakai has larger leaves and is only represented so far by small trees. 'Pendulum' is a promising but slow-growing and rare form, with weeping branches.

CERCIDIPHYLLUM JAPONICUM 'PENDULUM' (above), is a slow growing graceful form, seldom seen in gardens and is well suited to the winter landscape.

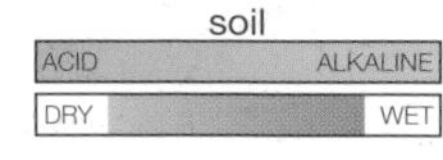

CERCIDIPHYLLUM JAPONICUM (left). When the leaves are dry after falling they have a strong smell of burnt sugar, not unlike candy floss.

Cercis siliquastrum L.

JUDAS TREE; E MEDITERRANEAN REGION. DECIDUOUS.

This small tree is excellent in the summer warmth of a courtyard or on a south-facing bank. In places like these it should ripen enough new shoots each summer to flower well in the following spring. It will be densely floriferous after a warm summer, when it will bear flowers not just on the outer, new shoots but back on to the branches as well, and down these on to the bole. Bunches of bright pink, short-stalked typical Pea family flowers bursting from the bark make it an unusual-looking tree from root to tip, at its best before the leaves unfold. The foliage is pleasant – rather greyish-green, nearly round leaves about 10 x 10 cm, arranged alternately on dark red-brown shoots. It has broad pods which are rich purple in summer and hang in bunches, some from the bole after good flowering. Autumn colours are pale yellow and brown.

Cultivation The Judas tree needs warmth to flourish and should be given a position in full sun in well-drained soil. It will not flower or grow well in cold areas.

Variants 'Alba' has white flowers, while 'Bodnant' has deep pink ones.

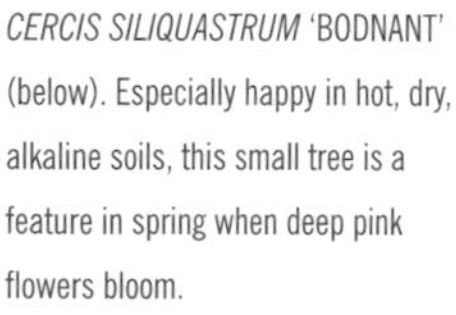

CERCIS SILIQUASTRUM 'BODNANT' (below). Especially happy in hot, dry, alkaline soils, this small tree is a feature in spring when deep pink flowers bloom.

Chamaecyparis/

Cypresses

TREES IN THIS GENUS are some of the most widely planted conifers, with numerous forms that vary in habit, size and foliage colour. The tiny, scale-like leaves are borne in flattened sprays. Male and female flowers are borne separately on the same plant and the males can be quite conspicuous in spring.

Cultivation These cypresses prefer a moist but well-drained soil and are lime-tolerant. Although they will tolerate light shade, forms with blue or yellow foliage will colour best in a sunny position.

CHAMAECYPARIS LAWSONIANA (MURR.) PARL.

LAWSON CYPRESS; CALIFORNIA, OREGON. EVERGREEN.

As the commonest and most gloomy conifer throughout the British Isles, this would merit no mention were it not also one of the most remarkable of all trees for its unceasing production of irreplaceable cultivars and its almost total adaptability. It was first sent to Britain in 1854, and by 1855 had thrown up a bright deep green, very erect form, 'Erecta Viridis', never seen in its home woods. More forms began soon after that and the most varied and bizarre trees poured out of British, Dutch and French nurseries at an ever-increasing rate. They are all as tough as the type and provide conifers of almost every possible colour, shape, and size, so are indispensable in garden design. Although few of the western trees in the USA can be grown in the eastern states Lawson cypress can, and so cultivars of this American tree have been sent back there from Britain and Holland. The 'ordinary' Lawson in the British Isles is, unlike those in the wild, very dark green, but the seeds so prolifically yielded by these trees give plants that are a great mixture of blue-greens and paler greens. None is normally sufficiently distinctive to be named, and hedges and lines grown as plain Lawson cypress vary from plant to plant.

The typical tree is usually much forked, grows heavy low branches when in the open and is not very windfirm. Numerous other conifers are greatly superior as single specimens. The Lawson cypress should never be planted in an avenue as it makes a gloomy tunnel between irregular, poorly shaped trees.

Variants 'Alumii', a common form that arose in 1880, is blue-grey and erect, neatly conic when young and bushing out at the base with age. It is good for small formal plantings but likely to attain 25 m in time.

CHAMAECYPARIS LAWSONIANA 'POTTENII' (above), has pale green feathery foliage and is useful in small-scale formal plantings.

CHAMAECYPARIS LAWSONIANA 'ALUMII' (far left), is good for small formal plantings but likely to attain 25m in time.

CHAMAECYPARIS LAWSONIANA 'STEWARTII' (left), is a popular form of vigorous growth and loose, conical habit, with spreading sprays of rich yellow foliage. It was raised by D. Stewart & Sons of Bournemouth about 1900.

CHAMAECYPARIS LAWSONIANA 'WINSTON CHURCHILL' (far left), is vigorous and densely conical with golden yellow foliage. It was raised in Kent before 1945.

CHAMAECYPARIS LAWSONIANA 'INTERTEXTA' (left). Among the best of the tall cypresses, 'Intertexta' is an elegant choice as both the tree and the foliage are attractive.

CHAMAECYPARIS LAWSONIANA 'ELLWOODII' (right), is a common small plant but is always growing, and quickly.

'Columnaris' arose in Holland in 1950 and makes a slender column, conic at the top. It grows 1 m every three years and is pale blue-grey. It is excellent in a formal group or as a spot plant, but in view of its growth, should not be used in small-scale settings. 'Ellwoodii' is a common small plant but is always growing. One reached 11 m tall after 30 years so caution is advised. It forms a narrow but multiple column, very tight at the base. The adult outer foliage is grey-green. 'Fletcheri' is a common plant that grows to 10 m and makes a medium-narrow multiple column to slender conic tips. Its juvenile fluffy foliage is dark grey-blue. It is a good spot plant in a large rock-garden or in a short line. 'Green Pillar' ('Green Spire') is very formal and attractive, with a stout silvery bole, tight, stiff, very erect branches and light or bright green foliage. 'Intertexta' is an elegant form which Lawson's Nursery found among plants raised from an early import of seeds. It forms a slender, tall crown with closely hanging foliage of curiously open, remotely twigged sprays. Although an undistinguished dull green, both the tree and the foliage are attractive, and it is among the best of the tall cypresses to give variety of form in a group. It should, however, be watched as it has a tendency to divide into two or three stems. Deal with this by singling as soon as the tendency becomes apparent, or the tree will not only lose much of its spire-like form but will become highly vulnerable to breakage in a storm. 'Lane' arose in Berkhamsted in 1938 and is one of the brightest and neatest of the golden forms, free with red male flowers and conic in crown. 'Lutea' is an early gold form, from 1873, and is as bright as any with a narrowly columnar and rather pendulous outer crown. It is ideal, with blue and green forms, in mixed eye-catcher groups. Unaccountably rare, 'New Silver' is a very tight fusiform plant with bright silvery blue, nodding shoot-tips. It is outstanding as a single specimen on a small scale. 'Pembury Blue' is often bushy to start with, but can make a tree. It is a unique powdery bright blue-grey, quite distinct from all the other blue-grey cypresses. A nursery in Cranbrook, Kent, raised 'Pottenii' in 1900. It has pale green feathery foliage that arches out from numerous erect stems or, less often, from erect branches on a single bole. It makes a narrow crown that looks neat and bright and is useful in small-scale formal plantings like short lines, avenues, false perspectives and eye-catchers. It goes on growing steadily, if rather slowly, and is 12 m tall in several gardens. It therefore outgrows a truly small-scale planting in time. Its upper branches are prone to being bent out by snow; if this happens they will not return but must be cut out. A 15 cm mesh net tied round the upper crown makes the foliage bush out and cover the net neatly as if the tree had been clipped. 'Stewartii' is a conic, sturdy golden form that is peculiarly decorative in the way it holds its fern-like sprays of rich yellow from a bright green interior. It is easily differentiated from all the other golds by these layers of long shoots. 'Triomf van Boskoop' is a relatively old form that is still deservedly popular because of its strong, single-stemmed growth and conic crown of bright blue-grey foliage. It is the most vigorous of the coloured Lawsons and some trees have already grown to 26 m. 'Wester-mannii' grows as an elegantly pendulous broad bush for some years, and looks most attractive with its pale lemon, hanging new shoots and lemon and green leaves. It goes on to make a broad columnar or conic tree and may grow fast, reaching 17 m in 70 years, with a big bole. 'Wisselii' is as remarkable for its growth as for its foliage. Dense tufts of thickened upright shoots are dark blue, much marked with white, and thickly covered in spring with pale crimson male flowers. For a few years newly struck cuttings look as if they will be dwarf trees but when put on a small rock-garden they go away at speed and are soon 20 m tall and 1.2 m through the bole. This is a good, unusual, columnar, turreted specimen to grow where there is room for a tall tree.

soil
ACID — ALKALINE
DRY — WET
6•12•30 M

CHAMAECYPARIS LAWSONIANA 'GREEN PILLAR' (below right), is very formal and attractive with very erect branches and light or bright green foliage.

CHAMAECYPARIS LAWSONIANA 'TRIOMF VAN BOSKOOP' (below). This vigorous blue-grey form is relatively old and still deservedly popular.

CHAMAECYPARIS NOOTKATENSIS (D. DON) SPACH

NOOTKA CYPRESS; NW NORTH AMERICA. EVERGREEN.

This sad-looking, dull, dark-foliaged tree has two strong points. It is imperturbably tough and hardy; and at all times and in all places it has a crown that is a perfect cone. This is enormously broad and obtuse tipped in the west of Ireland, and progressively narrower to the east until in East Anglia it is quite slender and very acute.

Variants 'Lutea' differs only in having yellow-flushed young foliage. 'Pendula' is a narrowly conic tree for many years. The small branches in wide U-shapes dangle the foliage in thin curtains, and are soon strung with navy-blue 1 cm cones. It is a good plant until it ages into a broad conic open crown, when the hanging shoots are spread too thinly to look healthy. Some trees age in better shape. Another form sometimes seen under this name is of much more compact habit.

C. OBTUSA (SIEBOLD & ZUCC.) ENDL.

HINOKI CYPRESS; JAPAN. EVERGREEN.

Seen at its best in areas of high rainfall, this is widely planted elsewhere as innumerable dwarf selections. It makes a broad conic crown, and the bole is straight with furrowed, rich red-brown bark and small level branches. The foliage is brilliant, shiny rich green, with tiny obtuse scales with fine white marks on the underside. In a humid area the good bark and bole and the shapely bright green crown make it an effective foliage tree of moderate size and growth.

Variants 'Crippsii' is a great improvement on the old Japanese form 'Aurea', and was raised in Tunbridge Wells in 1900. When grown in full sun it is as bright gold as any conifer. For some years it is loosely conic with nodding shoots, then it grows into a broad cone. Old trees are over 15 m tall. It is green tinged with yellow when it is grown in shade, and should be given full light. The shoots are fine, dense and square in section and when the outer ones are intense gold the inner are brilliant green. The tree ages from a loosely columnar growth to a broad, many-topped column of highly distinctive aspect and is a great adornment in the front rank of a group of small conifers.

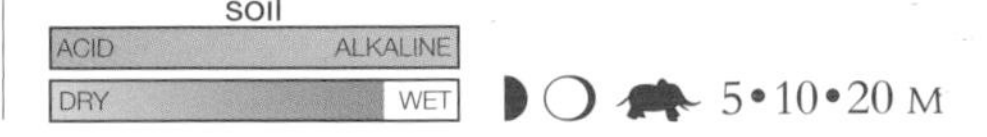

CHAMAECYPARIS NOOTKATENSIS 'PENDULA' (left), is the best and most ornamental form with long hanging shoots.

C. PISIFERA (SIEBOLD & ZUCC.) ENDL.

SAWARA CYPRESS; JAPAN. EVERGREEN.

This is another species that is seen more often as one of its many cultivars and has foliage so unlike theirs that it is often unrecognized as being the typical form. It has flat sprays of tiny, bright green, sharply pointed scales, with tiny, brightly silver marks beneath, borne on straight level branches from a bole with long-ridged brown bark.

Variants 'Aurea' is a far superior form and makes an attractive small tree because the new growth is bright yellow and does not fade completely before the next crop is out. No form is better than 'Squarrosa' for those who like fuzzy blue trees, and it is a pleasant variation among others. The soft 5 mm leaves are pale green above but broadly banded grey-blue beneath and stand out at all angles in angular dense sprays, giving a very blue fluffy appearance to the crown. The tree is sometimes 26 m tall. 'Boulevard' is similar and, although it is often planted as a dwarf, will eventually make a columnar tree at least 10 m tall.

CHAMAECYPARIS PISIFERA (left). This species is seldom grown in its typical form, and deservedly so, as it has been replaced by many improved selections.

CHAMAECYPARIS OBTUSA 'TETRAGONA AUREA' (above). Grown in full sun, this is an excellent choice for compact growth and bright yellow foliage.

CORNUS NUTTALI 'COLRIGO GIANT' (above). This vigorous but usually short-lived tree is a form of the Pacific dogwood. It prefers a sunny position in woodland in a moisture-retentive, humus rich and not too limy soil. The button-like heads of small green flowers (above right), in late spring are surrounded by usually 6 large white bracts, the whole flower head up to 15 cm across.

CORNUS CONTROVERSA (right), the tree is attractive in winter and summer, but is at its best in mid-June when creamy white flowers cover the branches.

Cornus controversa Hemsl.

TABLE DOGWOOD; JAPAN, CHINA, HIMALAYAS. DECIDUOUS.

Although the Table dogwood is very hardy and occasionally seen as far north as Edinburgh, the only large trees, to 15 m tall, are in Sussex, Gloucestershire and the south-west of Britain. The bark is grey in broad smooth ridges.From about 3 m up the bole bears long, level, well-spaced branches with short, dark red shoots proliferating on their upper sides. In season alternate broad, oval and abruptly pointed shiny bright green leaves hang from these. The tree is attractive in winter and summer, but is at its best in mid-June when creamy white flowers, massed in flat heads up to 15 cm across, are strung along the branches above the foliage giving a distinctly layered effect. The flowers turn into blue-black berries which do not remain long, but by then the leaves are turning soft yellow, pink and sometimes purple.

Cultivation The Table dogwood likes a good, deep soil with or without lime; it is best with trees that will provide some shelter, but must be open to the sun or it will not flower fully.

Variant 'Variegata' is a very special and highly sought after little tree. It is slow-growing and much prized by

the time it is 2–3 m tall. Bigger specimens are not often seen, but one in County Kerry was over 10 m tall with a clear bole 2 m long and 30 cm through. The level layers of foliage are striking because the leaves, only 4–5 cm long and often twisted, have broad clear white or pale cream margins.

Corylus colurna L.

TURKISH HAZEL; SE EUROPE, SW ASIA. DECIDUOUS.

This tree has been grown in Britain since 1580 or so but is only now being properly appreciated, and planted in urban areas both here and in the USA, for its splendid shape, vigour and foliage. It rapidly makes a medium-conic crown of sturdy level branches that are hung in summer with dense foliage of shining dark green leaves. These are cordate, 12 cm each way, on reddish petioles that are densely hairy like the shoots. Male catkins appear early in spring and are 6 cm long. The bunches of fruit, which are not always produced every year, have brilliant shiny green involucres with long slender lobes and prickles. The pinkish-grey or brown bark scales coarsely but attractively. Altogether this is a tree in the front rank for a specimen of moderate dimensions.

Cultivation Turkish hazel will grow on any reasonably good, well-drained soil and is particularly suitable for chalk soils. It grows vigorously and shoots of over 1 m can be grown in a season on sands or clays, acid or alkaline soils. It performs best in full sun.

CORYLUS COLURNA (left). The Turkish hazel is a highly ornamental tree with a stately shape and elegant foliage.

CRATAEGUS CRUS-GALLI (right). Autumn leaves turn to orange and red, while the small red fruits persist on the shoots through winter.

Crataegus/Hawthorns

THE HAWTHORNS provide a range of thorny trees that are tough enough to survive in city streets, exposed sites and difficult positions but which have enough ornamental merit to be worthy of the garden. The usually white flowers open in clusters in late spring and are often followed by highly attractive fruit. Some species also give excellent autumn colour.

Cultivation Hawthorns are easy trees to grow in almost any soil, even very shallow chalk. They perform best in sun but will tolerate shade.

CRATAEGUS LACINIATA (below). This highly ornamental small tree deserves to be more widely planted.

CRATAEGUS CRUS-GALLI L.

COCKSPUR THORN; E NORTH AMERICA. DECIDUOUS.

Widespread in its American range, the Cockspur thorn is quite rare in Britain and one of its presumed hybrids is usually planted instead. It makes quite a picturesque small tree with a distinctive flat, spreading head. The small long-cuneate leaves have a few teeth towards the blunt tips and are a glossy green, broadest near the tip. The feature that separates the Cockspur thorn from any of its hybrids is its glabrous flower and fruit stalks. In autumn the leaves turn to orange and red, and the small red fruits persist on the shoots through winter.

5•8•8 M

C. LACINIATA UCRIA

ORIENTAL THORN; SE EUROPE, SW ASIA. DECIDUOUS.

This highly ornamental small tree deserves to be more widely planted. It makes a compact head of spreading branches covered in deeply cut, glossy dark green leaves. The white flowers have conspicuous pink anthers and develop into relatively large fruit.

4•6•6 M

CRATAEGUS LAEVIGATA (POIR.) DC.

MIDLAND HAWTHORN; EUROPE. DECIDUOUS.

In Britain this species is less common in the wild than the Common hawthorn (*C. monogyna*), and differs from it in its shallowly lobed leaves and fruit that have two stones rather than one. It has produced a number of variants with pink or double flowers, some of which may be hybrids with *C. monogyna*. The one most frequently seen is 'Paul's Scarlet', which has striking, double, deep pink flowers but no fruit.

C. X *LAVALLEI* HERINCQ. ex LAV. 'CARRIÈREI'

CARRIÈRE'S HYBRID THORN; CULTIVATED ORIGIN. DECIDUOUS.

Frequently seen beside arterial and suburban roads, and formerly named *C. carrierei*, this fuzzy-topped little tree is distinctive in winter as well as in leaf. The bark is light grey with dark, scaly vertical fissures and the branches are level, their upper sides lined with congested, short spur shoots. Long shoots are dull green and sparsely hairy. The few thorns are 5 cm long and brown. The obovate leaves are dark glossy green above and pale with hairs beneath. The abundant flowers are borne in heads of about 20 each and are white, with pink anthers when fresh and a prominent red disc. They ripen late to orange-red fruit with brown speckles, which remain darker red through winter. The leaves stay green until late autumn then turn dark bronzy red, often rather briefly.

Splendid in flower and with good foliage, some late colour and fruit, and with a curious rather than beautiful winter aspect, Carrière's thorn is useful in restricted sites, the more so because like other thorns it is exceedingly tough and little concerned with niceties of soil. It is normally disease-free but could be attacked by fireblight, which kills the flower heads and the leaves nearest to them in early summer. These persist on the tree, withered and brown.

C. MONOGYNA JACQ.

COMMON HAWTHORN; EUROPE. DECIDUOUS.

It is hardly necessary to plant this in most British gardens as it is such a common feature of hedgerows where, unless it is regularly trimmed, it produces cascading shoots liberally covered with masses of white flowers and, in autumn, small, glossy red fruit. This very tough tree will thrive even in the most windswept coastal sites where it is shaped by the prevailing winds.

Variant Although less planted for ornament than the forms of *C. laevigata*, 'Biflora', Glastonbury thorn, is occasionally seen. This is derived from a tree which used to grow in Glastonbury. According to legend, Joseph of Arimathea planted his staff in the ground there on Christmas Day and it immediately produced leaves and flowers. This form will certainly come into leaf and flower early, but can be at any time during winter or early spring.

CRATAEGUS LAEVIGATA 'PAUL'S SCARLET' (above). Decorative, double, deep-pink flowers more than make up for an absence of fruit.

CRATAEGUS MONOGYNA 'BIFLORA' (left). Occasionally twice flowering, the Glastonbury thorn is derived from a tree which used to grow in Glastonbury.

CRATAEGUS X *LAVALLEI* (far left). This tree, splendid in flower and with good foliage, has a curious rather than beautiful winter aspect.

CRATAEGUS PEDICELLATA (above). The Scarlet haw is tough, dependable and worthwhile, and may occasionally be seen in small urban parks.

CRATAEGUS X PERSIMILIS 'PRUNIFOLIA' (far right). Less showy in flower than other haws, it has outstanding autumn colour and large dark red fruit add to the impact.

CRATAEGUS PHAENOPYRUM (below). This tough and very distinctive little tree has the daintiest foliage of any thorn.

C. PEDICELLATA SARG.

SCARLET HAW; NE NORTH AMERICA. DECIDUOUS.

This is perhaps the best of a group of North American species that were at one time confused under the name *C. coccinea*. It has large broad leaves, 8 x 6 cm, with large lobes, and hanging bunches of very big, bright red berries about 2 cm long. It is also quite striking in late spring when it bears relatively large white flowers. It has a broad, spreading crown and dark brown fissured and scaly bark. The Scarlet haw is tough, dependable and worthwhile, and may occasionally be seen in small urban parks.

C. X PERSIMILIS 'PRUNIFOLIA' (*C. PRUNIFOLIA*)

BROAD-LEAFED HYBRID COCKSPUR; CULTIVATED ORIGIN. DECIDUOUS.

Very often grown as a bush, this can be a broad, flat-crowned tree on a 2 m bole with dark brown bark. Unlike Carrière's hybrid (*C.* x *lavallei* 'Carrièrei'), it is not at all distinctive in winter although it can be identified easily enough at close quarters by its shiny purple glabrous shoots and dark purple thorns that are as sparse as those of the hybrid. It is distinctive in leaf as

its rich dark green leaves are broad-ovate and glossy, plane and smooth, neither folded along the midrib nor puckered by deep side-veins. In autumn it is outstanding as it turns rapidly from yellow to orange, then a striking burnished copper and finally crimson. The large, dark red fruit add to the effect and are then shed.

Although this is a twiggy, tangled, broad bushy plant when it is out of leaf, it is so good in leaf, and so spectacular in autumn, that it is of great value in an informal planting and in sites where conditions are difficult.

C. PHAENOPYRUM (L. f.) MEDIK.

WASHINGTON THORN; SE UNITED STATES. DECIDUOUS.

This tough and very distinctive little tree has the daintiest foliage of any thorn. Although it is much planted in many cities around its native range in the eastern USA, it is seldom seen in Britain. The biggest so far found is in Victoria Park, Bethnal Green, in east London. The tree's short bole with pale orange-grey cracked bark bears a low, open crown of red-brown shoots with numerous purple thorns 5–7 cm long. The leaves are 6 x 5 cm with 3–5 deeply cut lobes, each lobuled or toothed, and are smooth pale green, becoming dark and shiny. In autumn they turn orange and red. Numerous small flowers open in midsummer, late for a hawthorn. They are white with pink anthers and ripen into hanging bunches of 6 mm long glossy scarlet fruit which remain through the winter. As a small tree well able to cope with a paved root-run in a city, and one that has good foliage, autumn colour and long-lasting brilliant fruit, the Washington thorn has such obvious merits that it will hopefully be more commonly planted in the future. It needs a position in full sun to thrive.

soil

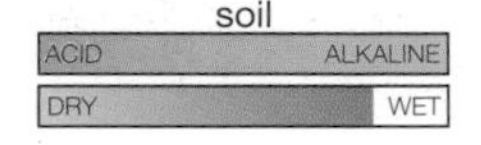

4•6•12 M

Cryptomeria japonica D. Don

JAPANESE RED CEDAR. JAPAN, CHINA. EVERGEEN

THIS IS REALLY A REDWOOD related to the Sequoias and is the chief timber tree of Japan. The bright, often yellowish, green of the hard, sharp in-curved, long-pointed scale-leaves and the fine chestnut-red stripping bole make it a good single specimen tree in sites where it will grow well and excellent for clumps or small groves where its good bole will be visible. The first form came to Britain from China, in 1842, and many of the oldest trees are identifiable as Chinese by their loose, hanging foliage. The Japanese form, planted after 1861, has shorter foliage in denser bunches. The foliage of the form 'Lobbii' consists entirely of dense bunches and is even shorter, but the tree is as tall as the Chinese and Japanese forms.

Cultivation The Japanese cedar will grow on any well-drained soil but is fastest and at its best on good, deep, moist ones in areas with cool, damp summers. It should be given some protection from strong winds.

Variant 'Elegans' has fuzzy pale green foliage which turns dark purplish-red in winter. It starts as an upright bush but, although it will make an attractive tree for many years, with age it sprawls around hopelessly or droops great branches everywhere. The bark is bright orange-red but that does not make up for its poor shape.

soil
ACID ALKALINE
DRY WET
8•15•30 M

CRYPTOMERIA JAPONICA (above). This sequoia relative has bright often yellowish, green scale-leaves.

CRYPTOMERIA JAPONICA 'ELEGANS' (left), has bright orange-red bark but a poor habit.

CUNNINGHAMIA LANCEOLATA (right). Very hardy and with an interesting habit, this redwood is seldom planted in Britain, although it makes a splendid, unusual specimen.

CUNNINGHAMIA LANCEOLATA 'GLAUCA' (below), has distinctive blue-green young foliage and may be hardier than the typical form.

Cunninghamia lanceolata (Lamb.) Hook. f.

CHINESE FIR; CHINA. EVERGREEN.

This is a redwood that looks somewhat like a Monkey puzzle (*Araucaria araucana*) and is very hardy, although little planted in Britain except in western gardens. Its very bright green leaves, up to 7 cm long, taper to a long sharp point and are hard and curved, with two silver bands beneath. The foliage is red-brown when it dies and many dead leaves are retained on the tree, adding to the crown and stopping it from being thin. The good straight, long-ridged bole is warm red-brown, and level branches carry a columnar crown which is domed at the top. It may be necessary to clear the crown of competing stems and low branches to make a splendid, unusual specimen.

Cultivation The Chinese fir prefers a moist but well-drained soil in a position sheltered from strong winds. It grows best in areas of high rainfall.

Variant 'Glauca' has distinctive blue-green young foliage.

soil

ACID ALKALINE

DRY WET

x *Cupressocyparis leylandii* (Jackson & Dallimore) Dallimore

LEYLAND CYPRESS; CULTIVATED ORIGIN. EVERGREEN.

X *CUPRESSOCYPARIS LEYLANDII* 'CASTLEWELLAN' (below left). More suitable for hedging, this has gold tipped foliage when young, and is less vigorous than other forms.

These extremely vigorous trees are hybrids between Nootka cypress (*Chamaecyparis nootkatensis*) and Monterey cypress (*Cupressus macrocarpa*). The first two occurrences of the hybrid were separated by 23 years but both were at Leighton Hall, Powys, Wales, in 1888 and 1911 respectively. It was another 29 years before the third occurred, at Ferndown in Dorset. The hybrids have now been extensively planted as hedges, screens, background and specimen trees, and demand is still insatiable. As spot-trees all the cultivars are of about equal value and make a slightly fusiform, variably slender column at 1 m per year for 20 years and 2 m every three years thereafter to, it must be assumed, around 40 m. The usual forms, 'Leighton Green' and 'Haggerston Grey', develop numerous strong, vertical branches all of which stop 2 m short of the very dominant, if rather wavy, slender leading shoot. For hedges and single specimens, 'Leighton Green' is indistinguishable from the better of the two Stapehill trees, grown as '21'. These are much the best of all the cultivars, with long, fern-like sprays and more vigorous growth in the diameter of the bole. 'Naylor's Blue' makes a fine unusual specimen slightly less rapidly. The golden forms are the most vigorous trees of this colour yet available. Their disadvantage is that they are too often planted in inappropriate positions. If more nurseries made their customers aware of the potential height of these trees, or of the difficulty of keeping a hedge trimmed, this might not be the case.

Cultivation Leyland cypresses will grow on virtually any soil that is not waterlogged. Hedges must be

X *CUPRESSOCYPARIS LEYLANDII* 'LEIGHTON GREEN' (below and right). One of the original hybrids raised at Leighton Hall.

X *CUPRESSOCYPARIS LEYLANDII* , 'NAYLORS BLUE' (below right).

trimmed by cutting only the young shoots, which is often necessary several times a year. The vigour and regular crowns of the trees make them suitable for planting in short avenues; a long one could be dull. As in any avenue of dark conifers, the trees must be planted or thinned so that the space between the crowns is equal to the width of each crown, to give light and form. No evergreen is better for a really tall hedge than the Leyland cypress. The only problem is the practical one of the need for ladders or raised platforms from which to clip it.

Variants The 'Castlewellan' seedling from the Golden Monterey cypress (*Cupressus macrocarpa* 'Lutea') was raised in 1963. It has the plumose foliage sprays of the common 'Haggerston Grey' with bright yellow new growth. The colour becomes disappointing with age, unlike the striking bright yellow of young plants, and may fade to yellow-green. This makes the next year's new shoots speckle the crown distinctively, but some trees in some years remain a good yellow through the winter. In the official trial, 'Castlewellan'' is so far keeping pace with the green forms. 'Golconda' is a

branch-sport of 'Haggerston Grey' and the brightest gold of any cypress. 'Haggerston Grey', a seedling of the Nootka cypress (*Chamaecyparis nootkatensis*) was raised in 1888 and is still the most numerous. It has plumose sprays of slender, rather distant, fine shoots, which are dark blue-green or dark green with a grey tinge. It flowers or cones very rarely, unlike 'Leighton Green' and the Stapehill trees.

'Leighton Green', a seedling of Monterey cypress (*Cupressus macrocarpa*), was raised in 1911. It is the second most frequent of the earlier plantings and is the best for hedges and single specimens. It grows a slightly broader crown in the open than others but is remarkably slender in light woodland shade. The foliage is in long, flattened sprays of regularly alternate flat systems of thicker, denser, ultimate shoots than in 'Haggerston Grey' and is a brighter green. Small golden male flowers are common in some years and most trees bear numerous cones. 'Naylors Blue', a seedling of Monterey cypress, was raised in 1911 from the same batch as 'Leighton Green'. It is a more slender tree with fine, grey-blue plumose foliage. The 'Robinson's Gold' seedling was found among rhododendrons in Belvoir Park near Belfast in 1975. Its foliage is of the pinnate 'Leighton Green' form and is bright yellow. It often appears brighter and more lasting than in 'Castlewellan' but some trees do fade. 'Robinson's Gold' seems to be at least as vigorous as other cypresses. 'Skinner's Green' ('Stapehill 21'), a seedling of Monterey cypress, was raised in 1940. It is a very vigorous form, distinguished from 'Leighton Green' only by its foliage which is harsh above. It flowers and cones freely. 'Stapehill' ('Stapehill 20'), a seedling of Monterey cypress, was raised in 1940. It is easily distinguished by its crown which is open internally and holds old brown foliage, and by the very rough foliage in the pinnate layout; the base of each minor spray is partly missing as if it had been chewed away. It flowers and cones freely.

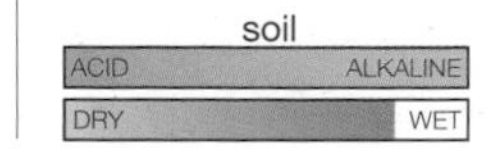

10 • 18 • 40 M

Cupressus/Cypresses

THE TRUE CYPRESSES are related to *Chamaecyparis* and, like them, have tiny, scale-like leaves. However, their foliage sprays are arranged all around the shoots, rather than in flattened sprays. A few species are intermediate and uncertainly placed. Their uses in gardens are rather different to those of *Chamaecyparis*. They do not respond well to clipping so are not as suitable for hedges. However, because they are usually of narrow habit with attractive foliage they are useful specimen trees.

Cultivation *Cupressus* will grow in any well-drained soil and should be planted in full sun. They will withstand considerable wind where winters are mild but are best given a little shelter where cold spells are possible.

CUPRESSUS GLABRA SUDW.

SMOOTH ARIZONA CYPRESS; ARIZONA. EVERGREEN.

This must be about the most useful of all conifers, other than Lawson cypress (*Chamaecyparis lawsoniana*), in garden planting. It is utterly hardy; it grows on limestone or extremely acid soil; it is resistant to drought; it always has a neat ovoid-conic crown of a lovely smoky blue-grey; and it maintains moderate growth. Male flowers spend the winter decorating the blue-grey foliage with dense patches of golden specks, and the fine dark purple-red bark rolls off to leave pale yellow smooth areas. The tree has no known faults and can be used for a large informal hedge or background of blue. 'Pyramidalis' is the best form, with foliage densely speckled with white and slightly thicker sprays erect around the crown.

CUPRESSUS GLABRA 'PYRAMIDALIS' (left), is the best form with attractive blue foliage and peeling red bark.

soil: ACID — ALKALINE; DRY — WET

5 • 10 • 20 M

C. MACROCARPA HARTWEG

MONTEREY CYPRESS; CALIFORNIA. EVERGREEN.

One of the Monterey trees which vastly prefers a damp climate to the long dry summers of its native habitat, this grows enormously faster and bigger in Britain than on its American homeland cliffs. There are more Monterey cypresses in most Devon parishes than in the two small headlands where they grew originally and they are widely grown throughout the British Isles. They are exceptionally useful in windswept coastal areas because they rapidly provide high shelter and a green background, even though the trees are mostly rough, heavily branched and liable to be broken or blown down in severe exposure. In eastern parts the Monterey cypress is much less branchy, narrower in the crown, seldom killed by freezing winds, less often blown down and, as a single specimen, is likely to be a shapely tree of moderately rapid growth. Superb specimens are produced if the lower bole is kept clear of

CUPRESSUS MACROCARPA 'DONARD GOLD' (far left) and 'GOLDCREST' (below), are arguably the best two yellow cypresses for hot, dry, sites, and both are popular choices.

CUPRESSUS MACROCARPA 'LUTEA' (above). Now less frequently grown since the introduction of superior forms, it is still useful for coastal planting.

branches. It grows best on light, sandy but damp, soil which is acid, but it will grow on almost any soil. It will not succeed in or very near towns and cities

Variants 'Lutea' is a broad bun in western Ireland but columnar in England, and is less vigorous than green forms. The foliage is yellow, and often bright. In some places 'Lutea' has been better than the type in resisting salt-laden winds. It is often too twiggy and untidy below to compete as a specimen with some other golden conifers, and needs watching in youth or it may grow several stems and become a bush. 'Donard Gold' is an improvement on 'Lutea' as it is a brighter yellow and shapely. 'Goldcrest' is perhaps the best yellow form, with bright gold foliage.

C. SEMPERVIRENS L.

ITALIAN CYPRESS; MEDITERRANEAN REGION. EVERGREEN.

This species is variable in habit and in the Mediterranean region its forms can vary from the common, narrow tree to those with spreading or drooping shoots. The narrowly conic form is the most usual one in Britain and it comes true from seed, although some trees are narrower than others. While some of these turn out to be from Arizona or Monterey cypresses, which are also frequently grown in those parts, seeds extracted from others by putting the cones briefly in a warm oven will usually yield fine slender fastigiate plants. Within two years they are 1 m tall and soon grow nearly 1 m a year. Long ago the Italian cypress was regarded as being tender, but quite big trees in cold places have been unaffected by very severe winters, and the 20 m ones in some Sussex gardens have shown no signs of frosting. Seedlings can be burned back 30 cm or so in their first few years and, with a little judicious help from secateurs, will make a new leader. Italian cypresses are fine trees to place at each end of a group of shrubs or in a tight group. They can also be temporary features among small shrubs or semi-dwarf conifers.

Variants 'Green Pencil' is a particularly narrow and compact tree, while 'Swane's Gold' is an excellent small tree with bright yellow foliage.

CUPRESSUS SEMPERVIRENS (far right). Characteristically narrow, this tree has a distinct Mediterranean air, and is ideal for hiding telegraph poles.

DAVIDIA INVOLUCRATA (left and below). Translucent delicate bracts surround dark flower centres and are a real joy. The dove tree is a treasure, although good flowering is seldom an annual affair.

Davidia involucrata Baill.

DOVE TREE, HANDKERCHIEF TREE; CHINA.

PÈRE DAVID FOUND the Dove tree, with soft white down on the underside of its leaves, in 1867 in Sichuan, China. Ernest Wilson also found this form which, because it was the first to be described, is the typical form, and sent it to Britain in 1903. However, Père Farges had already sent another form with the leaf underside shiny and smooth to France in 1897. This second form, var. *vilmoriniana* (Dode) Wanger, is much the commoner, and is usually of greater vigour than the typical form but otherwise similar to it.

The Dove tree's gaunt winter aspect of sparse branching and spiky shoots is offset by dark purple bark which flakes and crumbles to pale brown. The large leaves have coarse triangular teeth and are broad-ovate drawn out to the tip. They are leathery dark green with scarcely any autumn colouring, although they occasionally turn pink. The true flowers are tiny and purple in bud, yellow when they open, and are clustered in a globular head on a long stalk that hangs between two bracts. These bracts open yellow in late spring then soon turn clear white. They make the tree a unique sight for two or three weeks, as one bract is the same size and shape as a big leaf and the other is about half this size.

Cultivation The Dove tree is among the first to show signs of severe stress during a long drought and should be planted on a damp site. It grows best in a rich, moist soil although it manages well on lighter and sandy ones if they do not dry out readily. It is tolerant of lime but will languish if the soil is dry and chalky. Older trees in some shelter are 18–20 m tall, less if they are much exposed. The Dove tree's tendency to heavy low branching or even forking must be watched, for it can, and should, be made to grow into a shapely tree with a good bole. On lighter soils a mixed or nitrogenous fertilizer is of benefit for some years in spring.

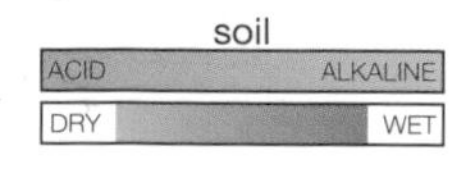

6•10•20 M

Drimys winteri Forst. & Forst. f.

WINTER'S BARK; CENTRAL AND SOUTH AMERICA. EVERGREEN.

The name comes from one of Sir Francis Drake's captains, John Winter, who found in 1578 that the inhabitants of the region around the Strait of Magellan used the bark of the tree to treat scurvy, which made it valuable on board ship and as a spice for meats. Older trees, 15 m tall in Irish gardens and ones in the south west of Britain, are attractive when the large evergreen, aromatic leaves are relieved by masses of large, loose heads of small, fragrant, white flowers with 5–7 or more decurved narrow petals and yellow stamens. The form more usually planted now is a different matter; even with no flowers at all it is very decorative, with whorls of level then upswept branches making a regular, conic crown and veinless, smooth, light green leaves that are bright silver-blue beneath.

Cultivation Except in the mildest areas Winter's bark should be grown against a wall. However, it shows its shape and worth fully if it is grown where it can stand as a tree. It can take about 15 years to start flowering and this may be irregular for some years after that. It grows at moderate speed with or without lime in the soil, but does prefer a moist soil in a sheltered site.

soil
ACID ALKALINE
DRY WET
◐ ○ 3•6•15 M

DRIMYS WINTERI (right). A tree for protected sites, with ivory-white, highly scented flowers in late spring.

Embothrium coccineum Forst. & Forst. f.

CHILEAN FIRE BUSH; ARGENTINA, CHILE. EVERGREEN.

A well-grown specimen of this striking tree always attracts a great deal of attention when in full flower, in late spring or early summer. It is fast-growing and of upright habit and its leaves are very variable, but always more or less oblong, without teeth and rather leathery. Their length varies from 10–15 cm to 20 cm or more on some trees, and although they are often evergreen they can be deciduous or partly so. The glory of this tree, however, is the bunches of bright orange-red flowers, 5 cm long, that open in late spring and early summer; each flower then splits and four lobes curl backwards.

Cultivation The Chilean fire bush is at its best in mild, moist parts of Britain, notably in the west where it can be grown in a sunny position. In drier, colder areas it needs protection – in woodland, for example. It does not flower so freely when shaded.

soil
ACID ALKALINE
DRY WET
5•8•10 M

EMBOTHRIUM COCCINEUM 'LANCEOLATUM' (below). This particularly hardy selection is distinct in its long, lanceolate leaves and, like other forms, prefers full sun.

EUCALYPTUS CORDATA (far right). The juvenile foliage on this species is retained even on old plants and is a useful identification tool.

Eucalyptus/

Eucalypts or Gum trees

THIS HUGE GENUS of the Myrtle family is the hallmark of the Australasian flora, but is not native to New Zealand. In many parts of Australia's desert interior eucalypts have ribbon-like ranges as they are confined to river banks and this makes the populations particularly liable to split into numerous closely related species. By most reckonings there are more than 500 species and identifying them is a problem in the field and garden.

Eucalypts can be difficult to place in a landscape, and some people do not like to see them at all. Their evergreen and distinctive crowns and their strange bark are conspicuous at all times and they should not be scattered about. In a large garden a eucalyptus grove can be a fine feature; in a smaller garden a single specimen can be impressive – or it can look out of place. Some of the tender species have pink flowers, but those of all the more hardy ones are white, without petals but with numerous long stamens. When produced in abundance, usually in late spring or early summer, they can be effective.

Most gum trees have two distinct types of foliage during their lives. Typically, seedlings start with juvenile foliage, in which the leaves are usually silvery, rounded and opposite on the shoots. As they age the adult foliage develops, in which the leaves are usually long and narrow, greener and alternate. There are notable exceptions to this and *E. cordata* retains its juvenile foliage throughout its life.

Cultivation All gum trees should be planted as small as possible, at about 60 cm. Unfortunately, it is not always easy to obtain them at this size. Large plants are liable to blow over easily in strong winds before they get established. If this occurs it is best to cut them down to ground level and they will resprout from the base the next year. This can be done every few years if it is the juvenile foliage that is required.

In Ireland hardiness is no problem with any of the 40 or so species that grow there; even the blue gums as far north as Belfast were unaffected by the hard winter of 1979. In other parts, even in Cornwall, hardiness is a necessary consideration. Very cold winters can kill many of the less hardy species, and even some of the hardy ones. It is not the cold that is lethal, but a sudden drop in temperature, as when it fell from above freezing to -19°C early on the first day of 1979, on the south coast of Cornwall where the more tender trees were concentrated. However, really cold winters do not come to Britain that often, perhaps every 15 years or so, and eucalypts can make enormous growth and give great pleasure in the run of mild winters that can be expected in between.

EUCALYPTUS DALRYMPLEANA (below). One of the most impressive of the gums, this is a large stately tree with stark white winter bark.

EUCALYPTUS CORDATA LABILL.

SILVER GUM; TASMANIA. EVERGREEN.

This vigorous conical tree is striking in leaf because it retains its juvenile foliage into old age, unlike most species. The angled, bloomy shoots bear opposite, stalkless, powdery blue-grey, aromatic leaves. Another unusual feature is that its creamy white flowers are usually borne during winter. The Silver gum is proving to be very hardy.

E. DALRYMPLEANA MAIDEN

BROAD-LEAFED KINDLING-BARK; SE AUSTRALIA AND TASMANIA. EVERGREEN.

This can be regarded as a poor man's Blue gum (*E. globulus*), and grows nearly as fast for some years with equally big, 20–25 cm falcate leaves which are leathery blue-green, and similar but more yellow-pink bark which peels in large strips leaving a creamy bole. After juvenility the spot difference between the two is this species' tiny flower buds and seed capsules in threes; during juvenile growth it has much smaller, more tapered leaves than the blue gum, which are yellowish and pinkish-green. It is also much hardier but its hardiness is variable, probably because of the altitude of the parent stand; in 1979 a completely unharmed tree could be in the same garden as another that had been scorched right back to the bole or killed.

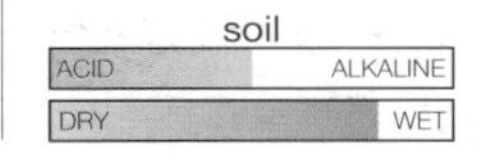

EUCALYPTUS GLOBULUS LABILL.

BLUE GUM; SE AUSTRALIA AND TASMANIA. EVERGREEN.

In its native Tasmania this is no record-breaker but in many parts of the world, in tropical and sub-tropical or Mediterranean climates, it is the fastest tree to 30 m and one of the very few to be 60 m tall. In Ireland and the Isle of Man this is the gum to plant for an enormous specimen; anywhere else it is unlikely to survive more than four or five winters so it will scarcely achieve 12 m. Juvenile plants are well known as annual spot-plants in bedding schemes, with big, floppy, broad silver-blue leaves joined in pairs around the square, flanged stem. Adult foliage is hard, leathery, dark blue-green, often over 20 cm long and curved. The flower buds are usually solitary on a stout short stalk and are 2–3 cm long. They open by extruding bunches of white stamens at almost any time of the year. The seed capsules become black with an intensely blue-white bloom, and are twice the size of any other eucalypt capsules in Britain.

15•25•40 M

E. GUNNII HOOK. F.

CIDER GUM; TASMANIA. EVERGREEN.

The standard eucalypt of suburban and other gardens throughout Britain, this is perfectly hardy in normally severe winters but may occasionally be caught by freak falls in temperature. Juvenile foliage is in opposite pairs, nearly round and is blue-grey or bright blue-green. It soon yields to alternate, elliptic leaves on slender yellow petioles. Young trees have a conic acute crown and become rounded with age. Growth is variably rapid; some trees make shoots of 2 m each year but others grow at about 1 m anually for some years. In one form derived from a narrow-leafed tree at Whittingehame, East Lothian, the branches are distinctively warm brown.

12•20•25 M

E. JOHNSTONII MAIDEN

TASMANIA. EVERGREEN.

This is another gum that is safe only in Ireland, where it should be grown with the Blue gum (*E. globulus*) for its superior shape. It keeps a slender conic crown until it is about 40 m tall and the bole is so smoothly cylindric that it appears to be a machined pole. The foliage is unusual in being bright deep green and glossy. Growth is often more than 2 m a year. Juvenile trees are narrowly erect with rough, deep red shoots and stalk-less dark green leaves. This Tasmanian gum has survived some hard winters in south Devon and Cornwall but the worst winters exact a heavy toll and it is unlikely to last long in parts of Britain that are much colder.

12•20•40 M

E. NICHOLII MAIDEN & BLAKELY

PEPPER GUM; SE AUSTRALIA. EVERGREEN.

In most areas the Pepper gum is likely to be killed by any winter that is less than mild, but it is so attractive when juvenile or as a small bushy tree that it is worth replacing when necessary. Its very slender little ribbony leaves, to 5 x 0.5 cm, are grey-green and bloomed red-purple, on red-purple shoots.

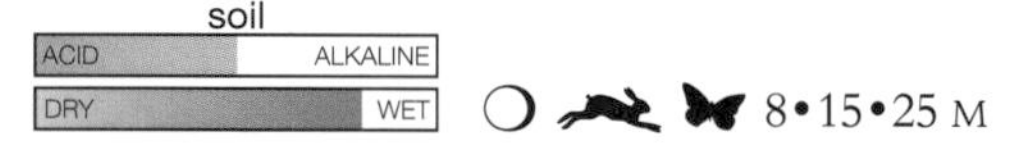

8•15•25 M

EUCALYPTUS GLOBULUS (far left). The tender *E. globulus* is more common in bedding schemes.

EUCALYPTUS JOHNSTONII (above). This tender gum has survived hard winters in Devon and Cornwall.

EUCALYPTUS NICHOLII (below). The Pepper gum is unlikely to survive on mainland Britain.

EUCALYPTUS GUNNII (bottom). The most widely planted gum in suburban gardens, it quickly outgrows its site.

EUCALYPTUS NITENS (above). Although supposedly one of the hardiest gums, it may not survive severe winters

EUCALYPTUS PAUCIFLORA subsp. *NIPHOPHILA* (right). This snow gum is extremely hardy, fast growing and not too large, with exceptionally ornamental bark.

E. NITENS MAIDEN

SHINING GUM; SE AUSTRALIA. EVERGREEN.

In its early years this is the fastest gum grown in Britain and trees have reached 20 m in nine years. It had proved hardy everywhere until 1979 but almost all the Shining gums were badly scorched in that year. Its very broad, large juvenile leaves are blue-grey on square stems. It makes a broad columnar crown with regular, ascending, rather big branches from which the adult leaves hang.

E. PAUCIFLORA SIEBER ex. SPRENG

SNOW GUM; SE AUSTRALIA. EVERGREEN. 15 M.

The typical form of the species, which also occurs in Tasmania is not always reliably hardy as it can occur at low altitudes. The commonly grown form is subsp. *niphophila* (Maiden & Blakely) L. Johnson & Blaxell (*E. niphophila* Maiden & Blakely). This Australian tree raised from seeds collected at the highest parts of its range came through the winter of 1979 quite unscathed. It is the only gum for which no death or damage was reported. It has no distinct juvenile foliage and new leaves on young plants emerge rich orange-brown on glossy red-brown shoots. The leaves are soon grey-green with a fine margin of dark red; they are elliptic and falcate, to 14 x 5 cm. The shoots become brilliantly blue-white and the bole and branches, a striking combination of grey, blue-grey and cream, are the main attraction of the tree. The Snow gum takes a few years to grow fast and is variable but can make shoots of 1.3–1.5 m for a few years before it rounds into a broadly domed tree which will occasionally throw up vigorous shoots at its base, subsp. *debeuzevillei* (Maiden) L. Johnson & Blaxell (*E. debeuzevillei* Maiden) was recently introduced and is promising. A 12 m tall tree was unharmed in a Devon garden in 1979. It is rather similar to the Snow gum with darker leaves and orange patches where the bark flakes, and has a more shapely columnar crown. It is the most attractive of all the gums.

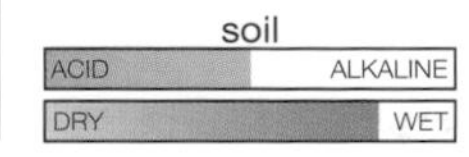

10•15•15 M

Eucommia ulmoides Oliver

GUTTA-PERCHA TREE; CHINA. DECIDUOUS.

This is a good and unusual, if not spectacular, foliage tree, that grows into a broad dome with deep glossy green leaves. These are lanceolate-elliptic, to 18 x 10 cm, with elegantly tapered apexes and are shallowly toothed. They have a party trick, which is as well because otherwise they would be hard to place when received as detached specimens; when a leaf is torn gently across the middle, latex from the veins hardens in the air and one half of the leaf can hang 5 cm below the other on the threads. Only the Table dogwood (*Cornus controversa*) has a similar trick. Trees are either male with little tufts of brown stamens for flowers or female with a single pistil and then winged fruit.

Cultivation The Gutta-percha tree is perfectly hardy and amenable to most soils, even shallow chalk. It prefers full sun and shelter from strong winds.

EUCOMMIA ULMOIDES (below). Is more of a novelty than a desirable landscape plant, its claim to fame is its ability to produce rubbery latex.

EUCRYPHIA GLUTINOSA PLENA GROUP (above). Seeds of *Eucryphia glutinosa* often gives highly desirable plants with double or semi-double flowers.

Eucryphia x *nymansensis* Bausch 'Nymansay'

CULTIVATED ORIGIN. EVERGREEN.

This hybrid between *E. cordifolia* and *E. glutinosa* first arose at Nymans in Sussex and makes a dense, columnar and fast-growing tree. The glossy, very dark green leaves have from one to three leaflets and are pale green beneath. Fragrant white flowers, 7.5 cm across and rather like dog-roses, are produced among the leaves during summer. They have centres of numerous conspicuous stamens tipped with pink anthers. The flowers open during late summer and autumn.

Cultivation Although this splendid hybrid is at its best in mild, moist gardens it will grow in all but the coldest areas given a good, moist soil and protection from cold winds. It ideally likes to be kept shaded at the base and will flower most prolifically if allowed to grow into full sun.

Other species *E. cordifolia* Cav. from Chile differs in having grey leaves that are always undivided and hairy beneath. It is more tender than the hybrid and only suitable for mild gardens. *E. glutinosa* (Poepp. & Endl.) Baill., also from Chile, is deciduous. Its leaves have three to five leaflets and turn orange-red in autumn. It is more hardy than both the hybrid and *E. cordifolia* and requires a lime-free soil. Plena Group is distinct for its double flowers.

soil

ACID ALKALINE

DRY WET

5•8•15 M

Fagus/Beeches

The beeches form a distinct group of deciduous trees, native to temperate regions of the Northern Hemisphere. Only Common beech (*F. sylvatica*) is frequent, together with its many forms, but ther species are occaisionally seen in collections. Male and female flowers occur separately on the same tree giving rise to woody fruits which can be profuse in some years.

Cultivation Beeches are easy to grow in most soils that are not waterlogged. They are especially suited to chalky soils.

FAGUS ENGLERIANA SEEMEN

CHINESE BEECH; C CHINA. DECIDUOUS.

This is an elegant, small tree, similar to the Common beech (*F. sylvatica*), and highly desirable for its foliage in summer and autumn. It has a tendency, which should be checked, to fork at its base or very low down, but can make a shapely tree, so far to 15 m; none in Britain is yet 70 years old and most of the few seen are much younger. The buds are very slender, almost needle-like, and the leaves taper at each end. They are fresh light green above, slightly silvered beneath and have a somewhat crinkled margin. In autumn they turn gold, then the outer ones turn orange and russet-brown.

5•8•15 M

F. ORIENTALIS LIPSKY

ORIENTAL BEECH; SE EUROPE, SW ASIA. DECIDUOUS.

This very uncommon tree is a shade more vigorous than the Common beech (*F. sylvatica*), and is similar except that the leaves are further apart, have seven to ten parallel veins each side instead of up to seven and are more slender-tapered and entire with a less marked wavy margin. They are also larger, up to 14 x 7 cm but usually 10 x 4 cm. The autumn colour is a rich orange-brown. The bole is fluted and the crown is an upswept ovoid. It is an interesting change from the common beech and makes a good specimen. However, it is not as effective as the common tree in a group as it lacks its smooth bole.

soil
ACID ALKALINE
DRY WET

6•12•25 M

FAGUS ORIENTALIS (above). Bolder in leaf than the common beech, this uncommon species requires similar conditions.

FAGUS ENGLERIANA (far left). This elegant small tree has attractive foliage in both summer and autumn.

FAGUS SYLVATICA 'DAWYCK' (right) is a vigorous tree with a distinctive flame-shaped habit.

FAGUS SYLVATICA 'DAWYCK GOLD' (far right). This impressive, slow growing, yellow leaved beech, has a tight columnar habit that may be enhanced by clipping. In line with current trends to use more native species in our landscapes, the native beech is becoming more widely planted.

F. SYLVATICA L.

COMMON BEECH; EUROPE. DECIDUOUS.

This, one of the most valuable of all the big trees has manifold uses and many landscapes, clumps and fine woods would not be possible without it. One of its advantages for wide-scale amenity use is that it is native to England. Its one major defect, which is less of a drawback in large plantings, is the dangerous way in which it decays at senility after what is not a very long life for a large tree. In the open, or spaced widely apart, few beech live for much more than 200 years. However, their life and their period as safe trees will be prolonged if in their early years they are grown closely spaced, about 1.5 m apart, and gradually thinned to the best boles – beech make long clean boles which are supremely attractive. They must also be prevented from growing heavy branches at a wide angle to make their crowns far less vulnerable to breakage and decay. Some fine examples of beechwood remain in the Cotswolds, but the best ones on the South Downs were blown over in the storm of 1987. One of these woods, at Slindon near Arundel, dated from about 1830. It had many trees to 40 m, which were clean boled for 20 m, and after all inferior trees had been removed in 1950 had been a source of top-quality seed.

Never less than pleasing at any time of the year, the best time for beech is when the leaves are freshly out. They are then of a brilliant shiny green which is most effective with the silvery grey bark. Autumn comes a close second.

Variants Because they are native trees with a vast population from seed, beech vary far more than most of the exotics, which have been raised from samples of a few hundred seeds in original imports that came from only a few trees in a range. Some beech are thus well in leaf when others are still bare, and the time when leaves change colour in autumn, and the shades they turn, vary greatly. Beech grow well in city parks. 'Aspleniifolia', Fern or Cut-leafed beech, was previously named 'Heterophylla' and 'Laciniata'. The majority of the leaves have a slender central lobe that makes a long apex beyond 4–5 deeply cut, acuminate, forward-pointing lobes and are only 4–5 cm long; some late season leaves at the tip of the shoots are linear or strap-shaped. These are all grafted trees and each shoot has a chimaeral structure – that is, it is made of tissues from two different forms. The interior tissues are of the beech type and shoots regrowing from breakages in the crown come mainly from this and bear normal beech leaves. Some sprouts are variably modified by the fern-leafed tissues outside and bear leaves with varying degrees of lobing. This beech could be identified in winter, even were every one of the half million or so leaves of a big tree to be swept away, by the fine shoots that sprout from its branches and bole and by its generally finer and more dense crown. It is a good tree as a lawn specimen, but makes less impact in a group and is wasted in a wood.

Atropunicea Group, the Purple beeches, are usually grown from seed and there is variation in their colour. They are about as fast as the green form and become nearly as big. Although they are very popular for clumps, lines and avenues no Purple beech should ever be planted in these settings. For six months of the year, when the garden is most admired, these would be heavy, dark masses, garish without being bright, and blending their shared failings. Such a grouping has but one ideal position: on someone else's lawn half a mile away, with the top just visible.

The paler, browner Cuprea Group flush a curious pinkish colour for a day or two, an interesting hue that is hardly suited to a garden. 'Riversii' is a much deeper red selection and is quite presentable at a distance.

'Aurea Pendula' is among the elite of weeping trees and makes a slender column of bright yellow with branches hanging vertically against its trunk. It can burn in too much sun and will be too green if given a lot of shade, so needs careful siting. The parent tree from which all the 'Dawyck' beeches are raised as grafts stands by a gate at Dawyck, a fine garden and enormous tree collection in Peeblesshire. Like a Lombardy poplar (*P. nigra* 'Italica') but flame-shaped, tapering from the base, this has greater presence than other beeches with its more solid crown, heavier foliage and superior autumn colours. It is a splendid tree as a mark of emphasis on a fairly large scale – at an entrance (one on each side) or a cross-rides or path junction, or planted as a tight group. Five to ten trees at 4–5 m spacing – five for a close feature and larger numbers only for distant prospects – will add character to the end of a vista. 'Dawyck Gold' is similar but slower growing and more

FAGUS SYLVATICA 'AUREA PENDULA' (left). This is a first class, golden weeping tree. Unfortunately, its foliage may scorch in full sun, so a shady, wind protected location is required.

FAGUS SYLVATICA 'PENDULA' (below), has an unusual habit. Natural growth layers develop around the main trunk forming a distinct ring of branches.

FAGUS SYLVATICA 'ZLATIA' (above), is a slow growing form with light yellow foliage, fading to green with age.

FAGUS SYLVATICA ATROPUNICEA GROUP (far right), covers the many purple leafed forms that have been raised and selected from seed. They often match the growth of the green forms and can be heavy in the landscape.

columnar, with bright yellow spring foliage that turns green during summer. 'Dawyck Purple' is narrower with deep purple foliage. Both need careful placing. 'Laciniata' ('Quercifolia'), the Oak-leafed beech, was found in a beech hedge in Saxony in 1792. It is rather rare but can make a large tree. The leaves are the same size as those of normal beech but a little darker and edged by regular triangular lobes. Similar leaves are found here and there in the crowns of 'Aspleniifolia' but in 'Laciniata' the entire crown is of this form of leaf. It is a pleasant variant on common beech.

'Pendula', the Weeping beech, is one of the best of all large weeping trees. It soon grows a stout silvery grey bole from which two or three rather sinuous erect branches arise at about 2 m and tower to 20–25 m; small branches arch out and weep to the ground. When the shoots reach the ground they rest on it and send up a vertical shoot or two. These eventually root, and the layers become a ring of big trees around the old stem. Unlike some weeping trees this beech can look after itself and needs no splinted leading shoot. Other trees are tall and slender without layers.

This is a fine specimen from a moderate distance, so it needs to be on an extensive lawn or down a vista. It is rather overwhelming at close quarters and casts a wide area of shade.

'Rotundifolia' is round-leafed, and scarceamong the many variant foliage-forms of the beech. It grows into a broad crowned tree 20 m tall and so needs a large space, but it is well worth it for its unusual foliage. The neat, small leaves are nearly round and 1–3 cm across; in the similar 'Cockleshell' they are only 1 cm across.

If any of the beech cultivars has not been planted as much as it deserves to be, it is 'Zlatia', the Golden beech. It is very vigorous and grows anywhere that ordinary beech will. Found in Serbia, and considered to be a hybrid with the Oriental beech (*F. orientalis*), it has been available in Britain only since 1890. The older trees are confined to botanic gardens and a few collections, but it has been used more widely lately. It comes into leaf soft yellow and just about achieves a good gold before midsummer when it turns green, with paler shoot-tips. The new growth sometimes keeps the outer crown golden. It is a refreshing variation on the common beech and the countryside would be vastly improved if for the next 150 years every intended planting of purple beech were required by law to be 'Zlatia' instead.

soil
ACID ALKALINE
DRY WET 6•10•35 M

Fitzroya cupressoides (Molina) Johnson

ALERCE; CHILE, ARGENTINA. EVERGREEN.

Named after Captain Fitzroy, who commanded the *Beagle* on which Charles Darwin sailed, this little tree is like a juniper but has hanging, dark blue and white foliage. The little 3 mm leaves, arranged in threes on the shoots, curve out their thick blunt tips, dark blue-green with two prominent white stripes on each surface. The vase-shaped crown branches low from the bole and arches out.

Cultivation *F. cupressoides* will grow on a wide range of soils but is best in areas with cool, moist summers. Although fairly hardy, it is a little tender when young. On damp, acid soil in shelter it is a pleasant and unusual foliage tree of rather slow growth.

FITZROYA CUPRESSOIDES (below). Seldom attaining its full height in Britain, this remarkable tree is rarely seen outside botanic gardens.

Fraxinus/Ashes

THE ASHES ARE A GROUP of fast-growing mainly large trees with pinnate leaves arranged oppositely on the shoots. Although most have fairly inconspicuous flowers, without petals, there are exceptions to this and the Manna ash (*F. ornus*) is an outstanding flowering tree.

Cultivation Ashes prefer a well-drained soil in full sun and are particularly good for alkaline soils.

FRAXINUS ANGUSTIFOLIA (far right). Although this species is grown, cultivated selections are more commonly seen.

FRAXINUS ANGUSTIFOLIA VAHL.

CAUCASIAN ASH; S EUROPE, NORTH AFRICA. DECIDUOUS.

Although this species is cultivated it is now most commonly seen as the following forms. It is fast-growing with graceful foliage; the leaves have slender, glossy green, often drooping leaflets.

Variants subsp. *oxycarpa* (M. Bieb. ex Willd.) Franco & Rocha Alfonso (*F. oxycarpa* M. Bieb ex Willd.), Caucasian ash, is a smooth-barked, more shapely, smaller tree and is scarce but highly attractive for an ash. Its attraction is in its light grey branches and decorative bright, glossy green foliage of 5–7 slender leaflets. Although it is basically opposite-leafed, as are the entire family, this tree often has some leaves in threes. 'Raywood', a very vigorous form that came to Britain from Australia in 1925, is becoming popular.

FRAXINUS EXCELSIOR 'DIVERSIFOLIA' (below). Although the common ash is seldom planted in gardens, there are some delightful forms like the one-leafed ash.

F. EXCELSIOR L.

COMMON ASH; EUROPE. DECIDUOUS.

Although useful in places as a framework tree, good in city parks, on chalky soils and in exposure, this native tree is a coarse one for a garden. It is late into leaf and sheds early with a minimum of autumn colour. It is prone to being misshapen and having canker. Altogether it is best left in the countryside, where it has its place, although some of its cultivars are worth growing.

Variants Known as the one-leafed ash, 'Diversifolia' has simple, long-stalked, irregularly toothed leaves to 20 x 12 cm and a good straight bole with rather remote branching so that it has an open, shapely crown. It can be 27 m tall, making a handsome, unusual specimen. 'Jaspidea', Golden ash, is a tall-growing tree with yellow to orange shoots that contrast with its black buds in winter, and golden leaves in spring and autumn. It is seen to 20 m tall and is conspicuous in winter and autumn. It might suit the edge of a prospect but is not a specimen for a prominent position. 'Pendula', Weeping ash, is a sad-looking tree, too often seen on or around small lawns.

FRAXINUS ORNUS (below). Its flowering qualities, and insect attracting scent, make this the most commonly grown ash.

F. ORNUS L.

MANNA ASH, FLOWERING ASH; S EUROPE, SW ASIA. DECIDUOUS.

Ash trees are in the Olive family, the more familiar members of which are lilacs, privets, forsythia and jasmines, all of which have tubular, often fragrant, flowers. The common ash is wind pollinated, so has no need for petals or scent. However, a small group of ashes does have flowers with petals and scent to attract insects. The only one frequently seen in Britain is the Manna ash. It can be raised from seed but is slow-growing and nearly all garden trees are grafted on to common ash. Since the rootstock of this has a ridged bark and the Manna ash has a smooth grey one, the union is evident even if the graft was made at ground level,when there is a sprouty boss.

The Manna ash makes a broadly domed tree distinguished from the Common ash (*F. excelsior*) in winter by its shape, its smooth bark and by buds that are not jet black but two shades of brown and covered in grey pubescence.

Genista aetnensis (Bivona) DC.

MT ETNA BROOM; SARDINIA, SICILY. DECIDUOUS.

This is the largest species of hardy broom and makes a small rounded tree with an open head of slender, arching and drooping shoots, on a short bole. Although it is deciduous, the green stems give it an evergreen appearance. Young shoots do bear small leaves but these are mostly lost by flowering time. In late summer it produces golden, fragrant pea flowers along the young shoots.

Cultivation Mt Etna broom should be grown in a well-drained soil in full sun. As it is very open in habit and does not cast a dense shade, a variety of plants can be accommodated beneath a mature specimen.

soil
ACID ALKALINE
DRY WET
5•8•10 M

GENISTA AETNENSIS (below). This hardy broom will make an open branched, round headed tree. In summer an explosion of highly scented, yellow flowers, weigh heavily on the branches.

GINKGO BILOBA (right). This unusual, ancient relic has distinctive, two lobed leaves, and butter yellow autumn tints.

Ginkgo biloba L.

MAIDENHAIR TREE; CHINA. DECIDUOUS.

Only this single species survives of all the species, genera and families of Ginkgos in the order Ginkgoales, which dominated tree-life 200 million years ago. It is thus botanically a very isolated plant with no relatives, and no other tree resembles it. It is probably still growing wild in China today where monasteries have preserved it from the felling for firewood which devastated woods in long-settled areas. It was introduced into Japan a thousand years ago and was first seen by a European in that country in 1689. The first Maidenhair tree in Britain was raised in 1754 and moved in 1760 to Kew when part of the palace grounds was opened as public gardens. It was planted against the wall of a boiler-house which was demolished in 1860, and the tree stands free and in full health today. It can be almost any shape, from a straight flagpole with one or two side-arms to a fan like a burst of spray, but is usually quite narrow with a good central stem. It is deciduous with thick leathery leaves which evolved before the pinnate branching system of veins, so their shape is determined by a fanwise arrangement of veins that spreads from a narrow cuneate base to a broad two-lobed tip. The leaves turn bright gold when and where a warm summer is followed by a sunny, warm autumn.

Every garden with room for a narrow tree or two should have a Maidenhair tree. The spiky crown and fresh bright green new leaves go remarkably well with buildings whether red brick or grey stone. Some old male trees bear thick yellow catkins and a few females in a number of cities and gardens bear blue-green plum-shaped fruit which ripen yellow then orange-brown, and decompose with a highly unpleasant smell.

Cultivation The Maidenhair tree is extremely hardy but needs hot summers to thrive. It will grow on any well-drained soil, acid or alkaline, and is well suited to growing in cities. It is almost the only tree able to withstand the peculiarly severe conditions created by the canyons between skyscrapers and it is a downtown tree in many city centres.

Variants 'Fastigiata', Sentinel ginkgo, is as narrowly and densely crowned as an acute-tipped Lombardy poplar(*P. nigra* 'Italica'). There are a few in London parks but they are frequent in Philadelphia, Pittsburgh and New York, where they grow to 30 m tall.

Several trees have also been selected for their fine habits or autumn colour and some are now planted.

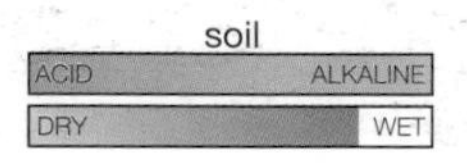

Gleditsia triacanthos L.

HONEY LOCUST; NORTH AMERICA. DECIDUOUS.

This tree is so tough that it alone can compete with the Maidenhair tree (*Ginkgo biloba*) in the downtown parts of North American cities and is widely used (except in the far south-west) as far north as Toronto. In Britain it is seen only occasionally, mostly in Cambridge and London, two places where it is warmest in good summers.

Although it may thrive in warm city centres its ability to grow there does not necessarily recommend it for planting in a garden. It has an open, none too shapely crown and too thin a foliage to make a feature. However, its narrow compound leaves of tiny leaflets have a good, bright green colour and provide a brief flash of gold in the autumn. The fat pods, often curved and bent, are 30 cm long in the tree's native habitat, but are rare and much smaller in Britain. They are, anyway, a nuisance on paths. The Honey Locust has obvious value for a hot dusty, dry corner with rubbly soil or paving. It is also possible to use this spiny tree with its ferocious bunches of sharp, branched thorns – the newer growth on them green – for interest in a position not close to a path

Cultivation The Honey locust will grow in any well-drained soil in a hot, sunny position.

Variants For street and town planting the thornless f. *inermis* (L.) Zab. is advisable. It has a dark red-brown bark with wide, scaly flanges and is known to 23 m tall. Unfortunately it does not always come true from seed and plants may turn out to be thorny. 'Sunburst' is a thornless form that is as tough as the green tree and is planted in many suburban and larger gardens. It comes into leaf bright yellow and stays that colour as long as growth continues, while the early, interior leaves turn bright green – a most effective contrast. Even where an older plant makes no late growth and all its leaves are green, the colour is bright and tinged yellow so it is still a good tree.

GLEDITSIA TRIACANTHOS, the Honey locust is widley planted as a street tree in North America, but thorns on stems are ferocious. 'Sunburst' (left) is more appealing as a garden tree, due to its yellow, feathery foliage, and lack of thorns.

Gymnocladus dioica (L.) K. Koch

KENTUCKY COFFEE TREE; E UNITED STATES. DECIDUOUS.

In winter this is an ungainly, gaunt tree with dark grey bark in big scales, but it has stout shoots with a good lilac-blue bloom. Late in spring the leaves unfold pink, and turn pale yellow, nearly white, then become a good fresh green above, silvery beneath, when they expand fully. The leaves are hugely and doubly compound, about the biggest of any hardy tree. Over 90 cm long, they branch, and branch again, before bearing entire, ovate leaflets. Rather oddly, when all the leaflets and minor leaf stems are shed in autumn, the central leaf stems remain radiating from the branch ends.

The flowers, male and female on separate trees, are pretty but not spectacular. They are rarely produced except in areas with very hot summers.

Too stark in winter to occupy an important position, this scarce tree deserves to be grown more often, among other trees but not crowded by them as it needs full light.

Cultivation The Kentucky coffee tree prefers a good, deep soil and only grows well in areas with hot summers. Elsewhere it is very slow-growing. In Britain the largest specimens are all in south-east England.

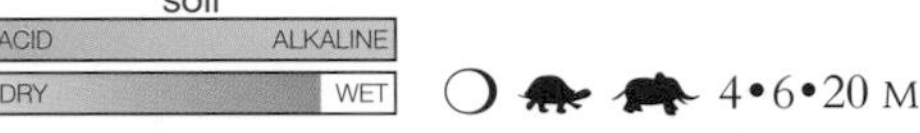

GYMNOCLADUS DIOICA (right and top right). This is a wonderful, large leafed tree with bold architectural foliage. It requires a sunny climate to attain its full height.

Halesia monticola (Rehder) Sarg.

SNOWDROP TREE; SE UNITED STATES. DECIDUOUS.

Although it was not introduced in Britain until 1897, this tree is widely planted. When young it makes a sinuous bole with a grey, fissured bark and a crown that is broad near the base and tapered to the top. The foliage is coarse and dull with yellowish-green leaves about 20 cm long. However, the Snowdrop tree is worthy of a place in a mixed planting for its two or three weeks in flower. In late spring slender pink buds hang in threes from every joint and open to white, 3 cm, bell-shaped flowers. They are in such profusion that the tree is a fine sight. The four-winged fruit, each 1 cm wide, hang in green bunches during summer.

Cultivation The Snowdrop tree likes an acid soil that is damp but well-drained, and grows well on sands if they are not dry. All forms need attention in early life to keep a good dominant single stem.

Variant 'Rosea' is a pale rosy-pink flowered form.

5•8•12 M

HALESIA MONTICOLA (below). Provide an acidic, moist soil and you will be rewarded with a breath taking display of snowdrop-like flowers in spring.

IDESIA POLYCARPA (above). With foliage rivaling the Indian bean tree, this Chinese treasure is seldom grown, and often difficult to establish.

Idesia polycarpa Maxim.

CHINA, JAPAN. DECIDUOUS.

In leaf this resembles a bright, shiny *Catalpa* and it is too rarely seen in Britain. Where summers are hotter, female trees produce red, berry-like fruit in conspicuous bunches and is not just a foliage tree, as in the British Isles. As such, it ranks high with glossy, yellowish dark green, hook-toothed, cordate, ovate leaves 20 x 20 cm on scarlet petioles, 12–30 cm long.

Cultivation Best on a good, deep, acidic or neutral soil in full sun but will grow on alkaline soils if they are not too shallow.

soil

ACID	ALKALINE
DRY	WET

5•8•15 M

Ilex/Hollies

THE CULTIVATED HOLLIES include some of the most popular broad-leafed evergreen trees for the garden. Their range of ornamental features includes attractive, sometimes variegated, foliage and, on female plants, showy berries and makes them of great value for several purposes. They can be effectively planted for shelter and hedging, as single specimens, and in avenues or groups. As a single specimen, one of the Highclere hybrids is preferred, but in a group the Common holly is better.

Cultivation Hollies can be planted on almost any soil that is not waterlogged, from clay to chalk, and will withstand considerable exposure, city gardens and coastal sites. Male and female flowers are usually on separate plants and both must be present in order to obtain fruit.

ILEX X ALTACLERENSIS (HORT. ex LOUDON) DALLIMORE

HIGHCLERE HYBRID HOLLIES; CULTIVATED ORIGIN. EVERGREEN.

About 200 years ago a popular plant for red winter berries in conservatories was the Madeira holly, *Ilex perado* Ait. and its subsp. *platyphylla* (Webb & Berth.) Tutin, from the Canary Islands. To bear berries, the flowers had to be pollinated and for that purpose, the hollies were grown in big tubs which were trundled out on to the terrace in spring to be visited by bees. But the bees had often been on the common native holly first, so when the Madeira holly berries were sown to raise more plants some of these were hybrids. This happened in many places and several nurseries began to raise and select different forms, especially in Derbyshire and Northern Ireland. The first hybrid to be named arose at Highclere House on the Berkshire–Hampshire border and hence all became forms of *Ilex* x *altaclerensis*.

The hybrids are mostly very sturdy, exceptionally tough and rather tall hollies with big, thick, broad and flat leaves that are spined, unspined or with one or very few spines and often have purple stems.

'Belgica Aurea' is a vigorous female, conical tree. The margins of the few-spined leaves are yellow when young and turn to creamy white. Berries are red. 'Camelliifolia' makes a splendid isolated specimen because it has excellent shape and foliage as well as being female with large, darkish red berries in good clusters. It grows as a shapely cone with regular, light and level branches, and its leaves are glossy green, bronze when young, and are entire or with a few teeth. The relatively big flowers have white petals with prominent violet marks at the base. 'Golden

ILEX X ALTACLERENSIS 'GOLDEN KING' (above) is one of the most widely planted of the golden leafed hybrid hollies, although contrary to its name, it is in fact female.

ILEX X ALTACLERENSIS 'HODGINSII' (left). With considerably variable foliage, some very spiny, others less so, this male form with purple stems is somewhat of a curiosity.

ILEX X ALTACLERENSIS 'WILSONII' (right). With its evenly spined leaves, and domed habit, this is still one of the most popular of the hybrid hollies.

ILEX X ALTACLERENSIS 'CAMELLIFOLIA VARIEGETA' (below). This must be one of the most desirable hybrids with an attractive habit and glossy, gold margined leaves.

King' is a female tree with large leaves, often decurved at the margin. These are mainly entire and are broadly margined, or wholly, deep yellow. Berries are red. 'Hodginsii', Hodgins's holly is a very robust male form, often 15–17 m tall with a good bole that is 40–50 cm in diameter and clear for 3 m. It is identifiable by the dull sheen on its broad, 9 x 8 cm leaves which vary on each tree from entire to many spined, usually asymmetrically; and by its large bunches of male flowers, which are dark purple in bud in winter. It is singularly resistant to sea winds and industrial atmosphere so is seen in promenade gardens and inner city parks and churchyards. It is a handsome tree throughout the year and gives substance to a group of small trees or tall shrubs, on any soil. 'Lawsoniana' is female and may be bushy, and makes a fine splash of colour as the 10 x 6 cm leaves are marbled two shades of green with most of the centre bright and pale yellow. It has a tendency to throw green-leafed shoots which must be cut out to the base. Berries are red. 'Nobilis' is male, similar to 'Hodginsii' and as sturdy and tall, but with even more purple on the shoots and more varied toothing; many of the smaller leaves have none. The big leaves have more spines that are more symmetrically placed. 'Wilsonii' is a broadly conic female bush or tree that grows to 12 m and has glorious foliage. The new shoots unfold purple and the leaves open out to as much as 14 x 9 cm. They are bright green and flat, with 4–10 spines each side. Grow it near a path where its foliage can be admired. Berries are red.

soil
ACID ALKALINE
DRY WET

5•8•20 M

ILEX AQUIFOLIUM L.

COMMON HOLLY; EUROPE, NORTH AFRICA, W ASIA. EVERGREEN.

Although this can be a straggly tree that flowers and fruits little when it grows in woodland, in the open it makes a tall, spired crown and female plants fruit heavily. In some years both sexes are so thickly wreathed in flowers along the shoots that it qualifies as a flowering tree.

Variants 'Argentea Marginata' is a vigorous female with white-margined leaves. 'Argentea Marginata Pendula', Perry's weeping holly, a tall, long-pendulous mound with leaves that have broad, nearly white, margins. 'Bacciflava', Yellow-berried holly, is a lovely sight when its shiny black leaves form the background to long clusters of bright, lemon-yellow berries. 'Golden Queen' is the commonest variegated male, with yellow-edged leaves. 'Handsworth New Silver' is female with dark purple shoots that set off the dark-centred and clear white margined spiny leaves. 'Laurifolia' can be grown where a tall, neat spire of a crown is wanted. Old plants are usually 18–20 m tall and taper to a long point, or perhaps to two or three. The dark and glossy leaves, 6–8 cm long, are nearly all ellipses with sharp pointed apices. It is male, so no berries. 'Pendula', the Weeping holly, makes a bower to the ground, is 8–9 m tall, and the long hanging shoots are lined with spiny, buckled leaves and plenty of bright red berries. It may need shaping at first as there are some untidy ones around, but this may be because they are partly shaded and 'Pendula' does need full light. 'Pyramidalis' is desirable as a specimen, with lighter, bright green leaves. These are rather crowded, often curled, and almost all of them are entire and broad. It grows in a shapely, conic form and is prolific with big, bright red berries. 'Pyramidalis Fructu Luteo' is similar but with profuse yellow berries.

soil
ACID ALKALINE
DRY WET
4•6•20 M

ILEX AQUIFOLIUM 'PYRAMIDALIS FRUCTU LUTEO' (above left) is similar to 'Pyramidalis' although instead of red fruits it produces yellow ones.

ILEX AQUIFOLIUM 'HANDSWORTH NEW SILVER' (above) a splendid specimen small tree.

JUGLANS AILANTHIFOLIA var. *CORDIFORMIS* (right). Walnuts are difficult to move as they produce a single tap root and very little root fibre.

JUGLANS CINEREA (below). The butternut is similar to the common walnut, but the shoots are sticky to the touch.

Juglans/Walnuts

THESE SPLENDID FOLIAGE TREES have bold, pinnate leaves and make magnificent specimens. Male and female flowers are borne separately on the same tree as the leaves emerge, the males in drooping catkins.

Cultivation Best planted into their permanent position when small, as early in life walnuts put down a taproot which can be damaged if they are moved.. They like deep, well-drained soil in full sun. Their foliage can be damaged by late spring frosts.

JUGLANS AILANTHIFOLIA CARR.

JAPANESE WALNUT; JAPAN. DECIDUOUS.

This hardy foliage tree makes broad, dense, leafy domes of dark green, huge leaves. The shoots and leaf rachises are densely covered in sticky, dark red hairs. The leaves can be 1 m long with 17 oblong leaflets and are, shiny green but appear darker in the mass. The female flowers are remarkably attractive and appear as 10 cm erect heads on the young shoots, they show bright, deep red stigmas and ripen to globose 5 cm, sticky fruits.

J. CINEREA L.

BUTTERNUT; E NORTH AMERICA. DECIDUOUS.

No known specimen of this American walnut is bigger or better than one at Cliveden, Buckinghamshire, which has reached 25 m. The bark of the Butternut is similar to that of the Common walnut (*J. regia*). The leaves are up to 60 cm long with 15–17 leaflets which are finely toothed and stalkless on a slender, densely pubescent central stalk. The buds are white or pink and the female flowers and the fruit are on 15 cm spreading catkins. The leaf-axis and leaflets, which decrease in size towards the base of the leaf, distinguish it from the black walnut.

JUGLANS MICROCARPA BERL. (*J. RUPESTRIS* TORR.)

TEXAN WALNUT; SW UNITED STATES. DECIDUOUS.

Very scarce and apt to be bushy, this has made a splendidly decorative tree 11.5 m tall at Cambridge Botanic Garden in 56 years. The bark is very dark brown and deeply fissured into rectangular plates. The foliage is the Texan walnut's best feature: delicate, drooping and bright glossy green, turning yellow in autumn. Each leaf has 15–25 obliquely based, closely set, slender leaflets with fine, mucronate teeth and is 30–40 cm long.

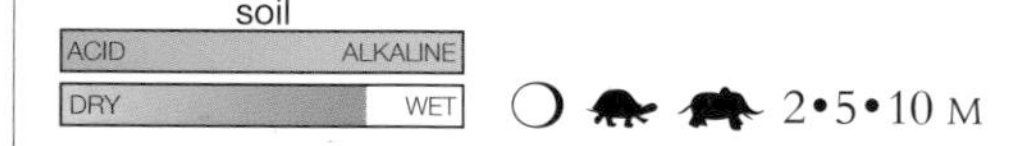

J. NIGRA L.

BLACK WALNUT; E UNITED STATES. DECIDUOUS.

This native of the eastern USA is one of the most stately and handsome trees that can be grown in Britain. The bark is dark brown, deeply ridged and fissured on young trees and becomes black on old trees, with deep holes among the crossing ridges. The leaves have about 15 ovate-lanceolate, shallowly toothed, rich shiny green leaflets which are longest in the middle length of the leaf where they are about 9 x 3 cm. This luxuriant foliage is well spaced all over the crown and hangs on the outside. It briefly turns bright yellow in the autumn.

To raise a Black walnut, it is best to use fresh nuts imported from the USA in damp peat. They should be sown early in spring or even, because they are woody and slow to germinate, on arrival in autumn. The tree is put in its final position after a year's growth, when the shoot will be around 1 m long. This should be cut back to ground level – hard though it may seem.

J. REGIA L.

COMMON WALNUT; SE EUROPE TO CHINA. DECIDUOUS.

As a specimen of very moderate size, the Common walnut has a picturesque, Chinese aspect with twisted branches and soft pale grey, platy bark. This is the only walnut with untoothed leaflets but a shaded leaf will sometimes have a few small-toothed ones. When the foliage comes into leaf, very late in spring, it is orange-brown then pale brown. Crushing a leaf gives rise to a strong scent like polish which is said to be a repellent to flies, even if the leaf is from a sprig placed in a jar

Variants 'Laciniata' is an attractive form with dark purple rachises that bear leaflets which are deeply and very irregularly lobed with slender, often curved points.

JUGLANS MICROCARPA var. *MAJOR* (far left), is more vigorous and tree-like with larger leaves.

JUGLANS NIGRA (below). A fast growing species of noble habit with age, when it develops characteristic deeply furrowed bark.

JUGLANS REGIA (below) is the most widely grown of the walnuts for both the timber and edible nuts.

JUNIPERUS CHINENSIS 'NEABORIENSIS' (above), slowly grows into a column, often multiple-topped.

JUNIPERUS CHINENSIS 'KETELEERI' (far right), is a fast growing columnar female tree with foliage reaching 12 m.

JUNIPERUS DEPPEANA (below). This delightful, small juniper has vivid blue foliage when young.

Juniperus/Junipers

THE JUNIPERS ARE DISTINCTIVE among conifers in the fleshy, berry-like cones produced by female plants. They have prickly juvenile foliage and scale-like adult foliage, sometimes both on the same tree. Although mostly shrubby species are grown in gardens there are a few which make good specimen trees.

Cultivation Junipers like a well-drained soil in full sun and are particularly good on dry and chalky soils.

JUNIPERUS CHINENSIS L.

CHINESE JUNIPER; CHINA. EVERGREEN.

In its typical form this makes a conical tree with brown peeling bark, and dark grey-green foliage which is both juvenile and adult on the same tree. There are many cultivars, including shrubs and trees, and these are better garden plants.

Variants 'Aurea', Golden Chinese juniper retains its bright golden foliage to the baseand has copious male flowers, which are present from autumn until early spring. 'Kaizuka', the Hollywood juniper, is generally shrubby but can be tree-like with age. It is

female with arm-like branches and bunched foliage that give it a twisted appearance.

soil
ACID ALKALINE
DRY WET
4•6•15 M

J. DEPPEANA STEUD.

ALLIGATOR JUNIPER; SW UNITED STATES, MEXICO. EVERGREEN.

This tree is proving to be quite hardy in Britain and is worth trying in full sun. Its bole has beautiful, checkered brown bark. The tree's outstanding feature is the soft blue foliage, bearing both prickly and scale-like leaves.

soil
ACID ALKALINE
DRY WET

3•5•8 M

JUNIPERUS DRUPACEA LABILL.

SYRIAN JUNIPER; SW ASIA. EVERGREEN.

The only juniper with sufficient character to make a good single specimen tree. It grows well on any soil but prefers limestone. Most of the taller trees are very narrow, although a few are broad-columnar. The leaves are in dense whorls of three on twisting shoots from the erect small branches and are 2.5 cm long. They are bright fresh green above with two white bands beneath. Occasionally a tree is found bearing distinctive cones, which are the largest of any juniper – up to 2.5 cm long

soil
ACID ALKALINE
DRY WET ◗◯ 3•6•15 M

J. RECURVA BUCH.-HAM. ex D. DON var. *COXII* (JACKSON) MELVILLE

COX'S JUNIPER, COFFIN JUNIPER; EVERGREEN.

This tree is more vigorous and attractive than the Drooping juniper, the typical form of *J. recurva* from south-west China and the Himalayas. It has orange-brown bark that hangs in loose strips as it ages, bright green long-pendulous shoots and strong, low branches that arch to make a vase-shaped crown. The leaves, in whorls of three, are well spaced on the slender green shoot, 1 cm long and fresh bright green above and banded greenish-white beneath. This is a good, small specimen tree. Female plants bear glossy, blue-black, berry-like cones.

◗◯ 3•5•15 M

JUNIPERUS DRUPACEA (above) has the best foliage of any juniper.

JUNIPERUS RECURVA var. *COXII* (left, above and below). This Himalayan gem is most beautiful when young with arching branches and long pendulous foliage.

JUNIPERUS SQUAMATA 'MEYERI' (above) is one of the bluest of all conifers in foliage.

JUNIPERUS VIRGINIANA 'BURKII' (far right). Although the foliage is purple tinged in winter, in spring it returns to its steel blue colour.

J. SQUAMATA BUCH.-HAM. ex D. DON

FLAKY JUNIPER; HIMALAYAS TO CHINA. EVERGREEN.

This is grown in a wide variety of forms in gardens, many of them dwarf. All have needle-like leaves arranged in threes on the shoots. One form in particular can be tree-like in gardens.

Variant 'Meyeri', Meyer's juniper, is named after the plant collector Frank Meyer who found it in a Chinese garden in 1910. It grows unexpectedly fast for a juniper up to 6–8 m tall with up-curved spires from a low-spreading crown,with drooping shoot-tips. Young trees are conic and steely blue and, planted in a small feature, will need replacing after some years. They root easily from cuttings and grow well on any soil, however poor.

soil
ACID ALKALINE
DRY WET
2•4•10 M

J. VIRGINIANA L.

PENCIL CEDAR; E NORTH AMERICA. EVERGREEN.

This is similar to the Chinese juniper (*J. chinensis*) and like it usually bears both juvenile and adult foliage in the same plant. It is less frequently seen but increasing use is being made of a few cultivars. The foliage varies from green to blue-green and the small cones are covered in a glaucous bloom.

Variant 'Burkii' is dense and columnar and grows to 10 m. Winter foliage is tinged with purple.

soil
ACID ALKALINE
DRY WET
5•8•20 M

J. WALLICHIANA HOOK. F. ex BRANDIS

WALLICH'S JUNIPER; HIMALAYAS. EVERGREEN.

This little Himalayan juniper remains narrow and dense into old age. Young trees are the same neat shape and the dense foliage is brightened by bunches of juvenile deep green leaves which mostly show their silvered undersides. The adult scale-leaves are dark grey with white edges and the berry-like fruit ripen black.

soil

ACID ALKALINE
DRY WET
3•5•10 M

JUNIPERUS WALLICHIANA (far right) makes a delightful small specimen tree in any garden.

Kalopanax septemlobus (Thunb.) Koidz. (*K. pictus* (Thunb.) Nakai)

CASTOR ARALIA; NE ASIA. DECIDUOUS.

For a tree which looks to be tender when in leaf, it is extremely hardy and is especially valuable where more tender trees cannot be grown. Although strangely gaunt in winter, with few branches and few stout, spiky shoots, it is luxuriant in leaf and curious in flower and fruit. The bark is thickly ridged and dull grey. The bole has many short but sharp, broadly based spines, which are most prominent when the tree is young.

Cultivation The Castor aralia grows poorly on very dry soils so needs one that is reasonably moist, but well drained. It is best sited among other trees in sun or semi-shade.

Variants There are two extreme forms of foliage and many trees bear leaves that are somewhere between them. The typical form has maple-like leaves with three broad, shallow, finely pointed lobes and two small ones at the base, on slender 12–15 cm petioles which are green and glabrous. The var. *maximowiczii* (Van Houtte) Hand.-Mazz from Japan has 5–7 deeply cut ,elliptic-acute lobes and a red-brown pubescent and rough petiole 10–20 cm long. The leaf-blade may be 20 x 20 cm. The margins of both forms have hard, very sharp, thick but fine toothing. The flowers open in late summer and are small and white in umbels of about 25 on thin stalks 8 cm long. About 30 such stalks radiate from the tip of the shoot. In late autumn each umbel is a cluster of 5 mm black berries.

KALOPANAX SEPTEMLOBUS (left) adds splendid foliage effects to any planting.

KOELREUTERIA PANICULATA (above). A true summer tree, large panicles of bright yellow flowers are followed by distinct lantern-like fruits.

Koelreuteria paniculata Laxm.

GOLDEN RAIN TREE, PRIDE OF INDIA; CHINA, KOREA. DECIDUOUS.

Since this tree is not Indian but Chinese, and as several other trees are called Pride of India, the name more often used in America – Golden rain tree – is preferred. Gaunt with dark red-brown bark in winter, late into leaf and early to shed. The leaves are dark red from the bud, up to 45 cm long, and pinnate with broad and lobed or doubly toothed leaflets, to 8 cm long, on a red rachis. They turn briefly yellow and pale orange in autumn. Late summer flowering is the tree's best point and is best when summers are warm. Great open panicles, 30–40 cm long, grow out beyond the foliage and bear 1 cm, bright yellow, four-petalled flowers; these ripen into bladder-like fruit 4–5 cm long, which can be bright pink in autumn. This late flowering, of a colour unusual in any tree after spring, earns the Golden rain tree a place in the garden – but not a prominent one as it is undistinguished for much of the year.

Cultivation Best on good soils, including very dry ones. Not very demanding, but must have full light.

soil
ACID ALKALINE
DRY WET
❍ 5•8•12 M

+ *Laburnocytisus adamii* (Poit.) C. Schneid.

ADAM'S LABURNUM; CULTIVATED ORIGIN. DECIDUOUS.

Not many species are first-rate conversation pieces and tenth-rate trees but Adam's laburnum can, without doubt, make this claim. For 50 weeks of the year it stands shapeless, its meagre shoots apparently afflicted by a witch's broom and its foliage, when present, dark and scanty. Single-handed it could ruin any group or prospect. During the two weeks that remain it is an eye-catching harlequin of a tree. The 'witches' brooms' become 25 cm bunches of little, 4 cm racemes of soft rosy-purple flowers. These are spread randomly through a crown which is mostly hung densely with 15 cm racemes of pale pinkish-purple or coppery-pink flowers but which also bears, at random, normal, bright yellow laburnum racemes.

Monsieur Adam grafted the Dwarf purple broom (*Cytisus purpureus*), on a leg of Common laburnum (*Laburnum anagyroides* Medik.) at his nursery near Paris in 1825 and one branch grew out with the pinkish laburnum flowers, which are yellow-based with purple overlay. When this was propagated by grafting, the new plants began to produce the flowers of each parent tree here and there. A shoot from any part of the tree will do the same if grafted. M. Adam's shoot was evidently a 'chimaera': the two parent tissues remained unaltered and some of the flowers were derived from both.

A place has to be found for such an interesting tree, preferably where it is not obtrusive when out of flower – like the interior of a large, well-spaced group for example, or as a single tree in a planting of large shrubs that are attractive all through the year – and where it can be ignored as a minor player until it flowers.

Cultivation Adam's laburnum is an easy tree to grow on any well-drained soil in a sunny position.

+ *LABURNOCYTISUS ADAMII* (left). An eye-sore 50 weeks out of the year, the remaining two weeks find it smothered in large bunches of soft rosy-purple flowers.

Laburnum x *watereri* (Kirchn.) Dipp. 'Vossii'

VOSS'S HYBRID LABURNUM; CULTIVATED ORIGIN. DECIDUOUS.

This hybrid between the Scotch laburnum (*L. alpinum* (Mill.) Bercht. & Presl.) and Common laburnum (*L. anagyroides* Medik.) has almost replaced its parents in most gardens. It is so superior to both of them, and to other forms of the cross, that only it needs to be considered. The flower racemes are usually 45 cm long and can be 60 cm, and do not shorten as the tree ages to the extent that occurs on the common laburnum. They are densely strung with big, bright yellow flowers and last well. The seed-pods are brown and dull in autumn, but there are few of them and they do not disfigure the tree. The superior foliage is dense along the branches, with 10 cm leaflets, and does not thin noticeably with age. The hybid is neverthless a poor tree when not in flower, and thus difficult to place.

LABURNUM X *WATERERI* (right).
In June, few trees surpass the flowery display of the laburnum.

Larix/Larches

THESE DECIDUOUS CONIFERS are fast-growing and very tough trees. All bear foliage of two types: whorled leaves on short side-shoots and long, leading shoots with spirally arranged single leaves. Most give good colour in autumn when the leaves usually turn yellow. Male and female flowers are separate on the same tree in spring before the leaves emerge and the females develop into woody cones.

Cultivation Larches prefer a well-drained soil and are at their best in areas of high rainfall. They may be stunted and grow poorly on very dry sites.

To be as fast-growing and shapely as it should be, a larch must be planted when it is two or, at the most, three years old and 1 m tall; provided it is looked after, it is better still to plant a one-year seedling, which can be 30 cm tall. On light poor soils larches respond strongly to fertilizer, especially nitrate in spring, and young trees should not be allowed to be dry.

LARIX DECIDUA MILL.

EUROPEAN LARCH; EUROPE. DECIDUOUS.

Few garden trees can have more numerous desirable features. It makes a fine specimen tree with very rapid early growth and its bole is soon smooth and handsome. It bears pink female flowers in quantity at no great age, and leafs out a striking bright fresh green very early in spring before most trees. It attracts many birds for feeding and nesting, especially redpolls, crossbills, goldfinches, blue-, coal- and great-tits, goldcrests and, when older and in groups, birds of prey. It colours gloriously and late in the autumns. It is very wind-firm and good in exposure.

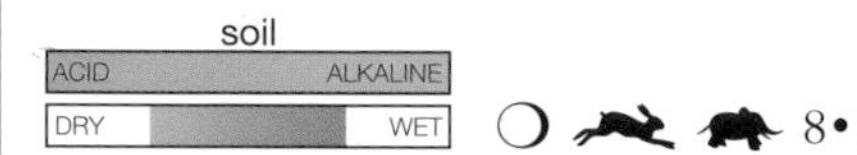

8•15•40 M

L. X *EUROLEPIS* HENRY

HYBRID LARCH; CULTIVATED ORIGIN. DECIDUOUS.

This hybrid of the European and Japanese larch has the same qualities as the former (*L. decidua*) except that on the poorest and most difficult sites it is more vigorous, and it usually bears more cones from an even earlier age. Trees planted as two-year-olds can grow leading shoots 1.3 m long two years later, with leaves up to 8 cm long. It differs from the European larch mainly in its variably pale orange shoots and broader leaves and tall cones with the edges of the scales curved outwards.

10•18•35 M

L. KAEMPFERI (LAMB.) CARR.

JAPANESE LARCH; JAPAN. DECIDUOUS.

This differs from the European larch (*L. decidua*) in its sturdier, more branched, often broader crown; dark orange or purple shoots; broader, grey-green to blue-green leaves; cream and red female flowers; and more squat, rosette-like cones. As a garden tree it casts more shade and its leaf fall is heavier, so it is much less useful as an over-storey of high shade.

Variant 'Pendula' is sometimes seen with long, hanging shoots.

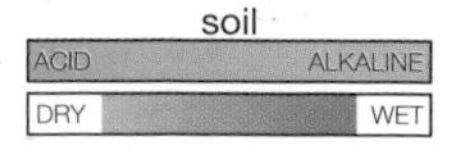

10•15•30 M

LARIX DECIDUA (far left). Long grown in this country this deciduous conifer colours gloriously with vibrant yellow autumn tints.

LARIX X EUROLEPIS (above). This large tree is of great commercial value due to its fast growth. In gardens it is seldom too big.

LARIX KAEMPFERI 'PENDULA' (far left). This distinguished tree has wonderful pendulous branches. Unfortunately, it is often grafted, resulting in an unsightly bole below the union.

Ligustrum lucidum Ait. f.

GLOSSY PRIVET, CHINESE PRIVET; CHINA. EVERGREEN.

This is one of the choicest and most continuously attractive hardy evergreen trees, and one that is able to thrive in cities. It probably needs warm summers to do well, for it grows well in these conditions but it little seen in cold areas. However, the relatively cool summers of Devon are adequate, for the tallest specimen – over 20 m tall – is in a garden above an estuary in the far south-western corner of the county.

Apart from being very amenable to soil and site, the points on which this tree scores so well are its good crown, foliage and flowers, strong scent and long season. The crown is a high dome, leafy and evergreen, but not dense as it is open inside with straight ascending branches; it provides shade without gloom, and the light glinting on the leaves makes it appear to be flowering all season. The leaves, in opposite pairs, are ovate and taper-pointed, entire, about 10 cm long and glossy dark green. The flowers begin their display as pale green, conic panicles in early spring, continue as ivory-white buds through summer and open in autumn when they are whiter and intensely sweet-scented. Fruit does not develop in Britain and the panicles remain, tinged dark red, until early spring when more buds appear.

Cultivation The Glossy privet grows best on a well-drained soil in a sunny position and does particularly well on chalk soils. It should ideally be planted in a position that is sheltered from strong winds.

Variants Variegated forms sometimes seen include 'Excelsum Superbum', the leaves of which have creamy yellow margins that become creamy white; and 'Tricolor', which is similar but has pink leaf edges when young.

LIGUSTRUM LUCIDUM (right). A wonderful, evergreen tree both in foliage and in flower and is the best privet for general planting.

Liquidambar styraciflua L.

SWEET GUM; E UNITED STATES, C AMERICA. DECIDUOUS.

The Sweet gum with its heavy crown of rich green, shiny, big, star-like leaves has few equals for summer foliage and autumn colours. It never grows particularly fast but it keeps on upwards for 100 years or more. Each leaf can be 15 x 15 cm and may be deeply 5–7 lobed on some trees. The bark is deeply furrowed and dull grey. The crown is conic and fairly broad at its base. With age the top broadens to a big dome. Small branches and shoots on some trees, and suckers from most trees, have corky wings, probably because the trees were raised from suckers. However, these wings can also occur on seedlings.

Flowers open with the young leaves in spring, but are seen profusely only in areas with hot summers. Males are in little globes on 5–10 cm erect stalks and are soon shed. Females are more prominent with yellow-green dense clusters of globes. The globes are 1 cm across on 5 cm stalks and become dark brown, woody, spiky and hanging in late autumn.

Autumn colouring is notoriously variable but rarely fails altogether. It is best on trees in full light in a damp, rich soil. Some turn early, scarlet then deeper red. Others turn later and are soon deep red. Others turn later still, to a grand marbling of pale orange, red and purple, while as late as mid-November a few are mixed green, pale yellow and plum-purple.

LIQUIDAMBAR STYRACIFLUA (above). One of the most reliable North American trees for autumn colour. Round fruits only occur after exceptionally hot summers.

LIQUIDAMBAR STYRACIFLUA 'VARIEGATA' (far left) has foliage striped and mottled yellow.

Cultivation Sweet gums prefer a good, moist, but well-drained, acid or neutral soil and colour best in full sun.

Variants A few variegated forms have been named such as 'Golden Treasure' with yellow-margined leaves and 'Silver King', which has leaves margined creamy white. 'Variegata' is faster and its leaves are blotched and streaked with pale yellow-green. Several forms such as 'Lane Roberts' and 'Worplesdon' have also been selected for their autumn colour.

Other species *Liquidambar formosana* Hance, the Chinese sweet gum, is a really choice tree but rarely seen. Young trees are quite vigorous, narrowly crowned and conic. The leaves are glossy red-brown when they unfold, then have a crimson cast before turning blackish-green. The veins remain deep purple and the petioles deep red. The leaves are hard and very three-lobed, and their margins are finely cut into sharp, hard teeth. This makes the foliage distinguishable, if not very exciting, but in autumn it stands out with a unique mixture of orange, deep red and bright purple. The tree can reach 20 m tall.

5•10•25 M

LIQUIDAMBAR STYRACIFLUA 'WORPLESDON' (below) is a form selected for its orange and yellow autumn tints.

LIRIODENDRON TULIPIFERA 'AUREOMARGINATUM' (above). Although the foliage of this form is highly ornamental, it does not provide a foil for the flowers.

LIRIODENDRON TULIPIFERA (right). A massive tree in its native habitat, it seldom attains such heights here.

LIRIODENDRON TULIPIFERA 'FASTIGIATUM' (above). A delightful, large tree with a distinct habit and foliage held low down on the stem.

LIRIODENDRON CHINENSE (below). Often the best species on which to view the flowers as it rarely loses its lower branches.

Liriodendron tulipifera L.

TULIP TREE; E NORTH AMERICA. DECIDUOUS.

The American name tulip or yellow poplar aptly describes the way this tree grows in its native habitat, for it has an open, conic, lightly branched crown until it is 30 m tall, and then makes a dense dome to 50 m on a clear bole of 30 m. In Britain it grows quickly to 25 m in the south but is slower, less free-flowering and lower in the north. The bark is grey and well-fissured until a tree is very old.

Although this is a superb foliage tree, it is less spectacular in flower. The tulip-shaped flowers are mainly green, with an orange band at their base, and are produced in summer when the tree is in full leaf. Trees often need to be 25 years old before they flower, although some flower younger than this.Perhaps the Tulip tree's best season is autumn, when the distinctively lobed leaves, quite unlike those of any other tree, turn bright yellow before they fall. The persistent, pale brown, cone-like fruit are a feature in winter and often remain until early spring.

Cultivation The Tulip tree is suitable for any good, deep, well-drained soil in full sun. It prefers soil that is not too dry and a nearby pond or stream can be beneficial. Small, container-grown plants are best, but may grow slowly at first. The roots are fragile, and they do not move well, but if moving is necessary it should be carried out in early spring. Any damage to the base should be avoided as wounds there rarely heal.

Variants Several selections are available. 'Aureomarginatum', is less vigorous, but striking in late spring with broad, bright yellow margins on the leaves that fade to green after midsummer. 'Fastigiatum' is erect, and usually broadens at a narrow angle from the base. It tends to splay a little at the top but is effective in a group, particularly when gold in autumn.

Other species *L. chinense* (Hemsl.) Sarg., the Chinese tulip tree, is similar to *L. tulipifera* and will reach about the same size, but is much less common. It is just as vigorous and differs in its more deeply lobed leaves (although similar ones can be seen on stump sprouts of *L. tulipifera*), rich brown young foliage and its smaller flowers, which are green with yellow veins. It is an excellent specimen tree but is best given shelter as it can suffer breakage.

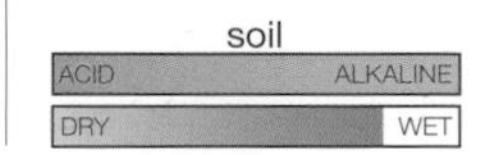

8•15•30 M

Lithocarpus henryi (Seemen) Rehder & Wilson

CHINA. EVERGREEN.

This slow-growing relative of the oaks (*Quercus*) is rarely seen outside collections but is worthy of wider planting. It is a splendid foliage tree with bold, dark green, untoothed leaves that end in long, tapering points and makes a spreading, domed head with age. *Lithocarpus* differ from the oaks in their upright catkins. In this species these are borne in late summer or autumn and are occasionally followed by acorns that are densely clustered in spikes.

Cultivation *Lithocarpus* prefers a warm site sheltered from cold winds and is not recommended for alkaline soils. Like oaks, it should be planted when young.

Other species *L. edulis* (Mak.) Nakai, sometimes grown as *L. glaber* or *Quercus glabra*, has smaller leaves and its fruits are more reliable but it is often only a shrub.

soil
ACID ALKALINE
DRY WET
3•6•15 M

LITHOCARPUS HENRYI (below). One of the most impressive, ornamental foliage trees this Lithocarpus is difficult to obtain.

LUMA APICULATA (right). This delightful suckering bush has year 'round appeal with attractive bark, flower and fruit and, in a protected location, will attain tree status.

Luma apiculata (DC.) Burret (Myrtus luma hort.)

MYRTLE; CHILE, ARGENTINA. EVERGREEN.

This tree from South America runs wild in the gardens of Counties Cork and Kerry and grows to 15 m in Devon, Cornwall and Argyll. Further east and even along the south coast in Britain, it struggles and becomes progressively smaller until it is only a bush in Kent and not reliably hardy east of Dorset, although it will survive for many years in sheltered positions. Well grown, it is splendid as a background with neat black, evergreen foliage setting off bright orange boles which strip in patches to leave white areas. The shoots are densely pubescent and dark pink above, and bear opposite pairs of oval, 2.5 cm, entire leaves. A single, slender-stalked, red and green bud projects from every axil of these and opens pure white in late summer. The black crown then becomes mixed with a starry white cloud and, held on the orange branches, it makes an arresting sight.

Cultivation This myrtle prefers a moist but well-drained soil and flowers best in a sunny position. It will only thrive and form a tree in areas where winters are mild and summers moist.

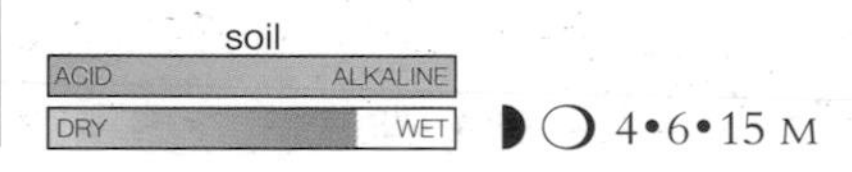

◗ ❍ 4•6•15 M

Magnolia/Magnolias

THE MAGNOLIAS GIVE US SOME of the most striking hardy trees for flower. They start to bloom in late winter and, depending on the species, will continue until late summer and autumn. The parts of the flower are not distinguished into petals and sepals and are collectively called tepals.

Cultivation Most magnolias prefer a well-drained, acid to neutral soil rich in organic matter and not too dry, but *M. delavayi* and *M. grandiflora* will grow well on alkaline soils. Species that flower early can have the flowers damaged by late spring frosts, which in some years can also damage newly emerged foliage.

MAGNOLIA ACUMINATA L.

CUCUMBER TREE; E NORTH AMERICA. DECIDUOUS.

Although this is a member of the Magnolia family – a name that conjures up visions of huge flowers – this is strictly a good foliage tree. The flowers are relatively inconspicuous. They appear among the leaves in early summer and are smallish, yellow-green or blue-green and seldom numerous. The Cucumber tree grows quite rapidly at first, then rather more slowly to become a tree with a straight, 2–4 m bole with well-furrowed, dark brown bark.

M. CAMPBELLII HOOK. f & THOMS.

CAMPBELL'S MAGNOLIA; HIMALAYAS. DECIDUOUS.

This is the biggest of the Asiatic magnolias and can be well over 30 m tall – some say 45 m – in the Himalayas. From the Thames Valley south and westward, and in southern Ireland, it makes a large tree. The flowers open in January in some years and places but usually appear a month or two later. The buds protect them through the hardest winter frosts but once these begin to open the flowers are vulnerable. In a frost-free spell they reach 25 cm across, like great, rose-pink waterlilies, each at the end of a still-leafless shoot. The outer tepals then droop, to show the inner ones standing in a cone shape and give the flower its characteristic cup-and-saucer shape.

Seed-raised plants can take 20 or more years to flower but several selected forms are propagated by grafting and will flower much sooner.

Variants 'Charles Raffill' was raised at Kew in about 1945 and is a cross between Campbell's magnolia and its smaller-flowered Chinese form, subsp. *mollicomata* (W.W. Sm.) Johnstone. This form should bear some flowers when it is 10 or 12 years old. These are not quite as big as those of Campbell's magnolia. Described as deep purple outside and pink-purple and white inside, they are usually the same bright rose-pink as

MAGNOLIA ACUMINATA (left). The cucumber tree is quick to establish, but slows with age. A foliage tree, it is the least spectacular in flower of the magnolias.

MAGNOLIA CAMPBELLII (below) One of the most beautiful and exotic of blossoms, the magnolia flower gains its dramatic form from its outer tepals which burst outward to expose a crown of inner ones.

MAGNOLIA CAMPBELLII subsp. *MOLLICOMATA* 'LANARTH' (right). Flowering from a young age, this form has rich, deep purple flowers alighting on naked branches.

MAGNOLIA DAWSONIANA (below) In contrast to the *M. campbellii* (opposite), the flowers of this species point horizontally after they are open.

MAGNOLIA DELAVAYI (below right). Boasting the largest leaves of any hardy evergreen, it is often grown with wall protection.

Campbell's and on a vigorous, shapely crown. 'Lanarth' has rich, deep purple flowers; subsp. *mollicomata* produces its flowers when it is a younger plant.

M. DAWSONIANA REHDER & WILSON

CHINA. DECIDUOUS.

Among the earliest of magnolias to flower, this species develops a rounded, spreading head in the open, but can have an oval crown with numerous upright branches in woodland. Unlike Campbell's magnolia (*M. campbellii*), the flowers point horizontally after they open.

M. DELAVAYI FRANCH.

CHINESE EVERGREEN MAGNOLIA; CHINA. EVERGREEN.

This is grown in the same way as the Bull bay (*M. grandiflora*), against a wall, in the south of England and Ireland and is a lawn specimen only in the far south-west. It makes a very stout bole with a thick, corky, cream or white bark and heavy low branches. The leaves, much bigger and very different from those of the common species, are broad ellipses, 25 x 18 cm. They are silvery grey-green and unfold coppery brown. The cream flowers, 25 cm across, are regular but not prolific and are short-lived, opening at night and fading the next day. It is as a superb foliage plant that this magnolia is desirable and it should certainly be more widely planted.

soil

ACID	ALKALINE
DRY	WET

4•6•12 M

MAGNOLIA DENUDATA 'PURPLE EYE' (above) is probably a hybrid, and was widely used as one of the parents for many magnolia crosses.

MAGNOLIA DENUDATA DESROUSS.

YULAN, YULAN LILY; CHINA

This broad, much-branched, domed Chinese tree opens its fine, pure white flowers two or three weeks before the common, bushy, Saucer magnolia (*M.* x *soulangeana* Soulange-Bodin). It has a gracefulness absent from the other, so is possibly more attractive than it when not in flower. The leaves are 8–15 cm long, obovate, broader than those of the Saucer magnolia, abruptly acute and more grey-green.

Variant 'Purple Eye', with large, white flowers blotched purple in the centre, is probably a form of the usually shrubby *M.* x *soulangeana*.

5•8•10 M

MAGNOLIA GRANDIFLORA (above). Although commonly seen against a wall, it will make a very attractive evergreen tree in protected locations.

MAGNOLIA X LOEBNERI (above right). One of the best magnolias for general planting as it will thrive on a wide range of soils. Shown here is 'Neil McEachern'.

M. GRANDIFLORA L.

BULL BAY; SE UNITED STATES. EVERGREEN.

Most commonly seen close against a sunny wall, the Bull bay will grow as a free-standing tree in areas with mild winters. The glossy dark green leaves, to about 25 cm long, are covered beneath with a variable amount of rusty hairs. Pure white, very fragrant flowers, which can be up to 30 cm across, open from midsummer through to autumn, but the tree never bears many flowers at the same time.

Variants A number of selected forms are planted including 'Exmouth', which is particularly hardy and flowers when young, and 'Goliath' which has very large flowers and wavy-edged leaves.

MAGNOLIA OBOVATA (right). This magnolia should be more widely grown as, although the flowers open after the leaves, the scent hangs heavy

M. X LOEBNERI KACHE

CULTIVATED ORIGIN. DECIDUOUS.

Hybrids between *M. kobus* and *M. stellata* first arose in Germany. Several selected forms of the cross are now grown in gardens and generally combine the characters of the parents in various ways. All flower before the leaves emerge.

Variants 'Leonard Messel' is a small and rather bushy tree of the highest class when in flower. It arose at Nymans when the pink-flowered *M. stellata* 'Rosea' crossed with a *M. kobus* which had a crimson patch at the base of the tepals. The hybrid opens fairly early and its rich, rose-pink buds expand to form numerous, narrow, soft pink petals which become pale pink shading to white as they spread. For two or three weeks, the variation in the stages of the prolific blossoming present a charming spectacle. It thrives in any garden soil that is not too dry, even in limestone areas. 'Merrill' is much more vigorous and upright, with large white flowers that are flushed pink when they open. 'Neil McEachern' is a vigorous, bushy small tree or large shrub with pink-flushed flowers.

M. OBOVATA THUNB.

JAPAN. DECIDUOUS.

With the wide range and popularity of cultivated spring-flowering magnolias, the deciduous species that flower in summer are hardly given a chance. This is among the

MAGNOLIA SPRENGERI (left). With tidy rose-pink flowers blooming on bare branches and a more compact habit than *M. campbellii*, this spring flowering magnolia is worth talking about.

best of these and is fast-growing and hardy. The bold leaves, as big as 45 cm long and broadest above the middle, are arranged in large whorls at the ends of the shoots. The large, cup-shaped flowers, 20 cm across, are almost overpowering in their fragrance and open in early summer. In autumn they are followed by bright red spiky fruit clusters up to 20 cm long.

MAGNOLIA SPRENGERI PAMPAN. 'DIVA'

In many respects this is the best of the big-flowered tree magnolias. It grows fast and flowers relatively young. A tree at Westonbirt in Gloucestershire was 17 m tall after 15 years and bore five flowers. The next year it had 550. *M. sprengeri* is a shapely, conic open-crowned tree with broad obovate leaves 17 x 12 cm. The flowers open on the bare shoots and are a little smaller than those of Campbell's magnolia (*M. campbellii*) but tidier and a purer bright rose-pink. It is only by a quirk of its taxonomic history that it has to be named as a variety. It derives from a single tree at Caerhays Castle, which was raised from the batch of seed sent by Ernest Wilson from near the Ichang Gorge in western China in 1900. All the others chanced to be white-flowered and much inferior and are called var. *elongata* (Rehder & Wilson) Stapf.

Malus/Crab apples

THIS RELATIVELY SMALL genus has given rise to numerous hybrids, many of which are commonly planted. They have ornamental flowers in spring ranging from white to pink or red, single or double. Many are also attractive in autumn when their fruit ripen.

Cultivation Crab apples are very hardy and tough and provide good trees for small gardens and difficult sites. They will grow on any soil that is not waterlogged, even dry chalky soil, and will withstand considerable exposure. In spite of the large and ever-increasing range of hybrids in cultivation there are still several highly attractive and distinct species which deserve to be more widely grown.

MALUS FLORENTINA (ZUCCAGNI) SCHNEID.

ITALY TO GREECE AND TURKEY.
DECIDUOUS.

This distinctive species is rare both in the wild and in gardens but is very attractive with several ornamental features and is suitable for small gardens. It is so different from other species that it has been thought to be a hybrid between a crab apple and the Wild service tree (*Sorbus torminalis*). The bark is red-brown and flaking, and the crown is densely columnar. Clusters of small white flowers open in spring amid hawthorn-like, lobed and toothed leaves, which turn purple in autumn as the small fruit ripen to orange-red.

MALUS FLORENTINA (right).
This species' small white flowers make it as attractive for its blossoms as for its fruits. Native to southern Europe, it takes its name from the Tuscan capital.

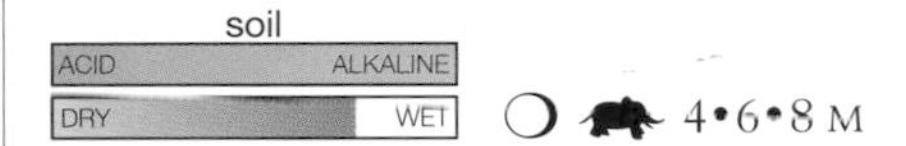

M. FLORIBUNDA SIEBOLD ex VAN HOUTTE

JAPANESE CRAB APPLE; CULTIVATED ORIGIN.
DECIDUOUS.

This tree cannot be omitted despite its formless twiggy crown, which is no adornment to any planting in winter or summer, for nothing else can quite replace its foaming mass of deep pink buds and pink then white flowers in spring. Very early in the season, it unfolds bright green, little lanceolate leaves, and it seems impossible that any abundance of flower could hide them. But it does, always. As with the laburnums, the problem is how to hide the tree when it is not in flower. Nothing must crowd or shade it as it will become thin, straggling and poor in flower and hence only bonfire-worthy. One possible solution is to plant a bed in front of it with tall annual or biennial herbaceous plants.

soil
ACID ALKALINE
DRY WET
3•4•5 M

MALUS FLORIBUNDA (below)
Seasonal in appeal, this crab apple is a mass of cloudy floss-pink when in bud and white in flower. However,it has little to recommend it when it has lost its blossoms.

MALUS HUPEHENSIS (PAMPAN) REHDER

HUBEI CRAB; W CHINA. DECIDUOUS.

A number of strange crabs can be found growing under this name in British and – far more – in American collections, but the one intended here is unmistakeable, at least when in flower. Ernest Wilson, who discovered it, regarded it as the finest of all the flowering trees he sent from China and in the hot summer of 1979 many must have agreed with him. A profusion of large pink, globular buds radiate from a broad, level-branched crown on slender, 4 cm stalks. They open to pure white, cup-shaped flowers that spray out from long sectors of shoot, then open further to broad-petalled 4 cm stars with golden anthers at their centres. The buds are well spread among bright green leaves with enough flowers beyond them to turn the whole crown into a dense cloud of white. In autumn the glossy red, cherry-like fruit are almost as striking.

This superb tree has other merits. It is a triploid and will not cross with other species within bee-flight, so is true to seed. Seedlings grow straight and fast, about 1 m a year for a few years, and soon make sturdy, well-boled trees over 10 m tall. The bark is good in winter: orange-brown fissured into big plates. A few trees have pink flowers, a frequent form in the wild, and are grown as var. *rosea*, but the white form is preferable.

M. 'JOHN DOWNIE'

CULTIVATED ORIGIN. DECIDUOUS.

'John Downie's' starry white, rather small, flowers from pink buds are attractive but would not on their own earn this tree a place here. It is the great bonus of the fruit that qualifies it as a specimen tree. Strung along the ascending branches of a young tree in long-stalked bunches, they are ovoid and ripen yellow, orange and scarlet with a high gloss. They are spectacular among the green leaves and can put growers in a quandary, for they make the most delicious and beautifully coloured apple-jelly jam. The best idea is to plant several trees. They are narrow when young, and so stand well as a group, but will spread with age. The name 'cherry-apple' is sometimes given to this tree and, although the fruit are bigger than any cherry, the long-stalked bunches do give the two some similarity.

soil
ACID ALKALINE
DRY WET
5•8•10 M

M. 'MAGDEBURGENSIS'

MAGDEBURG APPLE; CULTIVATED ORIGIN. DECIDUOUS.

This broad, low and rather pendulous crab apple bears large clusters of big, semi-double, rosy pink flowers with paler interiors, which contrast very effectively with its soft grey-green young leaves. It is beautiful in flower but not good at other times and is generally seen more in village gardens than in bigger gardens or parks.

MALUS HUPEHENSIS (above). One of the finest flowering trees, this species has white cup-shaped flowers and bright green leaves.

MALUS 'JOHN DOWNIE' (left and below). Prized for jam and display, long stalked "cherry apples" ripen yellow, orange and scarlet.

MALUS 'MAGDEBURGENSIS' (left). Large, semi-double, rosy-pink flowers dance above glossy green leaves.

M. X *PURPUREA* (BARBIER) REHDER

PURPLE CRAB; CULTIVATED ORIGIN.

With the exception, perhaps, of the variety mentioned below, the Purple crab is so unsightly, badly shaped and miserably foliaged that it has no place in a well-ordered garden. For the brief and uncertain period in which it is presentable, enough examples can be seen in streets, parks and other people's gardens. It is exceedingly resistant to harsh conditions and a big array has been raised in the prairie states of Canada and the USA. Few of them will reach Britain, but 'Royal Red' is good and might be welcome.

Variants 'Liset' has been raised from 'Profusion' and promises well, as its flowers fade less readily than those of the species to a poor purplish colour. 'Profusion' was bred partly for improved foliage, and is also superior in having dark red flowers that sprayout and wreath long sectors of shoot around the deep red opening leaves.

M. TRANSITORIA (BATAL.) SCHNEID.

NW CHINA. DECIDUOUS.

Although this vigorous tree is small it will spread quite widely and occupy a good deal of room. It has the advantage of several ornamental features. The foliage is light and elegant with leaves, deeply cut into three lobes at least on vigorous shoots, that turn clear yellow in autumn. Small white flowers are very profuse in late spring. They open from pink buds and in autumn each produces small yellow fruit on red stalks.

MALUS X PURPUREA (right). The purple crab is so unsightly that it is best ignored, although future breeding does hold some promise.

MALUS TRANSITORIA (below and below right). This short but wide tree has tiny yellow fruits amongst clear yellow autumn leaves. Profuse small white flowers open in late spring.

MALUS TRILOBATA (LABILL.) SCHNEID

GREECE, SW ASIA. DECIDUOUS.

This eastern Mediterranean crab apple is scarce in Britain and highly distinctive. It is easily mistaken for a Wild service tree (*Sorbus torminalis*). The bark is closely cracked into small, light and dark brown squares and the crown, which grows quite fast, is open and narrow-conical to 12 m tall. Leaves are on 6 cm petioles and are deeply three-lobed, almost maple-like, cut to 1 cm of the base of a 7 x 6 cm leaf. The central lobe has 3–5 lobules, and the spreading basal lobes have one lobule each side; all have a few small, triangular teeth and are grey-green. In autumn the leaves turn yellow and red to blackish-purple with bright, deep red veins. The white flowers are 5 cm across and bunched in terminal heads. They open in early summer, later than most crabs, and are followed by small fruit which are green with a red flush.

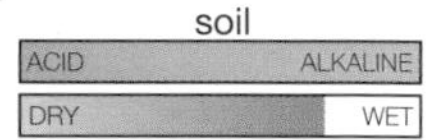

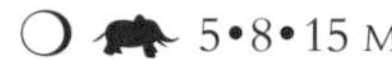 5•8•15 M

M. TSCHONOSKII (MAXIM.) SCHNEID.

PILLAR APPLE; JAPAN. DECIDUOUS.

This Japanese tree is almost tailor-made for planting in streets and courtyards, precincts and small gardens. It makes a very vigorous young plant and can be moved when it is quite big. It is able to thrive in very poor or compacted soils and withstands cold and drought. Its neat, strictly, but not too tightly, upright crown keeps its foliage away from lampposts and enables it to fit into small spaces. Its buds open silvery with hairs and produce firm, grey-downy leaves. These are substantial, but not big enough to be a nuisance in gutters and drains. Its flowers are pleasant, small and white with pink at the tips of the petals, and yield small 2 cm glossy yellow and red fruit but not in quantities that will litter paving.

Above all, in autumn the leaves turn bright yellow then scarlet and deep red, making it one of the very best trees for an autumn display, all the more so because this type of colouring is unusual in a fastigiate tree. It is formal enough in shape to make a good line among buildings. Groups of three are also suitable there or as a feature in formal gardens; large-scale settings will require bigger groups.

soil
ACID ALKALINE
DRY WET
6•10•15 M

MALUS TRILOBATA (above). Easily mistaken for the Wild service tree, autumn leaves turn yellow, red and blackish-purple with bright red veins.

MALUS TSCHONOSKII (far left). A perfect choice for restricted spaces, the tidy Pillar apple has attractive features and will withstand poor conditions and treatment.

MALUS 'VAN ESELTINE' (above and above right). This unobtrusive, columnar tree blooms attractively and sports small yellow and red fruits in autumn.

M. 'VAN ESELTINE'

CULTIVATED ORIGIN. DECIDUOUS.

This is like a small, columnar Japanese crab apple (*M. floribunda*) but has bigger, 5 cm, double, rosy pink flowers. It is exceedingly attractive in flower and because it is narrow and small is unobtrusive for the rest of the year. It can add a vertical motif of value in a group of shrubs, although it does open up a little with age. Although the flowers are double the tree often produces a few small fruit which are yellow with a red flush.

soil
ACID ALKALINE
DRY WET

4•6•8 M

M. YUNNANENSIS (FRANCH.) SCHNEID.

SW CHINA. DECIDUOUS.

This distinctive and unusual species is rarely seen. It makes a small tree with flaking bark and upright branches that bear bold leaves up to 10 cm long. These colour attractive shades of orange to red and purple in autumn. It produces flattened heads of small white flowers in spring and small, red fruit dotted with white lenticels. Some trees belong to var. *veitchii* Rehder, which differs in its more distinctly lobed leaves.

5•8•10 M

MALUS YUNNANENSIS (right). With several feature of interest including flaking bark, delicate flowers, fruit and autumn colour, this unusual species deserves more attention.

MALUS YUNNANENSIS var. *VEITCHII* (far right). The small white flowers appear in flattened heads in spring.

Maytenus boaria Molina

MAITEN; SOUTH AMERICA. EVERGREEN.

This tree is really quite unlike any other and although hardy except in the coldest areas of Britain is rarely seen. It is variable in habit: some trees are upright columns while others are rounded with slender pendulous shoots. The foliage is attractive throughout the year but particularly in spring, when the glossy dark green, slender leaves are highlighted by numerous clusters of tiny, pale green flowers or the pale green young foliage. Most trees appear to be mainly male or female and the latter produce small, orange-red fruits.

Cultivation Maiten will grow in any well-drained soil. It prefers full sun in a position sheltered from strong winds, but will tolerate partial shade. It can produce suckers at some distance from the parent tree.

soil
ACID ALKALINE
DRY WET
5•8•10 M

MAYTENUS BOARIA (below). One of a handful of extremely versatile and useful trees, this small leafed evergreen should be more widely planted.

MESPILUS GERMANICA (above). Dramatic both in autumn colour and in fruit, curious the medlar is seldom grown today.

Mespilus germanica L.

MEDLAR; SE EUROPE, SW ASIA. DECIDUOUS.

The medlar is an old-fashioned tree long cultivated for its fruit. Related to the hawthorns (*Crataegus*), it differs from them in its singly borne flowers and large fruit and makes a low wide-spreading tree. It is most commonly seen as cultivated forms selected for their fruit. 'Nottingham' is an example. These cultivars have oblong, short-stalked leaves up to 15 cm long which turn yellow-brown in autumn. White flowers about 5 cm across appear in early summer and ripen in autumn to distinctive russet-brown fruit crowned by persistent sepals that surround their open, sunken ends. Medlars can be eaten when half-rotten after the first frosts but are best made into jelly.

Cultivation Medlars will grow in any reasonably fertile well-drained soil, in sun or partial shade.

soil
ACID ALKALINE
DRY WET

3•5•6 M

Metasequoia glyptostroboides Hu & Cheng

DAWN REDWOOD; CHINA. DECIDUOUS.

METASEQUOIA GLYPTOSTROBOIDES (below), with sparkling autumn colour and spectacular fluted bark, this prehistoric relic is suitable for only the larger garden or park.

This deciduous redwood was a sensational discovery because it is a familiar and very widespread fossil in rocks 200 million years old and there was no reason to assume that it was still with us. It was found in central China in 1941 but not described and published, or generally known, until 1944. Because of the traditional largesse of the Arnold Arboretum in Boston every major garden in Britain had the opportunity to plant one or more in 1949 from seed received in January 1948. Nearly all the great gardens did so and, except in the colder areas, growth has been vigorous.

The Dawn redwood seems to like warm summers as most of the biggest trees are in Cambridge, Kent, Sussex and Surrey. Ready access to water must also be important because these are all by lakes or rivers or in woodlands with springs or wet hollows. There is less need for such receiving sites in high rainfall areas but cooler summers restrict growth and the tree is not always very successful in Cornwall, and rarely vigorous in Scotland.

Despite its poor appearance in winter, this is a good specimen tree as it is early into leaf and keeps its foliage late into autumn, when it is pink, deep red or red-brown. Through the summer it is fresh green, markedly darker and greyer than the finer, densely twigged foliage of the Swamp cypress (*Taxodium distichum*).The Dawn redwood is the only surviving redwood with an opposite arrangement of foliage and branching. A young tree has a long violet-pink leading shoot and holds out the level side-shoots in pairs, each at right angles to the ones above and below.

Cultivation Dawn redwood will grow on most soils and in most areas but is fastest when summers are warm and when it is near water or in areas of high rainfall. It tends to produce a thin crown when shaded and so should be given full sun with some protection from strong winds. It should always be planted when young and small – at 20–30 cm tall it needs no stake and grows fast. Bigger trees check badly and must be staked.

Michelia doltsopa Buch.-Ham. ex DC.

MICHELIA; HIMALAYAS, W CHINA. EVERGREEN.

Michelias are a genus related to the Magnolias but bear their flowers in leaf-axils instead of terminally. This grand evergreen is reliably hardy only in very mild gardens where it grows very fast and makes a shapely tree with an upswept medium-conic crown; it is nevertheless worth risking in favoured sites for its handsome foliage and fragrant flowers. The bark is smooth and grey, shoots are bright green, and the long conic buds are purple-brown. The glossy deep green leaves are 15 x 6 cm and untoothed; the undersides are glaucous with orange-pubescent veins. The flowers are pale yellow or white and 10 cm across, with about 15 petals. The flower buds, prominent through the winter, are 5 cm long with orange-rusty hairs on pale green scales. *M. doltsopa* was sent to Britain from western China in 1918 by George Forrest and was in flower by 1933.

Cultivation Michelia needs a moist but well-drained lime-free soil in sun or partial shade, with shelter from strong winds. It is successful only in gardens with very little frost.

MICHELIA DOLTSOPA (above right and right). Grown commonly in Cornwall, this evergreen magnolia relative has attractive foliage and flower.

Morus nigra L.

BLACK MULBERRY; ASIA. DECIDUOUS.

Many mulberries look venerable before their time because they were raised by a curious method used for this tree alone: the planting of truncheons. These are big branches from an old tree which are cut into lengths of 1.5 m and planted with about 50 cm in the ground. As a result, relatively young trees are often thought to be of a great age. The dull orange, scaly bark is attractive, as is the broad dense crown when it bears its heavy, rich green, rough foliage in summer, or pale then bright yellow leaves in autumn. The fruit is copiously borne after some 20 years and would be more effective if all were the same bright red but, over a long period, a proportion are deep red then black when they fall. Delicious to eat when fully ripe black, the fruit attract birds and a mown lawn or hard surface beneath the tree becomes messy. This detracts somewhat from its value in a courtyard but it is a fine foliage subject in long grass or a shrub bed.

Cultivation Mulberries grow well on any reasonable well-drained soil. Their main requirement is full sun.

Other species The White mulberry (*Morus alba* L.) from China is the one preferred by silkworms. It has glossy, quite smooth leaves that are more given to fancy lobing than those of the Black mulberry, but is not so hardy. It really needs hotter summers and is exceptionally liable to damage so cannot be recommended. Unlike the Black mulberry, however, it has some interesting forms, such as 'Pendula' which makes a mound of steeply pendulous shoots.

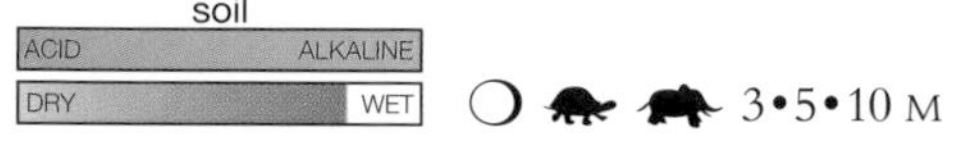

MORUS NIGRA (below). Its delicious red-ageing-to-black fruit are produced with maturity and will attract both bird and human interest.

Nothofagus/
Southern beeches

THESE SOUTHERN HEMISPHERE trees provide some fast-growing specimens, both evergreen and deciduous, in Britain. They are attractive in foliage – the deciduous sorts colour in autumn – and bear male and female flowers separately on the same plant. These are small, but can be conspicuous *en masse.*

Cultivation Southern beeches prefer a moist but well-drained soil in sun or partial shade and are generally at their best situated in woodland among other trees, in areas of high rainfall. Unlike the true beeches (*Fagus*) they do not grow well on dry, chalky soils.

NOTHOFAGUS ANTARCTICA (FORST. F .) OERST.

ANTARCTIC BEECH; CHILE. DECIDUOUS.

As befits a tree which ranges south into Tierra del Fuego, this is absolutely hardy anywhere. However, it looks delicate because of its sparse, branching carrying-systems of short fine shoots and tiny leaves and because the crown often bends out to one side. There are often shoots 1 m or more long in the second year from planting but this rate of growth does not last and few trees exceed 15 m in height, while many end up as shrubs. In most trees the bark is very soon rough and fissured into grey-brown, flaking plates but in a few it remains dark red with shiny, smooth areas between bands of lenticels. In winter, therefore, although the tree is very bare-looking and a wandering rather than a positive decisive shape, there is an attractive look about it. It is even better as the leaves unfold a shiny, bright green. Only 3 cm long, they are crinkled by four pairs of veins and become deep green, and still shiny, then yellow and pale brown in autumn. They have irregular, shallow toothing.

NOTHOFAGUS ANTARCTICA (far right) Small in both leaf and stature, this southern beech produces a distinctive leaning shape with age.

NOTHOFAGUS DOMBEYI (below). This ultra hardy southern beech is the perhaps the most suitable evergreen tree in both habit and size for general landscape planting.

N. DOMBEYI (MIRBEL) BLUME

COIGUE, DOMBEY'S SOUTHERN BEECH; CHILE, ARGENTINA. EVERGREEN.

This Chilean tree is the best hardy evergreen *Nothofagus* and remarkably vigorous: it has reached 25 m in less than 50 years. The bark of young trees is dark grey and smooth but horizontally wrinkled. Older trees have rich brown and red-brown plates and strips. The slender shoots bear irregularly toothed, oval, 3–4 cm leaves. These are hard and shiny blackish-green with smooth, matt, veinless undersides. The Coigue is unusual among evergreen trees in Britain in having such small foliage and reaching such a size. The smallness of the leaves prevents the big blackish crown from being oppressive and makes this beech a grand specimen tree. Planted in groups, it would be too dark.

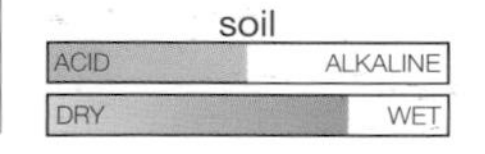

5•10•30 M

NOTHOFAGUS FUSCA (HOOK. F.) OERST.

RED BEECH; NEW ZEALAND. SEMI-EVERGREEN.

This semi-evergreen New Zealand tree is remarkably hardy and grows in Edinburgh, but is best in milder gardens. For much of the year some of its leaves colour yellow and dark red, preparatory to being shed, and this livens up the rather sparse crown of dull, pale green younger leaves. The leaves are thin and papery, 4 x 2 cm, with a few big in-curved teeth on each side, and are unlike those of any other tree grown in Britain.

N. NERVOSA (PHIL.) DIM. & MIL. (*N. PROCERA* (POEPP. & ENDL.) OERST.)

RAULI; CHILE, ARGENTINA. DECIDUOUS.

Except on very acid or alkaline soils, those that are very dry and in some exposed, cold places, the Rauli is superior to the Roble beech (*N. obliqua*) as a specimen. At its best in areas of high rainfall, it is a superb tree and has reached 30 m tall at Brodick Castle on Arran. Many young plants add shoots 1.5–2 m long and one was 15 m in nine years from seed. Its form is very different from that of the roble, as it rapidly grows a stout bole with strong upswept branches and stout spreading shoots. Its leaves, the best of the deciduous southern beeches, are prominently marked by 15–22 parallel straight veins on each side of the midrib and are up to 10 cm long. They open orange-brown from the bud early in spring, then turn fresh light green and become darker and grey-green in late summer. In autumn they turn yellow and pale orange with some dark red leaves.

On any loamy or not too dry sandy soil, in a little shelter, the Rauli makes an imposing specimen more quickly than any but a few eucalypts and willows. In a damp, sheltered site it will go on to become a very big tree, some 25 m tall in 40 years.

N. OBLIQUA (MIRBEL) BLUME

ROBLE BEECH; CHILE, ARGENTINA. DECIDUOUS.

This is a tree of remarkable vigour even on poor sandy soils, where it does better than the Rauli (*N. nervosa*).

NOTHOFAGUS FUSCA (top left). Distinct in leaf, this is one of the easiest southern beeches to identify with the conspicuous, occasionally large, in-curved teeth.

NOTHOFAGUS NERVOSA (above). This tree was once tested in England as a timber tree due to its incredible straight growth; it will often surpass the tallest gums in stature.

NOTHOFAGUS OBLIQUA (above and right). Dark green foliage in summer becomes yellow, orange, and crimson before falling. Unfortunately, this tree is susceptible to storm damage when larger, although it can be protected by planting in mixed stands.

Leading shoots of 1.3 m are seen and the Roble has reached 26 m in 22 years. Specimens over 30 m are rare, largely because the branches are usually weak and tall trees are liable to breakage high in the crown. There are few that are older than 40 years but many trees have been planted since 1950 and there are some – mainly experimental – small forest plantations.

Slender shoots spray out at a sharp downward angle from the upper crown and taper regularly in outline as the straight laterals, close and parallel, decrease in length towards their tips. The leaves are oblong-elliptic and 5–8 cm long with 7–11 pairs of impressed parallel veins and sharp, irregular toothing. Dark green in summer, they turn yellow, orange and crimson before falling. The Roble is easily distinguished from the rauli by the number of veins in its leaves.

N. SOLANDERI (HOOK. F.) OERST.

BLACK BEECH; NEW ZEALAND. EVERGREEN.

Together with the following form, this is the only evergreen southern beech with entire leaves. Both are strange trees with small, slender branches that arch out maybe 1 m apart, with a shallow layer of dense twiglets and tiny 1 cm leaves above each branch, and boles with smooth, blackish ribs. The Black beech is very vigorous in the west but less so in the east. The biggest, at Benmore, Argyll, is 20 x 0.8 m.

Variant var. *cliffortioides* (Hook. f.) Poole, the Mountain beech, differs only in that its equally small leaves, are buckled, and it is hardy almost anywhere.

soil
ACID ALKALINE
DRY WET
6•12•20 M

NOTHOFAGUS SOLANDERI var. *CLIFFORTIOIDES* (far right).
This hardy, vigorous tree has dainty, fern-like foliage.

Nyssa sylvatica Marsh.

TUPELO, BLACK GUM; E NORTH AMERICA. DECIDUOUS.

The Tupelo is grown entirely for its autumn colour. The glossy leaves, 5–18 cm in length and equally variable in width from lanceolate to broad elliptic, retain their high gloss as they turn gold, after which the outer leaves turn through orange to scarlet. It is then at its distinctive best, but later the whole crown is scarlet and dark red. On some trees, and in some autumns, shades of orange are as far as the leaves will go but they are still a fine sight.

The major planting of Tupelo in Europe was the one at Sheffield Park in Sussex, where 400 were planted in 1909, but many were lost in the gales in 1987. 'Sheffield Park', which colours a brilliant orange-red reliably and early in the season, came from there.

Cultivation The best trees are generally seen in areas with hot summers on a good, deep, not too dry, acid soil. The Tupelo is usually slow-growing at first and the early years should be tolerated for it has a long, healthy life and in sunny autumns will be the most spectacular plant in the garden.

Other species Chinese tupelo (*N. sinensis* Oliver) is similar but rare in gardens. Its leaves are larger than those of the Tupelo, up to 20 cm long, and it gives at least as good autumn colours of orange, red and yellow.

NYSSA SYLVATICA (left). Grown entirely for its reliable autumn colour of a brilliant orange-red, leaves change early in the season.

Ostrya carpinifolia Scop.

European Hop-hornbeam; S Europe, W Asia. Deciduous.

This is included entirely for its unusual appearance in summer when the crown of dark, quite handsome foliage is varied by white fruit clusters – 5 cm broad-cylindric bunches of bladders like a big hop fruit. Otherwise it is rather a dull tree with a broad crown from level branches low on the fissured and flaky brown bole. The leaves, which are good at close quarters, are 10 x 5 cm ovate with about 15 mostly parallel pairs of veins to very sharp teeth; there are smaller teeth between those at the vein-ends.

Cultivation Grow the European hop-hornbeam on any good, well-drained soil. Because it is a woodland tree it will stand a good deal of shade as well as full sun.

soil
ACID ALKALINE
DRY WET
5•8•20 M

OSTRYA CARPINIFOLIA (below). Unusual white fruit clusters contrast sharply against handsome dark green foliage in summer.

Oxydendrum arboreum (L.) DC.

SOURWOOD, SORREL-TREE; E NORTH AMERICA. DECIDUOUS.

Where it can be grown well, this is worth planting where a small tree is required because of its unusual combination of autumn colour and flowers. Although slow-growing, it may flower well when only a few years old. The leaves are oblong-elliptic, acute and finely serrated, and are deep glossy green above and smooth, greyish-green beneath with only the midrib showing white. In autumn they turn scarlet then deep red but, like the Tupelo (*Nyssa sylvatica*), they need full sun if this is to happen in Britain. In their native woods they colour brilliantly beneath quite a dense canopy.

The flowers are a feature and spray down at a slight angle from the branch-ends on slender 25 cm panicles, each with about six branches. Each flower is a tiny pendulous white urn and they open over a long period from midsummer. Since the fruit are almost the same colour – ivory-white until they go woody – the tree seems to be, and probably partly is, in flower when in full autumn colour. The bark soon fissures into dull grey ridges and the crown becomes an open dome on ascending, twisting branches.

In a small planting, it warrants a fairly prominent position and must be unshaded. On a larger scale, it must be planted in groups if it is to have much effect, particularly as it grows slowly.

Cultivation The Sourwood is a member of the great Rhododendron family, *Ericaceae*, and it is therefore not unexpected that, unlike most of the trees grown in Britain, it really does need a moist acid soil and cannot tolerate any lime. Given these conditions it will grow on even poor soils, but needs full sun to colour well.

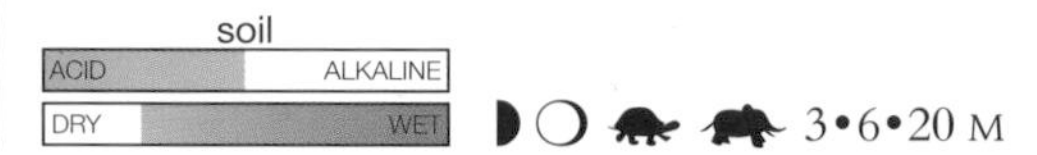

OXYDENDRUM ARBOREUM (left). Suitable only for acid soils, the sourwood turns scarlet red in autumn, in stark contrast to the ripening white fruits.

PARROTIA PERSICA (right). Shedding bark, brilliant autumn colour, and interesting winter flowers, make this a highly ornamental tree.

Parrotia persica (DC.) C.A. Meyer

PERSIAN IRONWOOD; CAUCASUS, N IRAN.

This is often no more than a tall, wide-spreading bush, but it can make a bole 2–3 m long that shows the mottled brown, flaking, plane-like bark well. As a garden tree the Persian ironwood is planted for autumn colour, but it would make more of a show if the upper crown of long, shallowly arched branches did not colour and shed before the rest of the crown has properly started. The thick, wavy-edged leaves broaden from the base to near the tip. They are a lush, dark green until some turn yellow in early autumn. By mid-autumn they have become orange and then crimson and dark red and the top branches are bare.

The flowers are little bunches of dark red stamens which often open in January. However, their value is diminished because they are small and inconspicuous. Winter flowers are most appreciated near a much-used path or near buildings, but these are not usually the best places for this plant at other times of the year.

It is very effective when planted in groups, but these can only be accommodated in large gardens.

Cultivation The Persian ironwood grows best on a good, deep, moist but well-drained, neutral to acid soil. It is shade-tolerant, but colours best in a reasonably sunny position.

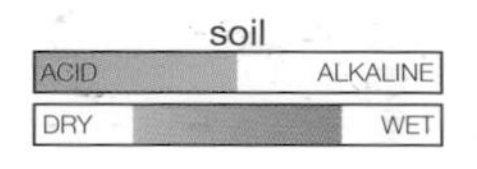

5•8•10 M

Paulownia tomentosa (Thunb.) Steud.

Empress tree; China. Deciduous.

Bold in foliage and flower, this is a striking tree when well sited. The leaves of an adult tree are hugely long – up to 40 cm – triangular, entire and cordate and are softly white pubescent all over on 10–15 cm pinkish and densely pubescent petioles. With its smooth, grey or purple-grey bark and a good cylindric bole, this makes an attractive foliage tree.

The flowers are on panicles which are prominent in winter as orange pubescent buds. These survive cold winters but can be killed in spring if a sharp frost follows a mild spell during which they begin to open. In Britain the panicles are 20–30 cm long and each carries 15–20 flowers, but in hot climates they are 40 cm in length with far more flowers, and are much more numerous. The flowers open in late spring before the leaves emerge and are trumpet-shaped, 6 cm long and violet-blue or pale purple. They ripen to shiny green, later brown, globular, beaked and horribly sticky 3 cm fruit.

Cultivation The Empress tree needs the warmest summers it can have in Britain if it is to grow well and flower abundantly, so is largely restricted to areas which provide these. It needs shelter in order to grow tall as its branches are brittle, but it also needs full sun to flower well.

As the flowers are terminal they are mostly above the crown, and it is not easy to see them from beneath the tree. It should therefore be positioned on the lower slopes of a bank with a prospect from above.

The Empress tree should ideally be planted out at the end of its first year from seed, when it may be 50 cm tall, and cut back late in spring to a basal bud. If this is done it should grow a rod to 2.5 m long that carries great broad leaves, 45–50 cm each way, with several shallow, triangular lobes. If the first-year cutting back is omitted it should be done on trees planted out two, three or many years previously since they will not have made strong straight growth if left uncut. Because the tree grows on through the summer, nearly into October, the tip of the shoot cannot be hardened against winter frosts and always dies back. New growth starts from one or two whorls of paired buds some way below the tip, and to ensure a longer bole the strongest must be selected and the others cut out. After cutting back, the foliage on the one-year shoot is so luxuriant that the plant can be grown just for its leaves, especially in cooler areas where it cannot be expected to be a good flowering tree. In this case, two or three rods can be left and cut down each spring.

soil
ACID ALKALINE
DRY WET
8•15•15 M

PAULOWNIA TOMENTOSA (left). Beautiful for its large, lilac flowers and bold foliage, this is the only woody member of the foxglove family.

Phellodendron amurense Rupr.

AMUR CORK TREE; N CHINA. DECIDUOUS.

PHELLODENDRON AMURENSE (below). Conspicuous yellow flowers are followed by black aromatic fruits, before the leaflets turn golden yellow in autumn.

Although this fast-growing member of the Citrus family is very hardy, it needs hot summers to thrive and so is only seen at its best in sunnier gardens. It gets its name from the thick corky bark which develops with age. Its bold leaves are divided into up to 13 glossy dark green leaflets and turn yellow in autumn before they fall. The flowers are small individually but are borne in large clusters and, with their yellow anthers, can be quite conspicuous in midsummer. They ripen to green, finally black, aromatic berries which are carried in dense clusters.

Cultivation Grow the Amur cork tree on good, well-drained soil, in full sun.

soil
ACID ALKALINE
DRY WET
5•8•15 M

PHOTINIA SERRATIFOLIA (above). Bright red shiny growth is sometimes damaged by late frosts.

PHOTINIA VILLOSA f. *MAXIMOWICZIANA* (above left). Clusters of hawthorn-like flowers in late spring are followed by small, glossy, red berries in autumn.

PHOTINIA X *FRASERI* 'ROBUSTA' (left). Bronzy young foliage, turns to red before fading to dark, glossy green; this effect can be encouraged by annual pruning.

Photinia

TOO INFREQUENTLY SEEN in gardens, except as shrubs or hedges, some of the deciduous and evergreen species in this genus related to the hawthorns (*Crataegus*) will make respectable trees. The evergreens are valuable for their bold foliage while deciduous species give good flowers, fruit and autumn colour.

Cultivation Deciduous Photinias need a lime-free soil, while evergreens are happy on most soils.

PHOTINIA SERRATIFOLIA (DESF.) KALKMAN (*P. SERRULATA* LINDLEY)

CHINA. EVERGREEN.

This splendid small tree, now sadly mostly replaced by its hybrids, is at its most striking in spring when the young foliage emerges. It is very variable but the best forms have bright red young growths. The growth can emerge so early in the year that it is sometimes damaged by late frosts. Mature plants have red-brown bark that peels in flakes and bear plate-sized heads of small white flowers in early summer. These can be followed by long-persistent red berries.

Other species The hybrid of *P. serratifolia* with the shrubby *P. glabra* (Thunb.) Maxim. is known as *P.* x *fraseri* Dress and is grown in three forms – 'Birmingham', 'Red Robin' and 'Robusta' – for their bronzy young foliage. All can reach tree-like proportions with age.

P. VILLOSA (THUNB.) DC.

CHINA, JAPAN, KOREA. DECIDUOUS.

This very variable species is grown in several forms. It is typically seen as a small, spreading tree with bronze-red young leaves, which has clusters of hawthorn-like flowers in late spring. Its finest moment, however, is in autumn when the leaves turn to brilliant orange and red and the small, glossy red berries ripen. A variant of this, f. *maximowicziana* (Levl.) Rehder, also distributed as *P. koreana*, is very distinctive, and more shrubby, with arching branches and deeply veined leaves that turn orange-yellow in autumn.

PICEA ABIES 'CUPRESSINA' (above), is a very unusual form of Norway spruce found in Germany before 1904 and which should be more widely planted. It is very dense and narrowly conical with upright branches and can reach 20 m tall.

PICEA BRACHYTYLA (far right). A fine and vigorous tree, this has perhaps the most stunning foliage of any of the spruces.

PICEA ABIES 'CRANSTONII' (below). Large, conspicuous, conical cones hang firm from long drooping, unbranched stems.

Picea/Spruces

THESE EVERGREEN CONIFERS ARE mainly fast-growing and hardy. They are superficially similar to the firs (*Abies*) but differ in that their needle-like leaves are borne on short woody pegs which remain after the leaves have fallen and make the shoots rough to the touch. They also have pendulous rather than upright cones which fall intact. While several species are really only suited to forestry others are highly ornamental. Male and female flower clusters are borne separately on the same tree and the females are often very conspicuous in spring before they develop into cones.

Cultivation Spruces will grow on most soils except those that are very dry and alkaline, and should be given full sun. They are generally at their best planted among the shelter of other trees and the largest specimens of most species are in areas of high rainfall.

PICEA ABIES (L.) KARST.

NORWAY SPRUCE; EUROPE. EVERGREEN.

Among the first conifers to be introduced in Britain, this is very common but not inspiring. It can be a background tree if it is used in moderation in a broad coniferous landscape but it becomes progressively less attractive with age and is not very wind-firm. Many are grown on from Christmas trees, most of them absurdly planted in a shady corner or a tiny suburban garden. Properly placed, the Norway spruce will grow 1 m a year

and is quite a bright green but of coarse growth. There are several preferable species for ornamental purposes.

Variants The Norway spruce is mainly represented in gardens by numerous dwarf forms. One of the most striking of the larger-growing forms is 'Cranstonii' which has long, drooping, mainly unbranched shoots.

P. BRACHYTYLA (FRANCH.) PRITZ

SARGENT SPRUCE; CHINA. EVERGREEN.

Seeds from this spruce were first sent to Britain from western China in 1901 and there were three or four more batches from different regions during the next decade. There are several forms from the different seed-lots. The best is a very fine and vigorous tree, with an open crown of slender branches on a pale grey bole and perhaps the most beautiful foliage of all the spruces. The leaves are abruptly spine-tipped, hard and pressed forward over white shoots: they are bright light green above and so solidly silver-white beneath that the normally green midrib between the two white bands is silvered right across.

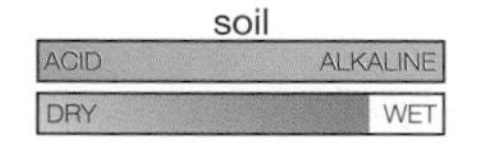

PICEA BREWERIANA (far left). Avoid grafted plants to achieve graceful, balanced specimens

PICEA BREWERIANA WATS.

BREWER SPRUCE; CALIFORNIA, OREGON. EVERGREEN.

Confined in the wild to a few small groves perched at around 2000 m on shelves in the Siskiyou Mountains, the Brewer spruce is a much sought-after lawn specimen. It is a remarkable sight when well-grown and not in shade: broad-columnar with up-curved branches from which hang long curtains of dark foliage. If seedling trees can be obtained they should always be grown. These will grow slowly and uninterestingly for 10–15 years but after that will be faster and start to show their characteristic weeping habit. Although grafted trees are much more attractive when young they make leaning, slow, one-sided plants of no beauty. Brewer spruces are superb in some gardens over chalk, but do need a damp soil and some side-shelter for their best growth: given this, they thrive anywhere except in a city park where they will grow but are thin and ineffective.

P. JEZOENSIS (SIEBOLD & ZUCC.) CARR. VAR. *HONDOENSIS* (MAYR) P. SCHMIDT

HONDO SPRUCE; JAPAN. EVERGREEN.

The Japanese variety of *P. jezoensis* is the hardy tree grown in many collections and gardens. The Hondo spruce is a broad conic tree and its outstanding feature is its bold foliage. The stout shoots are white turning cream, and the 1.5 cm leaves are densely set on each side above them; there are none below. The leaves are deep or bright shining green above and broadly banded, bright slightly bluish-white beneath. This white flashes out as the shoots move to show the close ranks of leaf-undersides.

P. LIKIANGENSIS (FRANCH.) PRITZ

LIKIANG SPRUCE; W CHINA. EVERGREEN.

Like the Sargent spruce, this was sent from several different areas of western China in differing forms – from 1910 to 1930. The Likiang spruce is among the most striking conifers in flower, when masses of crimson male flowers and bright red females stand out from the dark blue-grey foliage in spring. The females develop

PICEA JEZOENSIS var. *HONDOENSIS* (far left). The hondo spruce is grown for its bold foliage and attractive habit.

PICEA BALFOURIANA (left), is similar to *P. likiangensis* but makes a narrower tree with purple young cones and longer blue-grey leaves.

PICEA OMORIKA (above), has a decorative weeping habit.

PICEA ORIENTALIS 'AUREA' (below right). Slender new shoots pour out bright gold over the dense crown, before fading to dark green with age.

PICEA ORIENTALIS (below), is more attractive in habit than the Norway spruce, both as a garden tree and as a Christmas tree.

into equally profuse cones 10 cm long. The crown is very open on strong branches that ascend at a low angle from the bole. The bark is pale grey with a few black fissures. The foliage is a dense fringe on the outside of the crown; grey pubescent shoots bear flattened leaves that are blue-grey above and white-banded beneath.It needs acid, moist soil, but does not mind underlying limestone provided this is well below ground level.

Other species *P. balfouriana*.

soil
ACID ALKALINE
DRY WET 6•12•20 M

P. OMORIKA (PANCIC) PURKYNE

SERBIAN SPRUCE; BOSNIA, SERBIA.

One of the most useful and decorative of the conifers, this tree grows fast on any soil from limestone to deep peat. It varies somewhat in the slenderness of its crown but is always narrow-spired and compact: even the tallest is only 4 m through. The flat leaves are rich deep green above and broadly banded bright blue-white beneath. It is one of the best conifers in towns as it casts little shade and copes with poor soils. The many merits of Serbian spruce make it the more sad that it is often seen dead or dying. In many collections, trees that were 20 m tall and rather thin in 1970 were found dead in 1981 or had already died and been removed. It is known to be highly susceptible to honey fungus, which is inevitably present in all woodland areas, but there is little risk from this in long-established gardens in towns. It is a normal hazard in the country and sometimes kills young plants.

P. ORIENTALIS (L.) LINK

ORIENTAL SPRUCE; CAUCASUS, N TURKEY. EVERGREEN.

This is far preferable to the Norway spruce (*P. abies*), even as a Christmas tree. Its shoots are more slender and are arranged most symmetrically in a spire of whorls of decreasing length, and its leaves are shorter and held much closer so they don't snag the loops of Christmas decorations. As a specimen tree it is as vigorous as the Norway spruce and more tidy, with tiny, bevel-tipped, dark glossy leaves. It is still a neat, conic tree when 30 m tall, but is very slow-growing by then and has a tendency to die back at the top.

Variant In summer 'Aurea' can be distinguished only by the odd leaf that retains some yellow, but in May or early June it is briefly superb. Slender new shoots pour out bright gold all over the dense, dark and shapely crown and contrast with the old foliage.

PICEA PUNGENS ENGELM.

COLORADO SPRUCE; W UNITED STATES. EVERGREEN.

In the wild the Colorado spruce varies in foliage colour from dark green to bluish. The most commonly grown forms are those now called Glauca Group, selected from the wild and grown in a garden at Harvard, Massachusetts. Shoots were brought by Anthony Waterer to his nursery at Knaphill in 1877. It makes quite a robust, fairly narrow conic tree with level branches and rigid upstanding leaves which are blue-grey on both sides on stout orange or brown shoots. It is very hardy and withstands heat and drought but outside cool damp regions it loses its decorative value with age: it sheds leaves when they are only two years old and so becomes twiggy and thin, often due to a profusion of green spruce aphid. It is therefore fine for small-scale plantings where it can be removed when it outgrows other small trees, at about which time it will be starting to deteriorate. In more favourable sites it is well-furnished and highly attractive and is a very good specimen tree.

Variants Several forms have been selected in gardens for the intensity of their foliage colour. 'Hoopsii' is so startlingly blue-white that it must be mentioned although it has been seen so far mostly in the USA where some specimens are bushy conic plants that grow to 3 m and may qualify as trees one day. It is now available in Britain. 'Koster' is seen most frequently but several similar forms may be grown under this name. Its shoots are purple, brown or orange and its leaves are bright blue-white, although not as strikingly so as 'Hoopsii'. It grows slowly, and few trees are yet 20 m tall.

PICEA PUNGENS 'KOSTER' (above). New, striking blue-white foliage contrasts dramatically with old leaves. This is the most popular form of the blue spruce

soil
ACID ALKALINE
DRY WET
3•6•25 M

PICEA PUNGENS 'HOOPSII' (left) is an excellent, slow growing form with startling blue foliage and an attractive habit.

P. SITCHENSIS (BONG.) CARR.

SITKA SPRUCE; W NORTH AMERICA. EVERGREEN.

This is the standard species for maximum timber production in all western mountainous areas of run-down peaty soils in Britain, and no other conifer has ever been found to challenge it. The wavy leading shoots can be 1.5 m long and whole hillsides of 1 m leaders project from hitherto barren slopes swept by sea winds. It obviously has great value for shelter in some exposed places where other trees are hard to grow. It is, however, strictly for areas of cool summers and high rainfall and only reaches its largest size there. Anywhere else it will be thin and poor, except in the occasional spring-fed dell. Only the Sequoias are in the same class as monumental specimen trees of great height that keep a conic top and are wind-firm. As a young tree, shooting upwards, it is a little open and gawky at the top but the lower crown is better covered and the dark blue foliage, bright white beneath, is attractive.

Large gardens in the areas specified should make room for a specimen somewhere, probably at their edge. A small group will be a feature in extensive gardens and parks. In the Scone Palace Pinetum near Perth a square of four was planted in 1851 with a side of about 30 m. Now almost uniformly 45 m tall and 1.9 m through, they are a stirring sight. The foolish prejudice against this tree should be forgotten. Forests of Sitka spruce thrive bursting with promise, where few trees will grow. Any tree in full vigour, growing more than 1 m every year, would be pleasing to see, even were the foliage not as lovely as that of the soft, dark-blue Sitka. How fortunate that it produces timber so fast and that Britain's forests, more productive than any others in the world on the same latitudes, look so well in the process.

PICEA SITCHENSIS (right), although more widely planted as a timber tree, the bold shape and foliage make this tree hard to surpass in the landscape.

P. SMITHIANA (WALLICH) BOISS.

MORINDA SPRUCE; W HIMALAYAS. EVERGREEN.

This could be regarded as a giant Brewer spruce (*P. breweriana*), although it weeps in a much less exaggerated way when young. The foliage differs from that of the flat-leafed Brewer spruce in that the slender, dark green leaves, which are up to 4 cm long, are nearly square in cross-section. They spread all round pale-coloured, stout shoots and, with the Morinda's vigorous early growth, make it a superior specimen to the Brewer for at least 20 years. Given a damp woodland soil, it starts well even in drier warmer parts but will eventually become thin in the struggle to stay alive, and slowly die. In areas of high rainfall it remains well furnished and weeps more with age.

PICEA SMITHIANA (right). This delightful, pendulous tree grows best in areas of high rainfall.

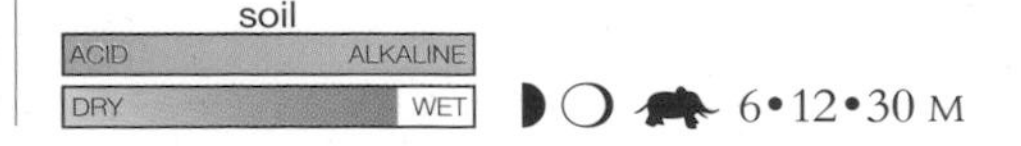

Picrasma quassioides (D. Don) Bennett

QUASSIA TREE; E ASIA. DECIDUOUS.

PICRASMA QUASSIOIDES (above). A small tree with ash-like foliage, the quassia tree is especially showy in the autumn.

This little tree is rare in gardens but adds distinction to a planting with its foliage, fruit and, particularly, its autumn colours. Its leaves are rather like those of an Ash (*Fraxinus*) with 11 broad-ovate leaflets but are glossy, rich green on crimson central stalks. They turn yellow and bright red in autumn, when there may also be numerous flattish heads of tiny berries, orange-red turning black. These arise from little, yellow-green, four-petalled flowers. Winter interest is added by dark purple-brown shoots with scarlet buds.

Cultivation Grow the Quassia tree in a not too dry, lime-free soil in sun or partial shade. It is particularly good positioned among other small trees.

soil
ACID ALKALINE
DRY WET
3•5•10 M

Pinus/Pines

THE PINES ARE evergreen conifers which are distinctive in that all their foliage, except on seedlings, is borne in bundles on short shoots. These bundles usually consist of two, three or five needle-like leaves. While there are shrubby species, those that make trees are conical, at least when young, and sometimes broaden with age. Cones are a characteristic feature and are ornamental in many species. Sometimes, as on pines with three needles, they are retained on the tree for many years.

Cultivation Most pines are very adaptable and require only a well-drained soil in full sun. Those with five needles are generally not satisfactory on very shallow chalk soils. All are best planted as young trees.

PINUS AYACAHUITE EHRENB. ex SCHLDL.

MEXICAN WHITE PINE; MEXICO, C AMERICA. EVERGREEN.

This five-needled pine is one of the trees that was introduced in Britain by Theodor Hartweg as a result of his first tour of Mexico in 1839–1840. As a foliage pine with blue needles it is particularly attractive when it bears its cones as a young tree. These are freely borne from the age of about 20, on stout 2 cm stalks. They are long, tapering almost from the base to a narrow apex and are heavy, firm and leathery, then become woody. They are bright blue-green for a year then turn pale orange and are much daubed with resin. A few trees bear cones only 15 cm long but 25–30 cm ones are more usual and 40 cm may be seen in var. *veitchii* (Roezl) Shaw. The scales around the stalks are strongly reflexed and the remainder are generally straight, pointing somewhat outwards However, all the scales are reflexed in some of the bigger cones.

The Mexican white pine grows very vigorously for many years on acid soils in good drainage and has a conic crown that is broad at the base for the first 30 years, and long, level but sinuous branches. In older trees these may be shed and the upper crown can be a shapely, narrow and dense cone. On less acid loam or clay, the tree's growth rate falls earlier and its life span is shorter. In either case a measure of shelter is of great benefit. The shoot is pale brownish-green, thinly covered with fine pale pubescence, and is more slender than the stout, blue-white bloomed, glabrous shoot of the Himalayan pine (*P. wallichiana*). The needles are also shorter, about 15 cm.

soil

ACID ALKALINE

DRY WET

6•12•25 M

PINUS AYACAHUITE var. *VEITCHII* (below). This variety of *P. ayacahuite* bears the longest cones. It also has needles which are an attractive blue-green in colour.

PINUS BUNGEANA (far left). Grown mainly for its striking bark, this tree is best cultivated as a multi-stemmed specimen.

PINUS BUNGEANA ZUCC. ex ENDL.

LACEBARK PINE; N CHINA. EVERGREEN.

'Lacebark' is not a good description of this tree at any stage but at least it calls attention to the feature for which it is grown. The bark is mottled with pale patches from shed scales almost from the start and becomes more colourful with age until a clean bole, 30 cm through, has a smooth background of blue-grey or pink, with patches of yellow, brown, red-brown or dark purple-red where scales have been shed. The crown has many nearly erect, straight slender branches and may be an ovoid pointed bush or variously conic. The foliage is good; the rich, dark, shiny green leaves are in threes and are sparsely borne, but each bundle is closely held together on smooth olive or grey-green shoots with short, curved lateral shoots that spread perpendicularly. It is so attractive and unusual that it is an ornament to any group of small trees or large shrubs.

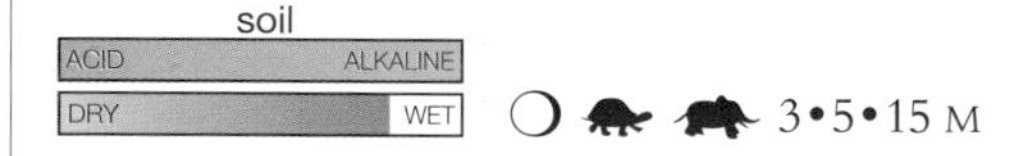

P. CEMBRA L.

AROLLA PINE, SWISS STONE PINE; ALPS OF EUROPE. EVERGREEN.

The Arolla pine is a snow-line tree in the Alps where it is planted to control avalanches. It grows at only about 30 cm a year but even when old can have a conic top to its neatly columnar crown with short, level branches.

PINUS CEMBRA 'JERMYNS' (left), is a slow growing and bushy form of the Arolla pine with good blue foliage, but is usually shrubby.

Needles, in bundles of five, densely cover the thickly hairy, orange-brown shoots. Blackish from a distance, they are dark shiny green on the outer surfaces and blue-white on the inner. The tree has to be some 40 years old to fruit, if it does so at all, and the cones, which are borne near its top, are squat-cylindric, 8 x 6 cm and deep blue when young. The Arolla pine is a neat, tough tree which is able to grow above chalk or in peat or poor sands.

soil
ACID ALKALINE
DRY WET 3•6•25 M

P. COULTERI D. DON

COULTER PINE, BIG-CONE PINE; CALIFORNIA.

This pine was sent to Britain by David Douglas in 1832 and, as all the original trees have died, it does not appear to be long-lived. It grows very rapidly and is gaunt for some years with a 1 m leading shoot, but soon makes a broad conic crown that is open but well-furnished on the outside. Apart from its early robust growth its appeal lies in both its foliage and its cones. The stout, blue-white shoots bear stiff grey needles, 25–30 cm long, in bunches of five around their tips. From about the tenth year the Coulter bears the most massive cones of any tree. These are sporadic at first, become more numerous with age, and are long-ovoid and pale shiny brown, with each scale ending in a broad-based, up-curved, stout but exceedingly sharp spine. Each cone may weigh 2 kg and be 35 cm long. This tree can be grown anywhere in the southern half of the British Isles on well-drained neutral or acid soils. It makes a bold foliage specimen.

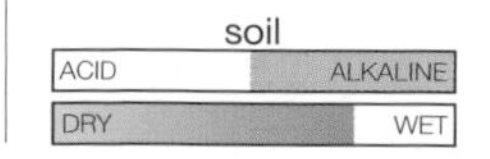

PINUS COULTERI (below). Although seldom long lived, this must have the largest and heaviest cones of any pine. Luckily, they stay attached for many years.

PINUS DENSIFLORA (right), a sacred tree in Korea with an uncanny resemblance to our Scots pine, it has familiar dark red, scaly bark, and a shapely habit.

P. DENSIFLORA SIEBOLD & ZUCC.

JAPANESE RED PINE; JAPAN, KOREA. EVERGREEN.

This makes an attractive young tree with slender, dark green, paired needles on slender, bright green shoots. It is a pleasant variation on the Scots pine (*P. sylvestris*) which it resembles in cone and dark red scaly bark, but is better furnished and more shapely with its narrow-conic, deep green crown.

Variants 'Aurea' is uncommon but young plants are exceptionally bright gold and neat. 'Umbraculifera' makes an upright bush on a 20 cm bole and may slowly achieve 8 m. Its bark is prominent because of the open crown and half-dozen or so stems and is bright orange-red with patches of dark brown scales.

soil
ACID ALKALINE
DRY WET
5•10•20 M

PINUS X HOLFORDIANA A.B. JACKSON

HOLFORD PINE, WESTONBIRT HYBRID PINE; CULTIVATED ORIGIN.

At Westonbirt in Gloucestershire, Sir George Holford extracted seeds in 1904 from the extra-large cones that distinguish Veitch's form of the Mexican white pine, *P. ayacahuite* var. *veitchii*. Some of the plants raised were given to friends while others were planted in 1908 in four groups, three in the arboretum and one in Silk Wood at Westonbirt. When these first coned, 20 years later, it was seen that they were hybrids with some features of the Himalayan pine (*P. wallichiana*), a specimen of which had been growing behind the Mexican white pine at that time.

The Holford pine is very vigorous, and makes a broad-based conic crown with long, level wandering lower branches and an upswept narrow top. The bole is often curved at the base and has orange-brown scaly bark. It is best to clean the bole of branches as soon as possible. The needles hang 15 cm long in bundles of five from shoots that are pale green and covered in fine buff hairs. Cones can be 30 cm long and are cylindric, tapered to the tip. They are orange and become dark brown and very resinous. The original trees grow on about 1 m of loam or sand above limestone and have been much depleted by losses from honey fungus.

Holford pines as found in a number of collections vary from the true form, which must be grafts or first cross seedlings from Westonbirt, to forms approaching each parent which are second generation trees raised from seeds of Holford pines.

P. JEFFREYI BALF. ex A. MURRAY

JEFFREY PINE; W UNITED STATES. EVERGREEN.

One of John Jeffrey's many fine discoveries, this pine is an exceptionally tough tree and maintains a nearly perfect, conic narrow crown until it is 30 m tall. It grows fast on any well-drained non-limy soil and makes a very handsome specimen from the start. The stout blue-bloomed shoots bear hard, 20 cm long pale blue-grey needles in threes and cylindric, acute, red-brown buds. In their first year the cones are purple-brown, big heavy ovoids 12 cm long. In their second year they are pale brown and broad ovoid with a flat base, part of which is left on the tree when the cone is shed, and open out to 20 x 15 cm. Although this tree is unlikely to flourish within a city, it is worth a trial in a town park and in any garden that needs a large, shapely pine with big cones.

soil
ACID ALKALINE
DRY WET
6•12•30 M

PINUS X HOLFORDIANA (below left). A vigorous hybrid with orange-red scaly bark, the needles hang in 15 cm long bundles.

PINUS JEFFREYI (below),is an exceptionally tough tree with blue-grey foliage and large cones.

PINUS LEUCODERMIS (above). Growing well on any well-drained soil, the Bosnian pine has bright blue cones.

P. LEUCODERMIS ANT.

BOSNIAN PINE; BALKANS. EVERGREEN.

Although botanically closely related to the Austrian pine (*P. nigra*), the Bosnian pine is quite unlike that scaly-barked, rough tree and is clean and smooth. It grows steadily on any well-drained soil, from pure chalk to strongly acid sand or peat, to make a beautifully neat and regular ovoid with upswept branches on a sturdy bole and pale grey bark that is finely cracked into squares. With age the bark becomes paler and finely fissured, and the branches smooth and grey. The shoots are bloomed pale grey then pale brown and the leaves, in pairs, are stiff, densely borne and dark green.

PINUS MONTEZUMAE (far right). With slender 30-40cm blue-grey foliage that stands upright on radiating branches, this is the most spectacular Mexican pine.

PINUS MURICATA (below). The Bishop pine is a close relative of the Monterey pine but has much stouter needles arranged in pairs.

P. MONTEZUMAE LAMB.

MONTEZUMA PINE; MEXICO. EVERGREEN.

A well-grown specimen of this Mexican tree is the most spectacular of any pine, if not of any conifer. The form that does best in Britain has a great, broad dome on level and radiating branches, with huge brushes of long, blue-grey needles thatstand straight out from stout, shining orange-brown shoots. The needles, in fives, are crowded on to the outer third of the annual shoot and are slender and 30–40 cm long. Despite the giant scale of the foliage, the cone is of no account in Britain; it is prickly and 8 cm long.

soil
ACID ALKALINE
DRY WET
6•12•20 M

P. MURICATA D. DON

BISHOP PINE; CALIFORNIA. EVERGREEN.

This tree grows in scattered relict colonies by the coast of California. The largest patch in the north includes the Pygmy Forest where soil conditions reduce the normally towering coast redwoods and Douglas firs to some 10 m in height. But not the Bishop pines. They soar – narrow, shapely and blue – to 28 m or more. In groves to the south, however, they are short, broadly domed and dark green. Theodor Hartweg sent the first seeds from a southern source to Britain in 1846 and the early trees are of this form. A later introduction from northern populations gave extremely fast-growing plants with blue-green foliage. No conifer withstands the maritime blasts on Britain's west coast as well as the Bishop pine. It has rarely been seen to scorch from salt or frost. Either the southern or northern form will rapidly provide dense outer shelter although there may be a few losses from wind blow, but for specimen trees or feature groups the blue, northern form is much to be preferred.

Bishop pine is like the closely related Monterey pine (*P. radiata*) but has its much stouter needles in pairs. It has a similar very fissured, but dark grey, bark and holds whorls of cones even more tenaciously. The cones are smaller ovoids; unlike those of Monterey pine, the scales bear strong, sharp spines so it is difficult to wrench cones from the branches. Like most south-western American pines, these are 'fire-climax' trees – dominant after fires. The cones hold viable seeds for 60 years or so and release them only when the crown of the tree is on fire. The seeds fall to the ash-enriched soil and the stand regrows. Cones picked in Britain require a spell in a warm oven if the seeds are to be extracted.

soil
ACID ALKALINE
DRY WET
8•15•25 M

PINUS NIGRA ARN.

AUSTRIAN PINE; C & S EUROPE. EVERGREEN.

The typical form of this species is a dark-foliaged and very tough tree which, although it can be straight-boled narrow, and conic, is more often heavily branched from low down with an irregular or bushy crown. The foliage is very dense with 12 cm, stiff, in-curved needles that are well bunched in close whorls on the shoots. Mixed with Sycamore (*Acer pseudoplatanus*) they are the best trees to give shelter on high, exposed ridges of chalk or limestone – but only because few other species can compete there. Elsewhere, the Austrian pine is too coarse and grimy-looking to earn a place in a garden.

Variant subsp. *laricio* (Poir.) Maire (var. *maritima* (Ait.) Melv.), Corsican pine, is the best tree for the rapid production of commercial timber on southern heathlands. It is also the best one for amenity planting, particularly in city parks on difficult soils – but not in vast numbers as it gives thin shelter and is dull *en masse*. Rather, it should be planted as a small group in a shelter-belt or, better, as a roundel or clump. Rapid growth is well maintained and occurs not only on acid sands, but also on clay, gravel, shallow peat and very shallow soil over chalk. Moreover, the tree is tailor-made for forestry, with a bole that is never crooked and rarely forked, and with light, level branches through to the persistent long conic top. Hence Corsican pine makes a splendid and shapely specimen tree almost anywhere. In addition, it can tolerate more soot and pollution than most trees, and many Midland parks and gardens once planted with a range of conifers are now dominated by Corsican (and Austrian) pines twice the size of any other survivors. Its brown shoots bear long, twisted, dark grey needles 15 cm long, in well-spread pairs that give an open, airy crown. The Corsican pine makes a sparse root system and does not transplant well. The best results come from planting three-year-old pot-grown trees in July.

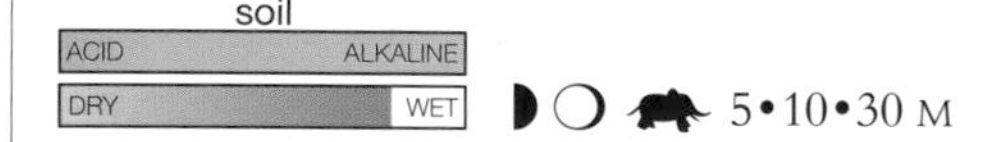

PINUS NIGRA subsp. *LARICIO* (left). Tolerating more atmospheric pollution than most trees, the Austrian pine makes a splendid specimen tree almost anywhere.

P. PARVIFLORA SIEBOLD & ZUCC.

JAPANESE WHITE PINE; JAPAN. EVERGREEN.

When Japan was first opened to collectors the available area was limited and mostly around Tokyo and Yokohama. The collectors were nurserymen and the plant-nurseries they visited were full of the huge range of extreme cultivars that Japanese gardeners had been selecting for many hundreds of years. It was only to be expected that cultivars formed a large part of the first acquisitions. The Japanese white pine is a cultivar and was sent to Britain in 1861. It was much planted and became familiar as a low, spreading tree with level branches that hold layers of very blue and white twisted needles in fives. It is well suited to Japanese-style gardens and rock-gardens and hardly exceeds 10 m in height. It bears innumerable whorls of up to four erect ovoid cones which are bright green in their first year. The wild form, however, was not sent to Britain until about 1880 and is not so often seen. It is a straight and much taller tree with lighter branches, also level, that bear layers of less twisted, much greener, needles and fewer cones.

Variants There are several selected forms, some shrubby. 'Gimborn's Ideal' makes a small tree with good blue-green foliage.

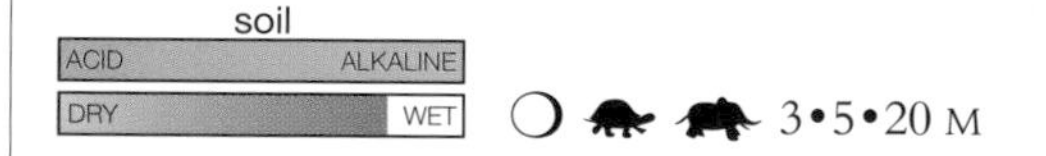

PINUS PARVIFLORA 'GIMBORN'S IDEAL' (below). This select form of the Japanese *P. parviflora* is bushy with blue-green foliage.

P. PEUCE GRISEB.

MACEDONIAN PINE; SE EUROPE. EVERGREEN.

This five-needled pine is singularly consistent and healthy. It grows at a steady rate of about 45 cm a year, whether on the richest soils and in the shelter of a Sussex garden or at 600 m on windswept mountain slopes in north Wales. Always columnar with a conic top, it makes a well-foliaged, densely crowned tree and it is very rare to see one in anything but vigorous good health. The bark, either very pale grey or purplish-grey, is shallowly divided into small squares. Fresh leaves are bright green on outer surfaces, blue-white on inner, and are densely borne in bundles of five on smooth green shoots. The cones, which are numerous on trees 20 years or more old, are slightly curved, tapered cylinders 10–15 cm long, with convex scales. This is a tree of some distinction.

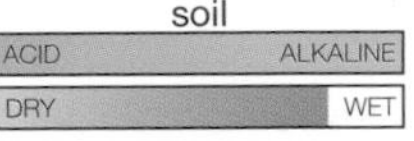

PINUS PEUCE (far right). A five-needled pine which is singularly consistent and healthy. It is rare to find it in anything but a vigorously good condition.

PINUS PINEA (below). Common in the Mediterranean region, the stone pine is perfectly hardy here. Cones contain edible pine nuts.

P. PINEA L.

STONE PINE, UMBRELLA PINE; MEDITERRANEAN REGION. EVERGREEN.

This is the pine with the wide umbrella crown and sinuous, orange, platy-barked bole that is common around the Mediterranean. Despite coming from a warmer climate, it is very hardy in Britain where it grows at least to the Scottish border in the east. It looks best as a small group in a wide open space. The seedlings are remarkably attractive for a few years when they are upright bushy plants with long, soft, flat juvenile leaves which are silvery-blue. When they are about 1.3 m high the shiny, dark grey-green adult needles begin to take over. At about 20 years the tree is almost globose on a short stem and begins to bear cones. Big, heavy and woody, these are nearly spherical, 10 x 10 cm, pale shining brown and yield edible pine nuts. A well-drained sandy soil may suit the Stone pine best but there are also good specimens on gravels and heavier soils. The male flowers are 1.3 cm long ovoids and cluster around a long basal sector of the new shoots. They are quite a good orange-brown before they shed pollen.

soil
ACID ALKALINE
DRY WET

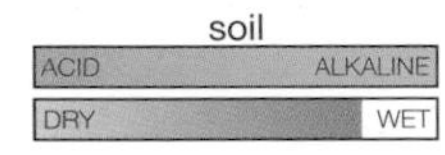

PINUS PONDEROSA LAWSON

WESTERN YELLOW PINE, PONDEROSA PINE; W NORTH AMERICA. EVERGREEN.

Mature trees of this species make grand specimens that often remain regularly conic to a single, stout leading shoot. The needles, in threes, are greyish or yellowish-green, stiff or slightly drooped and 20 cm long on stout, shiny brown shoots. The bark is sometimes black but usually develops into long pink or yellowish plates with age and is very scaly. Ponderosa pine will not grow well in limy or chalky soils but grows fast in any well-drained acid ones. Young trees with their shapely crowns and bold foliage add greatly to any group, and big specimens are full of character, with imposing boles and good crowns. The cones vary in size. At their largest they approach Jeffrey pine (*P. jeffreyi*), a close relative, but they are never so broad at the base and are usually 8 x 5 cm ovoids. As in the Jeffrey pine, each scale has a small, downward-pointing prickle. The deep purple clusters of male flowers can be striking in late spring.

P. RADIATA D. DON (*P. INSIGNIS* DOUGL. ex LOUD.)

MONTEREY PINE; CALIFORNIA. EVERGREEN.

The old name, *Pinus insignis,* means 'remarkable pine' and in some ways this is one of the most remarkable trees in the world. When confined to its native habitat – a few thousand hectares around Carmel in Monterey County and a smaller area around Cambria, 100 km to the south – the Monterey pine is generally only some 20 m tall, infested with dwarf mistletoe and short-lived. However, on an irrigated lawn in San Francisco one grew 15 m after five years. In New Zealand one was 61 m in 41 years, the youngest recorded conifer to achieve 60 m. The great domes of dense foliage, dark from a distance but bright green closer to hand, are part of the accepted scenery of Devon and Cornwall. Big rough trees are common inland in Kent, but less frequent north along the eastern side of Britain to Northumberland and Perthshire where the Monterey pine is scarce and not so big.

Young trees of good form are highly decorative – brilliant green, with regularly whorled, narrow conic crowns and very long leaders. The bark is soon very coarsely ridged, deeply fissured and scaly dark grey, heavy branches are ringed by whorls of big, thickly woody ovoid-oblique cones, and pale green slender shoots bear dense tufts of slender, bright green needles in bunches of three. On shallow soil over chalk growth will be as fast as elsewhere, but after some 30 years the foliage will become yellow and the tree will soon die. Otherwise, any well-drained soil, however sandy, gives good results.

In western coastal areas exposed to sea winds this pine is valuable for the quick provision of good shelter. In spells of freezing winds its needles may scorch brown (unlike those of the Bishop pine, *P. muricata*) but new shoots will sprout as usual the following spring. The rough, branchy aspect of so many Monterey pines does not matter in a shelter-belt by the sea, and its snaggy, bare lower crown can be hidden from the interior of a park or garden by other trees. On its own, a branchy tree will droop heavy branches and remain locally densely foliaged as a huge, apparently ancient, highly picturesque feature. If a tidier and less spreading specimen is preferred, early pruning high up the bole will usually give a splendid tree. Some gardeners may like to collect cones from one of the narrow conic trees occasionally seen, warm them until the seeds can be shaken out, and raise their own specimens.

soil
ACID ALKALINE
DRY WET
10•20•40 M

PINUS PONDEROSA (far left). Big specimens are full of character, with imposing trunks and rounded heads.

PINUS RADIATA (left). This "remarkable pine" is more at home in our gardens than it is in its native California.

PINUS SYLVESTRIS (above and below). The upper bark of the Scots pine glows ember red in the evening light, contrasting with the blue-green foliage. It provides light shade to plantings below.

P. SYLVESTRIS L.

SCOTS PINE; EUROPE, ASIA. EVERGREEN.

This species is native in a variety of forms throughout Europe and Asia. The only British trees that are native are those that grow wild in woods on the little islands in Loch Maree, Wester Ross, and south and east from them through Glenfinnan, for example, to the Black Wood of Rannoch. To reach those places it must, of course, have migrated through England, where it was eventually eliminated by the improving climate and subsequent arrival of more successful species. In England it is thus a 'secondary native' that spread from cultivation, and the first known re-introduction appears to be the planting of a few trees in north-eastern Hampshire soon after 1660. It was first planted in the New Forest after 1770 with trees from Morayshire. When the light sandy areas of Bagshot Sands and Lower Greensand in south-eastern England had been cleared of their woodland cover by early settlers, and had degenerated into sandy heaths subject to fires, the Scots pine spread rapidly through them and became a dominant feature of the West Surrey Desert and its extension through the army-owned lands from Aldershot to Chobham and into Berkshire.

Heathland sites preserved for Dartford warblers, smooth snakes and natterjack toads, as well as numerous plants, are under constant threat from the advance of Scots pine and conservation in these parts is largely a matter of felling them. They not only shade out the heather but are surprisingly thirsty trees in summer and winter, and dry out the bogs needed by the toads and many other forms of wildlife.

In the mid-eighteenth century Lancelot 'Capability' Brown used the Scots pine in landscaping and frequently planted groups on the tumps and knolls raised with the spoils from his lakes. Relatively few conifers were known at the time – certainly none of the fine species from western North America – so his choice was limited. The Scots pine was a good tree to choose as it makes some of the best clumps for distant viewing. It grows fast when young, adding annual shoots of around 1 m whether it is on poor acid sand or quite heavy clay, and if the bole is cleaned of low branches early in life it can make a reasonable specimen tree of moderate size. However, it lacks the stature, shape and presence required in a single specimen on a large scale.

In young trees the bark is pale orange-brown and flakes in tiny, papery scales. In old ones the bark on upper branches is reddish-orange but variable on the bole. Some trees have smooth, flat, big, pink-brown or dark red-brown scales, while others have dark red, scaly thick ridges.

Variants Several selections are popular dwarf conifers but the following will make trees. 'Aurea', the Golden Scots pine, is slow-growing with a tendency to be bushy. It looks rather unhealthy in summer and autumn. As winter approaches, however, the leaves turn bright gold and the tree stands out until early spring as a splash of fine colour. There are better golden conifers, but none is a pine, so this deserves a place either in a winter garden where it will be little seen in summer, or at a moderate distance and in front of dark evergreens. 'Fastigiata', the Erect Scots pine, is a neat little tree that is strangely rare in British gardens. It remains tightly erect and well-foliaged until it is at least 8–10 m tall. This is first-class as a feature in a small-scale planting, in any situation and on any soil, and should surely become popular once it is more widely known. It needs practically no room and, after some years of moderate growth, becomes very slow.

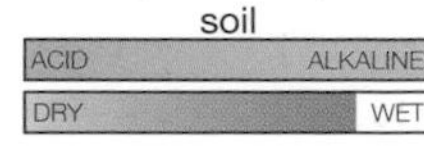

8•12•35 M

PINUS THUNBERGII PARL.

JAPANESE BLACK PINE; NE CHINA, JAPAN, KOREA. EVERGREEN.

This makes an excellent, neat, dark, narrow tree for its first 30 years or so, with silky, white-haired buds that are prominent among whorls of stiff, dark, paired needles. It is native to poor coastal soils so is unusually tough and resistant to sea winds, salt and difficult soils. It is strange that a species so neat and upright in youth should become so gaunt with age, but most old trees lean strongly and spread slender branches widely in thin, open crowns. Another curious feature is it stendency to flower excessively; in some trees every bundle of needles is replaced by a female flower. There may be 200 of them crowded on a length of shoot, with no room for the cones to develop properly. This adds to the interest of growing such a peculiar tree.

P. WALLICHIANA A.B. JACKSON

HIMALAYAN PINE; HIMALAYAS. EVERGREEN.

Although previously known as the Bhutan pine, to avoid confusion this name should be reserved for *P. bhutanica* Grierson, Long & Page, which was introduced more recently in Britain. For no obvious reason this is seen more than any other five-needle pine in older gardens around towns. It is good as a young tree but seldom as a specimen because as it ages it starts to lose branches and dies back at the top. It grows fast in youth, making leading shoots of 1 m, and may reach 20 m in 20 years but is much slower thereafter. In rural areas it remains well-foliaged and attractive for many years with long, 20 cm, blue-grey needles in lax long whorls on a very whorled branch system in a fairly narrowly conic crown. Cones may be borne within 10 years from seed and soon become numerous, hanging from shoots all over the crown. They are cylindric, narrow and curved, 20–30 cm long, and are bright green and blue-grey with much resin. They add much to the tree until its crown becomes thin when it seems to be all cone and little foliage. Unless there is room for a big, widely branching old specimen, the Himalayan pine should be regarded as a short-term adornment that will be replaced in 30 years or whenever it becomes too thin and open to be attractive. It will grow on any normal soil, but not on thin soils over chalk.

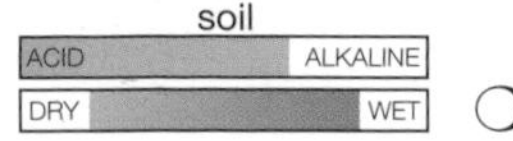

PINUS THUNBERGII (above). Native to poor coastal soils, it is a tough pine, tolerant of salt spray and nutrient poor soils.

PINUS WALLICHIANA (far left). Cylindrical long cones drip with resin as they hang among the pendulous needles of this widely planted Himalayan pine.

Pittosporum tenuifolium Banks & Sol. ex Gaertn.

NEW ZEALAND. EVERGREEN.

This is much the hardiest of a number of New Zealand plants seen in mild gardens, and grows as far east as London and northwards along the west coast to Argyll. In the mildest parts it is a tree that grows to 16 m with a smooth, dull grey bole and upright, dense ovoid crown. Elsewhere it is an upright ovoid bush valuable for foliage that is a different colour and texture from all others, and a useful evergreen screen, even in coastal positions. The slender, dark purple shoots bear rather remote groups of leaves which are bright pale green and deeply crinkled and waved, hard and 5 cm long. Dark purple cup-shaped flowers open in late spring. They are not conspicuous but are highly fragrant, especially in the evening, and ripen to black 1.5 cm fruits which contain sticky seeds. Many plants appear to be either male or female.

Cultivation Forms with coloured or variegated leaves develop their colour best in sun. In mild areas it is very wind-resistant but in cold areas it may need protection.

Variants A great many variegated selections are now planted for their ornamental foliage. They are all slower growing than the species but the more vigorous ones will make trees. Many, however, lack the crinkled leaves that is one of the attractive features of this species. Some of the more vigorous forms include 'Eila Keightley' which has a yellow-green blotch in the centre of the leaf, 'Purpureum', with pale green young leaves that turn glossy purple and 'Warnham Gold' which has pale green crinkled leaves that become golden in winter.

soil
ACID ALKALINE
DRY WET
5•10•15 M

PITTOSPORUM TENUIFOLIUM (right). Prized by flower arrangers, this small tree has glossy green foliage on dark purple shoots which often obscures the chocolate coloured flowers.

Platanus* x *hispanica Mill. ex Muenchh. (*P.* x *acerifolia* (ait.) Willd.)

LONDON PLANE; CULTIVATED ORIGIN. DECIDUOUS.

This presumed cross between the Buttonwood or American plane (*P. occidentalis*) and the Oriental plane (*P. orientalis*) has hybrid vigour combined with near indestructibility and a great life span. The oldest are nearly 300 years of age, immense and still growing fast. It is almost unknown for one to blow down, or even to die, so there will be gigantic trees throughout Britain's cities one day. This ability to grow fast in almost any conditions, together with ease of propagation from stool-beds, cuttings or seeds, makes the London plane nearly irresistible to those who have to plant in cities and many are therefore in unsuitable positions. No tree should be planted unless it has about a quarter of a hectare over which to expand without causing trouble. Planes tolerate pruning very well, but it does not make them look anything but grievously wounded and truncated. These considerations apply only in the southern third of England for the plane likes hot summers and does not grow so fast or reach great sizes in other parts. The giant trees are found in southern gardens like Mottisfont Abbey in Hampshire and Pusey House, Oxfordshire, and in towns around London such as Carshalton and Richmond. In cooler areas the plane is a more modest size.

To some, the large, much-lobed shiny leaves of London plane are out of place in a rural setting and bring the air of a city park with them. The first may be true but there is nothing of the city park about a vast plane or two on a mansion lawn, where they can be monumental specimens worth going far to see. On trees of great size the well-known mottled bark is no longer on the bole, but only high on the branches. The boles are warm red-brown and finely fissured, ridged or folded in patches.

Variants There are many different forms of London plane. The aristocrat among them is the uncommon 'Augustine Henry' which has a long, clean bole and straight, sparse branches, both with prominent pale yellow or white patches on the bark, and sparse, deep green, hooded leaves. 'Pyramdalis' is very common in London and has a sprouty, dark bark covered in burs. When young it usually has only a single large ball of fruit on each catkin. The huge old trees have big leaves, about 20 x 30 cm with five large, toothed lobes and 3–6 smaller fruit-balls on the catkin. 'Suttneri' is very rare and striking with leaves that are strongly variegated white or very pale yellow. It is now being grown a little more than it was but planting is still limited, perhaps by availability.

Other species. *P. orientalis* L., the Oriental plane, is from south-eastern Europe and is one of the world's biggest and longest-living trees. It has much more attractive foliage than the London plane with deeply cut, slender, pointed lobes and bronzy autumn tints, but is not a good specimen tree since it sprawls widely and rarely has a tall crown. Old trees are picturesque when they lean huge branches on the ground, but few plantings have room for this unless they are in the middle of a big park or on the side of an extensive prospect in a garden. 'Digitata', which may be a form of London plane rather than of the oriental species, is a delightful foliage tree of reasonably narrow crown and rapid growth when young. Its leaves are deeply divided into five widely parted, long slender lobes with lobulate margins.

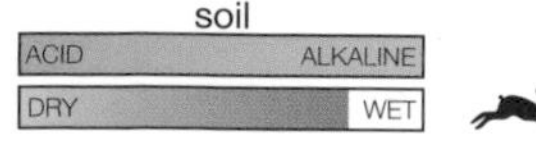

PLATANUS X *HISPANICA* 'AUGUSTINE HENRY' (left), has a clear white or yellow mottled stem, a good all-year-round attribute.

PLATANUS ORIENTALIS 'DIGITATA' (above), quick growing in youth, this is a delightful tree with deeply divided leaves.

PLATANUS X *HISPANICA* 'SUTTNERI' (far left), although rare, is worth seeking out for its striking foliage.

POPULUS ALBA (above). Fast growing and with an aggressive root system, P. alba is not recommended for the garden, but extremely useful on poor soils.

Populus/Poplars

While not generally suitable for small gardens the poplars provide some useful landscape trees which can be extremely effective in providing fast-growing shelter and screens. Male and female flowers are borne in catkins on separate plants. The males are often conspicuous with red anthers. The females are usually green and after the fruit have matured they often release clouds of white, hair-covered seeds.

Cultivation Most poplars are easy to grow in all but very shallow chalk or soils, or ones that are waterlogged, although they will tolerate moist conditions. They require full sun to grow well. As their roots are very invasive they should never be planted close to buildings: a distance of at least 30 m is recommended, particularly on clay soils.

POPULUS ALBA L.

WHITE POPLAR, ABELE; EUROPE AND AFRICA TO C ASIA. DECIDUOUS.

In its typical form this species can only be recommended as a temporary shelter tree on sea-blown sands. It makes a poor specimen as it is slender and leaning, although pretty when it first comes into leaf bright silver, and suckers widely, ruining a lawn. It is this suckering that gives the tree value for seaward shelter as it is profuse in the poorest soils and grows rapidly to a useful 5–6 m.

Variants 'Richardii' has a very unusual and attractive crown of pale grey-green, strikingly white-backed leaves with bright gold upper surfaces. It is exceptionally rare, although often mentioned, perhaps because of its excessive suckering. 'Pyramidalis' is a distinctly short-term tree since it tends to open out and disintegrate at no great age, but at considerable size. However, it can give 60–80 years of good, white-backed foliage on a narrow vase-shaped crown.

P. X *CANADENSIS* MOENCH

CULTIVATED ORIGIN. DECIDUOUS.

These hybrids between the North American *P. deltoides* and the European Black poplar (*P. nigra*) include some of the most commonly grown poplars. They are all fast-growing large trees, ideal for providing shelter.

Variants 'Robusta' is the best form for general planting. It has very luxuriant, heavy foliage of broad ovate, deep, glossy green leaves, and is exceptionally vigorous. Young trees usually grow shoots of 1.5–2 m and sometimes more. The bole should be pruned clean of shoots for 2 m by the third year and later for as high as can be reached. The tree's great merits in landscaping are its rapid growth and shapely crown, the abundance of deep bright red 10 cm male catkins in early spring, the bright orange of its unfolding leaves and its dense handsome foliage; also, because it is male, the absence of clouds of cottonwool in summer. The limitations on planting it, apart from those common to poplars near buildings on heavy clays, are that it does best in regions with warm summers and needs a base-rich moist soil. It makes a superb specimen by a lake or river and a group can be an important feature in an extensive landscape. 'Serotina' is altogether too coarse, fragile, short-lived and late into leaf to appear here and 'Robusta' excels it in every way. However, 'Serotina Aurea', the Golden black poplar, is a good tree with a denser and more tidy crown, slower growth and good foliage. The leaves are bright lemon yellow to butter-yellow. A 30 m high crown seen across a town, in sunshine but against a dark cloud, is spectacularly beautiful. It only rarely reverts to green foliage.

POPULUS X CANADENSIS (far right). The vigorous poplars are useful shelter providers, and quick growing natural windbreaks but should be sited carefully.

POPULUS X CANDICANS 'AURORA' (left). If pollarded this tree produces an oddly pleasing display of creamy-white, pink tinged leaves.

POPULUS X CANDICANS AIT. 'AURORA'

CULTIVATED ORIGIN. DECIDUOUS.

This female tree is prone to bacterial canker and can be short-lived, but if branches are cut back to the trunk every year it can be a striking, if odd, sight. It grows fast into a conic-crowned poplar, dark-leafed early in the season until new leaves, which often look like pure white waterlily flowers, grow at the tips of the shoots. As the shoots continue the leaves unfold. They are broadly splashed with creamy white, some with a pink tinge. The tree looks and grows well in the damp soil near the edge of a pool but will also grow on poorer soils.

8•12•15 M

P. X CANESCENS (AIT.) SM.

GREY POPLAR; EUROPE. DECIDUOUS.

Although this rapidly grows too big for smaller gardens or spaces this makes a better specimen than the White poplar (*P. alba*). It does not sucker so intensively and the leaf undersides are not quite such a clear white, but it is a splendid, robust tree thought to be a hybrid between the White poplar (*P. alba*) and the Aspen (*P. tremula*). It reaches its perfection in the limy alluvial soils of lowland valleys in southern England and central Ireland, but makes a very big tree even in Easter Ross, north of Inverness. The biggest ones have long boles and few strong, upswept branches which arch out to a high-domed crown. Grey poplars are a feature in very early spring as they are almost all male trees and the catkins swell and turn purple. Later, when they come into leaf the big crowns are silvery, and turn grey as the leaves unfold. On young trees the strong shoots bear ovate leaves 8–10 cm long, but the crowns of mature ones consist entirely of nearly round leaves with hooked teeth.

POPULUS X CANESCENS (left). In early springs grey poplars are easily spotted as the male catkins swell and turn purple.

soil

ACID ALKALINE

DRY WET

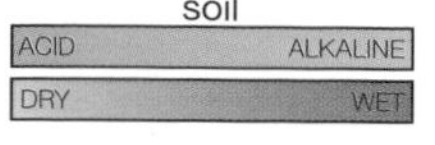

10•15•30 M

POPULUS LASIOCARPA (right). Although relatively uninteresting during the winter, it is a fine foliage tree in summer.

POPULUS NIGRA 'ITALICA' (below). Commonly grown as the Lombardy poplar, and universally used as large windbreaks, they seldom look

P. LASIOCARPA OLIVER

CHINESE NECKLACE POPLAR; C CHINA. DECIDUOUS.

Although this is gaunt and shaggily grey-barked in winter, it is a fine foliage tree during summer. First sent to Britain from China in 1900, it has been in short supply at times and some trees are grafted but have not grown well. Seedling trees are not fast either, except for a superb and shapely one in the Botanic Garden at Bath, which reached 25 m tall. The leaves are the largest of those of any poplar, to over 30 x 20 cm, and are bright shining green with red veins towards the base, on 20 cm pink petioles. The flowers are conspicuous and numerous: thick, yellow, 25 cm catkins of male flowers, often with 5–6 females at the base or, on female trees, 25 cm catkins with sparse green flowers and later globose green fruit that sprout huge clumps of cottonwool-covered seeds.

soil
ACID ALKALINE
DRY WET
5•8•20 M

P. NIGRA L.

BLACK POPLAR; EUROPE, W ASIA. DECIDUOUS.

The most commonly seen form of this species is 'Italica', the Lombardy polar, which is distinctive in its very narrow, acute-tipped crown with upright branches, often from near the base, and glossy green leaves which turn yellow in autumn. This very well-known tree was brought to Essex from Turin in 1758 and is highly adaptable as to site and soil. Planted in lines it is no ornament to the countryside because some trees will always be broken or stunted, but it is superb in a group and makes an impressive large-scale feature.

All trees derived from the true form are males with dark red catkins that open in March. Other forms exist, however, one which is much narrower and some, such as 'Gigantea', that are female and broader.

soil
ACID ALKALINE
DRY WET
10•15•30 M

Prumnopitys andina (Poepp. ex Endl.) Laub. (*Podocarpus andinus* Poepp. ex Endl.)

PLUM-FRUITED YEW; CHILE. EVERGREEN.

Although often a large erect bush, this can be a tree with 2–3 boles or, less often, a single bole. The bark is nearly black and smooth, with horizontal wrinkles. The branches are light and upswept. Its soft, 5 cm long leaves are densely held and bright fresh or slightly blued green above with two broad, pale blue-grey bands beneath. It is hardy and accommodating and should be more planted in gardens for it foliage. It is too likely to become a bush to be worth a place as a specimen tree, but is splendid for low shelter or different foliage in a group of shrubs, and a good change from the sombre Yew (*Taxus baccata*). Male and female plants both have slender erect heads of flowers at the tips of some shoots. These are yellow on males and bright blue-grey on females, which bear 2 cm apple-green fruit in small bunches.

Cultivation The Plum-fruited yew grows slowly on any soil.

PRUMNOPITYS ANDINA (left). A large spreading bush with very distinctive foliage resembling a large leafed yew. Large apple-yellow fruits develop on female plants.

PRUNUS 'ACCOLADE' (far right). Brilliant in both flower and autumn colour, this hybrid cherry owes much of its popularity to the Sargent cherry.

Prunus/

Cherries, plums, almonds

THE NUMEROUS ORNAMENTAL trees in this genus brighten many gardens with their spring flowers. As most of them are of modest size they are often suitable for fairly small gardens. The genus also includes several trees grown solely for their edible fruit and these are not dealt with here.

Cultivation *Prunus* are easy to grow on any reasonably good, well-drained soil. They prefer full sun or partial shade.

PRUNUS 'ACCOLADE'

CULTIVATED ORIGIN. DECIDUOUS.

A hybrid from Sargent cherry (*P. sargentii*), this wide-spreading tree is outstanding for its abundance of rosy pink, semi-double, fringed flowers that hang in clusters early in spring. Its thin straggly crown and sparse slender leaves are rather a let-down for the rest of the year until the foliage turns pale orange-red in autumn.

P. AVIUM L.

GEAN, WILD CHERRY; EUROPE, W ASIA. DECIDUOUS.

The Gean is a tree of great and varied amenity values. It grows best on chalky loams, but does very well on neutral clays or sands and adequately on fairly acid sands. It grows rapidly with a conic crown of whorled

branches that is unusual in a broad-leafed tree and has the proper cherry bark of mahogany red-brown in smooth shiny bands. Flowering is prolific in mid-spring and remarkable when seen on a large forest tree. The fruit feed birds. The foliage is dreary until it turns yellow, dull orange and dark red in autumn. As a specimen the Gean has a place in a spring or autumn planting but not in a mainly summer one. On a large scale it is good in a clump, as a single specimen among other trees or scattered in open woodland. A 'witch's broom' often bends quite large branches down, and should be cut out at first sighting.

Variant 'Plena', the Double wild cherry, flowers later than the single form, more or less with 'Kanzan', and is a good foil and diluter for it. Globular flowers hang in dense lines beneath bright green new leaves and last well. Although not quite so lavish a spectacle as any of the double white Japanese cherries, it has an elegance that they lack, and a central stem which can take the crown to over 20 m.

PRUNUS AVIUM (right). Our native cherry will thrive on chalk. It flowers prolifically in spring and has good quality autumn tints.

PRUNUS AVIUM 'PLENA' (far right). The double form of the wild cherry is superior in flower although less likely to produce valuable fruit for native and migrating birds.

PRUNUS CERASIFERA EHRH.

CHERRY PLUM; ORIGIN UNKNOWN. DECIDUOUS.

While the Cherry plum's profuse white flowers on bare stems adorn Britain's hedgerows in early spring, it is mainly seen in its purple-leafed forms in gardens. It is only of any value covered in flowers, when it lights up many suburban gardens and heralds the start of spring.

Variants Although 'Lindsayae' is hardly ever seen it is perhaps the best form, with a strongly upright habit, large pink flowers and green foliage. It should be much more widely grown. 'Nigra' is the frequent form with pink flowers and deep purple-red foliage, while 'Pissardii' has white flowers, slightly flushed pink as they open, and deep purple leaves. 'Pendula' is a rarely seen, but very picturesque, small tree with weeping shoots.

P. CERASUS L.

SOUR CHERRY; ORIGIN UNKNOWN. DECIDUOUS.

The Sour cherry is grown in gardens in many forms for its edible fruit but one form in particular is garden-worthy for its flowers.

'Rhexii' has been cultivated for nearly 400 years and is particularly valuable because it flowers in late spring or early summer. The flowers are tight rosettes, up to 4 cm across, of white petals that open from pale pink, long-stalked buds. It is only unfortunate in that it has a poor, flattish, untidy crown and dull-looking foliage.

PRUNUS CERASIFERA 'PENDULA' (above left). Arching branches make this one of the most picturesque cherry plums for the garden in winter and when in flower.

PRUNUS CERASIFERA 'NIGRA' (above). A frequently planted, pink flowered, cherry plum with deep purple-red foliage.

PRUNUS CERASUS (left). More commonly seen in gardens as one of its many forms, the species produces edible fruits.

P. DULCIS (MILL.) D.A. WEBB

ALMOND; AFRICA TO C ASIA. DECIDUOUS.

At its best in a hot, dry climate the Almond is frequently not long-lived in Britain, but many good trees are seen in warm city gardens. Its large flowers, up to 5 cm across, are normally white in the wild but often pink on cultivated trees. The long, slender-pointed leaves can be infected with peach-leaf curl which makes them red and unsightly.

soil
ACID ALKALINE
DRY WET
5•6•8 M

P. 'HALLY JOLIVETTE'

In flower this is a tree, or perhaps more often a shrub, of exceptional elegance. The delicate little flowers spray out in mid-spring, before the leaves. They are like snowdrops and are faintly pink then white, with purple calyces on slender, purple stalks. This makes only a small tree, slender when young and rounded with age.

soil
ACID ALKALINE
DRY WET
3•4•5 M

PRUNUS DULCIS (far right). Although generally not long lived in Britain, the almond will occasionally produce fruit after a long, hot summer.

PRUNUS 'HALLY JOLIVETTE' (right). Raised in North America, this is a small tree of exceptional elegance when in spring the naked branches are covered with delicate flowers.

PRUNUS 'KURSAR'

CULTIVATED ORIGIN. DECIDUOUS.

This first-class tree provides an early and long display of unusually bright pink, single flowers with dark red calyces and is among the finest of early-flowering cherries. Raised by Captain Collingwood Ingram, it was named when the parentage was assumed to be *P. nipponica* var. *kurilensis* x *P. sargentii*. Ingram later decided that the second parent was in fact *P. campanulata* but the original name must remain.

soil
ACID ALKALINE
DRY WET 6•7•8 M

P. LUSITANICA L.

PORTUGAL LAUREL; SW EUROPE. EVERGREEN.

Although this species is frequently grown as a shrub and used for hedging, it will make a respectable tree and is useful for being very hardy and for flowering in summer. Although often confused with the more shrubby Cherry laurel (*P. laurocerasus*), it can be easily distinguished by its red-stalked leaves and much later flowers. Its attractive, glossy dark green leaves highlight long racemes of fragrant white flowers in early summer. These are followed by shining red then black fruit.

PRUNUS 'KURSAR' (above and left). The most desirable of the early flowering ornamental Japanese cherries, outstanding flower and shape make its is easy to see why.

PRUNUS LUSITANICA (left), is a more familiar sight as a hedge than as a specimen plant, which is a shame, as the flowers are very ornamental.

PRUNUS MAACKII (above). Less commonly grown than the Tibetan cherry, this cherry comes a close second for winter bark effect.

P. MAACKII RUPR.

MANCHURIAN CHERRY; NE ASIA. DECIDUOUS.

The bark of a young Manchurian cherry is a unique glistening honey colour, and soon darkens with age to pale orange-brown, then dark orange with wide grey fissures. It grows too fast for its own good as the vigour-cracks soon detract from the bark for which it is grown. Little erect spikes of small, fragrant flowers emerge late in spring among minutely peg-toothed dark green leaves, but are not conspicuous and are followed by small, glossy black cherries. The bole can be 80 cm through in 40 years.

soil
ACID ALKALINE
DRY WET
◗ ◯ 6•8•12 M

PRUNUS PADUS L.

BIRD CHERRY; EUROPE, N ASIA. DECIDUOUS.

Native in northern and mountainous areas where it is often shrubby, this very tough little tree has much to recommend it. When young it has a conic crown of slender branches with shining, dark brown shoots. It flowers late in spring, when the leafy, 12 cm, clear white spikes spread abundantly from pale green, new leaves. In early autumn the leaves turn pale yellow, then the outer crown is tinged with red. This tree will grow among pavings and on limy or poor soils, but not on dry sands.

Variants 'Albertii' should be planted more frequently. It is upright in habit with short, erect flower spikes. 'Colorata', dark-crowned with blackish-purple leaves on red petioles, is worth a place for its curious foliage colour. It is lovely when the dark red-purple flower spikes open to show the pink and white insides of the petals. 'Purple Queen' is very similar. 'Watereri' is a coarse-growing, vigorous and spreading tree to 18 m with large dark leaves remotely set on long,

PRUNUS PADUS 'ALBERTII' (left). A cultivar of the bird cherry, this is a striking upright tree, with considerable landscape appeal.

PRUNUS PADUS (below). Although the species is infrequently planted, it has much to recommend it. It is a tough little plant and will tolerate most poor soils.

whippy shoots. It is redeemed only when its numerous, 20 cm long spikes of white flowers spray out in all directions. Unfortunately, it is too often planted close against a building, a site that is most unsuitable because of the tree's spreading habit.

PRUNUS PADUS 'COLORATA' (right and far right). This splendid form has attractive dark purple foliage that contrasts well with the coppery purple new shoots and pale pink flowers.

PRUNUS PADUS var. *COMMUTATA* (right), from E Asia, is useful as it is very vigorous and comes into leaf very early, one of the first trees to do so, and is in flower soon afterwards.

PRUNUS SARGENTII REHDER

SARGENT CHERRY; JAPAN. DECIDUOUS..

This Japanese tree is commonly planted in towns because it grows strongly, gives a reliable early display – a soft pink cloud of flowers opens amidst deep bronzy red young leaves – and is the best of all cherries for autumn colour, with scarlet, orange and deep red leaves. Hence its lack-lustre, hanging, summer foliage is a price worth paying, and its dark red bark in smooth bands tides it through the winter. Seedlings spread wide branches from the base, as do grafts made at ground level, so roadside trees are worked at 1.5 m or 2 m and have stout boles of Gean bark. Although the Sargent cherry is unsuited to a fully rural landscape, it is splendid for an extensive park planting where generous groups, 8–10 trees spaced 8 m apart, make spectacular features in early spring and early autumn. A single specimen will attain 12 m in time, with a widely spread crown, and needs much space.

Variant 'Rancho' is a selection from North America with a narrow, upright habit and large, pink flowers.

P. X *SCHMITTII* REHDER

GARDEN ORIGIN. DECIDUOUS.

This hybrid between the Gean (*P. avium*) and the shrubby *P. canescens* is a vigorous tree with a head of long, upright branches that is very narrow when young and broadens with age. It inherits ornamental bark from both parents, so has narrow bands of peeling purple-red punctuated by bands of corky lenticels. It is grown mainly for its habit. Although the small, pink flowers,

profusely borne as the young leaves emerge, are attractive close-up, they are too small to be effective on a tree of this size

P. SERRULA FRANCH.

TIBETAN CHERRY; W CHINA. DECIDUOUS.

This was sent from China to Britain in 1908 and 1913 and is scarce as an old plant, but has recently been much more used. Its bark, the most attractive of any tree, is deep mahogany-red or sometimes orange-brown on young plants, and is satiny-surfaced with shining, peeling bands between lines of lenticels. The boles expand rapidly and, although the branch bark looks after itself,

PRUNUS SARGENTII 'RANCHO' (above and above left). Introduced from North America and instantly recognised for its potential as an urban tree, it is now widely planted.

PRUNUS X *SCHMITTII* (far left). Although the bark is not as smooth as that of the Tibetan cherry, it has the advantage of higher quality flowers.

PRUNUS SERRULA (left). Unlike the Paperbark maple (*Acer griseum*), this tactile tree will tolerate a wide range of soils.

PRUNUS X SUBHIRTELLA 'AUTUMNALIS ROSEA' (above). The early flowering Winter cherries are a breath of fresh air during the dark winter months.

the boles can become hidden in blackish scales and numerous sprouts unless they are frequently smoothed and the papery rolls removed without being torn. Hence this tree is best planted by a well-used path where it will incite passers-by to stroke and smooth it. The lenticel bands have usually narrowed the shiny strips by the time the bole is some 40 cm through, and made it less attractive, but nothing can be done about this except perhaps to graft the tree on a less vigorous rootstock than the usual Gean and grow it more slowly.

Although flowers are never the reason for planting this tree – just a minor bonus – they are sometimes prolific, although never conspicuous. Slender-stalked, white and 2 cm across, they are borne in bunches of 2–3 among the open green leaves,.

PRUNUS X YEDOENSIS 'IVENSII' (below). This fascinating, short weeping tree, especially when snow laden in winter or when flowering

The Tibetan cherry has a twiggy, broad crown and slender, sharply toothed, dark green leaves. Despite its crown, and because the bark is always prominent and the tree never becomes big (or can be replaced when it does), this is a good single specimen for an enclosed, much-frequented area like a courtyard.

soil
ACID ALKALINE
DRY WET 3•6•15 M

P. X *SUBHIRTELLA* MIQ.

ROSE-BUD CHERRY; JAPAN. DECIDUOUS.

This is a hybrid that occurs naturally in Japan with its parents *P. incisa* and *P. pendula*. The following are some of the forms that are grown.

The tiny white flowers of 'Autumnalis', the Winter cherry, start to open in October, on very short stalks, among leaves that are by then turning yellow. They continue to open – a fresh set after each hard frost or continually and on longer stalks if mild – with a last burst in April. The buds are pink and the contrast with the white flowers makes this form preferable to the pink-flowered 'Autumnalis Rosea'. Although 'Pendula' is barely a tree it is a wonderful hummock submerged in white single flowers in April, and is best planted high on a rock-garden or on a tiny island in a pool. 'Rosea' seems to be the name of a superbly floriferous tree which is densely, if briefly, a rich uniform pink all over with starry single flowers, but which is not often seen.

P. X *YEDOENSIS* MATSUM.

YOSHINO CHERRY; JAPAN. DECIDUOUS.

This is believed to be a hybrid between two species native to Japan, *P. pendula* and *P. speciosa*. In early spring its arching branches are completely wreathed in profuse flowers 4 cm across, which open pale pink and fade to nearly white. In summer, the fruit are small cherries that ripen from red to glossy black. The tree's brilliant show in spring makes up for its rather lifeless appearance for the rest of the year.

Variant 'Ivensii' is among the most distinctive of several selections. It makes a wide small tree with branches that spread horizontally from the point of grafting and arch to the ground.

JAPANESE CHERRIES

The opulent-flowered Japanese cherries often listed as forms of *P. serrulata*, itself a garden plant, are of hybrid origin and much selected so are better called by their cultivar names alone. They all flower in the latter half of the cherry season, beginning in early April – Mount Fuji is the first – and continuing through May, and all are from Japan except for 'Pink Perfection' which is a hybrid between two Japanese cultivars and occurred at Bagshot, Surrey.

Only their salient features for landscaping purposes, and the most distinct and attractive types, will be mentioned here since Japanese cherries are an immense subject, better covered in books devoted to them. All the following trees are grafted on Gean (*P. avium*) and will grow on any fairly good soil including chalky soils and when they are surrounded by paving. They will not do well on light sands.

'Amanogawa' is strictly erect and columnar when young, but opens with age, and is ideal for very restricted spaces among buildings. In a garden it is better planted as a group than singly. Its pale pink, large, frilled, semi-double, fragrant flowers open in mid- to late season among slightly bronzed leaves which turn pale yellow and pinkish-red in autumn. It grows to 10 m tall.

'Fugenzo' is a useful change from 'Kanzan'. It flowers two weeks later on a lower, more spreading crown, and has short-stalked bunches of similar flowers but redder buds and leaves.

'Hokusai' is a sturdy tree that is often grown but little known to the public. It is probably regarded as an early 'Kanzan' as it flowers earlier, with more bunched, much paler flowers that open to show red eyes, among pale brown leaves. In autumn these are orange and fiery red. The tree will reach about 7 m.

'Kanzan' is the universal, double, pink 'Japanese cherry' of suburbia. Its strong upright branches later bend out, heavy with long-stalked bunches of very pink flowers that open from red buds among slightly brownish-red leaves. The heavy criticism this tree attracts is perhaps due less to over-planting than to the unvaried pink of its flowers. It cannot be faulted for reliability or sheer abundance of flower. 'Kanzan' can grow to 12 m tall.

'Mount Fuji', the first Japanese cherry in flower, is similar to an early-flowering 'Shogetsu' but its crown is wider and it has shining bright green leaves. It was previously grown as 'Shirotae'.

'Okiku' is the most beautiful of all Japanese cherries in some ways, but still very scarce. Its strong upright growth is wreathed in great clusters of frilled, semi-double, green-eyed, pale pink flowers in mid-season.

'Pink Perfection', the only Japanese cherry not of Japanese origin, is a cross between 'Shogetsu' and 'Kanzan'. It was raised in 1935 and is quite frequently

PRUNUS 'HOKUSAI' (above). A very early introduction into British gardens, this cherry has a stately habit and large semi-double, pale pink flowers.

PRUNUS 'FUGENZO' (below). This commonly grown Japanese favourite has coppery new growth and large, late, double pink flowers.

PRUNUS 'MOUNT FUJI' (far left), is a very distinct form, with snow-white, fragrant flowers and arching branches.

PRUNUS 'SHIROFUGEN' (left), is a strong growing form, with flowers that that open white and age to pale pink.

PRUNUS 'SCHIMIDUS' (above). With the exception of 'Tai Haku' this is the loveliest of the Japanese cherries as it contains masses of pure-white flowers.

PRUNUS 'KANZAN' (right) is an exceptionally popular pink form of Japanese Cherry.

PRUNUS SERRULATA var. *SPONTANEA* (far right) is a beautiful cherry with bronze young foliage and pink flowers in mid- to late spring.

seen in Surrey, its county of origin, but less so elsewhere. It comes into flower towards the end of the 'Kanzan' period and a few sprays sometimes open around midsummer. It improves upon 'Kanzan' in that its bright red buds among pale bronzy-green leaves open to form rich pink flowers that fade gradually to white and so avoid 'Kanzan's' uniform and unvarying colour. The flowers are in big, hanging bunches and in good years the tree is as laden with them as either parent. The one drawback is that not every year is a good one. At its best it is the most opulent of all the Japanese cherries as the big, tightly packed clusters have some flowers that are bright pink and others that are all shades to white. It will reach 8 m.

'Shirofugen', a glorious variation on 'Shogetsu', flowers at the same time but lasts much longer with occasional sprays until July. It is stronger, taller and equally spreading and has a three-colour trick. The buds are a good pink and, beneath deep red leaves, open to pink flowers for a few days then turn a shining pure white, superb against the dark leaves, for a week or more. As the leaves change to green the flowers turn pale pink again for another week or two.

'Shogetsu' ('Shimidsu') makes only a low-crowned, flat-topped spreading tree of slow growth, but is unsurpassed when in flower and among the last in the season. Copious big bunches of lilac-tinted buds hang beneath similarly coloured leaves which become bright green as the flowers, borne in bunches, open. Large, 6 cm long, these are very double, purest white and long-stemmed. The tree will reach 5 m.

'Tai Haku', the Great white cherry, was lost to cultivation in Japan around 1700. However, in 1923 Capain Collingwood Ingram discovered a single, nearly dead plant in a Sussex garden that had been planted in 1900 from a job lot of plants from Japan. He raised grafted plants from this one tree and now every 'Tai Haku' in the world, including Japan, is derived from it. Young plants have strong, raised branches and long shoots that are wreathed in big, wide, 7 cm, single white flowers among deep red leaves by mid-early season. On rather older trees the crown spreads widely and the flowers are in huge globular clusters. The leaves, like those of all Japanese cherries, have abrupt long tips and sharp, whisker-ended teeth. They differ from those of other trees in the group, except 'Ukon', in being very dark, well spaced, leathery and to 20 cm long. On occasional trees they turn bright red in autumn.

'Ukon' is the only generally planted cherry that has pale buff-yellow flowers for the first week of flowering in mid-season. They are semi-double, long-stalked and borne beneath pale brown or khaki leaves. They mature pure white with a red eye and then resemble the flowers of 'Tai Haku' although they are smaller and with more petals. The unusual colour of the flowers lasts longer if the tree is grown in a partially shaded position.

soil

ACID | ALKALINE

DRY | WET

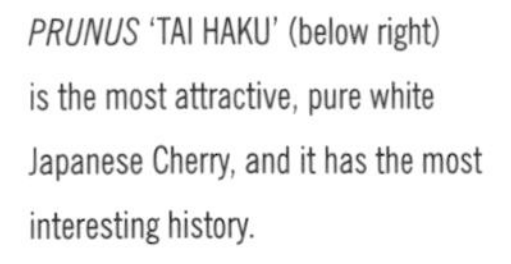

PRUNUS 'TAI HAKU' (below right) is the most attractive, pure white Japanese Cherry, and it has the most interesting history.

PRUNUS 'PINK PERFECTION' (below), is the only Japanese cherries not

Pseudolarix amabilis (J. Nels.) Rehder

GOLDEN LARCH; E CHINA. DECIDUOUS.

This relative of the true larches (*Larix*) is quite rare in gardens because there have been periods when there were no plants in the trade. It is very hardy once established, but not in its first few years of very slow growth when it can be damaged by late frosts, and large specimens are confined to milder gardens. Male and female flowers are borne separately on the same tree, but not when it is young. They are both yellow and females develop into cones up to 5 cm long which, unlike those of the true larches, break up before they fall.

The Golden larch has bolder foliage than the true larches, with 5–7 cm strap-like leaves in whorls on long, curved spurs which lengthen and broaden each year. The leaves are bright pale green and grey a little until, in autumn, they turn yellow, orange and red-brown. This autumn display is the brightest of any conifer and earns the Golden larch a place in a planting. In a good site it will make a broad tree with long level branches, pale grey deeply fissured bark and an attractive appearance.

Cultivation The Golden larch needs good, fertile and well-drained, lime-free soil in full sun. In a shady position it makes a narrow, thinly foliaged tree. Plants should be given protection from hard frosts when young.

soil
ACID ALKALINE
DRY WET
2•4•20 M

PSEUDOLARIX AMABILIS (below). Quite rare in gardens due to lack of supply, the golden larch is a delightful tree for acidic soils.

PSEUDOTSUGA MENZIESII (right). The Douglas fir is a fast growing tree commonly used for timber production, although it is a stately conifer for parks and gardens.

Pseudotsuga menziesii (Mirb.) Franco

DOUGLAS FIR; W NORTH AMERICA. EVERGREEN.

David Douglas sent the first seeds to Britain in 1827 from near Portland, Oregon, and, by a strange chance, of all the seeds imported from North America's western slopes, from British Columbia to California, those from a small area between Portland and the Puget Sound in Washington state have been found to give the best results. At Quinault Lake, also in Washington, there is a stand of Douglas fir unsurpassed by any group of trees, with clear boles 2.2 m in diameter that run 60 m to the first branch and with top heights of 85–90 m.

The Douglas fir is fast-growing and of the largest size, and is an important and commonly planted forestry tree. The slender, dark green, blunt leaves are soft to the touch and fragrant when bruised. They have two white bands beneath and are arranged all around the shoots. Its slender, conical buds, like those of beech (*Fagus*), make it easily distinguishable. The flowers are not usually noticed. Males are yellow and pendulous, beneath the shoots, and females are green flushed with red and ripen to very distinctive cones. These are abundantly produced on old trees and easily recognized by the three-pronged bracts that project from between the scales.

Grown as a single specimen, in the right area and in some shelter on a damp site, the Douglas fir needs plenty of room and, for the best effect, the bole must be kept clean for 3 m or more. Single trees have heavy dense masses of foliage that hangs from big branches. It is splendid in a group and, if the boles in the interior are kept clean, will make an impressive grove.

Cultivation Although the Douglas fir is very adaptable, it is at its best in areas of high rainfall and cool summers. It tends to become thin and chlorotic on dry, chalky soils, although it will occasionally do well.

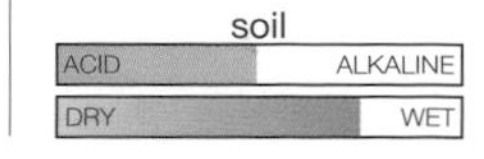

8•15•50 M

PTEROCARYA FRAXINIFOLIA (left). A very vigorous tree that will outgrow many of its deciduous counterparts, this hybrid wing nut makes a delightful large tree with butter yellow autumnal tints.

Pterocarya fraxinifolia (Lam.) Spach

CAUCASIAN WING NUT; CAUCASUS, N IRAN. DECIDUOUS.

To accommodate this immensely vigorous, superb foliage tree one needs either a large clear area or to be vigilant and severe with suckers. Left to itself it will disappear in a thicket which soon becomes high woodland. It makes a broad crown on level branches and a dense shade from the big compound leaves, which are bright shiny green with around 21 crowded and overlapping leaflets. These are narrowly oblong, slender-pointed and sharply toothed. The buds are peculiar. They have no scales but are two small, richly brown pubescent leaves held together; lateral buds are stalked and may sprout not quite within the axils. In spring the male catkins are thick, yellow and soon shed. The females, on the same tree, are up to 15 cm long, with pink flowers scattered on the basal parts and closer towards the tips. In summer the female catkins are 50 cm long and prominently strung with circular, winged, green fruit. In autumn the leaves turn bright yellow. This is a very remarkable tree in all seasons except winter.

Cultivation This wing nut grows best in moist, fertile soil and is handily planted on a waterside bank, which halves the area under siege by suckers. However, the bank should be wide and open as the view to water should be framed but not obstructed.

Other species *Pterocarya* x *rehderiana* Schneid. Hybrid wing nut, is a hybrid with *P. stenoptera* C. DC. It grows even faster than *P. fraxinifolia* – in fact, few trees grow more vigorously. It also keeps to one bole for longer as the suckering is less strong, although still extensive. The main distinction between the two is the channel along the hybrid's rachis, but for general effect of foliage and fruit it is just an extra- vigorous wing nut.

soil
ACID ALKALINE
DRY WET
10•15•25 M

PYRUS CALLERYANA 'CHANTICLEER' (far right). This North American introduction with attractive flowers and a conic shape is useful as a street tree.

Pyrus/Pears

THE CULTIVATED PEARS are remarkably tough trees that thrive in a wide range of sites. Of only small to modest size, they can be accommodated in many gardens and are largely grown for their flowers, although some are also planted for their ornamental habit or autumn colour.

Cultivation Grow in any soil that is not waterlogged. They tolerate extremes of heat well and are particularly useful in dry sites, industrial areas and exposed positions.

PYRUS CALLERYANA DECNE

CHINESE PEAR; CHINA. DECIDUOUS.

This species is represented in gardens almost entirely by forms selected for their habit in North America and commonly planted as amenity landscape trees.

Variants 'Chanticleer' is a seedling selected by that great connoisseur of town and street trees, Ed Scanlon of Ohio, and regarded by him as being among the very best that he found. It makes a tall, conic tree and has the following remarkable combination of star points: it is fast-growing in any soil; it bears masses of heads of small white flowers before the leaves unfold; the leaf buds expand bright silver-white; the leaves are a soft green and through the summer some often turn yellow, orange and red; late autumn or early winter colours are bright yellow, orange and red, and some heads of flowers may open at the same time. Although this is the common form in Britain, 'Bradford', the Bradford pear, is the one seen in North America where it has been widely planted. Broader than 'Chanticleer' it is like the Pyramidal hornbeam (*Carpinus betulus* 'Fastigiata') in shape.

8•12•15 M

PYRUS ELAEAGNIFOLIA (above). At first glance it may be mistaken for the willow-leafed pear, but it grows much taller, and does not have the same weeping habit.

P. ELAEAGNIFOLIA PALL.

SE EUROPE

At first sight this may be taken for the more familiar Willow-leafed pear (below) but it grows taller, is not weeping and has broader, 8 x 3 cm entire leaves that are greener above. It is a good silvery-grey and green foliage tree where a bigger tree than the willow-leaf, and one that is non-weeping, is required. It has spines on its shoot.

5•8•10 M

PYRUS SALICIFOLIA 'PENDULA' (right) is an interesting, although rather scruffy pendulous tree suitable for smaller gardens.

P. SALICIFOLIA PALL. 'PENDULA'

WILLOW-LEAFED PEAR. DECIDUOUS.

It is debatable whether this is a form entitled to a cultivar name or whether the typical tree is pendulous. The rather shapeless crown is not ornamental in winter but is attractive in early spring when the steeply pendulous branches, which hang to the ground, are covered in slender 7 x 1.5 cm silver-haired leaves. In late spring the effect is enhanced by heads of pure white 2 cm flowers, tipped scarlet in the bud.

soil
ACID ALKALINE
DRY WET

3•5•8 M

Quercus/Oaks

FOR TOO LONG, oaks have been regarded as plants which are part of the natural landscape, taken for granted but not planted. When a large one dies or has to be removed, it is often replaced by another species, something that will give more immediate impact but will not be as long-lived or as valuable to native wildlife. With a renewed interest in the genus this is now being corrected, and a wide range of oak species are planted. They are magnificent trees that show an extraordinary diversity in foliage, and it is easy to become passionate about them.

Cultivation Oaks prefer a good deep soil in a sunny or partially shaded position. While many are lime-tolerant, some will not thrive on shallow chalky soil. The taproot is important when the tree is young so they are best planted when they are small.

QUERCUS ACUTA (above). The glossy green leaves of this evergreen oak are covered in soft indumentum and resemble the leaves if rhododendrons.

QUERCUS ACUTA THUNB.

JAPANESE EVERGREEN OAK; JAPAN, KOREA. EVERGREEN.

This remarkable hardy species is generally shrubby in cultivation and looks more like a leafy Rhododendron than an oak until it bears spikes of big orange-brown acorns. The narrow, abruptly pointed, glossy green leaves are usually without teeth and when they unfold are covered in soft orange wool which rolls off by autumn.

Q. ACUTISSIMA CARRUTH.

SAWTOOTH OAK; JAPAN, KOREA, CHINA. DECIDUOUS.

This very hardy species is more commonly grown in the United States, particularly in the east, than in Britain. It is highly attractive in leaf and somewhat stark in winter with an open, few-branched crown and coarsely ridged grey bark. The smooth, pale green shoots bear big, handsome, glossy, chestnut-like leaves. These are rich dark green with about 15 pairs of prominent parallel veins each of which ends in a sharp, triangular, spine-tipped tooth.

QUERCUS ACUTUSSIMA (far left). Big, handsome, glossy, chestnut leaves make this hardy species especially desirable.

QUERCUS ALBA (far left). this magnificent oak has elegant lobed leaves and excellent autumn colour.

Q. ALBA L.

WHITE OAK; E NORTH AMERICA. DECIDUOUS.

One of the magnificent oaks of the eastern United States, where it can reach 25 m or more, this species is frequently seen as a native tree there but is less often

QUERCUS CANARIENSIS (above). This is a first-class oak and a highly distinctive, vigorous and shapely specimen tree for large gardens.

planted. Its merits are the elegant lobing of its leaves with deeply cut, curved sinuses. Often tinged with pink when young, they will turn a deep red-purple in autumn. The bark is dark grey and shaggy, with lifting plates or flakes. It is not recommended for alkaline soils.

Q. CANARIENSIS WILLD.

ALGERIAN OAK; SW EUROPE, NORTH AFRICA. SEMI-EVERGREEN.

Misleadingly named – it is not found in the Canary Islands – this is a first-class oak for a highly distinctive, vigorous and shapely specimen tree on a large scale. The dark grey bark is rough and fissured from an early age and the crown is a narrow, regular ovoid, with upright branches that spread only a little with age. The bold leaves, of considerable substance, have a dozen or more lobes on each side which decrease in size regularly from base to tip. In autumn about half of them turn yellow and fall while the rest remain green through the winter. It thrives over a wide area in Britain, but is rarely planted in North America.

Acorns are regularly produced but, judging by some plants grown under this name, will often give rise to hybrids with the Common oak (*Q. robur)* in Britain. The Algerian oak is suitable for a wide range of soils, including chalk.

Q. CASTANEIFOLIA C.A. MEYER

CHESTNUT-LEAVED OAK; CAUCASUS, IRAN. DECIDUOUS.

The original introduction of this species was planted in Kew Gardens in 1846 and has always been the biggest specimen known. One of the finest trees of its kind in Britain, it reached 32 m by 1979. A seedling raised from it grew to 16 m in 25 years, so this species is a very vigorous oak. Its handsome foliage consists of glossy dark green, chestnut-like leaves, that are blue-white beneath, with a dozen or so pairs of prominent parallel veins which end in triangular teeth. On young trees the bark is smooth and grey but with age it breaks into small square plates of dark grey on big ridges. Its vigorous growth and attractive foliage make it a valuable tree for parks and large gardens, but it has a dark crown in summer and is not remarkable when bare. Attempts to raise it from home-produced seeds often result in inferior trees, the result of hybridization with the Turkey oak (*Q. cerris)*. Many of the more recent plantings are of 'Green Spire', the form distributed by Hillier Nurseries, which has upright branches.

QUERCUS CASTANEIFOLIA (far right). Vigorous growth and attractive foliage make this tree suitable for parks and large gardens.

QUERCUS CERRIS L.

TURKEY OAK; S EUROPE, SW ASIA. DECIDUOUS.

The Turkey oak is useful as a fast-growing framework tree that thrives on poor light soils and in the parks of big cities. It is not in the top rank for beauty: big branches leave the bole from unattractive swellings, the foliage is a dull dark green and dead male catkins remain in the crown for months. However, its flowers are first visible as crimson buds on bunches of catkins, its leaves are cut variably deeply into many lobes and it can be sturdy and tall. The bark is dark, rough and knobbly and the straight shoots are coppery-grey and densely pubescent. Although the Turkey oak is perfectly hardy it grows best in areas with warm summers. In some years the leaves turn a pleasing orange-brown but they are more often dull brown before they fall.

Variant 'Variegata' is a very striking form in which the leaves open with a creamy yellow margin that turns to creamy white. It is much slower growing than the species and makes only a small tree. It can produce occasional shoots which revert to green.

Q. COCCINEA MUENCHH.

SCARLET OAK; E NORTH AMERICA. DECIDUOUS.

Although the Scarlet oak was first grown in Britain as long ago as 1688 it is rare to see any that are more than 25 m x 85 cm. This is partly because it is not long-lived – none is much above 100 years old – and partly because, even in its native Appalachian Mountains area, it is seldom very much bigger. The crown is open with a few big branches at wide angles from the sinuous bole,

QUERCUS CERRIS 'LACINIATA' (above). Deeply divided leaves give another interesting feature to this stately tree.

QUERCUS COCCINEA 'SPLENDENS' (left). This English raised form of the North American scarlet oak has reliable autumn colour in our climate.

QUERCUS COCCINEA 'SPLENDENS' (left). Though first grown in England in 1688, these oaks are seldom seen at a great height as they are not long-lived.

each with its own canopy. The red-brown slender shoots bear leaves that are glossy on both sides and widely and deeply cut into three lobes, each with a few big-spined teeth on each side. They have slender 3 cm petioles. In autumn they turn fairly reliably from bright scarlet to deep wine-red, and from leaf shedding until the New Year the tree can be recognized by the way it holds much of the dark red-brown foliage of the lowest branches. A somewhat wispy tree, the Scarlet oak is most effective planted in groups of at least five in parkland or flanking a long vista. It grows on any normal soil but is best on rather light ones.

Variant 'Splendens', raised at Knaphill, Surrey, is noted for even better autumn colours than the Scarlet oak: it turns a reliable deep red-purple. It also has larger leaves, up to 18 x 13 cm as against 12 x 10 cm in the typical form, and small tufts of whitish hairs in the vein axils on their undersides.

QUERCUS FRAINETTO 'HUNGARIAN CROWN' (far right). A vigorous and handsome oak, it has attractive large, rich-green foliage and a distinct habit.

QUERCUS DENTATA (below). Rarely growing in excess of 15 m, this relatively small tree has exceedingly large leaves.

Q. *DENTATA* THUNB.

DAIMIO OAK; JAPAN, KOREA, CHINA. DECIDUOUS.

This Japanese oak must be mentioned for its giant leaves, which can be 40 x 20 cm and cause some interest for their absurd size. In shape they are very like those of the Common oak (*Q. robur*) but are more tapered to the base and with stout, densely pubescent petioles.

Q. *FRAINETTO* TEN.

HUNGARIAN OAK; SE EUROPE. DECIDUOUS.

One of the most vigorous and handsome of all the trees grown in Britain, the Hungarian oak makes an outstanding specimen and is hardy enough to grow near Aberdeen. It has a stout bole with pale grey bark that is finely and evenly divided into small ridges, and the big straight branches begin to radiate from it at 2–4 m to form a huge, high-domed crown. The rich green leaves are crimson-tipped when they emerge from the bud and covered in grey hairs which are soon shed. They are deeply and closely lobed, about 12 a side, and even from a distance the tree can be recognized by the jagged edges of its big, 22 x 10 cm leaves.

Variant Most of the more recently planted trees are 'Hungarian Crown', a form selected for its upright branches and dense, ovoid head.

soil

ACID	ALKALINE
DRY	WET

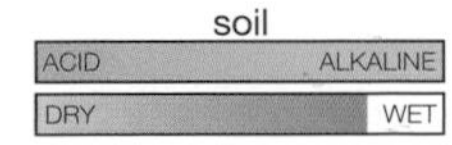
8•15•30 M

QUERCUS X HISPANICA LAM.

LUCOMBE OAK; S EUROPE. SEMI-EVERGREEN.

Although they occur in the wild, the various forms of this hybrid between the Turkey oak (*Q. cerris*) and Cork oak (*Q. suber*) are best known from ones raised in cultivation. The original form was first raised at Lucombe's Nursery at Exeter in 1765 and only it should be called 'Lucombeana', although others are also given this name. Grafts were made of the first cross and planted on several estates in the area. In 1785 Mr Lucombe felled the original seedling for his coffin and, when the first boards decayed, replaced them with a coffin made from one of the first grafts. He was buried in this when he was 102. Acorns collected from early grafts yielded more trees in 1792 and 1830. These were backcrosses to cork oak, and show this in their corky bark and small, very dark leaves which are bluish-white beneath. All are evergreen except in very hard winters. The true 'Lucombeana' is semi-evergreen and keeps a fringe of dark yellowish-green leaves around the outside of its crown.

None of the forms is a first-class tree for planting in numbers – a belt or avenue of Lucombe oak is gloomy – but the tree has value as one of the few completely hardy evergreen broad-leaves to reach a great size. The Lucombe oak is good in sea winds, it can be a fine specimen on its own, and it can show excellent boles when grown as a small clump or among other trees.

5•10•30 M

Q. ILEX L.

HOLM OAK; MEDITERRANEAN REGION.

This tree has been grown in Britain for some 400 years and is common in parks, gardens and churchyards. It has been planted in long belts and avenues on estates all round the coast as shelter from sea winds. It has black bark and foliage – the felted white undersides of the leaves hardly show. Only in June is it silvery white with new leaves at its periphery, and gold with dense bunches of male catkins. These are as decorative as they sound, but only briefly. As a young plant the tree is bushy-crowned and slow. There may be a place for it in areas of maritime exposure but, if available, the Lucombe oak (*Q.* x *hispanica*) is preferable. Away from the coast and in colder, inland areas, the Holm oak can occasionally be damaged in very severe winters.

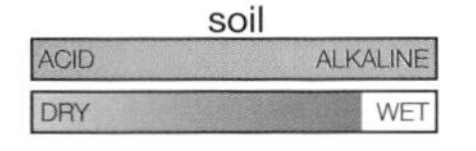

3•5•25 M

QUERCUS X HISPANICA (above). This is a useful semi-evergreen oak, that will reach a large size even if planted in exposed coastal locations.

QUERCUS ILEX (left). The holm oak has been grown in Britain for over 400 years. Many coastal gardens use it for their windbreaks.

QUERCUS LIBANI (above). This scarce tree has an open, shapely crown and very attractive foliage.

Q. LIBANI OLIVIER

LEBANON OAK; SW ASIA. DECIDUOUS.

This is similar to the Sawtooth oak (*Q. acutissima*) but is smaller and more suited to dry soils and hot summers. The leaves are smaller, 10–12 cm, with 10–12 pairs of hairy veins in triangular, whisker-tipped teeth, and are dark, glossy green above and pale beneath. They have short, slender stalks. The acorn is on a short, very stout stalk and hardly emerges from its deep cup, but will now and again mature into a big 4 cm seed. This scarce tree has an open, shapely crown and is very attractive when in leaf.

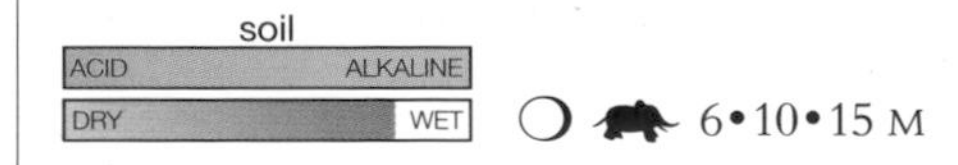

QUERCUS MACRANTHERA (left). A very hardy oak, it makes a shapely tree on any fertile soil.

QUERCUS MACRANTHERA FISCH. & MEYER

CAUCASIAN OAK; CAUCASUS, N IRAN. DECIDUOUS.

This robust tree has a slightly shaggy, silvery and dark grey bark and upswept branches. Its shoots are stout and densely orange-pubescent and bear firm, handsome, often hooded leaves, 20 x 12 cm, with shallow lobes that decrease in size regularly towards the tip. They are very like those of the Algerian oak (*Q. canariensis*) but have persistent grey pubescence on the undersides. It makes a shapely foliage tree on any fairly good soil and is very hardy. Occasional trees raised from seed in cultivation turn out to be hybrids with the Common oak (*Q. robur*) or the Sessile oak (*Q. petraea*).

Q. MYRSINIFOLIA BLUME

BAMBOO OAK; CHINA, JAPAN. EVERGREEN.

This graceful small tree is evergreen but with a light, airy crown. The distant, slender, lanceolate leaves, 10 x 2.5 cm, unfold reddish-purple late in the year and mature to hard, pale fresh green on the upper surfaces and silvery-green beneath. They are entire or with a few tiny sharp teeth. The Bamboo oak is hardy, very ornamental and interesting because it is, like the Japanese evergreen oak (*Q. acuta*), one of the Asiatic group of oaks known as Cyclobalanopsis. Like them it has concentric scales on its acorn cups, although these rarely mature in Britain.

soil
ACID ALKALINE
DRY WET
3•5•15 M

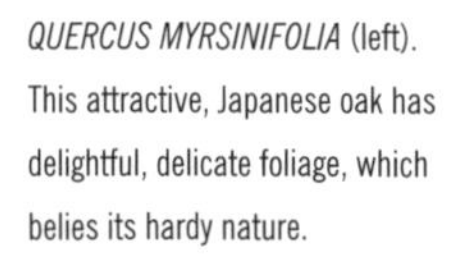

QUERCUS MYRSINIFOLIA (left). This attractive, Japanese oak has delightful, delicate foliage, which belies its hardy nature.

QUERCUS PALUSTRIS (above). Best suited for planting in nutrient poor soils, this oak revels in climates with long, hot summers.

Q. PALUSTRIS MUENCHH.

PIN OAK; E NORTH AMERICA. DECIDUOUS.

In Britain this oak is suited only to eastern and southern regions which have the chance of hot summers. It thrives in city streets throughout the eastern USA, especially in the hottest parts, but also in Pittsburgh and New York and in parts of the west. In England it grows fast as a young slender tree but becomes much slower with age, reaching around 25 m. The crown has a feature shared by no other tree here; it has a good clean bole for 2–4 m, then bears a dense crown of shoots which spray at a downward angle, straight for 2–3 m, as a sort of high skirt. The leaves, prettily and deeply cut into seven lobes, are very like those of the Scarlet oak (*Q. coccinea*) but are usually smaller and always with the vein-axils underneath prominently tufted with pale brown hairs. In autumn the tips of the shoots colour scarlet, then the whole crown follows. It finally turns dark red, but not reliably every year. Although it will also grow on dry soils, this oak is suited to very damp soils and makes a splendid group in a wet corner. It is also a good single specimen tree.

soil
ACID ALKALINE
DRY WET
6•12•25 M

QUERCUS PETRAEA (far right). The Sessile oak is a far finer tree than the common oak in growth, form and foliage.

Q. PETRAEA (MATTUSCHKA) LIEBL.

SESSILE OAK, DURMAST OAK; EUROPE, W ASIA. DECIDUOUS.

This colonized Britain earlier than the Common oak (*Q. robur*) and is in general the oak of mountains and high rainfall areas. Nonetheless it grows better on light sands than does the common oak. A small outlier from its main range is on the sandy hills south of Leith Hill summit in Surrey, and the biggest outlier is Enfield Chase on gravelly hills above the River Lee in Middlesex. The Sessile oak is a far finer tree than the common oak in growth, form and foliage. The bole is straight and clean without burs and the branches radiate mainly straight to make a high dome. The acorns are sessile, or nearly so, and the leaves have good, bright yellow, smooth stalks 2.5 cm long and taper from them. They have small auricles only where there is some hybridity with the common oak. They also taper to their tips, have regular symmetrical lobing and are firm, thick and healthy, usually free from the assortment of galls which disfigure the foliage of the common oak. The leaves are held evenly spread, not bunched.

The Sessile oak is the one to plant for landscaping, groups and specimens, except on the stiffest clays and in wildlife refuges. It is an uncommonly handsome tree.

Variant 'Columna' is very narrowly erect with shallowly lobed leaves, but is too strict for any but very formal plantings.

QUERCUS PONTICA (left). Positively noble leaves, long catkins, and mahogany red acorns grace this wonderful tree.

QUERCUS PYRENAICA (below). A striking display of golden male catkins accompany emerging dark, glossy green leaves in late spring.

QUERCUS PONTICA K. KOCH

ARMENIAN OAK; CAUCASUS, N TURKEY. DECIDUOUS.

This occasionally qualifies as a tree and, even were it always strictly a shrub, the rules would be bent shamelessly in order to include it. The green, stout and ribbed shoots stand up and hold out positively noble leaves, which are big, broad ellipses, 15 x 10 cm. They are bright green above with some 15 straight parallel yellow veins on each side running out to little hooked teeth. The undersides are soft blue-grey or glaucous green and in autumn the upper sides turn yellow, then yellow mixed with brown, and finally all brown. Male catkins can be 20 cm long and acorns, up to 4 cm, are mahogany-red. Occasional plants raised from seed in cultivation may turn out to be *Q.* x *hickelii*, the hybrid with the Common oak (*Q. robur*), which has smaller more deeply toothed leaves.

2•4•8 M

Q. PYRENAICA WILLD.

PYRENEAN OAK; SW EUROPE, NORTH AFRICA. DECIDUOUS.

This very distinctive tree is easily recognized as it is so late coming into leaf, usually long after most other species. The grey-green, often hooded leaves are

densely hairy beneath and emerge just as the tree is putting on a striking display of golden male catkins. Mature leaves are up to 15 cm long or more and are edged with 4–6 deep lobes on each side They are dark glossy green above, with characteristically sunken veins.

Variant The most commonly seen form is 'Pendula', which makes a spreading head of arching and drooping shoots.

soil

3•5•20 M

QUERCUS ROBUR 'FASTIGIATA' (right) is sometimes seed raised and thus too unreliable to call upright. If planting in a confined space choose the grafted 'Koster' instead.

Q. *ROBUR* L.

COMMON OAK, ENGLISH OAK; EUROPE, CAUCASUS. DECIDUOUS.

This is the oak of the clay lowlands of south-east England and the Midlands. Most of the famous old oaks are, or were, of this species except for some in Powys and Herefordshire. With its short, often burred bole, twisting branches, irregular broad-ended and much-galled leaves, it is generally not as desirable as the Sessile oak (*Q. petraea*) but on heavy clay soils it is invaluable as the main framework tree.

Variants The Common oak has produced a large number of forms that differ in habit and foliage, many of which have been introduced or reintroduced into cultivation recently. Most are rare but forms that are seen occasionally are 'Concordia', the Golden oak, with bright yellow leaves which turn green later, and 'Fastigiata', the Cypress oak, which, if raised from seed, varies from the shape of a Lombardy poplar (*P. nigra* 'Italica') to that of a huge goblet. Several reliably narrow forms have been selected, the most commonly grown of which is 'Koster'. This is splendid among buildings or in gardens, especially in groups, and grows quite fast to 24 m or more. 'Pendula', Weeping oak, is a form with pendulous branches.

QUERCUS ROBUR 'PURPURASCENS' (far right). Like many trees the English oak has a purple leafed variant, however, this form is slow growing.

QUERCUS RUBRA L.

RED OAK; E NORTH AMERICA. DECIDUOUS.

As a young tree the Red oak may live up to its name in autumn and be bright then dark red, but when older it is more likely to turn yellow and brown. It grows very vigorously on most soils, and will do so on light sandy soils where the common oak (*Q. robur*) might be no more than scrub. However, the Red oak is not a substitute for the common oak as it is so different in aspect. It does not fit into fully rural scenery but is a good framework tree in city parks and large gardens, in screens, shelter-belts or roundels and clumps. Trees grown fairly close for 20 years make good long boles, whereas one grown as a specimen in the open usually produces a broad crown that springs from big branches 1.5–2 m up the bole. The Red oak is also very different in aspect from the Scarlet oak (*Q. coccinea*) because its short bole is stout and straight and the strong, more regularly placed branches make a single dome of a crown: the leaves are coarser, larger, 20 cm long but vary in vigour of growth and are up to 30 cm on sprouts. They are less deeply or regularly lobed, and matt on both surfaces. As in scarlet and other 'red' oaks, the acorns take two years to ripen.

Variant 'Aurea' is a striking gold-leaved tree even though its display is relatively short. The leaves are at their best in May, soon after opening, and eventually turn green. It is excellent planted against a dark background.

QUERCUS RUBRA (left, above and below) The Red oak lives up to its name in autumn. When a young tree, its leaves turn bright red then a darker hue. The acorns, however, take two years to ripen. In the first year they are like brown buds on short stalks. Grown as a specimen in the open, the Red oak produces a broad crown. When planted close for 20 years, it makes good long boles.

QUERCUS RYSOPHYLLA (right). A real Mexican treasure. With large prominently veined leaves, this fast growing tree is unlike any other hardy oak.

Q. *RYSOPHYLLA* WEATHERBY

LOQUAT OAK; NE MEXICO. EVERGREEN.

Although this will reach 25 m or more in its native habitat it we can only guess at the ultimate size of this species in Britain. Trees introduced in gardens in 1978 have grown to more than 10 m tall. The Loquat oak is very fast-growing – young trees grow up to 60 cm or more a year – and is proving extremely hardy, although it will probably not survive in colder areas and is best with shelter. The crown is conical on young plants, and trees soon develop dark bark cracked into small squares. The young leaves emerge bronze-red and eventually become glossy dark green with deeply sunken veins and up to 25 cm long.This tree is undoubtedly one of the beauties of Mexico.

soil
ACID ALKALINE
DRY WET
5•10•20 M

Q. X *TURNERI* WILLD.

TURNER'S OAK; CULTIVATED ORIGIN. SEMI-EVERGREEN.

A hybrid between the Common oak (*Q. robur*) and Holm oak (*Q. ilex*), this very hardy tree deserves to be more widely planted. It makes a broad, spreading, domed head of dark green foliage with rather leathery leaves that are grey with hairs beneath and tapered to the base with shallow lobes. Many leaves are retained throughout winter and only fall as, or after, the young foliage emerges.

Variant Several forms have been raised, the most commonly seen of which is 'Pseudoturneri'.

QUERCUS X *TURNERI* (far right). Often semi-evergreen in warmer winters, this common oak hybrid should be more widely planted.

QUERCUS VARIABILIS BLUME

CHINESE CORK OAK; CHINA, JAPAN, KOREA. DECIDUOUS.

This all too rare species should be planted whenever it can be acquired, both for interest and as an exceptionally fine tree for foliage. The bark is deeply cavitied, corky pinkish-grey and more attractive than that of the Cork oak (*Q. suber*), which is a very dreary tree. The crown is open and level-branched. The leaves are elliptic, 20 cm long on a yellow 3 cm petiole, and remarkably handsome. The rich glossy green upper surface is marked by a white midrib with 18 pairs of parallel veins running to the margins, where each ends in a whisker that projects from the otherwise straight edge. The underside is covered in a fine silvery pubescence.

4•6•15 M

Q. VELUTINA LAM.

BLACK OAK, QUERCITRON OAK; E NORTH AMERICA. DECIDUOUS.

This eastern American oak has a nearly black bark, much roughened between orange-brown fissures. It is more effective as a foliage tree when it is young and the leaves are low enough to be seen at close range before they fall. They resemble those of the Red oak (*Q. rubra*) but are hard, parchment-like, softly downy on the veins beneath and have stout, yellow 4 cm petioles. They are usually bigger and are always glossier above. In North America they are a distinctive, very dark blackish-green but are usually paler in Britain.

Variant 'Rubrifolia' is a rather remarkable form that is sometimes seen as a graft from the original seedling found in a Hammersmith nursery. Its leaves are up to 40 cm long and hang vertically.

soil
ACID ALKALINE
DRY WET

8•12•25 M

QUERCUS VARIABILIS (above left). This all too rare oak should be planted whenever the opportunity arises, as it is a first-rate tree.

QUERCUS VELUTINA 'RUBRIFOLIA' (above and left). The leaves of this form of the black oak are similar to those on the red oak, although they hang vertically and are larger.

Rhus verniciflua Stokes

VARNISH TREE; E ASIA. DECIDUOUS.

Remarkably hardy for such a luxuriantly large-leafed tree, this is beautiful in summer and autumn. In winter it is gaunt but from close by this gauntness is relieved by its stout, pale lilac-grey shoots which are thinly freckled with orange, its shiny brown buds and the sometimes persistent fruit. The bark is dark grey and fissured and becomes flaky with curved plates. The leaves, up to 80 cm long, have around 14 big leaflets and a 20 cm terminal one. Leathery and hanging, they are rich glossy green on a scarlet rachis, and turn yellow, red and crimson in autumn. In midsummer small, yellow-green flowers radiate on 50 cm panicles which are axillary to the leaves near the tips of the branches. Some trees bear small glossy cream-brown berries in autumn and these can hang in clusters from the shoots all winter. One disadvantage is that the sap from this tree can be extremely irritating, so great care should be taken when handling it.

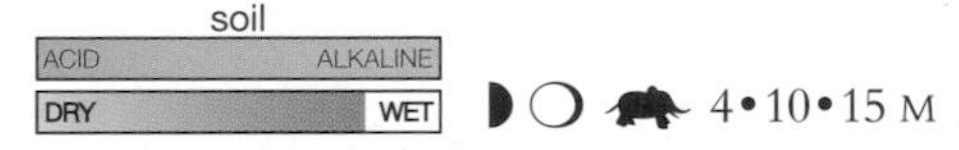

RHUS VERNICIFLUA (below). Although the sap of the sumacs can be irritating, it would be more irritating if we lost this fiery autumnal tree for any reason.

Robinia pseudoacacia L.

Locust tree, False acacia; E United States.

This hardy species will tolerate soils that are too dry, hot, poor or compacted to suit almost any other. It is thus a necessary pioneer tree on hot coal-tips ('bings') and made-up ground consisting largely of brickbats, and is a useful alternative to London plane (*Platanus* x *hispanica*). Its feathery, light green foliage is even a good foil to grimy Portland limestone buildings and it sometimes manages to cover itself in fragrant white flowers. In no other circumstances is there any use for this tree. It is graceless, rough and brittle; it is very late into leaf and early to shed without noticeable change of colour; in the cool climate of Britain it fails to flower more often than it succeeds; and the spiny suckers it sends up continue to appear long after the original tree has gone.

Variants 'Frisia' is so good that the outbreak of this form in new suburban gardens is enough to put some people off it as a cliché. Its fresh butter-gold foliage may green a little, or not at all, until it turns orange in autumn. It is as tough as the species, and grafted on it, but is not as vigorous. 'Frisia' can be grown anywhere except in the coolest summers of the far north and west. It may sucker and is no beauty in winter, but it is worth planting for its great splash of gold. Another form is the thornless 'Umbraculifera'. This makes a dense mop of dark green foliage and has no flowers, so has only its shape to recommend it.

ROBINIA PSEUDOACACIA 'FRISIA' (left). A very common garden tree planted for its feathery golden yellow foliage and its ability to grow on poor soils.

Salix/Willows

THE TREE WILLOWS are best known as waterside plants and although they will grow elsewhere it is here that many are at their best. The individually tiny flowers are borne in catkins, males and females on separate plants, and make an attractive feature in some species.

Cultivation Willows mainly require a moist soil, except for *S. caprea* which will grow on any soil, and need full sun. Several forms of *S. alba* are grown for their coloured winter shoots which remain most effective if they are cut back hard every few years in early spring.

SALIX ALBA (far right). This tree whose bark was once chewed for pain relief has spawned many good forms.

SALIX ALBA L.

WHITE WILLOW; EUROPE, W ASIA. DECIDUOUS.

This tree is far less common along British riversides than the Crack willow (*S. fragilis*). It is taller, with a conic crown until it billows out with age, and distinctively blue-grey. It is a good tree by a waterside but rather thin as a specimen elsewhere and the cultivars below are preferred.

Variants 'Britzensis', the Coral-bank willow, also known as 'Chermesina', is a fine waterside tree with shoots that glow orange-red in winter. 'Sericea' ('Argentea'), the Silver willow, grows much more slowly, but still quite fast and to almost the same size. It is fairly broad with a silvery-grey, densely leafed crown. It stands out among other trees and sets off golden foliage particularly well.

S. BABYLONICA L.

CHINESE WEEPING WILLOW; CHINA. DECIDUOUS.

Before the advent of *S.* 'Chrysocoma', which has largely replaced it, this was the original weeping willow. From China, its typical form is now known only in cultivation and is mainly grown in warm countries.

Variant 'Tortuosa' (*S. matsudana* 'Tortuosa'), the Dragon's claw willow, has twisted leaves and shoots and is now deservedly very popular. For a few years at least, it grows very rapidly on any soil, even rather dry sands. One of the first trees into leaf, it flushes bright green and becomes paler during the season. With very little change except a little yellowing, it holds its leaves as long as any willow, well into December in some years. The sharp sinuosities of its shoots show in summer as well as winter and in older wood – branches and bole – are progressively smoothed out but still visible. This willow may grow as a bush if allowed to do so. Although it does not need a long bole, and would look top-heavy if it had one, it is a better plant with about 1 m clear at the base.

SALIX BABYLONICA 'TORTUOSA' (below). Growing rapidly on any soil, this twisted branched willow is a popular tree that may be coppiced regularly.

soil
ACID ALKALINE
DRY WET
6•10•12 M

SALIX CAPREA (far left). A fast growing, shrubby tree for a variety of soils, only the male forms warrant space in the garden.

SALIX CAPREA L.

GOAT WILLOW, SALLOW; EUROPE, W ASIA. DECIDUOUS.

Although it is often shrubby, this native Goat willow is the only one of several similar native species to grow into a genuine tree. It is quick to colonize bare ground, especially on damp soils, and is common on the edges of woodland that spreads into wet grassy land in hill country. Although it is too coarse and untidy to be grown as an ornamental tree, both male and female plants are valuable in giving early shelter to a new garden with their rapid early growth. The males are worth a permanent place because of their early spring display of golden flowers, which sometimes starts in December but is variably held back until April. The silvery-grey flowered females should be removed in the first thinning. Unfortunately the Goat willow cannot be raised from cuttings, but comes easily from seed: hence the sex of the plant cannot be chosen from the start. 'Kilmarnock' is a male weeping form only about 2.5 m tall with steeply pendulous branches.

S. 'CHRYSOCOMA' (*S. ALBA* L. 'TRISTIS')

WEEPING WILLOW; CULTIVATED ORIGIN. DECIDUOUS.

This is the familiar Weeping willow and not the Babylon willow – the name it is often known by – and is probably a hybrid between that Chinese tree (*S. babylonica*) and the White willow (*S. alba*). It grows almost as well on sandy soils away from open water as it does by a poolside, for its roots find all the water it needs: in a garden it will often find it in, or leaking from, water mains and sewers. It soon becomes too big for a small garden and even in a street it can be 20 m tall and still spreading. It is easily raised from cuttings made from a short length of fairly stout shoot. These must be cut back to the ground and the next year's shoots singled early.

soil
ACID ALKALINE
DRY WET
6•12•20 M

SALIX 'CHRYSOCOMA' (below). Avoid planting the weeping willow too close to buildings as it will quickly outgrow all but the largest gardens.

S. FRAGILIS L.

CRACK WILLOW; EUROPE, ASIA. DECIDUOUS.

This is the common waterside willow everywhere, and is sometimes seen growing among other trees. On a good damp soil it holds its place as a foliage tree. Its leaves, often 16 x 4 cm, are rich glossy green. In autumn many are bright shiny gold, but the crown as a whole does not turn and many leaves remain green. It is a very vigorous tree and, with attention from secateurs, could be given a splendid bole. However, it is all too often allowed to be bush at the base. The hybrid with White willow (*S. alba*) is *S.* x *rubens* and is frequent and intermediate.

SALIX FRAGILIS (right). This, the frequently seen waterside willow, is a worthy foliage tree, although all too often it is grown as a shrub.

S. PENTANDRA L.

BAY WILLOW; EUROPE. DECIDUOUS.

This lovely tree is seldom seen in gardens and should be planted more. It has deep glossy green leaves with yellow midribs. The Bay willow flowers when it is in leaf and the bright yellow, erect catkins on male plants look well against the dark, shiny foliage.

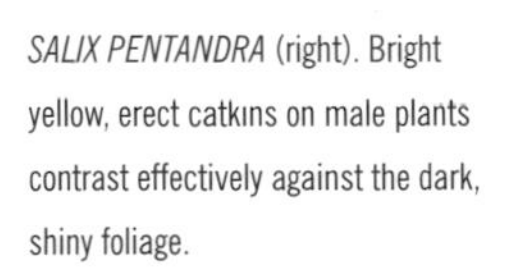

SALIX PENTANDRA (right). Bright yellow, erect catkins on male plants contrast effectively against the dark, shiny foliage.

Sassafras albidum (Nutt.) Nees

SASSAFRAS; E NORTH AMERICA. DECIDUOUS.

The Sassafras has grey, much-fissured bark and a need for heat which limits reasonable growth to regions with warm summers. A member of the Laurel family, it is aromatic and crushed leaves yield a scent and taste of vanilla and oranges. In Britain, as in its homeland where it proliferates by suckers and makes long hedges, the crown is bare and open below, with twisting, upright branches that hold aloft a shallow dome of very dense leafage. The leaves are unique in that their shapes vary on the same tree, from elliptic and entire through one large ovate lobe on one side only (the 'mitten' leaves) to three-lobed with a fairly deeply cut ovate lobe on each side. The undersides are pale blue-grey. In autumn the foliage turns to fine yellows, pinks and then orange, but Britain does not see the brilliant display of mixed orange, scarlet and crimson that it gives in Pennsylvania. Tiny yellow flowers open in spring before the leaves have expanded, males and females on separate plants.

Cultivation The Sassafras needs a good, deep, lime-free soil and only really thrives in areas with hot summers. Suckering can sometimes be a problem in gardens.

Variant Some trees belong to var. *molle* (Raf.) Fern., which has shoots and leaves with grey hairs.

soil
ACID ALKALINE
DRY WET
3•5•15 M

SASSAFRAS ALBIDUM var. *MOLLE* (below). Given a lime-free soil and hot summer, the aromatic, often fig-like leaves turn a bright yellow, pink and orange in autumn.

SAXEGOTHAEA CONSPICUA (right). This shade tolerant conifer is an attractive little tree, with fountains of dark green foliage in warmer climates.

Saxegothaea conspicua Lindl.

PRINCE ALBERT'S YEW; CHILE, ARGENTINA. EVERGREEN.

This very attractive little tree from Chile grows best in warmer but not too dry areas where it makes fountains of rich dark green, elegant foliage to 18 m tall. In other areas it tends to be slender and small. The bark is similar to that of the common Yew (*Taxus baccata*) but smoother and mottled pink, brown and dark red. The outer shoots are strung with rather scattered bunches of dense foliage and hang on slender, bright green shoots with white stripes. The leaves unfold tinged purple and are 2 cm long, curved, hard, spine-tipped and broadly white-banded beneath. Powdery-blue, 1 cm ovoid female flowers are common through much of the year.

Cultivation Shelter and a damp, acid soil are important for this tree. It will tolerate considerable shade but very little exposure.

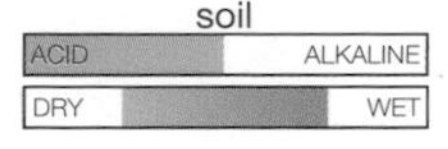

3•5•15 M

Sciadopitys verticillata Siebold & Zucc.

JAPANESE UMBRELLA PINE; JAPAN. EVERGREEN.

This strange tree, a member of the Redwood family (Taxodiaceae), is unique in having its leaves fused together in pairs and borne in whorls rather like the ribs of an umbrella. The fused leaves are 10–12 cm long, deep, shining green above and yellow-green beneath. Young plants are upright and narrowly conic. They may need guidance to form a shapely tree for some have been allowed to become many-stemmed and bushy. In either case, the foliage is unusual and attractive, even in some shade. This pine is normally slow or very slow in growth, but can occasionally be surprisingly fast.

Cultivation The Japanese umbrella pine will grow on any damp non-alkaline soil in sun or partial shade, with some protection from strong winds. It is usually at its best in high rainfall areas with warm summers.

soil
ACID ALKALINE
DRY WET
4•8•20 M

SCIADOPITYS VERTICILLATA (below). The unusual Japanese umbrella pine has leathery needles borne in whorls around the stem.

Sequoia sempervirens (D. Don) Endl.

COAST REDWOOD; CALIFORNIA. EVERGREEN.

The tallest tree in the world is a 114 m Coast redwood at Redwood Creek in north-west California, where entire stands are 90 m tall. In the sea-fog areas of the foothills of the Coast Ranges the trees stand very close together, but groups in Britain's drier climate need to be at wider spacing: 8–12 m will give superb rich deep red boles. Grown in the open, a single tree maintains a narrow, columnar crown of light branches. Growth will cease at a certain height, between 25 m and 35 m depending on exposure and hence the height of surrounding trees. Young plants on damp, deep soils make annual shoots of around 1.3 m and at that speed some trees are gaunt, open and too narrow,. However, the ones that thrive are good to see with their long, rather pendulous, broadly leafed deep green foliage, and deeply fissured, fibrous bark, which is either dark chestnut all over or, as in California, pale grey on the ridges.

SEQUOIA SEMPERVIRENS 'ADPRESSA' (right). This selection is slower growing and smaller than its mammoth parent.

SEQUOIA SEMPERVIRENS (far right and below). Growing to only 25-35 m in Britain the coast redwood attains over 100 m in its sea-fog eclipsed California home. This gentle giant has soft fibrous, chestnut or pale grey bark.

This tree is excellent for a short avenue of massive boles in the shelter of woodland but in open country, for example along a drive between fields, it is too thin to be effective.

Cultivation Grow the Coast redwood in any good, well-drained soil, in sun.

Variant 'Adpressa' is relatively slow – it takes about 100 years to reach 22 m – and small, and is sometimes planted as a dwarf. The new shoots are slender and cream-coloured, and one-year leaves are small and banded bright blue-white beneath with a single white band above. It is good in a group of middle-sized trees.

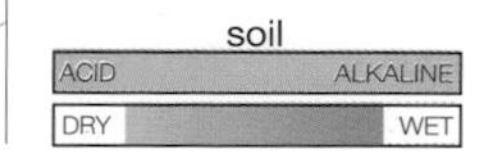

8•15•35 M

Sequoiadendron giganteum (Lindl.) Buchholz

SIERRA REDWOOD, GIANT SEQUOIA, WELLINGTONIA, BIG TREE; CALIFORNIA. EVERGREEN.

The name Sierra redwood is preferred by Californian foresters since it distinguishes this species, by origin, from the Coast redwood (*Sequoia sempervirens*) which is only found at least 200 km to the north, across the Central Valley. In gardens the two are frequently confused, in name at least, but the Sierra redwood is quite distinct from the coast redwood in its rough foliage and sharp-pointed, scale-like leaves.

The Sierra redwood is not quite the tallest, the stoutest or the oldest tree in the world but its combination of height and bole diameter make it the biggest. Seventy-two small groves are scattered along the southern parts of the western flanks of the Sierra Nevada. A few of them are in private ownership: the rest are State Forest Parks or National Parks. No tree has been felled this century and all are closely protected. Although it was noted in 1833 by a traveller, J. Leonard, in a diary which remained obscure until recently, the Sierra redwood was re-found in 1850 and only brought to the notice of the world in 1853, a by-product of the 1849 gold rush.

This is an ideal tree for plantings on a monumental scale, in avenues, lines, roundels and as a single specimen or in groups. Early growth can be variable and is not very rapid in height – 60–80 cm a year is more usual than 1 m – but is often extremely rapid in diameter after a few years. Some old trees have layered branches or many big ones low on the bole, and would have been good specimens had they been cleaned up when young, but the Sierra redwood generally looks after itself very well. Trees in Britain are half the height and one-third of the diameter of the best specimens in California, but only one-thirtieth of their age ('Grizzly Giant' is reckoned to be 3400 years old), so how long they will live and what sizes they will reach are open and intriguing questions. Some of the British Sierra redwoods are already the biggest trees of any kind in Europe.

SEQUOIADENDRON GIGANTEUM (above). A dramatic tree for plantings on a monumental scale.

Cultivation Sierra redwoods will grow on almost any kind of soil except solid chalk. Honey fungus kills a few trees here and there, and lightning strikes many, but there seem to be no other problems and they are rarely blown down.

Variants 'Aureum', a slower, more upright form with dull yellow new shoots, was raised in County Cork from one of the earliest seed-lots in 1856. It is only a curiosity and has no place as a golden tree. 'Pendulum' is a freak with short branches that emerge and continue almost vertically downwards. The main stems of a few trees of this form remain erect as with the 32 m tree in the ravine at Bodnant, but most of them arch over to make a hoop 10–12 m high like a grazing giraffe.

SEQUOIADENDRON GIGANTEUM 'PENDULUM' (far left) is a freak, and lacks any will to produce an upright leader. Well established specimens often require support.

8•12•40 M

SOPHORA JAPONICA 'VIOLACEA' (above) is a delightful, spreading, small tree with feathery foliage.

SOPHORA JAPONICA 'PENDULA' (below) is a small weeping tree with a torous head of branches, often top grafted on a clear stem.

Sophora japonica L.

PAGODA TREE, SCHOLAR'S TREE; CHINA. DECIDUOUS.

In old China there was a strict hierarchy of permitted trees for graves. Only the emperor could have a pine; a princess could have a *Paulownia* and a scholar or a priest, still fairly high in the order of things, could have a *Sophora*. The Japanese borrowed the tree long ago and it was first known to botanists as a Japanese tree, hence the specific epithet. The original tree in Britain came from China and was moved to Kew in 1760, where it survives with a horizontal bole. It is still far from common to see a Pagoda tree in Britain but there was a great vogue for it in the streets and squares of the eastern USA some years ago, evidence that it survives well in hot cities and poor soils. It is not a great tree for foliage, nor for shape; in fact, it is very like the Locust tree (*Robinia pseudoacacia*) except that it is thornless and has blue-green shoots and acute leaflets. It scores over the locust tree by never suckering and by flowering in September. The flowers are similar – white, pea forms on panicles – but are longer, 20 cm, and spreading. The fruit are much superior – not dull brown pods, but long, bright green ones that swell by each seed like a few large beads on a string. However, they seldom develop in Britain.

Cultivation The Pagoda tree thrives and flowers best only in areas with hot summers.

Variants 'Pendula' is a mop-head of violently contorted shoots on a stem of rootstock, and is usually some 3–4 m tall, with long shoots hanging to the ground all round. It rarely flowers. 'Violacea' has flowers flushed with violet.

6•12•20 M

Sorbus

THIS DIVERSE and widely distributed genus includes the mountain ashes and whitebeams. Mostly small trees, many are grown in gardens for their spring flowers, as well as their fruit and foliage.

Cultivation Sorbus will grow in any reasonably good, well-drained soil. The rowans (those with pinnate leaves) prefer lime-free soil, while the whitebeams, such as *S. aria* and *S. intermedia* are good on shallow chalk soils.

SORBUS ALNIFOLIA (SIEB. & ZUCC.) K. KOCH

ALDER WHITEBEAM; CHINA, KOREA, JAPAN. DECIDUOUS.

This has unusual and attractive foliage for a whitebeam and is a fine sight in autumn as well as during winter. It has dark or pale grey bark finely striped in buff. The dark green leaves are ovate, up to 9 x 6 cm, and are on red petioles with silky hairs. The flowers are prolifically borne and mature to bright orange and red around the fruit, which remain a good colour well after the leaves fall.

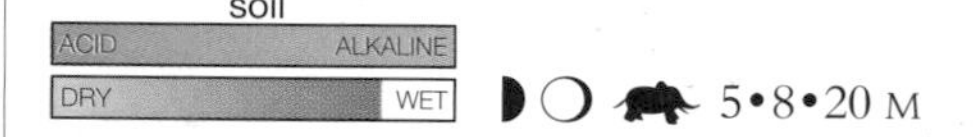

S. ARIA (L.) CRANTZ

WHITEBEAM; EUROPE. DECIDUOUS.

This tough and hardy tree is normally conic in shape with ascending branches. The leaves are rather variable in shape but are unlobed or shallowly lobed, and edged with sharp, small teeth. Grey with hairs above when they emerge, they become glossy dark green, but remain white-hairy beneath and can turn yellow in autumn before they fall. The bright red fruit are about 1.2 cm across in clusters.

Variants Numerous minor forms, most of them rare are grown. The most commonly seen is 'Lutescens' which has very silvery-grey young foliage.

Other species *S. intermedia* (Ehrh.) Pers., the Swedish whitebeam grows to 15 m and differs from *S. aria* in that its leaves are lobed, particularly towards the base. *S.* x *thuringiaca* (Ilse) Fritsch is a naturally occurring hybrid between *S. aria* and *S. aucuparia* and has deeply lobed leave. It grows to 12 m.

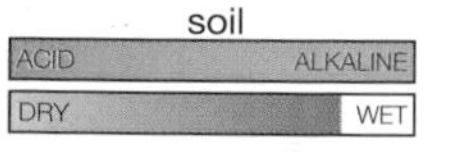

5•8•15 M

SORBUS ALNIFOLIA (left). A distinctive, and very attractive small tree with glowing autumn colour and bright orange-red fruits.

SORBUS ARIA (below). The whitebeams come in a variety of shapes and sizes, but all are tolerant to some degree of dry, chalk soils.

SORBUS AUCUPARIA 'SHEERWATER SEEDLING' (above). Large creamy-white flowers are followed by followed by orange-red fruits that are quickly devoured by birds.

S. AUCUPARIA L.

MOUNTAIN ASH, ROWAN; EUROPE, N ASIA. DECIDUOUS.

This tree is at its best in areas with cool summers where it gives its brightest autumn colour, turning reds of a variety and quality that it seems incapable of achieving in warmer gardens. Every few years it provides large orange-red berries in numbers that sate and defeat even suburban blackbirds. It will tolerate very hard conditions and has a place in town parks and streets. Since it is also common in most sorts of countryside there is no need for it in a large garden. Better rowans can be found. It is usually short-lived and the upper crown soon becomes thin and open.

Variants Superior ones include the following two cultivars. 'Beissneri' is a very choice tree with pale yellow-green foliage and, at least on young trees, a shining dark orange bark. It has a faint bluish wax finish which is completely translucent when wet so that in sunshine after rain the stems shine out a brilliant clear orange. The leaflets are prettily serrated and turn yellow, amber and pink in autumn. 'Xanthocarpa' has big, clear yellow berries and numerous domed flower heads late in the season. It is a tall-growing tree. 'Sheerwater Seedling', one of several similar superior forms, is remarkably neatly narrow-conic and upright in crown and has good foliage and fruit.

S. COMMIXTA KOEHNE

SCARLET ROWAN; JAPAN, KOREA. DECIDUOUS.

This variable species has 2 cm long shining red, conic smooth buds. Its leaves, up to 25 cm long, consist of 15 broad lanceolate leaflets, each 8 x 2.5 cm and serrated to within 2 cm of the base.

Variant The most commonly seen form, originally grown as *S. discolor*, is 'Embley', which is distinguished by its smaller, 15 cm long leaves and much narrower leaflets. In autumn the leaflets assume rich, dark purple borders which spread across them and turn scarlet until the whole crown is a blaze of scarlet before it darkens to deep red. In summer 'Embley' is easily recognized by its crown of slender branches that arch out to the horizontal, with deeply toothed leaves in thin layers.

SORBUS COMMIXTA (right). One of the best rowan for autumn tints, leaves change from dark purple, then scarlet, to deep red.

SORBUS DOMESTICA L.

TRUE SERVICE TREE; S & E. EUROPE, W ASIA, NORTH AFRICA. DECIDUOUS.

This tree somewhat resembles the Mountain ash (*S. aucuparia*) but is broader with level, lower branches from which hang its larger, rather yellowish leaves. Its rich brown bark is vertically ridged and the buds are glossy green ovoids. Another striking difference from the mountain ash is the service tree's big, 3–4 cm fruit that are green tinged red-brown, and can be either apple- or pear-shaped.

It is unusual and its stature, bark, bold foliage and fruit earn it a place among specimen trees, where the bark and its large heads of 1.5 cm flowers can be seen. The dull colour of its foliage and its open crown render it less useful in groups. It grows well on any normal soil in some degree of shelter.

S. FOLGNERI (SCHNEID.) REHDER

CHINESE WHITEBEAM; CHINA. DECIDUOUS.

Introduced in Britain in 1901, this is an elegant specimen and foliage tree. It is scarce, but worthy of more frequent planting. The dark purplish bole with peeling fissures holds a crown of slender branches that arch out

to the horizontal in the very few old trees known this can be 16 m high. The leaves are lanceolate, up to 10 x 5 cm, and taper to a narrow point. They are very dark green above and variably but, in the best trees, well silvered beneath. Late autumn shows this tree at its best. When most other trees have lost their colour its leaves turn orange, scarlet and crimson and many fall to lie with their still-silver undersides showing. The small red berries often persist on the tree long after the leaves have been shed. The Chinese whitebeam seems to grow well on slightly acid, moist loams or sands, but may be more adaptable than has yet been found.

S. HUPEHENSIS SCHNEID.

HUBEI ROWAN; CHINA. DECIDUOUS.

This sturdy tree from western China transplants well when it is a big plant and is finding favour with public authorities as well as with gardeners who want good, rather unusual foliage and very unusual fruit. It has a broad-conic crown of stout rising branches and shoots from which hang 25 cm long leaves with 13 broad-oblong leaflets which are entire on their inner halves and very sharply toothed on the outer. They are slightly silvered grey-green above and glaucous grey beneath on pink, grooved rachises. The flowers, on big, open domed heads, are white with yellow centres and pale purple anthers. The stalks in the flower head turn bright red as the 6 mm berries turn white with a slight pink stain or, in 'Rosea', bright rose-pink, and hang in bunches 12 cm across. The leaf rachis turns deep red and the leaflets yellow with some red, and they fall before the fruit. Birds sometimes eat the berries but more usually they leave them alone, perhaps thinking they cannot yet be ripe. From a distance a well-laden specimen with pink fruit resembles a tree in full pink flower.

SORBUS DOMESTICA (left). Prized on its own for stature, bark, bold foliage, and 3-4 cm fruits, it also works well in groups.

SORBUS FOLGNERI (below). This tree blazes orange, scarlet, and crimson later than most other whitebeams.

SORBUS HUPEHENSIS (far left). A real gem of a garden tree, white and pink berries persist long into autumn after the deep red leaves have scattered.

SORBUS 'JOSEPH ROCK' (above). Distinctively scented flowers are followed by large clumps of lemon yellow fruits and attractive, fiery autumnal tints.

SORBUS SARGENTIANA (right). This is a delightful garden tree. The foliage is bold for a rowan but casts only a light shade, allowing under planting.

S. 'JOSEPH ROCK'

CHINA. DECIDUOUS.

First-class as a small specimen tree and outstanding in autumn, 'Joseph Rock' is also ideal in streets as it has a slender crown and very small leaflets that do not block drains. It was sent to Britain from China by Joseph Rock, an American, but only one seedling reached its destination, in a batch of seeds of another species. The leaves have about 17 narrow, rather crowded leaflets on a stalk which is crimson at its base early in the season and increasingly down its length. A narrow-crowned, dark, somewhat yellowish-green tree in summer, it becomes a pillar of fire – orange, scarlet and purple – in autumn. At the same time the little berries are bright lemon-yellow so the tree is, to put it mildly, quite a sight. 'Joseph Rock' is growing well in gardens on light sandy soils, as well as in streets on heavier soil, and seems to be adaptable.

soil
ACID ALKALINE
DRY WET

6•8•10 M

S. SARGENTIANA KOEHNE

SARGENT ROWAN; CHINA. DECIDUOUS.

Ernest Wilson sent this to Britain among many other splendid trees from western China in 1908, during his third collecting trip and his first for the Arnold Arboretum in Boston. It is usually seen grafted on to a stem of Mountain ash (*S. aucuparia*) from which its stout shoots spread out and up into a flattened globose crown. It has glossy deep red big buds that exude clear resin, and leaves 35 cm long and nearly as broad, with 11 large taper-pointed leaflets. The flower heads are broad and low-domed, to 20 cm across, and bear some 200–500 bright red but small fruit in autumn. These are quite impressive but this tree is usually grown for its autumn foliage. The big leaves turn dull orange then, in good years, uniform bright scarlet; in other years they are pale orange, mottled with red, and are nearly as attractive and less usual.

soil
ACID ALKALINE
DRY WET

3•5•10 M

SORBUS SCALARIS (far left). Distinctive foliage and domed heads of scarlet fruits, make this a first class tree of moderate size.

SORBUS SCALARIS KOEHNE

LADDER-LEAF ROWAN; W CHINA. DECIDUOUS.

This tree of very distinctive foliage was found and introduced in Britain in 1904 by Ernest Wilson when he was in West Sichuan, China. It is unfortunately rare in gardens. The leaves are well displayed along level, spreading branches and tend to hang. They are dark glossy green with around 30 slender oblong leaflets, each with a deeply impressed midrib. In autumn big domed heads of scarlet fruit stand above the green leaves, an attractive contrast, before the leaves turn red and purple.

The tree has a tendency to grow long branches from near the ground, but if it is kept to a single clean bole for 2 m before being allowed to spread it makes a first-class specimen tree of very modest size, at home on a wide range of soils provided they do not dry out too rapidly. It is good in a group if planted at wide spacing to give the spreading branches the room and light they need to flower. At maturity the spread can be at least 10 m, so the trees should not be planted more closely than that.

6•8•10 M

S. THIBETICA (CARDOT) HAND.-MAZZ.

SW CHINA, HIMALAYAS. DECIDUOUS.

This variable species is grown in several forms, most of which are rare in gardens except for 'John Mitchell', originally known as *S.* 'Mitchellii', which is named after the last curator under the Holford family at Westonbirt in Gloucestershire. This form has massively orbicular leaves up to 20 x 18 cm which are a striking silvery grey for several weeks after they unfold. They then turn to glossy dark green above but remain silvery beneath. These are its most attractive feature as the flowers and fruit are inconspicuous, but it is increasingly planted as a fast-growing medium-sized tree with bold foliage.

soil
ACID ALKALINE
DRY WET 8•15•20 M

S. TORMINALIS (L.) CRANTZ

WILD SERVICE TREE, CHEQUERS TREE; EUROPE, NORTH AFRICA, SW ASIA. DECIDUOUS.

This has many features of interest and others of garden merit. It was formerly grown for its fruit – checkers – from which a drink was made. Many inns specialized in this drink, and most of them have, through an etymological error, a splendid but irrelevant chessboard for their sign. In Britain it was a late arrival as a native and is distributed along the woods under the North Downs and thinly elsewhere, around the chalk-beds

SORBUS THIBETICA 'JOHN MITCHELL' (left). With the largest leaves of any sorbus, this form is a fast growing, medium-sized foliage tree of considerable merit.

SORBUS TORMINALIS (left). Once prized for its fruits (chequers), this native tree has delightful autumn colour, although now surpassed by many new introductions.

SORBUS TORMINALIS (above) bears open heads of white flowers with yellow anthers in late spring or early summer.

SORBUS VESTITA (above right). A splendid foliage tree with a light green overall colour, and orange autumn fruits.

and north on limestones in the Pennines to near Carnforth. Where it occurs in the wild is of particular interest to ecologists, and carefully mapped, because it is believed that it sows itself and grows wild only where the land is primary woodland, that is, it has never been cleared or ploughed and is not a plantation.

The leaves have a pair of big triangular lobes and 1–3 pairs of smaller ones, not unlike some maples but these are held alternately and not in opposite pairs. They have slender, yellow-green stalks and are shiny dark green and hard, turning yellow, dark red and purple in autumn. The bark is dark brown with grey scales.

In late spring or early summer the Wild service tree bears open heads of white flowers with yellow anthers, and then a few 1 cm, brown speckled fruit. It is a splendid and unusual specimen tree for any garden with the necessary space, and grows quite fast from seed. It prefers a rather rich soil, damp but well-drained, although it will tolerate lighter, poorer soils.

S. VESTITA (G. DON) LODD. (*S. CUSPIDATA* (SPACH) HEDL.)

HIMALAYAN WHITEBEAM. DECIDUOUS.

This makes a vigorous, tall, narrowly conic crown to 20 m, with rather few nearly erect branches and stout shoots. It is a very splendid foliage tree with a distinctive light grey-green overall colour. The thick, heavy leaves are elliptic and tapered at both ends and up to 22 x 14 cm. They are silvery at first and soon somewhat shiny deep green above and white beneath with dense pubescence. The tree grows well on moist, limy or sandy soils, and has heads of 2 cm fragrant flowers with dull purple anthers. In autumn 2 cm green fruits are borne in heavy clusters that weigh down the branches and slowly become flushed with orange as they ripen.

S. VILMORINII SCHNEID.

VILMORIN ROWAN. DECIDUOUS.

SORBUS VILMORINII (below). Although sold through nurseries as a single stem specimen, it is much more reliable if grown as a shrub.

This little tree is not at all demanding as to soil or climate, although it prefers a damp soil and high rainfall, and in good conditions can sow itself freely.

The bole of grey and brown flaking bark is short and often curved. It bears a low, wide head of shallowly arching branches with spurs that bear sprays of 12 cm long leaves, each with some 23 small leaflets elegantly placed. The leaves emerge brown and become dark grey-green until late autumn when they turn dark crimson. Each spur bears a slender head of small white flowers which ripen into 1 cm ovoid fruit. These are deep red in late summer, become pale through the autumn, and then turn from dark to pale pink and, finally, nearly white.

This tree is too small and low to be used as a single specimen. On a larger scale, a group of three, five or seven on a shallow bank, for example, makes a feature that is pleasant in summer and moderately spectacular in autumn. Some plants are grafted on to the Mountain ash (*S. aucuparia*) and may sprout at the base; these sprouts should be cut back annually.

STUARTIA MALACODENDRON (left), was an early introduction from the United States and first flowered here in 1742 but has never been common and is really only a success in southern England.

STUARTIA SINENSIS (below) with attractive flesh pink flaking bark, this is the most under utilised of this group.

Stuartia

RELATED TO THE CAMELLIAS, Stuartias give us some striking flowering trees which, with their attractive bark and autumn colour, spread their ornamental characters over several seasons.

Cultivation Stuartias require a reasonably moist but well-drained lime-free soil in a sunny position, ideally in a woodland site among other trees that give shelter from winds.

STUARTIA PSEUDOCAMELLIA MAXIM.

JAPAN. DECIDUOUS.

This species has a minor oddity in that its leaves are dull above and glossy underneath, which is a reversal of the normal arrangement. Its merits are more obvious: good bark, late flowers, and autumn colour. The bark is mainly dull orange-brown but it grows purplish scales and when these are newly shed they

STUARTIA PSEUDOCAMELLIA var. *KOREANA* (below). A true year-round performer with attractive bark, delightful flowers, and splendid autumn colours.

leave patches of bright orange. The open, flimsy crown bears layers of very dark leaves, round-toothed on the outer half and up to 8 cm long. Numerous cup-shaped white flowers, 6 cm across, open after midsummer to show an orange boss of stamens. In autumn the leaves turn yellow and red then, in good sun, deep bright red all over.

Variant The best form in gardens is var. *koreana* (Rehder) Sealy (*S. koreana* Rehder), which has slightly larger flowers.

Other species *S. sinensis* Rehder & Wilson, Chinese stuartia, is broader with rather larger leaves and flowers but is grown mainly for its bark. This is flaky in youth and smooth, bald and flesh-pink later when it has shed all the flakes. Some boles are more cream and grey.

soil
ACID ALKALINE
DRY WET
3•5•35 M

STYRAX JAPONICA (left). Plant this woodland tree close to a path so the pendulous flowers can be viewed from beneath.

Styrax japonica Siebold & Zucc.

JAPAN, KOREA, CHINA. DECIDUOUS.

No woodland garden should be without this beautiful and very elegant flowering tree. It is often seen with several branches from the base, but is equally effective as it is often on a single stem. Several forms are cultivated varying in leaf shape. The leaves are dark green, pale and glossy beneath, often with a long, tapered point, up to 8 cm long, but much smaller on flowering shoots. In early summer the white, fragrant flowers hang beneath the branches on long, slender stalks and have a centre of yellow anthers. Originally introduced from Japan in 1862, a later introduction from China, known as 'Fargesii' has broardly oval to nearly rounded leaves with a short point and bears earlier flowers on pink stalks. 'Pink Chimes' is a form raised in Japan with pale pink flowers.

Other Species *Styrax obassia* Siebold & Zucc. is a sturdy tree to 12 m tall. Young plants bear remarkable leaves, 20 x 15 cm, which are either truncate across the top or obtuse with three large triangular teeth each side. Adult foliage is orbicular, abruptly acute, 15 x 15 cm, and pale green above and densely glaucous pubescent beneath. The winter buds are enclosed by the swollen base of the stout 2 cm petiole, which is densely hairy. Twenty to 25 flowers are borne on one side of a nodding, pale green, 15 cm stalk and each is white, 2–3 cm across, fragrant and bell-shaped. However, they are often almost hidden by the large leaves. The fruit, which bend the racemes over further with their weight, are 1.5 cm ovoids. They are pale brown densely pubescent and cupped in a broad-lobed calyx.

Cultivation Grow in a moist but well-drained lime-free soil. Site this tree in light, high shade next to a path, so that the flowers can be viewed from below.

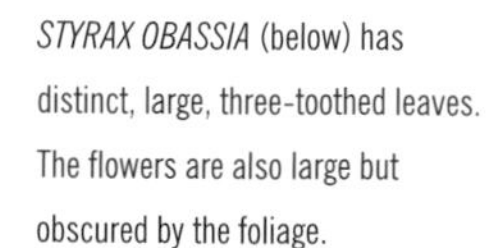

STYRAX OBASSIA (below) has distinct, large, three-toothed leaves. The flowers are also large but obscured by the foliage.

Taxodium distichum (L.) Rich.

SWAMP CYPRESS, BALD CYPRESS; SE UNITED STATES. DECIDUOUS.

Seldom in noticeable leaf before mid-June, the Swamp cypress is eventually a bright, fresh green over a twiggy, bluntly conic crown until it darkens and then, in November, turns foxy-brown. The slender leaves, 2 cm long, spread on either side of the young shoots and both are shed in autumn. Only trees planted by water or in flooding ground will grow the woody termite-hills, known as 'knees' or pneumatophores, which arise from their roots and were at one time thought to supply them with air.

In its native range, the Swamp or Bald cypress grows by tidal creeks along the coast from Virginia to Mexico, and in freshwater swamps along the Mississippi bottomlands north to Illinois. That great range could, no doubt provide hardier trees than those that are currently grown in Britain, but even these would still need hot summers for the best growth. There are rather few north of the Midlands and in Ireland. Many of the best specimens, which reach 35 m x 1.3 m, stand beside lakes or streams but some are not even in damp positions. No Swamp cypress in Britain is known to be growing in tidal or even brackish water – few gardens run to this anyway. Growth is best around London and in East Anglia and is moderate for a tree that reaches such a large size. Swamp cypresses look much better grown together than singly; they look bare and untidy among other conifers, whereas a group repeats the shape of the tree and makes a feature of it. A group is also preferable to a line by a waterside. It has substance and does not straggle, and is unspoiled by a tree or two of poor growth, which would be fatal to a line.

TAXODIUM DISTICHUM 'NUTANS' (far right) has striking upswept branches and foliage that turns russet in autumn.

TAXODIUM DISTICHUM (below). Best planted in groups, this deciduous conifer will often grow knees if cultivated in or near water.

Other species *Taxodium ascendens* Brongn, Pond cypress, also from the south-eastern United States, is less hardy and slower growing and makes a narrow tree to 20 m. In 'Nutans', the form seen in cultivation, the branch-tips curve downwards. The shoots emerge in summer as slender spikes that hang from the down-curved branch-tips and stand vertically along the branches. At this stage the tree is at its quaint best. Through the summer it is delicately foliaged in light green that turns a rich red-brown in late autumn. The leaves are only 8 mm long, slender and finely pointed and arise in spirals from the shoot.

Cultivation Although these cypresses grow naturally in areas where their trunks are submerged in water for at least part of the year, this is not a necessity and they grow well on a moist, lime-free soil, in a sunny position. They are at their best in regions with warm summers – this applies especially to *T. ascendens* – and look particularly good planted near water.

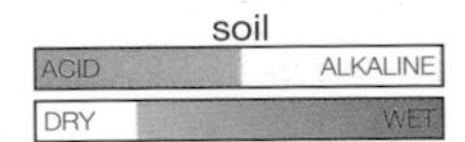

5 • 10 • 30 M

Taxus baccata L.

YEW; EUROPE; AFRICA, W ASIA. EVERGREEN.

The common Yew has one of the strongest and most elastic timbers of any tree. This enables a very old, very hollow bole to hold together and support long branches when other trees would collapse, until a specimen is well over 1000 years old. The Yew is much longer-lived than any other species in northern Europe. It is also very nearly indestructible and will happily tolerate intensive clipping, cutting and shaping while remaining clothed with green to the ground, since it is able to bear shade in a way that few trees can. All these features make it unrivalled for background work on an intimate scale in the garden. As a backing to a herbaceous border running away from a house, as a subject for topiary and for the alcoves behind marble statuary, and for screens and divisions within the garden and dense year-round shelter, what owner with thoughts of succeeding generations would not choose the plant which can be most closely clipped and lasts for over 1000 years?

Churchyards in a crescent from Kent to Devon, Wiltshire, Gloucestershire, Herefordshire, Powys and Clwyd are the homes of hundreds of vast old yews, bigger than any known elsewhere in the world, which range from 2 m to over 3 m in diameter. Their presence in so many churchyards was formerly attributed to very early planting to give shelter to the path and the porch; to yield, where male, the 'palm' still used in Ireland; to symbolize eternal life; and to grow bow staves where they would not poison grazing cattle. But, as shown by stone vaulting over a root from the Tandridge yew, which stands 8 m from the church wall today in the building's Saxon foundations, the yews hugely pre-date even the original churches built 1000 years ago. Many are now believed to be 3000 years old or more. The shelter a Yew gives to a church arises from the building being sited to benefit from the tree's big, evergreen crown and so that is could appropriate the ancient aura of the pagan sacred ground.

The Yew's upward growth is usually 15–25 cm a year at best then slows to a few centimetres for perhaps 300 years, when the tree may be 20 m tall. A few examples, in woods or close lines, are over 25 m and appear to still have short leading shoots. Really old specimens have such spreading crowns that there is no leader at all, but shoots 10–15 cm long may sprout from all parts of the tree. Growth in diameter is very variable. Some yews of known date have grown for 100 years at the standard rate of 0.8 cm a year, while others have grown at much less than half this rate. Very old yews may add 1 cm in 20 years. Such rates can be accurately discovered only by an individual taking his or her own

TAXUS BACCATA 'FASTIGIATA' (far left). Tolerant of chalk soil, this tightly conic form can be clipped to accentuate its habit.

TAXUS BACCATA 'HESSEI' (below). Raised in Germany, this is a dense and rather upright form with long, broad, dark green leaves.

measurements, for early figures were so unreliable that some records spanning 100 years or more in the growth of a tree give each succeeding figure as less than the one before. Gilbert White, however, was probably accurate, when in 1777 he recorded the girth of the Selborne yew as 7 m at a height of 1 m on the bole; it was exactly 7.6 m in diameter at that height 200 years later.

Cultivation Yews will grow on chalk, clays or sands. Although they never grow fast they will grow anywhere, in severe exposure or shade, in damp or dry soils, and they never blow down. Male and female flowers are borne on separate plants, so trees of both sexes need to be present to produce fruits.

Variants 'Adpressa' is a female form with a central axis and wide-spreading, slightly upswept level branches from which hang shoots lined with tiny leaves. Too open for use as a screen, this form makes a pleasant variation in foliage and should be beside a path or building where the minute leaves will be seen. It can be 11 m tall. 'Adpressa Aurea' is a beautiful golden-leafed form of 'Adpressa' but is more bushy and less open. It is bright, fresh yellow in winter and a deeper, slightly orange colour in early summer. At all times its golden foliage is among the best. 'Dovastoniana', the West Felton yew, is a strange plant with a history that makes it a talking-point in a garden. In 1777 Mr Dovaston bought it for sixpence from a pedlar to put by his well-head at West Felton, Shropshire. It grew strangely, with a good central stem and long, level branches that wandered out and hung their foliage in curtains. It is still there, 17 m tall and 117 cm in diameter, with a good bole. It is male but a female shoot was found on it. Every Dovaston yew comes from this one and a gold-leafed form, 'Dovastonii Aurea', is among the brightest of yews. 'Fastigiata', the Irish yew, is in every churchyard and every specimen is derived from one of the two female erect trees found in 1780 on a hillside in County Fermanagh. In the far west this grows numerous slender conic tops to 16 m tall, but it is broader and more squat towards the east. Avenues and lines of this yew are common in Cornish gardens and are sometimes successful, but the trees are generally broken out of shape if in the open, and straggly and dull if in shade. The twelve at Dartington, Devon, are superb and cleverly spaced but are clipped into shape. Yellow-leafed forms such as 'Fastigiata Aurea' and 'Standishii' are slower growing but make striking specimens. 'Lutea' is also of Irish origin. While the normal yew typically has red fruits, this form has yellow ones and is very striking when fully laden.

Tetradium daniellii (Benn.) Hartley (*Euodia daniellii* (Benn.) Hemsley, *E. hupehensis* Dode, *E. velutina* Rehder & Wilson)

CHINESE EUODIA; CHINA, KOREA. DECIDUOUS.

This tree has some unusual features which help to identify it. There are no bud-scales but spend the winter with the leaf folded tightly and covered in red-brown hairs. The compound leaves are in opposite pairs and the petioles do not cover the side-buds as in the related cork trees (*Phellodendron*). The flowers are in flat male or female heads which are rather randomly placed over the tree. The flowers open in autumn. The bark is grey and very smooth, but not shiny.

Its late flowering, which is profuse, handsome and valuable when so few other trees are in flower, and its very vigorous, sturdy growth on soils which are far from good, make this an important tree to consider when planting, but it has other good points. The 5–9 leaflets are a glossy dark green and often cupped, which enhances the effects of light, and their stalks are dark pink. Despite the late flowering the fruit ripen from mid-autumn and are bright orange-red then dark red. The form previously known as *Euodia daniellii*, which is seen mainly in collections, differs only in that its leaflets have shorter stalks and the fruit ripen purple.

Cultivation The Chinese euodia is absolutely hardy and will grow well on any well-drained soil. It is at its best given hot summers, so prefers plenty of sun, and is a good choice for planting in city gardens and parks. It will spread quite widely when mature so needs plenty of space.

TETRADIUM DANIELLII (left). This hardy, unusually tough tree, seldom attains a great height in our climate. It flowers quite late, but still develops fruits.

THUJA KORAIENSIS (far right). This little tree with delightfully scented leaves, adds distinction and grace to any shrub border.

Thuja/Arborvitae

THIS SMALL GROUP of evergreen conifers is closely related to *Chamaecyparis* and as its trees have similar tiny, scale-like leaves in flattened sprays they are often confused with cypresses. They can be distinguished from them quite readily with practice and easily recognized by their ovoid, upright cones. They have similar uses to cypresses, from specimen trees to hedging, and numerous forms have been selected for their coloured foliage or dwarf habit.

Cultivation Grow thujas in any well-drained, preferably not too dry, soil, in sun or partial shade. Hedges of *T. plicata* can be trimmed in spring before growth starts, and again in late summer.

THUJA KORAIENSIS NAKAI

KOREAN THUJA; KOREA. EVERGREEN.

This little tree grows slowly into a narrowly conic plant with up-curved branches that are heavily foliaged but often only close to the branch. The foliage may be fresh yellowish-green or deep blue-green bloomed silver, and the underside of each scale-leaf is thickly coated pure white all over. An added attraction is that crushed foliage emits a strong scent of rich, lemony, fruit-cake with almonds. This is valuable as a single specimen to add distinction and interest to a small-scale collection such as in a shrubbery, where only little trees can be grown.

soil: ACID – ALKALINE; DRY – WET 2•3•10 M

THUJA OCCIDENTALIS (right). First discovered in Virginia, this shapely conic tree has given rise to many excellent garden forms.

T. OCCIDENTALIS L.

EASTERN THUJA, NORTHERN WHITE CEDAR; E NORTH AMERICA. EVERGREEN.

'Eastern thuja' conflicts with the species name 'occidentalis', which was given to the tree because when it was first discovered, in Virginia, it was considered to be very 'western'. Another 250 years passed before the Western thuja or Western red cedar (*T. plicata*) was found by the Pacific Coast, and it was some time after this that the names Eastern thuja or Arborvitae were used. It is of minor use as it grows slowly and is short-lived. Meanwhile, it is a shapely conic tree with thin, pale bright green foliage in curved plates, without white markings beneath. During winter the foliage often assumes a bronze tinge.

Variants 'Lutea' is a far superior form: sturdy, upswept and with bright gold new foliage in curled fronds. 'Malonyana' is a narrow columnar form and its bright green foliage does not bronze in winter. 'Spiralis' is dark green and very narrowly conic-columnar. Its branches are fine and nearly level, and the tips bear spirally set upright sprays. A splendid, formal, small-scale tree, it is able to reach 12 m but takes some 60 years to do so.

THUJA ORIENTALIS L.

CHINESE THUJA; CHINA. EVERGREEN.

This is a dull, thinly foliaged, upright gaunt tree of little use in British gardens in its typical form, although it is commonly used for hedging in semi-arid regions. It does have several, mainly dwarf, selections which are better garden plants.

'Elegantissima' is very upright with vertically held plates of foliage. It is narrowly conic when young and eventually broadly columnar. Its foliage is bright yellow at the tips in early summer, then duller yellow until the first frosts when it bronzes a little. A young plant is neat and attractive in very restricted areas like patios and yards and small beds. Bigger plants (they can be 8 m tall) look well on a wall or beside a house. It flourishes on alkaline and mildly acid soils, but is not happy in very acid sands.

T. PLICATA D. DON

WESTERN RED CEDAR; W NORTH AMERICA. EVERGREEN.

This tree, introduced in Britain by John Jeffrey and William Lobb in 1854, is fast-growing but at its best in high rainfall areas. In damp weather the bright glossy green foliage will scent the air with an aroma of apple, acid-drop or pineapple. It is good on soil immediately above chalk and on damp clay, and is very widely used in shelter plantings. It will clip well to make a hedge and makes an excellent grove or roundel as, grown close, it remains shapely with a fine clean bole. A single specimen will often grow a big branch or two low from the bole, level then sharply up-curved, and can become untidy. The Western red cedar is much better as a line than in an avenue; in a line the trees can keep a wall of foliage but in an avenue the shade makes them thin and less attractive, with many bare twigs in the lower crown where they are most visible.

Variants 'Aurea' may not be the same as the tree first described under this name. It has bright golden foliage and provides a striking contrast among green-leafed forms. 'Zebrina', Golden-barred thuja, is one of the very best of the large-growing golden conifers. The oldest were planted a little over 90 years ago and while they are not really fast-growing trees they are often 20 m tall, sometimes 25 m, and still growing steadily.

THUJA ORIENTALIS 'SIEBOLDII' (top left) is a bushy form, barely a tree, long cultivated in Japan before it was introduced to Europe in 1859 by Siebold. It is very compact and particularly attractive when bearing its conspicuous bloomy cones.

THUJA PLICATA 'EXCELSA' (above). This very fast growing form was originally found in a Berlin cemetery and has been cultivated for 50 years. It is exceptionally hardy and densely conical, the rich green foliage not bronzing in winter, as in some forms.

THUJA PLICATA (above). The western red cedar is an excellent garden tree, as well as a valuable source of timber. It is also commonly grown as a hedge.

THUJA STANDISHII (right). Good bark and scented foliage redeem this, the least planted of the thujas.

There is considerable variation in the intensity of gold-barring on the foliage, but in most trees it is bright gold. In 'Irish Gold', seen more in Ireland, there is very little green between the bars.

8•15•35 M

T. STANDISHII (GORDON) CARR.

JAPANESE THUJA; JAPAN. EVERGREEN.

This cannot compete with the Western red cedar (*T. plicata*) in any of the roles of that tree but has a place, for interest and variety, in a collection or group of trees that are not intended to achieve great size. Its shoots are rounded and sprays, hanging from erect branch-tips, are often silvery with bloom on dark green. When crushed the foliage emits the most delicious sweet scent in which lemon, eucalyptus and cachou are combined. The crown is a broad cone with level branches that are up-curved towards their ends, and is open inside to display the bark. This is red-brown and stringy at first but in older trees has plates of smooth, rich, deep red. Old trees have distinctively yellow-green foliage and hanging shoots that make them look unhealthy; only their good bark and scented foliage redeem them at that age.

3•6•20 M

THUJOPSIS DOLABRATA 'AUREA' (left). As a tree or a shrub, this slow growing under-used form has handsome yellow flushed foliage.

Thujopsis dolabrata (L. f.) Siebold & Zucc.

HIBA; JAPAN. EVERGREEN.

The big, bright green reptilian scales on this rather slow-growing tree make very handsome foliage, hanging in sprays from branches bent upwards near the good single bole. The commoner bush form has between 12 and 20 stems of fairly even size and is broad and many-topped with thinner foliage. The Hiba is a good tree for a small-scale group of varied foliage. Both trees and bushes are very dense and broad-conic when young.

Cultivation The Hiba tends to be rather short-lived in dry, warm regions.

Variants 'Aurea' is a slower growing form in which the foliage is flushed with yellow and later turns dark green. 'Variegata' has too little variegation to affect its growth or make it worthwhile.

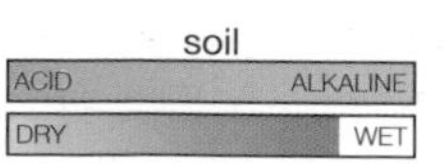

3•5•20 M

TILIA AMERICANA 'DENTATA' (far right) is a fast growing form of the American lime, with large, coarsely toothed leaves.

Tilia/Limes, Lindens

LIMES MAKE NOBLE TREES with handsome foliage and are ideally suited to large gardens and parks. They are particularly attractive when the small, yellow flowers open, usually in summer.

Cultivation Limes like a good and not too dry soil in full sun or partial shade and grow particularly well on alkaline soils. They are best not planted in full exposure.

TILIA AMERICANA L.

AMERICAN LIME, AMERICAN LINDEN; E NORTH AMERICA. DECIDUOUS.

The American lime is worthy of trial because of its luxuriantly rich green foliage. The leaves are moderately or very big, shiny and marked by pale, parallel straight veins. Unlike other lime leaves, they are the same rich colour beneath. The shoots and buds are apple-green and the big 10 cm bracts to the flowers are bright green. No doubt this tree thrives best where summers are warmest, but there are a few in areas with cool ones.

Young plants may suffer, as do some other trees with smooth bark, from great spotted woodpeckers sucking the sap – similar to the work of the sapsucker in America – which causes dense bands of pits in the bark, but does not generally harm the tree.

TILIA CORDATA 'GREENSPIRE' (far right). An excellent street tree with dainty, heart shaped leaves, and orange shoots, it is now becoming widely available.

T. CORDATA MILL.

SMALL-LEAFED LIME; EUROPE, W ASIA. DECIDUOUS.

This tree is native to limestone cliffs and woods and grows well on any moderately deep and moist soil that is not too acid. It is peculiarly well adapted to city streets. It has hardly been put to the test in Britain, but is among the most important city trees throughout the north-eastern USA. Big old ones share one bad feature with the Common lime (*T. x europaea*): they are very sprouty around the base. Until they are old the trees are a good conic shape, but they become irregularly domed and eventually have long branches that curve in to be quite erect, making a narrow-topped crown.

Red-brown shoots with red, shiny ovoid buds make a distinctive dense tracery of short jointed systems in winter. The leaves are daintily heart-shaped, around 6 cm long, and are dark shiny green above and pale, slightly silvered grey-green beneath, with large tufts of pale orange hairs in the vein-axils. The flowers immediately identify the tree in midsummer since they spray out at all angles in bunches of a dozen. They are white or ivory, clear and star-like, and as fragrant as those of the common lime, if less far-carrying. This species is increasingly being planted as a replacement for elms, and few trees could be such good additions to town and country.

Variants 'Greenspire', a recent form, is seen more often in America. It has a narrow, conic crown and orange shoots.

TILIA X EUCHLORA K. KOCH

CRIMEAN LIME; ORIGIN UNKNOWN. DECIDUOUS.

The Crimean lime is something of a disappointment after the high promise it gave. It is beautiful as a young tree, and until it is about 30 years old, with a smooth, pewter-grey, clean bole for 2 m and an ovoid crown of rich, glossy green leaves. These are obliquely heart-shaped with yellow sharp teeth, yellow 5 cm petioles and pale undersides with large tufts of pale brown hairs in the vein-axils. It grows excellently in streets and town gardens and the foliage is free from the aphids which infest the Common lime (*T.* x *europaea*) and to some extent the other common species of lime. It has a reputation, together with the Silver lime (*T. tomentosa*), of poisoning bees with its nectar but this seems to be based on a few observations of bumblebees rather than hive bees. Unfortunately it has two more substantial drawbacks. Some trees have a serious die-back of branches with something like a canker, and those that remain healthy develop unsightly crowns with branches that arch sharply down like hoops and become thickened and misshapen. The Crimean lime is therefore a splendid foliage tree, with good, big, yellow flowers, and worth planting, but may be less of a beauty in the long term.

soil
ACID — ALKALINE
DRY — WET
6•12•20 M

T. X *EUROPAEA* L.

COMMON LIME; EUROPE. DECIDUOUS.

It is not known whether this tree, which is a hybrid between the Small-leafed lime (*T. cordata*) and the Broad-leafed lime (*T. platyphyllos*), arose spontaneously in Britain as well as in Europe, migrated there with its parents or was brought there in the early seventeenth century. It is usually the tallest broad-leafed tree in any district with parks or gardens and can be 45 m tall with a narrow upper crown of several vertical stems and light level branches. The lower crown is broad. In such situations it is particularly useful for closely planted groups.

The Common lime's size and fragrant flowers, its adaptability to various soils, its long life and wind-firm nature earn it an assured place as a framework tree and parkland specimen, but it is the last one ever to consider planting in streets or small gardens. Any other lime is vastly preferable in these situations, and the Common lime is included only to warn against using it for any purpose except the two mentioned above.

soil
ACID — ALKALINE
DRY — WET
8•12•40 M

TILIA X EUCHLORA (far left). A delight as a young tree, the Crimean lime becomes unsightly with age.

TILIA X EUROPAEA (below). Exquisite in parkland and the countryside, the common lime should be avoided elsewhere due to its suckering habit.

T. 'MOLTKEI'

VON MOLTKE'S LIME; CULTIVATED ORIGIN. DECIDUOUS.

This hybrid is a cross between the American lime (*T. americana*) and the Silver pendent lime (*T. tomentosa* 'Petiolaris'), inherits the big leaf-size of the former and makes a very handsome foliage tree. Its rather pendulous shoots bear sharply toothed leaves, 25 x 15 cm, which are dark matt green above but silvery with close pubescence beneath. Young trees are very upright and vigorous and may grow leading shoots 1.5 m long.

TILIA 'MOLTKEI' (right). This very handsome foliage tree is a vigorous grower when young but spreads with age.

TILIA OLIVERI (below right). Perhaps the most choice of the limes, Oliver's lime prefers a damp site, and is free from aphid infestation.

TILIA MONGOLICA (below). Distinctive maple-like leaves and fragrant flowers cover this desirable tree.

T. MONGOLICA MAXIM.

MONGOLIAN LIME; NE ASIA. DECIDUOUS.

Still little known and uncommon in gardens, this very distinctive tree is worthy of much wider planting. The bark is at first smooth and grey but with age it becomes fissured and purplish. The shoots are slender and red and bear leaves which are highly distinctive and unlike those of any other lime. They are 5–8 cm long, almost maple-like with big triangular teeth or lobes and a slender, tapered, coarsely toothed central lobe. They are firm, dark green, on pink petioles 3 cm long, and are smooth beneath except for tufts in the vein-axils. With flowers like those of the Small-leafed lime (*T. cordata*) and pretty foliage, this is a highly desirable tree, hardy and adapted to any normal soil.

T. OLIVERI SZYSZ.

OLIVER'S LIME; CHINA. DECIDUOUS.

This fast-growing tree was one of the earliest sent to Britain from China by Ernest Wilson in 1900. It has exceptionally beautiful leaves that are large – up to 20 x 18 cm – on mature plants and, oddly, only around 15 cm long on young ones. They are soft pale green and very flat and smooth above with white peg-like sharp teeth; the undersides are bright silvery white. The leaves are well spaced on pendulous shoots and stand out level by a twist in the petiole. As with other limes with stout shoots, young trees that grow strong seem liable to breakage in the first few years and may need help from the secateurs to re-form a good crown. Some side-shelter is beneficial and any fairly damp soil will suffice. In some ways this is the most choice of all limes.

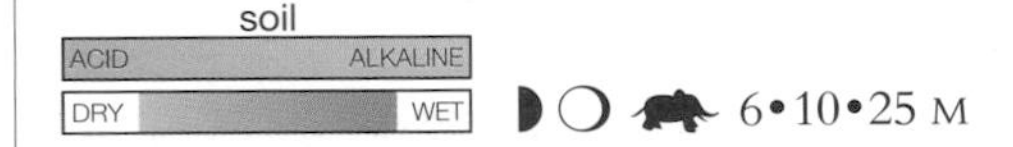

TILIA PLATYPHYLLOS SCOP.

BROAD-LEAFED LIME; EUROPE. DECIDUOUS.

This is distinguished from other limes by its shoots, which are densely hairy when fresh and nearly smooth by the end of winter, and hairy petioles and leaf undersides. The leaves are no larger than in the Common lime (*T.* x *europaea*) and often smaller. Its crown, which soon becomes a regular hemisphere or at least well domed, is also distinctive and the bole seldom has suckers around its base. In early winter the fringe of fruit that remains on the crown with the dead brown bracts clearly identifies this species. It is not a great specimen tree but it makes splendid clumps and roundels and is good in avenues, where it should always replace the common lime because of its clean growth and regular crown. It flowers much earlier than other limes, with only four or five biggish, very fragrant, pale flowers beneath each large pale bract.

Variants 'Laciniata', Cut-leaf lime, is of smaller growth. It is often prolific in flower and its deeply cut leaves are attractive. Although slow-growing, it can reach 15 m.

T. TOMENTOSA MOENCH.

SILVER LIME; SE EUROPE, SW ASIA. DECIDUOUS.

This is the best lime in cities and one of the best as a specimen on any site that has room for a big tree. It grows very vigorously and soon makes a dense, smoothly hemispheric crown with upswept shoots. It is as attractive in winter as it is in summer when it is heavily laden with dark leaves that are brightly silvered beneath. Its flowers are copious, heavily fragrant and short-cylindric with pale yellow petals and bright yellow stamens. The leaves turn pale yellow in autumn, then biscuit-brown in some years. One unfortunate characteristic is that the flowers are toxic to bumblebees and it is common to find many dead beneath it. However, this also applies to other limes including the Common lime (*T.* x *europaea*). A recent and hardly credible theory suggests that the bees die not from toxicity but from starvation.

Variant 'Petiolaris' (*T. petiolaris* DC.), the Silver pendent lime, is grafted, mostly on to the Broad-leafed lime (*T. platyphyllos*) which suckers less freely than the Common lime and Small-leafed lime (*T. cordata*). However, sprouts do occur at the base of many plants, and must be removed relentlessly. Invariably three or four huge branches rise steeply from 2 m on the bole and soon make a pendulous crown often 30 m tall. It is a splendid sight hung with big, dark leaves, 12 x 12 cm, that show their silver undersides. They are long-stalked – the slender petioles are about 12 cm – and deeply cordate. This is one of the best large-scale specimen trees and grows well in towns.

TILIA PLATYPHYLLOS 'LACINIATA' (above). Attractive, deeply cut leaves are produced by this slower growing form.

TILIA TOMENTOSA (far left). This lime doesn't seem to suffer from aphid infestations.

TILIA TOMENTOSA 'PETIOLARIS' (left) would be more widely planted except for the regular suckers which appear near the base and require regular removal.

Toona sinensis (A. Juss.) M. Roemer (*Cedrela sinensis* A. Juss.)

CHINESE CEDAR; CHINA. DECIDUOUS.

TOONA SINENSIS (below). Although often damaged by late frost in the spring, it is a delightful tree with fragrant white flowers.

The reason why this tree, which has very large pinnate leaves, is called a cedar is that any exotic tree with scented timber was originally given this name. The first Cedrelas, with which this species was once classified, was found in Cuba and was called Cigar cedar because its timber was good for cigar-boxes. When others of this genus were found elsewhere the 'cedar' part of the name was retained. The Chinese cedar is a rare tree with very handsome, onion-scented leaves up to 70 cm long. The 20–30 leaflets are up to 12 cm long and it usually lacks a terminal one. The bark breaks early into smooth grey plates tinged copper or purple, then becomes rough and shaggy. Although it is hardier than it looks, it is best in milder areas with warm summers. Its winter aspect is gaunt as it has singularly few branches. These are stout, and level then upturned towards the tips. It may produce large panicles of fragrant white flowers in hot summers.

Cultivation The Chinese cedar grows in any well-drained soil in full sun. It tends to come into growth early and can be damaged by late frosts.

Trachycarpus fortunei (Hook.) H. Wendl.

CHUSAN PALM; CHINA. EVERGREEN.

This is the only true palm that is hardy almost anywhere in Britain – no other can be grown unprotected north-east of Torbay. Its broad fan-leaves are on petioles hardly 1 m in length and are divided into 50–60 radiating slender lobes which are about 1 m long and fray at the ends. The cylindric bole is adorned with coconut-fibre around the big spiny stubs of the petioles. It does not increase in diameter through the addition of an annual layer of wood, as in other trees, but can expand minutely as a result of the slight thickening of internal bundles of tissues that run up the stem to each leaf. The tiny yellow flowers are on 60 cm, much-branched panicles and are borne on stout, twisting stems which are orange paling to cream. Several panicles emerge during summer and are generally either male or female but both sexes are found on the same tree. The globular, blue-black fruit are frequent only in the south and west.

Cultivation Chusan palm will grow on any well-drained soil in a sunny position. Although hardy, it prefers some shelter from winds in cold areas as it can be stubby and inelegant in exposed sites. It may superficially lend a tropical air to a corner, despite being so unlike most palms that actually grow in warmer climates. It is best in groups as a single tree can look odd, and better placed away from, rather than beside, a path as the spines on the petiole-stubs will cause pain if the bole is grasped.

2•4•10 M

TRACHYCARPUS FORTUNEI (left). Although tender looking, this, the hardiest palm, will thrive in many exposed locations as long as the huge leaves have wind protection.

Tsuga/Hemlocks

THESE ELEGANT EVERGREEN conifers are close relatives of the spruces (*Picea*) but differ in their normally blunt leaves and small cones.

Cultivation Hemlocks prefer a moist but well-drained soil, grow fastest and tallest in areas of high rainfall and are best with shelter from strong winds. They are among the best conifers for shady positions and so can be established beneath an existing canopy.

TSUGA CANADENSIS (L.) CARR.

EASTERN HEMLOCK; E NORTH AMERICA. EVERGREEN.

Although the Eastern hemlock is a shapely, slender, pale green tree through most of its wide native range, it is poorly shaped, dark and dull in Britain and cannot compete in any role, even as a hedge, with the splendid Western hemlock (*T. heterophylla*). Its bark is nearly black and coarsely ridged. The leaves taper from near the base and arrange themselves so that a line of leaves above the shoot lies upside-down. The tree should be avoided for general use.

soil: ACID – ALKALINE; DRY – WET; 5•8•25 M

T. HETEROPHYLLA (RAF.) SARG.

WESTERN HEMLOCK; W NORTH AMERICA. EVERGREEN.

In its native woods from southern Alaska to northern California this is an elegant narrowly conic tree, to 70 m tall in parts of Washington state. It grows in the same form but even faster, in Britain and in high rainfall areas will very soon be as tall as the Washington trees. Many are now over 40 m and none is more than 125 years old. It was introduced by John Jeffrey in 1851 but only two or three trees are known that were planted before 1860. It withstands considerable shade during early life and grows faster under well-thinned larch or oak than in the open. It cannot be recommended in dry areas, but is among the very best trees for groves, roundels and screens, and as a single specimen on the largest scale, in regions of high rainfall. There is hardly a tree of Western hemlock in these areas which does not taper regularly to a single long-spired tip or one with a misplaced branch. Single trees very rarely blow down or suffer damage from snow or gales. It makes an outstanding line of trees, and in an avenue the boles can give the effect of a cathedral nave – but the trees must be carefully spaced or the result will be shady and sombre.

soil: ACID – ALKALINE; DRY – WET; 8•15•40 M

TSUGA CANADENSIS (right). Although this tree suffers away from its native land, there are many fine forms available.

TSUGA HETEROPHYLLA (below). This will develop into a elegant tree, and is used in the south as a timber tree. If grown as a hedge it will excel.

TSUGA MERTENSIANA (above). Resembling a blue atlas cedar in growth, this small, neat tree has an attractive appearance.

TSUGA MERTENSIANA (BONG.) CARR.

MOUNTAIN HEMLOCK; W NORTH AMERICA. EVERGREEN.

This tree grows along the tree-lines of the highest ranges from Alaska to California, and on some inhospitable lavas where almost nothing else will grow, and should be remarkably tough. In fact, in Britain it seems to thrive only in areas of high rainfall and cool, moist summers. Elsewhere it grows very slowly. It can be strongly recommended as a small tree of neat and attractive appearance. With a few bushy exceptions, it grows as a narrow cone of light variably blue to grey foliage. Most trees are smoky grey and some, grown as 'Glauca', are blue-white. In their native range most are deep green. In Britain the older leaves become dark green or blackish, so the interior of the crown is very dark and shows off the pale new foliage. The leaves spread from all round the small shoots, unlike those in other hemlocks. Because the shoots tend to be short, in little bunches along the upper sides of the branches, they look like the spurs of a cedar, and the blue-grey leaf adds to the resemblance to the Blue Atlas cedar (*Cedrus atlantica* Glauca Group). The bark is dark orange-brown and flakes in small papery scales. The cones are much bigger than those of any other hemlock and are more like spruce cones.

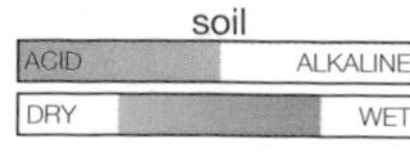

2•5•25 M

Ulmus/Elms

UNTIL 1970 THERE WERE several elms which could be strongly recommended as fine foliage trees, that were good in sea winds, very windfirm and made shapely and huge specimens. There were also several smaller elms of special habit or colour of foliage. Now, however, it is folly to recommend planting any elm as a long-term or important feature in Britain. As a result of Dutch elm disease nearly all the big trees in southern England have died. The exceptions are in west Devon and Cornwall, where a combination of sea winds that prevent big populations of the beetles that carry the fungus, and the higher resistance to it of the Cornish elm is, so far, holding the disease at bay.

Dutch elm disease has nothing to do with the Dutch elm in particular, or with Holland. English and American elms are, in fact, the most susceptible and the disease is thought to have an Asiatic origin, since elms from Asia are the most resistant. The name was applied because Dutch scientists were the pioneers in studying the fungus and breeding trees resistant to it.

When all the old elms are dead and removed the beetles will have nowhere to breed, and their population must collapse. Moreover, the suckers that arose wherever the elms grew are mostly below the level at which the beetles feed and spread the fungus, so these should reach tree-size. The disease will only be important again when these new trees are big and start to die, and by then it may have achieved an equilibrium with the elm as did the milder form in 1930.

Some species are either very resistant to Dutch elm disease or, it is hoped, immune to it. They are not immense trees and so it is justifiable to plant a few as individual specimens in the hope that they will survive, although they can never be regarded as replacements for the native elms.

ULMUS PARVIFOLIA JACQ.

CHINESE ELM; JAPAN, CHINA. DECIDUOUS.

The Chinese elm is a dainty and attractive tree with tiny 3 cm leaves that are fresh green in spring and dark in summer and remain so until the end of the year. This nearly evergreen crown is a light dome on a bole with remarkable bark that may be grey or brown at first, with small, orange, protruding flakes. It becomes paler with age until it is blue-white with orange flakes in warm climates, and pale grey, yellow or cream where it is less warm. The flowers, as tiny as the leaves, open in early autumn.

soil
ACID ALKALINE
DRY WET
5•10•15 M

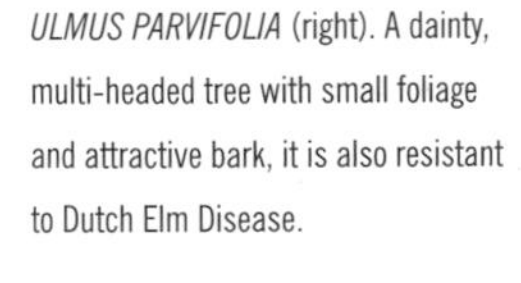

ULMUS PARVIFOLIA (right). A dainty, multi-headed tree with small foliage and attractive bark, it is also resistant to Dutch Elm Disease.

U. 'SAPPORO AUTUMN GOLD'

CULTIVATED ORIGIN. DECIDUOUS.

This Japanese-raised hybrid, a cross between two Asiatic, disease-resistant elms, *U. japonica* and Siberian elm (*U. pumila),* has now been planted on a small scale. It is upright and leafy with dark foliage that turns yellow-green in autumn.

8•12•15 M

ULMUS 'SAPPORO AUTUMN GOLD' (above). Resistant to Dutch Elm Disease this tree has been planted where susceptible trees have been removed.

Umbellularia californica (Hook. & Arn.) Nutt.

CALIFORNIAN LAUREL, OREGON MYRTLE; OREGON, CALIFORNIA.

This evergreen is rather dull except in spring when numerous umbels of small yellow flowers brighten the foliage. Although surprisingly hardy, it is mainly seen in milder, warmer gardens. It makes a tall, leafy, irregular dome on upright branches which are often lined with rows of slender sprouts. The leaves are held out well from the green shoots and are oblong-lanceolate, untoothed and about 8 cm long. They are pungently but sweetly aromatic and inhaling deeply from a crushed leaf may later bring on a sharp headache or feeling of nausea. Many of the largest trees in Britain were lost in the 1987 gales.

Cultivation The Californian laurel will grow in any well-drained soil. It prefers a sunny position, sheltered from cold winds.

4•6•20 M

UMBELLULARIA CALIFORNICA (below). Contrasting spring flowers enhance this otherwise dull evergreen. Graze on the leaves at your peril.

Zelkova

ZELKOVAS ARE MEMBERS OF THE elm family but largely escape Dutch elm disease. However, they are prone to wind blow and many of the biggest trees have been lost in recent gales. They are elegant, often of large size and ideal for large gardens.

Cultivation Zelkovas are very hardy but appreciate hot summers and so thrive best in warmer gardens. They prefer a good, deep, moist but well-drained soil in sun or partial shade, and it is best not to plant them in very exposed positions.

ZELKOVA CARPINIFOLIA (PALL.) K. KOCH

CAUCASIAN ZELKOVA; CAUCASUS. DECIDUOUS.

Old trees are huge and a unique shape: a stout bole of 1–2 m bears an immense brush of 100 or more vertical branches that rear up into a tall, ovoid crown. Although many much younger trees are becoming the same shape in Britain, this apparently does not happen in the species' native range and some British plants are also a more normal tree shape. The leaves are elliptic, with short pointed tips, and are prettily edged with round-based minutely pointed teeth. Variable in size and, particularly, breadth, around 8 x 5 cm, they are dark green and turn yellow, dull orange and brown in autumn. The Caucasian zelkova is outstanding as a single big specimen, mixed among other trees or in groups. It can sucker and make a long hedge, but should be kept clean.

soil
ACID ALKALINE
DRY WET
5•10•30 M

ZELKOVA CARPINIFOLIA (left). Although eventually quite large, this slow growing tree is an outstanding choice for southern gardens.

ZELKOVA SERRATA (above). Pollution tolerant and resistant to Dutch Elm Disease, this elegant large tree should be more widely planted.

Z. SERRATA (THUNB.) MAK.

KEAKI; JAPAN. DECIDUOUS.

This Japanese species is an elegant yet extremely tough and useful tree. It has so far rarely been affected by Dutch elm disease and is often healthy enough in badly affected areas to be worth the slight risk. It is seen in a few city parks and squares in southern England but has been used much more widely in North America, from Ontario to Georgia, and is the shade-tree in the car park at the Pentagon, Washington DC. Its smooth bole is pale grey, banded pink and orange in fine stripes on young trees, and becomes grey and stripping on older ones. It holds up a broad dome of slender, straight branches and shoots. The leaves differ from those of the Caucasian zelkova (*Z. carpinifolia*) in having long, tapered points, bigger teeth that are very rounded at the base but spine-tipped, and longer, 15 cm, smooth, pale yellow petioles. They hang very ornamentally on each side of long shoots on a young tree and generally turn delicate shades of yellow, amber and pink in autumn. As a young seedling it has a tendency to grow too many slender shoots, none of them dominant, so a little help may be needed to make a good crown. This also applies to trees bought on stems.

soil

ACID ALKALINE

DRY WET

5•10•20 M

INDEX

PICTURE CREDITS

Original photography by Anne Hyde

Additional photography courtesy of:

The Harry Smith Horticultural Photographic Collection
74 b, 76, 98 b, 123 tr, 131, 134 tl&cr, 158, 160, 174 c&cr, 181 b, 190, 197 t, 203 bl, 211 t&b, 212 t&c, 214, 217 t&b, 229 cl, 245 tr, 246 tl&r, 247 t, 249, 256 t, 267 bl.

Sir Harold Hillier Gardens & Arboretum © Justyn Willsmore
123 tl, 181 tr, 256 cr

The Garden Picture Library
10 br, 75 c, 81 t, 90 br, 167, 171 b, 172, 237 br